STATE B( ES

WIL

D0907085

SIBLING RELATIONSHIPS:
Their Nature and Significance
Across the Lifespan

SIBLING RELATIONSHIPS:
Their Nature and Significance Across the Lifespan

Edited by

MICHAEL E. LAMB
University of Utah

BRIAN SUTTON-SMITH
University of Pennsylvania

IEA LAWRENCE ERLBAUM ASSOCIATES, PUBLISHERS
1982   Hillsdale, New Jersey   London

Lawrence Erlbaum Associates, Inc., Publishers
365 Broadway
Hillsdale, New Jersey 07642

Library of Congress Cataloging in Publication Data

Main entry under title:

Sibling relationships.

Bibliography: p.
Includes indexes.
1. Brothers and sisters. 2. Developmental psychology.
I. Lamb, Michael E., 1953–   II. Sutton-Smith,
Brian. [DNLM: 1. Sibling relations. WS 105.5.F2 L216s]
BF723.S43S5   155.9′24   82-5091
ISBN 0-89859-189-9   AACR2

Printed in the United States of America
10 9 8 7 6 5 4 3 2 1

Contents

Preface

Since the emergence of developmental psychology early this century, theorists and researchers have emphasized the family's role in shaping the child's emergent social style, personality, and cognitive competence. In so doing, however, psychologists have implicitly adopted a fairly idiosyncratic definition of the family—one that focuses almost exclusively on parents and mostly on mothers. The realization that most families contain two parents and at least two children has occurred slowly, and has brought with it recognition that children develop in the context of a diverse network of social relationships within which each person may affect every other both directly (through their interactions) and indirectly (i.e., through A's effect on B, who in turn influences C). The family is such a social network, itself embedded in a broader network of relations with neighbors, relatives, and social institutions.

Within the family, relationships among siblings have received little attention until fairly recently. In this volume, our goal is to review the existing empirical and theoretical literature concerning the nature and importance of sibling relationships. Much of the work reviewed is discussed here for the first time, so recent is the emergence of interest among psychologists in the topic. In the 15 chapters that make up this volume, the contributors discuss what is known about the factors affecting the development and intensity of sibling relationships, their endurance over time, and the degree of influence siblings exert on one another—both directly and by way of their influence on the attitudes, expectations, and behavior of their parents. The picture the authors construct illustrates our growing awareness of the potential importance of sibling relationships, as well as pointing toward areas in which we remain grossly ignorant. Consequently, the book should be of value to academics, professionals, and students who want a thorough and up-to-date review of the available evidence concerning sibling relationships, as well as researchers and graduate students who would like direction toward fertile areas for future research.

In addition to the production staff at LEA, who made timely publication possible, we are grateful to Karen Boswell for preparing the subject index.

Michael E. Lamb
Brian Sutton-Smith

List of Contributors

Rona Abramovitch, Centre for Research in Human Development, Erindale College, University of Toronto, Mississauga, Ontario, Canada

Stephen Bank, Department of Psychology, Wesleyan University, Middletown, Connecticut

Audrey Begun, Department of Psychology, University of Michigan, Ann Arbor, Michigan

Brenda K. Bryant, Department of Applied Behavioral Sciences, University of California, Davis, California

Victor G. Cicirelli, Department of Psychological Studies, Purdue University, West Lafayette, Indiana

Carl Corter, Centre for Research in Human Development, Erindale College, University of Toronto, Mississauga, Ontario, Canada

Judy Dunn, Sub-Department of Animal Behaviour, Cambridge University, Madingley, Cambridge, England

Toni Falbo, Department of Educational Psychology, University of Texas, Austin, Texas

Susan Grajek, Department of Psychology, Yale University, New Haven, Connecticut

Michael D. Kahn, Department of Psychology, University of Hartford, West Hartford, Connecticut

Carol Kendrick, Sub-Department of Animal Behaviour, Cambridge University, Madingley, Cambridge, England

Michael E. Lamb, Departments of Psychology, Pediatrics, and Psychiatry, University of Utah, Salt Lake City, Utah

Joel I. Milgram, College of Education and Home Economics, University of Cincinnati, Cincinnati, Ohio

Lorraine Nadelman, Department of Psychology, University of Michigan, Ann Arbor, Michigan

Debra J. Pepler, Center for Research in Human Development, Erindale College, University of Toronto, Mississauga, Ontario, Canada

Ben G. Rosenberg, Dean of the Graduate School, Antioch College West, San Francisco, California

Helgola G. Ross, College of Education and Home Economics, University of Cincinnati, Cincinnati, Ohio

Sandra Scarr, Department of Psychology, Yale University, New Haven, Connecticut

Frances Fuchs Schachter, Department of Psychology, Barnard College, New York, New York

Stephen J. Suomi, Department of Psychology, University of Wisconsin, Madison, Wisconsin

Brian Sutton-Smith, Graduate School of Education, University of Pennsylvania, Philadelphia, Pennsylvania

Thomas Weisner, Departments of Anthropology and Psychiatry, University of California, Los Angeles, California

SIBLING RELATIONSHIPS:
Their Nature and Significance
Across the Lifespan

1 Sibling Relationships Across the Lifespan: An Overview and Introduction

Michael E. Lamb
University of Utah

OVERVIEW

More than a decade ago, Brian Sutton-Smith and Ben Rosenberg published a book entitled *The sibling* (1970). In this book, they summarized the results of research, much of it conducted by the authors themselves, on the effects of birth order and sibling status on personality and intellectual development. By the time the book was written, the accumulated evidence was impressive, but somewhat paradoxically, publication was associated with (if not causally related to) a temporary decrease in the amount of attention paid by researchers to sibling relationships and effects. The publication of the present volume, replete with chapters containing recent findings and the description of ongoing studies, testifies to the current resurgence of interest in sibling relationships and their formative significance. There are, however, several important differences between the research on sibling relationships conducted decades ago and the type of research that is now gaining popularity. These differences involve: a) a shift from the study of effects to the study of formative processes; b) the appreciation of cultural variability and the need to consider inter- and intraspecies diversity and similarity; and c) the growing concern with development across the lifespan, rather than only in childhood. Let us consider each of these issues in turn.

From Effects to Process

Whereas researchers were formerly concerned with the identification of sibling status effects, contemporary researchers are eager to determine the processes whereby effects are mediated. In the earlier work, the focus was on the effects of sibling status on personality and intellectual development, and the methodology adopted was very straightforward. Large numbers of people (usually high school or college students) were tested on standardized measures of some aspect of psychological or cognitive functioning. Groups of subjects differing with respect to sibling status were then compared, and any differences among the groups were attributed to sibling status. Since the research was exclusively correlational in nature, researchers could only speculate about the formative processes that had led to the emergence of the demonstrated group differences. Was it the behavior of older sisters that made younger brothers more cognitively competent, or did parents behave differently when they had an older daughter and a younger son? Did the enhanced masculinity of second-born boys with older brothers occur because the youngsters had additional male models with whom to identify, because the older brother and his predominantly male friends teased the young-ster whenever he behaved ''like a sissy'' and offered only male-typed activities for him to observe and/or engage in, because fathers (as adult role models) were especially salient and involved when they only had sons, or because parents could enforce clearer standards regarding sex-typed behavior when they only had children of one sex? It is clearly essential that developmental psychologists address questions regarding formative processes and that they evaluate the rela-tive explanatory power of the competing hypotheses raised by studies of sibling status effects. Unfortunately, the retrospective correlational strategy is not adequate for this task, and this has led to a change in the research strategies employed in studies of sibling relationships.

The new generation of research on sibling relationships is descriptive and process oriented. Many of the recent studies involve observational analyses of family and sibling interaction designed to determine how the effects revealed in studies of sibling status may have arisen (see, for example, the chapters by Nadelman and Begun, Dunn and Kendrick, Abramovitch, Pepler, and Corter, and Cicirelli). This is not to say that group difference studies are passé; on the contrary, several of the contributors to this volume rely heavily upon this strategy. However, researchers and theorists can now refer to a rapidly growing body of research focused on the elucidation of processes, and there is a general awareness that sibling status comparison studies can never in themselves demon-strate formative processes. Both group difference studies and process-oriented studies are informative, and the integration of these complementary strategies promises to advance understanding faster than exclusive reliance upon either one. Appreciation of the need to employ multiple research strategies is a distinc-tive feature of contemporary research on sibling relationships, which is amply reflected by the thoughtful contributions to the present volume.

Biological Influences and Intraspecies Variability

Current research on sibling relationships also reflects a growing awareness throughout the developmental sciences that we must look beyond the socializa-tion practices of modern western cultures if we are to attain a satisfactory and generalized understanding of formative developmental processes. Consequently, attempts have been made to identify species-typical patterns by studying intercultural consistencies and variations, and to identify biological constraints by intraspecies, interspecies, and behavior-genetic comparisons. Comparative anthropologists proceed by describing intraspecies variations and universals, comparative psychologists examine interspecies similarities and differences, while behavior geneticists attempt to quantify the relative contributions of heredity and environment by comparing similarities among people of varying degrees of relatedness to one another. Several of the chapters in the present volume exemplify the utility of these approaches. The chapter by Weisner focuses on sibling relationships in nonwestern societies, bringing to bear the interpretative framework of contemporary comparative anthropology. Weisner contends that one can obtain a broader and clearer understanding of sibling influences in any given culture by contrasting the behavior of siblings in that culture with their behavior in a variety of comparison cultures. Another chapter (that by Suomi) focuses on sibling relationships in nonhuman primates and exemplifies the perspective of comparative psychology in the course of building an animal model of sibling influences and relationships. Suomi believes that we can facilitate the understanding of sibling relationships and influences within our species by examining other, closely related species. He proposes that general biological and sociobiological principles are best understood by studying and comparing a variety of species facing diverse ecological challenges. Furthermore, it is possible to conduct experimental studies involving other species that would be ethically and practically impossible to attempt with humans.

Yet another perspective is offered by Scarr and Grajek, who review behavior genetic evidence suggesting that some similarities and differences among siblings must be attributed (respectively) to their shared and different genetic endowment. They note, quite appropriately, that in their single-minded focus on socially-mediated influences, developmental psychologists often lose sight of the fact that siblings share 50% of their genes. Consequently, many similarities among siblings may be genetically based, and Scarr and Grajek review evidence supporting this hypothesis. More provocatively, they argue that genetic differences between siblings help create different environments that exaggerate the phenotypic expression of these differences.

The Lifespan Perspective

A third perspectival change in the study of sibling relationships, again one which reflects a general trend in the study of development, has to do with a shift from a focus on children to a focus on people of all ages. Only recently, upon the insistence of lifespan developmental theorists, have psychologists become interested in development across the lifespan. For the most part, lifespan developmental psychologists have focused on methodological issues, or on the formative significance of "critical events" that take place in adulthood (e.g., marriage, parenthood, divorce, and various stages on the career trajectory). Compared with the "critical events" of interest to many lifespan developmental psychologists, family relationships are distinctive in that they themselves last over large portions of the lifespan—from childhood through adulthood. Unlike parent-child relationships, furthermore, sibling relationships are not predictably terminated by the death of one party while the other is still relatively young. Instead, sibling relationships often last an entire lifetime. Several of the contributions to this volume focus on this issue. In some chapters, the focus is on the preservation and perceived importance of the relationships among adult siblings (e.g., Bank & Kahn, Ross & Milgram, Cicirelli). In other chapters, the focus is on the extent to which sibling status effects are evident beyond adulthood (e.g., Rosenberg, Cicirelli). Whether these effects have their origins in earlier or contemporaneous interactions remains to be determined.

The emergence of lifespan developmental psychology has not only meant that adults must now be viewed developmentally; a broader change in perspective has occurred. The lifespan view proposes that development is continuous, with individuals continually adjusting to the competing demands of socialization agents and endogenous tendencies. Thus, even those concerned only with interactions among young siblings implicitly or explicitly acknowledge that all relationships change over time and that any "effects" may be eliminated, reinforced, or altered by later experiences. Thanks to the growing significance of lifespan theory, developmental psychology is currently witnessing a shift from emphasis on the long-term consequences of early experiences to a dynamic interactionist lifespan view. As the contents of the volume make abundantly clear, this revolution has had a marked impact on the study of sibling relationships.

SIBLINGS AS AGENTS OF SOCIALIZATION

None of the classical theories of personality or of psychological development portrayed siblings as important agents of socialization. Traditionally, psychological theories have emphasized parental influences on child development. (Parsons' theory [Parson & Bales, 1955] was, of course, an exception but it has always been of greater interest to sociologists than to psychologists.) However, a broader and more inclusive view of socializing agents has characterized the latest era of research on socialization and personality development (Zigler, Lamb, & Child, 1982), and in a recent review Belsky (1981) argued for the convergence of developmental psychology and family sociology. Besides parents, most attention has been focused on teachers and peers, but there has also emerged an appreciation that families are complex social systems, comprising a network of relationships within which each individual has the potential to influence every other member both directly and indirectly (i.e., mediated via the impact on third parties). However, most discussions of family influences still focus on the mother-father-child triad rather than four- and five-person families. As a result, an appreciation of the potential importance of sibling relationships has developed slowly.

Demographic statistics demonstrate that most children grow up with siblings. Even though the average family size has dropped in most western countries from the extreme fecundity of the "baby boom" that followed World War II, the modal family today contains two children, and a declining proportion contain three or more. The ubiquity of siblings and sibling relationships does not guarantee that siblings are of formative significance, of course, but it does necessitate attempts to determine just how influential they are.

Sibling influences begin even before the second child is born, for the anticipation of the youngster's birth affects the parents as well as their relationships with and availability to their first-born offspring. The subsequent arrival of the new baby further accentuates these effects (see Nadelman & Begun, chapter 2; Dunn & Kendrick, chapter 3). Usurpation of the first-born's unique status in the family sets the stage for resentment and rivalry, but although conflict between siblings is frequent, it usually occurs in the context of generally positive relationships between siblings. Among home-reared children, siblings are the most regular— often the only regular—playmates available to both older and younger siblings, and for the younger members of sibling pairs, older brothers and sisters are the primary models of interesting childlike activities (Lamb, 1978; Abramovitch, Pepler & Corter, chapter 4). When both parents are employed, siblings are likely to be placed with the same supplementary caretaker; although their social network is thus extended to include other children, the siblings' relationship is not disrupted.

Commonly, the first major threat to the sibling relationship occurs when the children enter the public school system—an institution that is notable for its extreme emphasis on age segregation. Nevertheless, as Ellis, Rogoff, and Cromer (1981) have shown recently, children regularly associate with both age-mates and non-age-mates outside school and so sibling relationships are not necessarily disrupted by schooling. Older children are increasingly likely to be given temporary responsibility over their siblings once they reach school age, and in nonwestern cultures, primary caretaking roles are often assumed by preadolescent siblings (Weisner & Gallimore, 1977). Younger children, meanwhile, increasingly find themselves being compared to their older siblings by teachers as well as by parents and relatives. Although these repeated comparisons may elicit attempts to differentiate between oneself and one's siblings in order to assert one's individuality, this individuation seldom occurs at the expense of the sibling relationship. On the contrary: siblings commonly become primary confidantes and sources of emotional support in preadolescence, and these mutually important relationships usually persist well into adolescence and young adulthood. During adolescence, when parents and children often have difficulty communicating about emotionally laden issues such as sexuality and the use of recreational drugs, and friends of both sexes prove fickle and unpredictable, siblings provide the most reliable and consistently supportive relationships. Sibling relationships may lose their urgent and unique importance in adulthood, although many young adults continue to find it easier to talk to siblings than to parents. In any event, as several contributors to the present volume demonstrate, it is not unusual for siblings to remain sources of emotional support, advice, and companionship into adulthood.

In contrast with the practices of the many cultures discussed by Weisner (chapter 13), modern western societies seldom assign specific roles in the socialization process to siblings. Wittingly or unwittingly, however, the evidence suggests that their influence is often profound. Siblings set and maintain standards, provide models to emulate and advice to consider, enact complementary roles in relation to one another through which both develop and practice social-interactional skills, and serve as confidantes and sources of nonjudgmental social support in times of emotional stress (e.g., break-ups with steady dates, menarche, pregnancy scares, etc.). Sibling relationships retain these qualities into adulthood, whereas parent-child relationships often retain a nonegalitarian and judgmental quality long after the children attain adulthood or parenthood themselves. Finally, besides marital relationships, sibling relationships are often the only heterosexual relationships in which western adults can express affection and closeness without eliciting disapprobation and gossip. Heterosexual sibling relationships may be especially important in adolescence and early adulthood, when long-term sexual commitments are commonly explored for the first time.

OUTLINE OF THE VOLUME

The chapters in this volume can be classified into four groups on the basis of their contents. The first and largest group (chapters 2 to 11) consists of chapters focused on the nature and significance of sibling relationships at specific points in the lifespan. These ten chapters are organized in rough chronological sequence, beginning with two chapters concerned with the effects of a second child's birth on existing family relationships, and ending with discussions of sibling relationships in mid- to late adulthood. There follows, in the brief second section, a single chapter concerned with children and adults who do not have siblings. The third set of chapters comprises various alternatives to the narrow perspective on sibling relationships that is obtained when we focus exclusively on western societies. This section includes contributions by a comparative anthropologist, a comparative psychologist, and two behavior geneticists. The book closes with a reflective epilogue written by one of the editors.

A Chronological Sequence

Chapters 2 through 11 form a chronological sequence; they are organized roughly by the age of the siblings who are the focus of the authors' research and speculation. Thus in the first chapter in this sequence, Nadelman and Begun (chapter 2) discuss the effects of younger siblings' births on the personality and perceptions of first-borns and on existing relationships between the older siblings and their parents. Dunn and Kendrick (in chapter 3) also address this issue, but their conclusions are based on naturalistic observational accounts of parent-child and sibling interaction whereas Nadelman and Begun base their conclusions upon projective doll play assessments of the older children, maternal reports, and global ratings made by observers. The studies also differ with respect to the ages of the first-borns and the amount of time elapsing between the birth of the second children and the assessment of the first-borns' adjustment. Because of the many methodological differences between these two attempts to determine how the birth of a second child affects existing family relationships, conclusions that are suggested by the findings of both studies are probably quite reliable.

In their chapter, Dunn and Kendrick also focus on individual differences in the quality of sibling relationships. They present evidence demonstrating that the quality of the mother-first-born relationships and the sex of the two siblings have an important impact on the quality of sibling relationships in the early years. In chapter 4, Abramovitch, Pepler and Corter, discuss several similar factors, in addition to the effects of age differences and maternal intervention and the issue of longitudinal continuity in the amount and quality of early sibling interaction. Again, the fact that Abramovitch et al. and Dunn and Kendrick rely upon different measures and analytic strategies adds credibility to those conclusions consistent with the results of both of these longitudinal studies.

In chapter 5, the focus shifts from preschool-aged children and their younger siblings to a concern with sibling relationships in middle childhood. Relationships with both older and younger siblings are considered here by Bryant, who offers a comparison between sibling and nonsibling relationships in the preadolescent years. She also relates sibling experiences to aspects of sociopersonality and intellectual development in both first- and second-born daughters.

The subjects of Schachter's research (see chapter 6) are either adolescents who are asked to review their sibling relationships in retrospect or mothers who are asked to describe specific aspects of the relationship between their children. Schachter employs these data to elucidate two processes that may help account for certain reliable differences between siblings. The processes of interest to Schachter are ''sibling deidentification'' and ''split-parent identification.'' Sibling deidentification involves attempts on the part of children to differentiate between themselves and their siblings in distinctive and salient ways so as to consolidate their individuality. These differences in children's aspirations and perceptions appear to be translated into differences that are evident on standardized and objective assessment instruments. Split-parent identification may have related origins and effects: the process involves the apparent tendency of children to identify with one of their parents because their siblings have identified with the other. This hypothesized process is especially interesting because it focuses on the entire family constellation, rather than just the parent-child and sibling relationships, in explaining child-parent identification and sibling status effects respectively. Both of the processes described by Schachter are not readily observable and are thus unlikely to be revealed by observational strategies like those employed by researchers such as Dunn and Abramovitch.

Sibling status effects are the focus of chapter 7, written by Brian Sutton-Smith, the person responsible for many informative studies of sibling status effects conducted in the 1960s. Among the factors that have been studied most intensively are the individual's position in the family birth order and the sex of the younger and older siblings. By contrast, age spacing has received much less attention. As dependent variables, most of the studies discussed by Sutton-Smith assessed performance on standardized measures of intelligence, school performance, and sex role adoption because these are constructs for which highly reliable instruments have long been available. Many of the findings described by Sutton-Smith in his review of sibling status studies are cited by other contributors and it is useful to have the evidence concisely reviewed by one of those who knows the literature best.

Sutton-Smith's collaborator in many studies of sibling status effects was Ben Rosenberg, and his chapter (8) follows that by Sutton-Smith. As might be expected, Rosenberg remains interested in sibling status effects, focusing in his chapter on a small sample of subjects studied longitudinally from early adolescence into mid-adulthood by researchers at the Institute of Human Development at the University of California (Berkeley). The personality characteristics of Rosenberg's 67 subjects were assessed four times over a period of nearly three decades using Q-sort techniques. The greatest temporal stability in personality characteristics was evident among the only children. As far as the subjects from two-child families were concerned, birth order proved more influential than the sex of the siblings, and stability was greatest among first-born girls and second-born boys. (Perhaps this is because sex role stereotypes and ordinal position combine to encourage nurturance in older girls, as well as independence in younger boys.) Sibling status effects were greatest in adolescence: they appeared to decrease with age.

In the chapter that follows Rosenberg's, Ross and Milgram (chapter 9) describe their attempts to define the factors accounting for individual differences in the quality of sibling relationships in adults ranging in age from their twenties to their nineties. From their studies has emerged a realization that the "closeness" of relationships is defined and appraised very differently at successive stages of the lifespan. This obviously has important implications for the conduct of research designed to explore the factors affecting closeness across the adult years. Nevertheless, Ross and Milgram are able to pinpoint two sets of factors influencing the quality of sibling relationships among adults: critical incidents (whether predictable, such as the death of a parent, or untimely, such as the unexpectedly early death of one of the sibling's spouses) and sibling rivalry—its presence, absence, and attenuation or perseveration.

Bank and Kahn (chapter 10) then present, with the provocative detail of a small-scale clinical study, their developing conceptualization of the origins of intense sibling loyalties. Bank and Kahn focus on three sets of intensely loyal siblings, and explore the origins of their intense loyalty and closeness. In every case, the sibling relationship had been strengthened by parental abandonment and/or abuse in childhood and by the absence of psychologically accessible adults with whom relationships could be formed instead. These findings are reminiscent of Freud and Dann's (1951) descriptions of extremely close peer relationships established among children who had been incarcerated in concentration camps. Because of the small sample size, the generalizability of Bank and Kahn's findings is uncertain, but these contributors certainly raise important issues and hypotheses for investigation in future studies.

Finally, in the last chapter in the chronological series, Cicirelli (chapter 11) attempts to review sibling influences across the entire lifespan. He focuses in turn on: changes in sibling relationships between early childhood and late adulthood; critical aspects of sibling relationships (including closeness, socioemotional evaluations of siblings, and sibling rivalry); the nature of sibling influences on personality and intellectual characteristics; and the sources of these influences.

Only Children

Although there is occasional mention of only children in the first ten substantive chapters, it is in chapter 12 that children raised without siblings come in for the closest attention. In her chapter, Falbo describes the negative stereotypes that many people hold about only children. Reading a volume on sibling relationships, it is easy to consider only children to be deviant. It is thus important to recognize both that only children are becoming increasingly common as the size of the average family declines (one-child families are modal in some of the low birth rate countries of western and eastern Europe) and that there is little empirical basis for the negative social stereotypes that many people hold about only children. In addition to discussing these issues, Falbo reviews the factors that lead some parents to have only one child, the effects of this decision on family functioning and parental behavior, and the effects of being an only child on aspects of psychosocial and intellectual functioning.

Alternative Perspectives on Sibling Relationships

In chapters 13 to 15, the focus shifts from the real or presumed effects of social interactions among western children and their parents to studies of other cultures and species. Comparative anthropologists and psychologists aim to assess the extent to which biological/hereditary influences either affect the potential for sibling relationships or mediate effects that are often attributed to social relationships. This section begins with a contribution by a comparative anthropologist

(Thomas Weisner) who has studied cultures in which children are explicitly assigned responsibility for the rearing of their younger siblings and often retain important roles in their siblings' lives. Weisner's (chapter 13) contention is that the sibling relationships characteristic of contemporary western societies are unrepresentative of our species (viewed in broader perspective), because siblings in industrialized cultures do not play an essential role in child rearing and are seldom involved in critical life choices. This situation contrasts with the status of siblings in many nonwestern cultures. A variety of practices that underscore the importance of siblings and are characteristic of many nonindustrialized cultures are described by Weisner in his review chapter.

From the focus on intraspecies variation that characterizes the chapter by Weisner, attention then shifts to interspecies comparisons in the chapter by Suomi (chapter 14). Actually, Suomi draws few parallels between humans and his rhesus monkey subjects, but his observational data illustrate the nature and importance of sibling relationships in nonhuman primates and raise some intriguing questions concerning the potential roles of siblings in human socialization.

Scarr and Grajek (chapter 15) then present a behavior genetic analysis of the similarities and differences among siblings. Drawing upon Scarr's own studies and those of other researchers concerned with the genetic and experimental bases of individual differences in personality, cognitive styles, and intellectual functioning, Scarr and Grajek conclude that many of the similarities and differences between siblings are demonstrably attributable (at least indirectly) to their partially shared and partially different genetic complement. They point out that genetic factors not only have direct effects on behavior, but also affect the treatment that children receive. Their conclusions are based on studies of same and opposite sex dizygotic twins, ordinary siblings, and adopted siblings.

Integration and Summary

The book concludes with a brief chapter by Brian Sutton-Smith presenting some final thoughts on the preceding chapters.

SUMMARY

In sum, the chapters in this volume provide a multifaceted account of sibling relationships. Using both observational and interview procedures to gather data regarding siblings varying in age from infants to pensioners, the authors attempt to define the diverse characteristics of sibling relationships. They also discuss the factors affecting the closeness and salience of sibling relationships as well as the type of influences siblings may have on one another. A common theme suggests that sibling relations must be seen in the context of family relationships, both because the parents' behavior helps determine the type of relationships that siblings develop, as well as because the distinctive characteristics of children shape the parents' differential treatment of each of their children and thus help account for the remarkable psychological differences that develop among siblings within families.

REFERENCES

Belsky, J. Early human experience: A family perspective. *Developmental Psychology,* 1981, *17,* 3-23.

Ellis, S., Rogoff, B., & Cromer, C. C. Age segregation in children's social interactions. *Developmental Psychology,* 1981, *17,* 399-407.

Freud, A. & Dann, S. An experiment in group living. In R. Eisler (Ed.), *The psychoanalytic study of the child* (Vol. 6). New York: International Universities Press, 1951.

Lamb, M. E. Interactions between eighteen-month-olds and their preschool-aged siblings. *Child Development,* 1978, *49,* 51-59.

Parsons, T., & Bales, R. F. *Family, socialization, and interaction process.* Glencoe, Ill: Free Press, 1955.

Sutton-Smith, B., & Rosenberg, B. *The sibling.* New York: Holt, Rinehart & Winston, 1970.

Weisner, T. S., & Gallimore, R. My brother's keeper: Child and sibling caretaking. *Current Anthropology,* 1977, *18,* 169-180.

Zigler, E., Lamb, M. E., & Child, I. L. *Socialization and personality development.* New York: Oxford University Press, 1982.

2 The Effect of the Newborn on the Older Sibling: Mothers' Questionnaires

Lorraine Nadelman and Audrey Begun
University of Michigan

Biblical stories of Cain and Abel, Esau and Jacob, and Joseph (of the many-colored coat) and his brothers indicate that an interest in sibling relationships is hardly a new phenomenon for the nonscientist. To say that social scientists were attentive to the mother, then the father, then the sibs, would be a tidy but not entirely justified summary.

Interest in the effects of sibship variables (like number of sibs, ordinal position, age spacing) on intelligence, achievement, creativity, personality, and health, resulted in over 2000 research articles published by 1979, summarized and integrated by Wagner, Schubert, and Schubert (1979). The major emphasis during the 19th and early 20th centuries appears to have been on primogeniture (first-borns contrasted with later-borns), with methodological advances then leading to investigations of four ordinal positions (only-born, eldest, inter-mediates, and last-born). Wagner et al. (1979) contend: "Investigators have become increasingly aware of the complexities in the number of sibship variables affecting personality development, of the interaction between the sibship variables, and of the influence of numerous demographic variables interacting with the sibships variables [p. 60]."

A major portion of the 2000 sibship articles reviewed by Wagner et al. (1979) focused on the individual, and on intrapsychic theories of development. Erik Erikson is credited by Hoffman (1980) for some shift away from this narrow focus. What distinguishes the newer work by clinicians and social scientists is the explicit recognition that the social sciences deal with complex problems which involve multiple interacting variables. Our personalities are influenced by (and reciprocally, influence) the relationships into which we enter. These relationships are shaped by, and in turn help to shape, the society in a continuing

13

dialectic. Psychologists, sociologists, ethologists, and many others now seem to be recognizing the need for integrating data about relationships on multidisciplinary, multicausal, multidirectional, cross-cultural bases. Words like "reciprocal," "dynamic," and "interactional" are key labels. Examples of these foci appear in Hinde (1979), Lerner and Spanier (1978), Toman (1976), Schultz (1976), Weisner and Gallimore (1977), and Whiting and Whiting (1975), to name but a few. Sib relationships are receiving increasing attention as *family systems* theory becomes more prominent.

Obviously, the topic of sibling relationships can be approached from a variety of theoretical perspectives in a number of different disciplines, e.g., psychoanalytic theory, ethological theory, social psychology (group dynamics, territoriality, personal space), sociology (family constellation), social work (family therapy), and so on. General system theory, in relation to role development in the family life cycle, possibly has the breadth and flexibility to integrate and conceptualize the complex interplay of numerous forces within the family (Carter & McGoldrick, 1980). Following is a brief history and description of family life cycle and family systems theory.

The first step toward a *family* view of the life cycle, according to Carter and McGoldrick (1980), was the work of Reuben Hill and Evelyn Duvall presented in their background papers written for the 1948 National Conference on Family Life. The *interdependence* of individual life cycles was stressed in these papers. The early studies by sociologists of the family life cycle and family development were primarily descriptive, and resulted in various lists of stages in family development. These stages were then used in research as classification variables, similar to variables like age, sex, and socioeconomic status. The number of stages in the family life cycle varied according to the conceptual scheme of the researcher and reflected the importance attached to particular developmental tasks by various researchers (Schultz, 1976). In the 1950s, Duvall broke the family life cycle into eight stages and applied the concept of developmental tasks to family function at each stage; thus attention shifted to the *process* aspect of the family life cycle. Examples of her family developmental tasks include establishment of a home, divisions of labor, communication system, and so on; in more recent years, many of these specified tasks have been criticized as culture-bound. At about the same time, Bowen, Satir, and others were attempting psychiatric treatment of the family unit. Explicit references to the family life cycle began appearing in the family therapy literature in the 1970s, in writings by Haley, Solomon, and Minuchin. At present, therapists and nontherapists alike agree that births of children are major nodal events in the family life cycle that can stimulate growth and strengthen a family system, or can stimulate dysfunction.

Dissatisfied with a linear model of causality (as in traditional S-R learning theory or in classical psychoanalysis), family therapists and researchers are turning to general system theory to understand change resulting from the process of interaction in the family (Stevenson, 1980). Conceptualizing the family as a dynamic system (a set of elements in interaction), it can be demonstrated that many principles of system theory relating to the maintenance and organization of systems have relevance to families. As a few abbreviated examples, which hardly do justice to Stevenson's exhaustive treatment of the parallels between general system theory and family functioning, consider the following paraphrasing by Stevenson (1980) of four aspects of natural systems; substitute "family" for "system" in the following: "a system is more than its separate parts, . . . it maintains itself in a steady state despite constant environmental pressures and internal constraints, . . . it is capable of change in response to spontaneous internal activity or environmental disruptions, . . . it develops generally in the direction of greater diversity of structure and function [p. 17]."

The most widely invoked principle of systems theory as it relates to family is the principle of organization known as *wholeness:* If the parts of a system are so interrelated that a change in one part creates change in every part and in the system, that system behaves as a whole. This is characteristic of fused or enmeshed families. If, however, a change in one part of a system does not change other parts, that system is characterized by *independence* or summativity. Another principle of organization of systems with relevance to families and sibs is *progressive segregation:* The change in living systems over time may be away from wholeness toward independence and summativity. Even researchers who do not use system theory language are often alert to system implications. For example, Lamb (1978a, 1978c) frequently studies "second-order" effects, pointing out that interaction within a dyad or triad is altered by the presence or absence of another individual.

As noted earlier, changing family composition can result in the stimulation of both growth and dysfunction. However, much writing on sibling relationships has tended to focus on negative aspects like sibling rivalry, from clinical reports (e.g., Levy, 1934, 1937) to modern children's books about sibs (reviewed by Begun, 1979). There has been, however, a growing recognition of the positive aspects and advantages of sibship. Bradt (1980) says that for an only child,

the experiences of symmetrical negotiation, multiplicity, diversity, and similarity are lost. Parents with only children, rather than a number of children, gravitate toward more egalitarian (peer) nonhierarchical relationships with their young. It could be asked if only children come out with less familiarity with organizational hierarchy and less appropriate reciprocal peering [page 132].

Other advantages of sibling status are: learning cooperation; practicing negotiation skills; competing and establishing territoriality; and learning that others have different rights and needs at different times. Bryant (1979) believes that "sibs . . . may play a particularly profound role in the development of successful modulation of aggressive motivation and expression in the context of enduring relations [page 10]."

Clearly, a large number of variables may affect the development and expression of sibling relationships: mother-child interactions; the temperaments, sexes, ages and spacing of the children; mother-father relationships; peer relationships; family history and ecology; and numerous other variables. According to systems theory, a new baby's arrival is viewed as a major change in a family system, with effects on individual family members and on their interpersonal relations. Because of the complexity of the system, how to target and measure these effects poses many difficult choices for the researcher.

Although our interest is in the emergence of sibling relations, we decided to start with a focus on the first-born, and attempt to answer a limited number of questions about the child's reaction to the expectation and arrival of a sibling. To answer the basic question—What are the reactions (behaviors) of the first-born?—a pre-post design was used. Data were collected both three to four weeks before and three to four weeks after the birth of the sibling. Like some others (Abramovitch, Corter, & Lando, 1979; Dunn & Kendrick, 1979), we utilized home visits rather than laboratory observations. To obtain a broad range of data, a multimeasure approach was chosen, utilizing mothers' reports, observations of projective doll play sessions by the first-born, and observer ratings of the global situation. In addition to the independent variable, pre-post birth of a sibling, we used classification variables to answer the questions: What are the effects of the child's sex, age (which is equivalent to the spacing of sibs), and the baby's sex? Boys and girls (26 to 66 months) were compared; children 40 months or older were compared to younger children; and the four dyad groups were compared (boys with new brother, boys with new sister, girls with new brother, girls with new sister). Importantly, in addition to the pre-post design in which each child serves as its own control, a control group of "only" children provided data to investigate whether changes in the experimental group related to the complex of events surrounding the birth of a sibling or were developmental changes.

In summary, the effect of the newborn on the older sibling was investigated in a pre-post design with only- and two-child families, with a multimeasure battery, with classification variables of sex, age, and baby's sex.

METHOD

Subjects

The sample was comprised of mostly middle-class, white, intact nuclear families from Southeastern Michigan. The final "experimental" group included 53 families who were expecting the birth of their second child and whose first-borns were about 2¼ to 5½ years of age at the time of the baby's due date. In practice, the age range at delivery date was 26 to 66 months, with a median of 39.25 months. The 17 control group families analyzed thus far had only one child and were not expecting a second child. (Three control group families were dropped from the sample earlier because the mother became pregnant, the parents separated, or an adoptive baby arrived between the first and second visits; nine families from the experimental group were dropped because of scheduling problems, serious unexpected birth defects, etc.).

Notices requesting volunteers were circulated through nurseries and day care centers, obstetrical practices and clinics, birthing classes, and newspaper interviews and announcements. In addition, a number of families volunteered after hearing of our study from other participants. Each family received a summary report of the group data as the only remuneration.

Material

The materials used in data collection at each visit included:

1. A two-part "Child's Behavior" questionnaire, with a series of eight open-ended questions followed by a 5-point behavioral rating scale (the latter adapted with modifications from a 5-point posthospitalization questionnaire by Vernon, Foley, Sipowicz, and Shulman, 1965; Vernon, Schulman, and Foley, 1966).

The expectant mother wrote answers to such open-ended questions as: What have you told, or do you plan to tell your child about the arrival of your expected baby? Have you found any books that were helpful in this? Other questions concerned the child's attitude toward the pregnancy, extent of contact with peers, and doll play. After the baby's birth, the mother was asked such questions as: To what extent, and in what ways, is your child involved with the new baby (for example, child helps with bathing, feeding, diapering, watches baby for you, etc.)? How did your child react to you when you came home from the hospital? What changes in behavior did you notice? The control group mothers were asked similar questions related to babies in general, such as: What, if anything, have you told your child about pregnancy, birth, or new babies? Did you use any books which you found helpful?

For the second portion of the questionnaire, each mother was asked to rank 26 items of her child's recent behavior on a 5-point scale (i.e., 1—my child *almost never* exhibits this behavior through 5—my child *almost always* exhibits this behavior). The specific items are listed in Table 1. This set of questions was identical on both the first and second visit questionnaires, and identical for both the experimental and control group families. The main modifications of the Vernon et al. (1966) instrument included two administrations rather than one; rephrasing 11 items in a positive mode (e.g., "Does your child obey" rather than "disobey"); dropping questions about child hospitalization; and adding questions about peer play, talking about babies, using baby talk, etc. Scoring on the positively phrased items was reversed, so that a higher score indicated more

TABLE 2.1
Mean Ratings of Firstborns on Mother Questionnaire
(Experimental Group, n = 53)

Item	Visit 1			Visit 2			Item Content
	Whole Group	M	F	Whole Group	M	F	
1	2.68	2.63	2.74	2.98	2.73	3.30	make a fuss about going to bed at night
2	2.36	2.67	1.96	2.36	2.50	2.17	make a fuss about eating
3	1.49	1.37	1.65	1.64	1.77	1.48	spend time sitting, lying around, doing nothing
4	1.25	1.30	1.17	1.26	1.07	1.52	use a pacifier or bottle
5*	2.53	2.63	2.39	2.74	2.70	2.77	look forward to being left with baby sitter
6*	1.06	1.07	1.04	1.11	1.13	1.09	alert and interested in what is going on
7*	2.62	2.70	2.52	2.47	2.63	2.26	stay dry at night
8	2.09	1.83	2.44	2.04	1.90	2.22	bite nails, or suck on fingers or thumbs
9	2.09	2.30	1.83	1.94	2.03	1.83	mind you leaving him/her alone for a few minutes
10	2.68	2.83	2.48	2.72	2.73	2.70	need a lot of help doing things
11*	1.40	1.53	1.22	1.43	1.47	1.39	easy to get child interested in doing things
12*	1.15	1.23	1.04	1.15	1.17	1.13	seem to enjoy new things or experiences
13*	2.17	2.23	2.09	2.25	2.30	2.17	find it easy to make up his/her mind
14	2.91	3.03	2.74	3.02	3.10	2.91	have temper tantrums, or end up crying
15*	1.40	1.43	1.35	1.59	1.70	1.43	easy to get child to talk to you
16*	1.70	1.93	1.39	1.94	2.03	1.83	seem to enjoy hearing talk about babies, brothers or sisters
17	3.32	3.43	3.17	3.00	3.10	2.87	follow you around the house
18	3.36	3.43	3.26	3.38	3.43	3.30	try hard to get your attention
19	1.55	1.80	1.22	1.64	1.70	1.57	break toys or other objects
20	1.94	2.00	1.87	1.77	1.93	1.57	have bad dreams or wake up at night crying
21	2.08	2.43	1.61	1.87	2.33	1.26	have toileting accidents during the day
22*	1.43	1.57	1.26	1.72	1.73	1.70	play well with other children
23*	2.34	2.37	2.30	2.34	2.20	2.52	talk about babies or the new baby
24	2.36	2.13	2.65	2.51	2.40	2.65	seem to be shy or afraid around strangers
25*	2.28	2.30	2.26	2.32	2.37	2.26	tend to obey you and your husband
26	2.15	1.93	2.44	1.93	2.03	1.78	talk baby talk or play baby
X̄	2.09	2.16	2.00	1.92	1.88	1.97	

*Scoring on this question is reversed. M = 30 males; F = 23 females Scale: 1 = almost never 5 = almost always

distress. The mothers rated the child's present or recent behaviors, rather than changes in behaviors.

2. A lightweight, portable, cardboard and vinyl doll house, and a family of four dolls, was used in a projective doll play measure. The doll house was marketed by Travel Toy Corp., Division of Prepac, Inc. (188 W. 230th St., Bronx, N.Y., 10463) and included the following rooms: bath, children's bedroom, parents' bedroom, kitchen, dining, living, and family rooms. Each room contained pertinent cardboard furniture. The Flagg Family of flexible dolls included a father, a mother, a boy or girl (depending on child's sex), and a nonsexed baby doll.

3. A six page recording form for a written sequential protocol during the 10-minute projective doll play session, divided into 30-sec sections.

4. A behavioral rating sheet on which the observer, immediately after the home visit, rated the child's general social and affective behavior throughout the visit. The 5-point scale ranged from "child almost never exhibited this behavior" to "almost always." The eight general categories of behaviors rated by the observer included seeking attention from mother, seeking attention from observer, exhibiting shyness, appearing relaxed, etc. The sheet was identical for each visit and for both groups.

5. A portable cassette tape recorder to record the child's verbalizations and some of the incidental auditory environmental cues that might influence the child's play response (e.g., baby crying, mother talking).

6. A device for observation timing (DOT), an auditory prompter that alerted the observer via a tone in the ear to the start of the successive 30-sec recording intervals during doll play.

Procedure

One of four trained female observers visited the expectant mother and child, in their home, about three to four weeks *before* the baby's expected due date ($\overline{X}$ = 23 days). A second visit, scheduled for three to four weeks *after* the baby's arrival, was made by the same observer ($\overline{X}$ = 29 days). Because of variance between due date and delivery dates, the time span between visits was variable; the mean span was 51 days. The events of the second visit parallelled those of the first. Control group visits were scheduled at a time when the child was the same age (plus or minus two months) as an experimental-group child of the same sex. The spacing of visits for each control group family was dependent on the spacing between visits for the matched experimental-group family (± two weeks).

Upon building rapport with both the mother and child during the first 10–15 minutes of the visit, the observer asked the mother to fill out the behavioral questionnaire. At the same time and in the same room, the doll play situation was set up on the floor with the mother nearby but out of the child's direct line of vision. In the case of second visits to the experimental group, the newborn was initially placed on the floor or in a baby seat between the mother and child; but some mothers were forced to pick up the baby if crying or serious fussing began.

After the observer opened the house and turned on the recorder the child was told and/or asked what each room was used for. Once the rooms had been identified in this interactive manner, each doll was placed in front of the child, each named in turn for the child ("This is the father, this is the mother," etc.). The child was then invited to play with the dolls and house while the observer wrote. If prompting was necessary the observer would say "Go ahead, you can make them do anything you like. What will they do?" The doll play protocol paralleled that outlined by Sears, Rau, and Alpert (1965) in their description of the "permissive doll play" session.

Timing and recording of the written sequential protocol (for 10 min of play segmented into 30–sec blocks) began when the child first touched the materials. The observer's protocol included information concerning which dolls the child used, what actions the dolls engaged in, the child's actions and expressions of affect, and the child's interactions with others (mother, observer, baby).

At the end of the doll play, the observer collected the mother's completed questionnaire, politely terminated the visit, and filled in the observation rating sheet of the child's behavior as soon as possible thereafter. The tape recording was then transcribed and collated with the written sequential protocol report.

Reliability.   Interobserver reliability was established prior to the collection of data through the use of videotape records of preschool-aged children engaged in free play with the doll equipment as well as several home visits with preschool-aged children. Reliability was reassessed periodically throughout the 24–month data collection period. Reliability was calculated for pairs of observers on their written sequential protocol records of doll play by dividing the number of statements in agreement by the number of total statements (agreements and disagreements). This ratio was multiplied by 100% for an observer reliability percentage for each pair of observers.

Reliability on the observation rating sheets was calculated by scoring one point credit for each exact agreement in rating between pairs of observers, ½ point credit for scores that were rated one number apart, and no credit for scores more than one rating apart. This was done with each item on the rating sheet. This score was then divided by the total number of items on the rating sheet, and multiplied by 100%, for a percent reliability estimate for each pair of observers.

Interobserver reliability on both measures was 85% or more for each pair of observers, prior to initial data collection. Reliability on periodic reassessment ranged from 85-93%. Intercoder reliability on the open-ended questions of the mothers' reports was established between two coders at the 90% level; then a single rater coded all open-ended responses.

The rationale for utilizing a small battery of measures directed towards both the child and mother was to combine the advantages of a projective nonthreatening technique for the child with the questionnaire technique for the mother, and the rating technique for observation of the total situation. We were not focusing on the emergence of sibling rivalry, but on whatever positive as well as negative behaviors and affects might surface. A multimeasure approach has proven valuable in recent research on social interactions and relationships (Clarke-Stewart, 1973). The information derived from the maternal questionnaire provided data on the child's routine behaviors, social relationships, and parentally observed changes in an economic fashion.

Since the newborn was only three or four weeks old at the time of the second visit to the home, and since funding was limited, the decision was made to concentrate on the older child in this preliminary study. Should a longitudinal follow up be possible, both children will be observed intensively, in reciprocal interaction with one another and with both parents.

RESULTS

The data presented in this chapter are limited to the mother's responses to the questionnaire. (The doll play and observer's ratings will be presented in future reports.) The data are presented in three sections: Ratings by the mothers in the experimental group; responses by these mothers to the open-ended questions on the questionnaire; and comparisons of the experimental and control group data.

Mother's Ratings, Experimental Group Only

First, the mothers' responses to the 26 behavior items are considered, and then the data from a factor analysis of these items are presented.

Behavioral Ratings, 26-item Questionnaire

Overall.   Children were rated relatively low on questions about behavioral distress. Half of the items on the second visit had mean ratings lower than 2, meaning that children almost never or did not often exhibit the distressed behavior. Mean scores ranged 1.06—3.38 on 1 to 5 scale of frequency. The only three items on either visit with a mean of 3 ("sometimes") or higher were temper tantrums or crying, following mother, and trying hard to get mother's attention (See Table 1).

Visit One to Visit Two.   In a repeated measure analysis of variance, when averaging across all 26 items, the mean rating for Visit 1 did not differ significantly from the Visit 2 mean. This absence of global differences was expected from previous research reports. There was, however, a significant interaction between visit and specific behavioral items [F (25,1125) = 1.73, $p < .014$], as well as a significant triple interaction of visit $\times$ sex of child $\times$ specific behavioral items [F (25,1125) = 1.63, $p < .026$].

Specific behavioral items for which ratings significantly differed between visits on paired-t analyses [$p < .05$] are described in Table 2 for the group as a whole, and for boys and girls separately. According to the mother's reports, the changes in boys' behaviors from Visit 1 to Visit 2 involved spending more time sitting or lying around doing nothing, and not being as easy to talk with. Following mother around the house decreased, but was still high. The girls, in turn, increased their use of pacifier or bottle, fussed more often about going to bed at night, less frequently played well with other children, enjoyed less hearing talk about babies or sibs, and decreased talking baby talk or playing baby. (Additional items significant at p levels $> .05 < .10$ for the whole group, for boys, and for girls also appear in Table 2.)

The global picture of change may perhaps be characterized for the boys as some withdrawal from the mother, and for the girls as some increased dependence.

TABLE 2.2
Visit 1 — Visit 2 Comparison: Ratings

Question	Paired t	p	Visit 1	Visit 2	Change
1. Whole Experimental Group (n = 53)					
15*	-2.11	.04	1.40	1.58	less easy to get child to talk to you
16*	-1.99	.05	1.70	1.94	enjoy hearing talk about babies and sibs less
22*	2.39	.021	1.43	1.72	play well with other children less frequently
17	2.61	.012	3.32	3.00	following mother around the house decreases (but is still high)
6*	-1.77	.083	1.06	1.11	less alert and interested
1	-1.66	.103	2.68	2.98	fuss more often about going to bed at night
2. Males (n = 30)					
3	-2.18	.04	1.37	1.77	spend more time sitting, lying **around** doing nothing
15*	-2.11	.04	1.43	1.70	less often easy to get child to talk to you
17	2.07	.05	3.43	3.10	following mother around the house decreases (but is still high)
24	-1.76	.088	2.13	2.40	more shy or afraid around strangers
3. Females (n = 23)					
1	2.13	.05	2.74	3.30	fuss more often about going to bed at night
4	-2.34	.03	1.17	1.52	use of pacifier or bottle increases
16*	-2.47	.022	1.39	1.83	enjoy less hearing talk about babies, sibs
22*	2.47	.022	1.26	1.70	play well with other children less frequently
26	3.04	.006	2.43	1.78	talking baby talk or playing baby decreases
5*	-1.90	.071	2.39	2.78	not look forward to being left with a sitter
21	1.89	.073	1.61	1.26	fewer toileting accidents during the day

*Scoring on this question is reversed.

Sex of Child. Multivariate analyses of variance (manova) on each visit's ratings, with age as a covariate, revealed significant sex differences on the first visit [F (26,23) = 2.27, $p < .025$] with girls having a less distressed mean rating than boys ($\bar{X}$ girls = 2.00, $\bar{X}$ boys = 2.16). On Visit 2 the significance of the sex effect diminished to $p < .077$ [F (26,23) = 1.81], with boys now rated slightly lower on global distress than girls.

Table 3 lists the specific behavioral items on each visit for which boys and girls significantly differed in mean rating. In addition, there is a list of specific items for which the *difference scores* (rating on Visit 2 minus rating on Visit 1) showed significant sex of child effects.

On Visit 1, there were significant sex differences on three items. Boys fussed more frequently about eating and broke toys or objects more often than girls; girls enjoyed hearing talk about babies more than boys. On Visit 2, girls used a pacifier or bottle more than the boys; boys had more daytime toileting accidents than girls.

From Visit 1 to Visit 2, boys and girls significantly changed in different directions. Boys lay around more, doing nothing; girls lay around a little less than before. Girls increased their use of a pacifier or bottle while boys decreased their use. Girls baby-talked less or played baby much less; boys changed little on

TABLE 2.3
Sex Differences on Ratings
(Age as Covariate on Manovas)

Question	F(1, 48)	p	Raw Means M	Raw Means F	
Visit 1					
2	6.96	.011	2.67	1.96	Boys fuss more about eating
16*	6.74	.012	1.93	1.39	Girls enjoy hearing talk about babies more than boys
19	9.73	.003	1.80	1.22	Boys break toys or objects more often than girls
Visit 2					
4	6.56	.014	1.07	1.52	Girls use a pacifier or bottle more than boys
21	7.92	.007	2.33	1.26	Boys have more day time toileting accidents than girls
Difference Scores (Visit 2 minus Visit 1)					*Change from VIsit 1*
3	6.99	.011	.40	-.17	Boys lie around more, doing nothing; girls lie around less
4	7.78	.008	-.23	.35	Girls increase their use of pacifier or bottle; boys decrease use
26	5.39	.025	.10	-.65	Girls baby-talk or play baby less
10	3.12	.084	-.10	.22	Girls increase their need for help in doing things

*Scoring on this question is reversed.

this. In addition, at marginal significance, girls more frequently needed a lot of help in doing things whereas boys didn't change much.

Despite the sex differences specified here, boys and girls did not significantly differ on most of the behaviors in the 26-item questionnaire.

Sex of Baby.   Not unexpected with infants so young, the babies' sex had no significant effect on overall ratings in a manova with age as a covariate. (One or two specific items of the 26 differed significantly, but this might have occurred by chance.)

Similarly, the sex of child × sex of baby interaction was not significant. The two or three specific items that were significant on the Visit 2 analysis, or on the analysis of the difference scores (Visit 2 minus Visit 1) were not consistent. Sometimes opposite sex pairs fared best, sometimes same sex pairs.

Age of Child.   When broken into two age groups (under 40 months; 40 months and over), overall age differences only reached $p < .109$ significance [RM anova, $F (1,45) = 2.67$]. However, the age × sex of child interaction, as well as the age × specific behavioral item interaction were highly significant [$F (1,45) = 6.0$, $p < .02$; $F (25,1125) = 3.16$, $p < .001$ respectively]. The younger children, particularly the boys, exhibited distress behaviors most frequently of the four age-sex groups.

Behavior items on which the younger group were rated as significantly worse than the older on Visits 1 and 2 were: Using a pacifier or bottle ($p < .04$, $p < .10$); not staying dry at night ($p < .001$, $p < .001$); and having toileting accidents during the day ($p < .001$, $p < .001$). These maturational differences are not surprising. However, the younger children had *more* toileting accidents on the second visit; the older children improved.

An item that significantly differed by age group on the first visit but not on the second was following mother around the house. Younger children did this more frequently than older children on the first visit only. Another item that significantly differed only on the first visit, with the older children getting the poorer rating (although both groups rated relatively well), was "easy to get child to talk to you."

Only one item surfaced marginally on Visit 2 that had not shown significant age differences on Visit 1, and that was needing a lot of help doing things ($p < .093$). The younger children were reported as needing more help on Visit 2 than the older children.

Factor Analysis of Questionnaire Items

On the basis of varimax rotated factor analysis of Visit 1 ratings, four factors were derived. These factors and their tentative labels are:

Factor 1—immature behavior—accounted for 37.2% of the variance

Factor 2—frustration/aggression—accounted for 29% of the variance
Factor 3—proximity maintenance—accounted for 18.9% of the variance
Factor 4—apathy, nondynamism—accounted for 14.9% of the variance.

These four factors utilized 18 of the 26 items; 6 items were repeated. Table 4 lists the items and their loadings.

Repeated measure anovas on the unweighted mean factor scores for each child, on each visit separately [2 sex × 2 ages × 4 factors], and a RM anova for 2 sex × 2 ages × 4 factors × 2 visits demonstrated numerous significant effects. Table 5 summarizes the analyses.

Most notably, the age difference in factor scores was prominent for boys, but not for girls; or put another way, sex differences were larger in the younger group

TABLE 2.4
Factors Derived from Mothers' Ratings
(Varimax Rotated Factor Analysis)

Factor 1	*(37.2%)*		*Immature behavior*
Item	4	.41	use a pacifier or bottle
	7*	.74	(not) stay dry at night
	16*	.63	(not) enjoy hearing talk about babies, sibs
	19	.29	break toys or other objects
	21	.49	have toileting accidents during the day
	23*	.48	(not) talk about babies or the new baby
	24	-.27	shy or afraid around strangers
	26	-.35	talk baby talk, or play baby
Factor 2	*(29.0%)*		*Frustration/aggression, hostility*
	14	.64	have temper tantrums or end up crying
	19	.35	break toys or other objects
	20	.59	have bad dreams or wake up at night crying
	21	.52	have toileting accidents during the day
	22*	.48	(not) play well with other children
	25*	.45	(not) tend to obey you and your husband
Factor 3	*(18.9%)*		*Proximity maintenance*
	2	.37	make a fuss about eating
	5*	.36	(not) seem to look forward to being left with sitter
	9	.90	mind you leaving him/her alone for a few minutes
	11*	.35	(not) easy to get interested in doing things
	17	.43	follow you around the house
	22*	.39	(not) play well with other children
Factor 4	*(14.9%)*		*Apathy, nondynamism*
	7*	.30	(not) stay dry at night
	11*	.54	(not) easy to get interested in doing things
	13*	.46	(not) easy to make up his/her mind
	26	.78	talk baby talk or play baby

*Scoring on this question is reversed

TABLE 2.5
Summary of Repeated Measures Anova on Factor[1] Scores
(2 sexes x 2 ages x 2 visits x 4 factors)

Source of Variation	df	F	P	Means
Sex	1, 49	3.93	.053	Males 2.15; Females 1.93
Age	1, 49	6.59	.013	Young 2.20; Old 1.90
Age x Sex	1, 49	7.45	.009	

	Young	Old
Male	2.37	1.89
Female	1.92	1.94

Source of Variation	df	F	P
Factors			ns
Sex x Factors			ns
Age x Factors	3, 147	7.04	.001

Factors

	1	2	3	4
Young	2.21	2.18	2.10	2.32
Old	1.78	1.91	2.15	1.77

Source of Variation	df	F	P
Triple interaction			ns
Visits			ns
Sex x Visit			ns
Age x Visit	1, 49	3.25	.077
Visit x Factor			ns
Sex x Visit x Factor	3, 147	3.06	.03

| | Young-Visit 1: 2.24 | Visit 2: 2.17 |
| Old | 1.87 | 1.94 |

		Factors			
Sex		1	2	3	4
M	V1	2.08	2.19	2.27	2.10
	V2	2.05	2.20	2.21	2.11
F	V1	1.91	1.83	1.87	2.07
	V2	1.92	1.88	2.08	1.90

[1]Factor 1 – Immature behaviors; Factor 2 – Frustration/Aggression;
Factor 3 – Proximity-maintenance; Factor 4 – Apathy

than in the older group. The young boys showed the greatest amount of distress on the mean factors score.

In addition, the older children were rated as less distressed than the younger group on all factors *except proximity maintenance,* where they had equal or worse mean ratings than the younger group. The greatest age differences occurred on the apathy factor. Differences between young and old groups tended to decrease in Visit 2 [$p < .08$].

Finally, the birth of the baby altered the girls' factor scores in the second visit more than the boys'. The boys' scores were relatively stable and worse than the girls. The girls increased in proximity maintenance and decreased in apathy.

Open-ended Questions, Experimental Group

Mothers' responses to the essay-type questions were coded by a rater. Frequencies and percentages were obtained, and chi square tests were performed to investigate the relation between sex of child and the mothers' responses, as well as age of child and responses.

All 53 children received some verbal preparation for the birth of the sibling, and 62% of the mothers reported using books to help prepare the child. Some contact by the child with other new-baby families prior to the birth of the younger sibling was reported by 74% of the mothers. Children's attitudes toward the pregnancy were reported as positive by 47% of the mothers and ambivalent by 40%. None reported wholly negative attitudes in their child.

Most of the mothers (72%) were hospitalized for 2-½ days or more for the birth. Father was most often the one who informed the child of the birth (55%); the caretaker (grandparent, neighbor, sitter) announced the news second most often (21%). Most of the children (79%) first saw the baby in the hospital. All knew where the mother was (three families had home births), and 81% had phone contact with the mother during hospitalization.

Children's reactions to the reunion with mother were coded as positive (49% of the children) and as mixed, ambivalent, or changing (26%). Initial reactions to the birth and new baby were reported as mainly positive (55%) or ambivalent (26%). Mothers reported general changes in their child's behavior during the few weeks after the baby's birth of a negative nature (64% of the children) and mixed changes in 19%. Most often changes were reported in the areas of affect (57%) and demanding of attention (60%). Ten to twelve children were reported as showing changes in sleeping or bedtime behavior, toileting routines, and discipline/obedience.

The mothers reported considerable involvement of the older child with the newborn: 71% of the mothers mentioned the child's helping to diaper or clothe the baby; 43% mentioned bathing; 38% mentioned feeding; 68% mentioned holding; touching or hugging the baby; 74% watching or supervising; and 53% entertaining or playing with the baby. Only 15% reported that the two children shared a room. Sleeping arrangements did change during the six months prior to the birth for 34% of the children. These changes usually involved a switch from crib to youth or "real" bed.

Two-thirds of the children had been in day care in nursery centers or classes; 45% had been in day care in a private home (a smaller setting). Only 4 boys and 3 girls were listed in neither experience.

All of the children played with dolls: 70% had baby dolls; 32% had family dolls; 43% had character dolls; 42% had Teddy bears or cuddley type dolls. The type of doll play was usually characterized as nurturant (85% of the children), but 15% were aggressive or abusive sometimes, and 28% played family scenes.

The firstborn's social behavior with familiar adults was characterized as positive by 91% of the mothers; social play with children was characterized as positive in 70% and mixed in 23%. Social behavior in unfamiliar situations was described as positive in 38%, shy or negative in 13%, and mixed in 42%. Three-quarters of the mothers judged the child's behavior with the observer to be the same as usual.

Sex.   More girls than boys role-played pregnancy [corrected χ^2 (1) = 4.06, p <.05], had baby dolls [corrected χ^2 (1) = 4.32, p <.04] and played family scenes [corrected χ^2 (1) = 3.39, p <.065]. More boys than girls played with dolls in an aggressive, abusive way [corrected χ^2 (1) = 5.29, p <.02], and were reported as having contact with peers who were relatives [corrected χ^2 (1) = 6.03, p <.014].

Age.   Almost all the older children were reported as having day care center or nursery experience, but only half the younger children [corrected χ^2 (1) = 8.12, p <.004]. More than half the younger group had changes in their sleeping arrangements as compared to very few of the older group [corrected χ^2 (1) = 9.56, p <.002]. Although the father was the modal informer about the birth in both age groups, more younger than older children were told by the caretaker [χ^2 (4) = 11.88, p < .02]. There was some tendency for more of the younger children to role play an older sibling (p <.06).

Experimental and Control Group Comparisons

Since data for only 17 control families (matched for age, sex, and time span between visits) have thus far been analyzed, current findings are stated with great tentativeness. The following data refer to the 17 control families and the 17 matched experimental families.

A 2 group × 2 sex × 2 visits × 26 questions repeated measures analysis of variance revealed no overall significant effects, except for questions. An item-by-item analysis indicated the following significant differences between the sibling and only child groups, on the *first* visit:

1. The children in the experimental group more often minded the mother leaving them alone for a few minutes (t, 32 df, p <.03).
2. Although both groups were reported as enjoying new things or experiences, the control group rated better in this respect (p <.04).
3. The experimental group (not surprisingly) talked more often about babies than the control group (p <.02).
4. The experimental group spent time more often just sitting or lying around and doing nothing (p <.075).
5. The experimental group was reported to enjoy hearing talk about babies, brothers, or sisters, more frequently than the control group (p <.097).

On the *second* visit, however, the only significant difference between the groups was how frequently they talked about babies or the new baby ($p < .01$).

Similarly, an analysis of the *change* scores (Visit 2 rating minus Visit 1 rating) indicated differences between experimental and control groups on: Needing a lot of help doing things ($p < .02$) where the experimental group improved considerably and the control group worsened slightly; objecting to mother's leaving child alone for a few minutes ($p < .073$), for which the experimental group improved and control group worsened; fussing about going to bed at night ($p < .107$) where experimental group worsened, control group improved; easy to get child to talk to you ($p < .102$), for which the control group worsened.

An analysis of the *factor scores* (2 groups × 2 sexes × 2 times × 4 factors) revealed two significant effects:

Group × sex × factors $F (3, 90) = 2.76, p < .05$.

Time × factors $F (3, 90) = 3.23, p < .03$.

The experimental boys were highest of all groups on the proximity-maintenance factor; the control girls were higher than the experimental girls on the aggression/hostility factor. The immaturity factor improved with time in both groups; proximity-maintenance became slightly more frequent.

On the *open-end* questions, it was clear from the chi square analyses that the experimental group used more children's books about births and siblings ($p < .006$), and the sib group had of course more involvement with a baby, in all facets (diapering, bathing, feeding, holding, watching, playing), $ps < .0003$. It is noteworthy that the modal response of both groups to the essay query about observed recent changes in the child's behavior was "more negative" changes and the small experimental and control groups did not significantly differ on this item or the specific areas of change in feeding, sleeping, toileting, discipline, or affect. There was a trend ($p < .10$) for the experimental mothers to mention changes in demanding of attention more than control mothers.

DISCUSSION

There can be little disagreement with the assumption that the birth of a second child is a stress time in a family system, nor with the recognition that stress is difficult, complex, and elusive to conceptualize and measure (Rieveschl, 1979). Some comment on the instrument and method employed in this portion of our study is in order, prior to the discussion of our findings.

Comment on the Questionnaire

Mothers' reports, one of our main measures and the one on which this paper focuses, were written questionnaires, containing both open-ended essay questions and 26 specific questions with a multiple-response format. The latter were modified versions of the Vernon et al. (1966) posthospitalization stress questionnaire, reported as a valid indicator of stress based on its agreement with independent clinician's interviews. Even in its original format, Vernon et al. (1966) reported that the significant group changes in psychological upset were small and varied only slightly from the mean, since means combine children who become more upset and children who appear to benefit from the experience. Similarly, even when dealing with *one* child's mean score, that mean combines specific items showing negative changes with those showing positive changes, and does not indicate the variability in scores to individual questions. Dunn, Kendrick, and MacNamee (1981) agree that a single index of "disturbance" that combined many different reactions would be inappropriate, particularly since they found that the prognostic implications of the various reactions differed. For example, they reported that signs of increased withdrawal in the first-born were associated with poor sibling relations later, whereas negative or demanding behavior changes showed no such association. Based on these considerations, we decided to pursue individual behavior items, even when the mean of the 26 combined ratings showed no statistically significant change.

Another decision that needed to be made about the questionnaire concerned derived factor scores. In view of the many modifications in the questionnaire items and style of administration and response, we decided not to adopt the six Vernon et al. (1966) factors and statistically derived our four. Although factor labels always involve some interpretation, there was an effort to use somewhat less psychodynamic interpretation and somewhat more direct description in choosing labels. Thus, "immature behaviors" might be labeled "regressions" by other investigators; "proximity-maintenance" could be viewed as "separation-anxiety."

Since our knowledge of the children's daily behavior was based on mothers' reports rather than direct systematic observation, the advantages and disadvantages of interview and observation techniques needed to be considered (Lytton, 1973). Dunn and Kendrick (in press) systematically compared information from different sources, and found good agreement (81–90%) between ratings of childrens' temperament from maternal interview and ratings by an observer (except for activity level, which mothers rated higher). They also examined the relation between the mothers' answers in the interview three weeks following the birth of the sibling and measures from the direct observations made in the home. Of the 11 comparisons, 6 were significantly related, including increases in tearfulness, clinging, demanding, and negative behavior towards the mother. Our use of mothers' reports as one of our measures has many precedents and reasonable justification.

Discussion of Findings

The sibling research most comparable to ours is the large English project by Dunn and Kendrick and their colleagues (see reference list). Even there, large differences between the studies require that comparisons be drawn with caution.

Their sample consisted of about 40 largely working-class English families; ours were 53 middle-class American families. Although both were longitudinal, involving visits pre- and postbirth of a second child, their more extensive study followed the family for 14 months postbirth. Both involved a multimeasure approach and utilized mothers' reports as one of the measures; ours included a doll play projective technique; theirs included direct observations of mother-child, father-child, and sib-sib interactions. The age range of our subjects was broader, and the median age older (39.25 months compared to 25 months). Their sample had 13 home deliveries; ours had 3. We used 5-point scales for the mothers to rate specific behavior items; they rated the mother interviews on 3-4 point scales.

It is noteworthy (but not surprising) that both studies found that mothers reported considerable distress in their firstborn. Our mothers, on the open-end questions, reported prebirth ambivalence in 40% of the children; mixed or ambivalent reactions to reunion with the mother after birth (26%); ambivalent initial reactions to the birth and new baby (26%); and general changes in the firstborn's behavior in the few weeks after the birth of a negative (64%) or mixed (19%) nature. The ratings portion of the questionnaire (see Table 2) gave less dramatic results, but seemed to yield a picture of withdrawal from mother in the boys and perhaps lessened independence in the girls. Dunn, Kendrick, and MacNamee (1981), with a younger sample of children, had more than half their 40 children reported as showing changes in demanding behavior and negative behaviors toward mother, 11–13 showing frequent or constant tearfulness and clinging, and increase in sleep problems. Twelve of the 26 children in their study who had been toilet-trained showed an increase in toilet-training problems after the birth.

It is important to state the following qualifications to this stress picture:

1. The mothers' essay answers gave a more stressed picture of the first-born than did their ratings on 26 specific behavior items.
2. The statistically significant negative changes in rated behavior items were limited to those listed in the Results section (see Tables 2 and 3).
3. The final ratings for many of these negatively changing items are relatively positive; that is, the mothers generally answered "almost never" or "not often" or "sometimes," and seldom answered "often" or "almost always."
4. Overall, mothers rated their children on the positive end of the scale.

Vernon and Schulman (1964) suggested that psychological upset and psychological benefit may be common in preschool children after a stress like hospitalization. We too were struck with how many items (of 26 items, 13 for boys, 10 for girls) and how many children showed no change or *improved* mean scores after a stressful experience such as separation from mother and presence of a new sib. Despite the signs of distress in some behavioral items in some children, it is possible to speculate from these improved scores that the birth of a sib can be a positive and maturing experience for the first-born and that transitions in family life, although stressful, can be beneficial. Some additional support for this proposition comes from the English study, in which 25 of the 40 children were reported to show some sign of being more "grown up"—more independent about feeding or toileting, improved language ability, and so on, even while 28 mothers were also noting signs of regression (Dunn, Kendrick, & MacNamee, 1981).

Although the previous pages have used words like *positive, negative,* or *improved,* the ascription of positive or negative labels to changes in behavior must be done cautiously. For example, the decrease in mean rating for "following mother around the house" seems positive when considered in isolation. However, when viewed in the context of other behavioral changes by the boys (Table 2: spend more time sitting or lying around doing nothing; less often easy to get child to talk to mother), the picture may be one of apathy or withdrawal. Whether one is a researcher or a parent, it is often difficult to know whether to take overt behavior at face value or to assume that appearances are deceptive. Motivated by fear of loss of love, a child can be overgood, overhelpful, overloving, and solicitous (Vernon et al., 1965).

Individual Differences.   There were differences in mean scores between children, and differences in item scores within children. This is consonant with earlier findings of both upset and benefit being reported by mothers for a sample and for individual children (Dunn, Kendrick, & MacNamee, 1981; Vernon & Schulman, 1964). Dunn (1981) also reports, from observational data of sibling interaction, great individual differences in the proportion of positive social approaches by the first-born and by the infant. The ambivalence of many of the children in our sample is captured by one mother's comment about her son during Visit 1: "[His] attitude seems to fluctuate between very caring and we'll lock it in the basement if it cries."

Sex of Child.   Sex differences in behavior ratings were more apparent in the mothers' reports on the prebirth visit than on the postbirth visit. Also, a comparison of Visits 1 and 2 ratings *within* each sex group showed a different pattern of changes for boys and girls, with the boys' pattern suggesting withdrawal from mother or apathy; Dunn, Kendrick, and MacNamee (1981), too, report more boys than girls showing an increase in withdrawal. The probability of an increase in withdrawal was higher in their subjects when the first-born was a boy; when the mother reported feeling tired or depressed; and when the child scored above the median on the temperamental trait of negative mood. Sex differences in our sample were also significant for the derived factor scores: Boys scored more poorly than girls on each factor score on each visit, particularly on the frustration/aggression factor and the proximity-maintenance factor. Girls, however, increased their proximity-maintenance factor score post sib-birth, while boys' factor scores remained relatively stable.

One can combine our data with information and suggestions from Baldwin (1947), Lamb (1977, 1978b), Legg, Sherick, and Wadland (1975), and Taylor and Kogan (1973) and speculate that boys and girls may react differently to the change in the pregnant mothers' style of relating to the first-born, and/or to the changes after parturition. These changes may include decreases in maternal attention and play, increases in confrontation, changes in the balance of responsibility for initiating interaction (Dunn and Kendrick 1980), decrease in mothers' infantilization of firstborn, and increased restrictiveness (Baldwin, 1947). In addition to maternal changes, the fathers' impact may be more salient after the birth of the second child, possibly being more involved with first-born sons than daughters (Lamb, 1977). This may help account for our findings that the boys' mean behavior ratings improved on the second visit (from 2.16 to 1.88), and that the birth of the baby altered the girls' factor scores more than the boys'.

Sex of Baby/Sex of Sibs-Dyad.   Neither the sex of the infant nor the sex of child X sex of infant interaction produced significant or consistent effects. There is no consensus in the research literature as yet. Some investigators reported more positive social behavior in same-sex than opposite-sex dyads (Dunn, 1981; Dunn & Kendrick, 1981, in press), but some did not (Santrock & Minnett, 1981); some showed sex of infant effects (Vandell & Wilson, 1981); some showed sex of older sib effects (Cicirelli, 1978), whereas some didn't (Pepler, 1981). The lack of a clear picture is not surprising, given the differences in ages of the dyads, in laboratory versus unstructured tasks, and in selection of dependent variables.

Age.   The age X item interaction and the age X sex interaction were highly significant, with younger boys faring the worst on both the behavior items and the factors scores. If the expected maturational differences between children above and below 40 months of age are removed from consideration (use of a pacifier or bottle, not staying dry at night), only a few items remain as distress signs: Younger children did increase their toileting accidents and did increase their need for a lot of help doing things on the postsib-birth visit.

It is possible that the potential for psychological disturbance and psychological benefit are relatively high for preschoolers (Solnit, 1960; Vernon & Schulman, 1964; Vernon et al., 1965; Vernon et al., 1966). One can make a case for greater vulnerability in younger children, especially boys, because of their greater immaturity and lesser grasp of reality concepts, and because of the developmental problems centering about the young child's relationship with mother (e.g., separation experiences, ambivalent feelings, control of bodily functions; Solnit, 1960). Younger children in the English study were more likely to be reported as showing a marked increase in clinging behavior (Dunn, Kendrick, & MacNamee, 1981).

On the other hand, it was striking that our older group was rated as less distressed than the younger on all factors *except proximity maintenance.* The pattern of significant age and sex effects on the two visits suggests that the degree of change may be less important, or no more important, for consideration than the *mode* of change. Emotional reactions of older children may be less dramatic, more indirect and complex, and/or may correspond less closely to the specific measures used to measure upset (Marlens, 1959; Vernon et al., 1965).

Prebirth Findings. Since age and sex effects were generally stronger on the first visit ratings than on the postbirth visit, it is possible that the anticipation of the birth had greater effects for some children than the *initial* adjustment to the new baby's actual presence. Anxiety and worry about the addition of a stranger—a rival, uncertainty about one's own role in the enlarged family, changed sleeping arrangements, etc., could raise psychological vulnerability. It is highly likely, too, that the child is reacting to changes in the pregnant mother's behavior (described earlier), or to her ambivalence about the anticipated complex consequences on family structure and function of a second child (Lamb, 1978b). The charged atmosphere of a late pregnancy may result in emotional contagion.

The above speculations receive some support from the preliminary analyses of the unfinished control group data where differences between control and experimental groups were more frequent on the prebirth visit than on the one-month postbirth visit. To resolve this issue, an investigator will need to reach the family much earlier in the pregnancy, preferably before the mother's figure changes, and before the child is informed (if possible). Ideally, one would wish to have prepregnancy data, but the long time span and developmental issues would complicate the interpretations.

Control Group. Dunn and Kendrick (1980) discuss the possibility that changes in mother and first-born interaction patterns reflect developmental changes rather than the complex of effects surrounding the birth of a sib. Lacking a control group, they used data for the 20 families whose pre- and postbirth visits were less than two months apart, and concluded it was "highly unlikely" that developmental changes in two months could account for the marked changes observed in behavior and interaction.

Our control group comparisons are highly tentative, since only 17 control families have been compared to 17 matched experimental families thus far. Most of the significant differences between the groups were evident on the *first* visit (not the second), leading us to speculate on the underexamined importance of the pregnancy period. The finding that the control girls were higher on the aggression/hostility factor than the experimental girls may indicate that the latter girls inhibit their naughtiness out of anxiety, or out of helpfulness to a pregnant or harried mother. The immaturity factor did show a small developmental change in both groups even over our short time span. It may also be a developmental finding that both groups of mothers listed negative changes frequently when asked about recent observed changes in the child's behavior. Not unrelated is the finding that control subjects in a hospitalization study also manifested some regression and disorganization (Rieveschl, 1979). Further evaluation and comment must be delayed until the data are in.

CONCLUDING COMMENT

Like most initial studies in a research program, this one raises more questions than it answers. A clear finding was that children, according to mothers' reports, exhibited both distress and benefit from the changes in the family system surrounding the anticipation and birth of the second child. Another clear finding was that sex differences were greater on the late pregnancy visit than on the postbirth visit. The incomplete control group data also revealed (thus far) greater contrasts with the experimental group on the first visit than on the second. The suggestion, therefore, is that late pregnancy is a stressful period for the first-born; for some children even more stressful than the few weeks following the birth of a sib.

The poor showing of the older children (40 months or more) on the proximity-maintenance factor was an important finding, reminding us that the *mode* of response may be more meaningful than the frequency or degree of change.

The meaning of some behavior changes is ambiguous. The finding that boys followed mother around the house less after the sib's arrival seemed initially like a "positive" change until considered as part of a pattern of changes that suggested withdrawal from mother. Yet, it is possible to look at this same pattern from a system theory stance and see it as "progressive segregation"—a child's differentiation from the family, an attempt to establish a new role and individual identity. Perhaps the kinds of "negative" changes that parents report at this juncture in the family life cycle represent for some children necessary disequilibrium preceding positive developmental outcome.

ACKNOWLEDGMENTS

Portions of this paper were presented at the meetings of the Society for Research in Child Development, Boston, April 1981, and the International Society for the Study of Behavioural Development, Toronto, August 1981. The data were collected by a team headed by Audrey Begun and consisted of Begun, Nancy Heather, Lucy Kirshner, and Sue Meister. D. Bruce Carter ran computer analyses. This research was supported in part by a University of Michigan Faculty Development Grant (No. 403958) to the senior author.

REFERENCES

Abramovitch, R., Corter, C., & Lando, B. Sibling interaction in the home. *Child Development,* 1979, *50,* 997–1003.
Baldwin, A. L. Changes in parent behavior during pregnancy: An experiment in longitudinal analysis. *Child Development,* 1947, *18,* 29–39.

Begun, A. *Sibling relationships as portrayed in young children's literature*. Unpublished manuscript, University of Michigan, Ann Arbor, Michigan, 1979.

Bradt, J. O. The family with young children. In E. A. Carter & M. McGoldrick (Eds.), *The family life cycle: A framework for family therapy*. New York: Gardner Press, 1980.

Bryant, B. K. *Siblings as caretakers*. Paper presented at the meeting of the American Psychological Association, New York City, 1979.

Carter, E. A., & McGoldrick, M. (Eds.). *The family life cycle: A framework for family therapy*. New York: Gardner Press, 1980.

Cicirelli, V. G. The relationship of sibling structure to intellectual abilities and achievement. *Review of Educational Research*, 1978, *48*(3), 365-379.

Clarke-Stewart, K. A. Interactions between mothers and their children: Characteristics and consequences. *Society for Research in Child Development Monographs*, 1973, 38 (6-7, Serial No. 153).

Dunn, J. *Infants and their siblings: Individual differences and family influences*. Paper presented at the meeting of the Society for Research in Child Development, Boston, April 1981.

Dunn, J., & Kendrick, C. Interaction between young siblings in the context of family relationships. In M. Lewis & L. A. Rosenblum (Eds.), *The child and its family*. New York: Plenum Press, 1979.

Dunn, J., & Kendrick, C. The arrival of a sibling: Changes in patterns of interactions between mother and first-born child. *Journal of Child Psychology and Psychiatry*, 1980, *21*, 119-132.

Dunn, J., & Kendrick, C. Social behaviour of young siblings in the family context: Differences between same-sex and different sex dyads. *Child Development*, 1981, in press.

Dunn, J., & Kendrick, C. Studying temperament and parent-child interaction: Comparison of interview and direct observation. *Developmental Medicine and Child Neurology*, in press.

Dunn, J., Kendrick, C., & MacNamee, R. The reaction of first-born children to the birth of a sibling: Mothers' reports. *Journal of Child Psychology and Psychiatry*, 1981, *22*, 1-18.

Haley, J. *Uncommon therapy: The psychiatric techniques of Milton H. Erickson*. New York: Norton, 1973.

Hinde, R. A. *Towards understanding relationships*. European Monographs in Social Psychology Number 18. New York: Academic Press, 1979.

Hoffman, L. The family life cycle and discontinuous change. In E. A. Carter & M. McGoldrick (Eds.), *The family life cycle: A framework for family therapy*. New York: Gardner Press, 1980.

Lamb, M. E. The development of parental preferences in the first two years of life. *Sex Roles*, 1977, *3*, 495-497.

Lamb, M. E. Infant social cognition and 'second order' effects. *Infant Behavior and Development*, 1978, *1*, 1-10. (a)

Lamb, M. E. Influence of the child on marital quality and family interaction during the prenatal, perinatal, and infancy periods. In R. M. Lerner & G. B. Spanier (Eds.), *Child Influences on marital and family interaction: A life-span perspective*. New York: Academic Press, 1978. (b)

Lamb, M. E. The development of sibling relationships in infancy: A short-term longitudinal study. *Child Development*, 1978, *49*, 1189-1196. (c)

Legg, C., Sherick, I., & Wadland, W. Reactions of pre-school children to the birth of a sibling. *Child Psychiatry and Human Development*, 1975, *5*, 5-39.

Lerner, R. M., & Spanier, G. B. (Eds.). *Child Influences on marital and family interaction: A life-span perspective*. New York: Academic Press, 1978.

Levy, D. M. Rivalry between children in the same family. *Child Study*, 1934, *11*, 233-261.

Levy, D. M. Studies in sibling rivalry. *American Orthopsychiatric Association*, Research Monograph, No. 2, 1937.

Lytton, H. Three approaches to the study of parent-child interaction: Ethological, interview and experimental. *Journal of Child Psychology and Psychiatry*, 1973, *14*, 1-17.

Marlens, H. S. *A study of the effect of hospitalization on children.* Unpublished doctoral dissertation, New York University, 1959.

Minuchin, S. *Families and family therapy.* Cambridge: Harvard University Press, 1974.

Pepler, D. *Naturalistic observations of teaching and modeling between siblings.* Paper presented at the meeting of the Society for Research in Child Development, Boston, April 1981.

Rieveschl, J. L. Regression in spatial and affective role-taking skill and its implications for young tonsillectomy patients. Unpublished doctoral dissertation, University of Michigan, 1979.

Santrock, J. W., & Minnett, A. M. *Sibling interaction in cooperative, competitive, and neutral settings: An observational study of sex of sibling, age spacing, and ordinal position.* Paper presented at the meeting of the Society for Research in Child Development, Boston, April 1981.

Satir, V. *Conjoint family therapy.* Palo Alto: Science and Behavior Books, 1964.

Schultz, D. A. *The changing family: Its function and future* (2nd ed.). Englewood Cliffs, N.J.: Prentice Hall, 1976.

Sears, R. R., Rau, L., & Alpert, R. *Identification and child rearing.* Stanford, Calif.: Stanford University Press, 1965.

Solnit, A. J. Hospitalization. An aid to physical and psychological health in childhood. *American Journal of Disturbed Children,* 1960, *99,* 155–163.

Solomon, M. A developmental, conceptual premise for family therapy. *Family Process,* 1973, *12,* 179–188.

Stevenson, N. *Family therapy and a theory of change.* Unpublished paper, University of Michigan, Ann Arbor, Michigan, 1980.

Taylor, M. K., & Kogan, K. L. Effects of birth of a sibling on mother-child interactions. *Child Psychiatry and Human Development,* 1973, *4*(1), 53–58.

Toman, W. *Family constellation: Its effects on personality and social behavior* (3rd ed.). New York: Springer-Verlag, 1976.

Vandell, D. L., & Wilson, K. S. *Sibling relations during the first year.* Paper presented at the meeting of the Society for Research in Child Development, Boston, April 1981.

Vernon, T. A., Foley, J. M., Sipowicz, R. R., & Schulman, J. L. *The psychological responses of children to hospitalization and illness: A review of the literature.* Springfield, Ill.: Charles C. Thomas, 1965.

Vernon, D. T. A., & Schulman, J. L. Hospitalization as a source of psychological benefit to children. *Pediatrics,* 1964, 694–696.

Vernon, D. T. A., Schulman, J. L., & Foley, J. M. Changes in children's behavior after hospitalization: Some dimensions of response and their correlates. *American Journal of Diseases in Children,* 1966, *111,* 581–593.

Wagner, M. E., Schubert, H. J. P., & Schubert, D. S. P. Sibship-constellation effects on psychosocial development, creativity, and health. In H. W. Reese & L. P. Lipsitt (Eds.), *Advances in child development and behavior* (Vol. 14). New York: Academic Press, 1979.

Weisner, T., & Gallimore, R. My brother's keeper: Child and sibling caretaking. *Current Anthropology,* 1977, *18*(2), 169–190.

Whiting, B., & Whiting, J. W. M. *Children of six cultures.* Cambridge: Harvard University Press, 1975.

3 Siblings and Their Mothers: Developing Relationships Within the Family

Judy Dunn
Carol Kendrick
Cambridge University

INTRODUCTION

He loves being with her and her friends—he's very fond of one of her friends. He trails after Laura. . . . They play in the sand a lot . . . making pies. She organizes it, and swipes away things that are dangerous and gives him something else. They go upstairs and bounce on the bed. Then he'll lie there while she sings to him, and reads books to him. And he'll go off in a trance with his hanky (comfort object). The important thing is they're becoming games that they'll play together. He'll start something by laughing and running towards some toy, turning round to see if she's following. He'll go upstairs and race into one bedroom and shriek, and she joins him. . . .

It's worse now he's on the go. He annoys her. They fight a lot—more than four or five big fights a day, and *every* day. They're very *bad tempered* with each other. He makes her cry such a lot.

Thus two very different pairs of siblings, each with a baby brother of 14 months and a sister of nearly three years old, are described by their mothers. In their relationship we see hostility, aggression, comfort, consolation, provocation, pleasure, amusement, and excitement. No one watching young siblings can fail to be impressed by the range and the intensity of emotions expressed by the children or by the great differences between sibling pairs in the quality of their relationships. But this range of expressive behavior, and the nature of the interactions between the children, raise many important questions for psychologists.

What *kind* of relationships do 2- and 3-year-olds have with their young siblings—children with whom they are extremely familiar, yet who are so different from the adults in their world? What kind of social understanding does this expressive behavior reflect? Clearly the quality of the sibling's relationships will be profoundly affected by the extent to which each child 'understands' the other. Do two- and three-year-old siblings show the very limited ability to perceive and respond to the feelings, wishes, and intentions of their siblings which, in the view of many psychologists, characterizes children of this age? What are the origins of the differences between sibling pairs in the quality of their relationship, clearly evident in the two examples given? Is the developing relationship between the siblings affected by the quality of the relationship between each child and its parents? How far do these individual differences persist over the early years of childhood? It is well established that by 5–6 years of age the position of a child in his or her family—the sex and age spacing of the siblings—influences his or her preferences, interests, style of thinking, and sense of self-esteem (Cicirelli, 1976; Sutton-Smith & Rosenberg, 1970). Sutton-Smith and Rosenberg have shown that differences between first-born and later-born children in interests, in sex roles, and conformity can be plausibly attributed to the influence of siblings. It is clearly important that we should investigate the development of these differences during the earliest years of the sibling relationship.

In this chapter these questions are considered in the light of findings from an observational study of young siblings carried out in Cambridge, England. Forty families were followed from a point late in the mother's second pregnancy and through the infancy of the second child. They were then visited again when the first child was six years old. The study was concerned with a variety of questions, both developmental and clinical: The impact of the birth of the sibling on the first born child; the prevalence and persistence of behavior problems arising after the sibling birth; the nature of the relationship between the young siblings; the development of individual differences in the sibling relationship; and, the mutual influence of the relationships within the family. Here we will consider three of these issues, and will give a brief overview of some of the main findings of the study in relation to these issues. The study is reported and discussed in full in Dunn and Kendrick (1982). Here we will first examine the quality of the relationship between the siblings at the stage when the second-born children were aged 14 months, and the first-born between 32 and 57 months. Second, we will discuss the nature of the social understanding revealed in the observations of the siblings—the young child's expressed beliefs about the baby, the child's sensitivity towards the sibling's affective state, and his response to the problems of communicating with the baby. Third, the mutual influence of relationships within the family will be considered, specifically the question of how far differences in the mother's relationship with each child are related to differences in the quality of the sibling relationship.

THE STUDY

Full details of the study, the sample, the methods of observation and of inter-view, and the reliabilities and stabilities of the measures are given in Dunn and Kendrick (1980; 1981a). The observation measures showed good stability from week to week, and the agreement between observation and interview was consid-erable (Dunn & Kendrick, 1982). In brief: The families were, in terms of the father's occupation, largely lower middle-class and working-class. There were 19 first-born girls, 21 first-born boys, 19 second-born girls, 21 second-born boys. There were 8 girl-girl pairs, 11 girl-boy pairs, 10 boy-boy pairs and 11 boy-girl pairs. The first-born children were aged 18–43 months at the birth of the sibling (median 24 months).

All observations and interviews were carried out in the homes. The families were visited at 4 time points in the main study:[1] During the mother's pregnancy with the second child; 2–3 weeks after the second baby's birth; 8 months later; and 14 months later. At each time point two hour-long observations were carried out and the mothers were interviewed. The observations were unstructured; precoded categories of behavior were recorded on a 10 sec time base. Only one observer was present at the observation. Verbal interaction during the observa-tions was tape recorded and transcribed after the observation by the observer. The temperamental characteristics of the first-born child were assessed at the pregnancy interview and when the baby was eight months old.

The Relationship Between Young Siblings

How we describe and interpret a child's behaviour depends crucially on our assumptions about the child's level of understanding and intention. Although there have been a number of studies of *interaction* between very young siblings (Abramovitch, Corter & Lando, 1979; Abramovitch, Corter & Pepler, 1980; Lamb, 1978a; 1978b) that refer to a wide range of items of 'prosocial' and aggressive behavior, attempts to describe the *relationship* between such young siblings in more 'global' psychological dimensions have usually been in terms of jealousy or rivalry for the parent (e.g., Levy, 1937; Ross, 1930; Sewall, 1930; Smalley, 1930). The assumption that jealousy is the key dimension in the sibling relationship reflects two presuppositions about the development of young chil-dren. First, it follows the assumption that the *mother-child* relationship is the central feature of a child's emotional and social development in the first three years—an assumption that means the relationship between child and sibling is

---

[1]Follow-up visits were made to the children when the elder sibling was six years old, as part of a study by Stilwell-Barnes (1982). I am grateful to her for permission to refer to her preliminary findings.

seen only in terms of a response to displacement from and competition for the mother. Yet clinical observations of children brought up together in institutions (Burlingham & Freud, 1944) suggest that a wide range of emotions are seen in the relations among the children:

> In a crowd of toddlers they have to learn unduly early to defend themselves and their property, to stand up for their own rights, and even to consider the rights of others. This means that they have to become social at an age when it is normal to be asocial. Under pressure of these circumstances they develop a surprising range of reactions: love, hate, jealousy, rivalry, competition, protectiveness, pity, generosity, sympathy and even understanding [p. 23-4].

Burlingham and Freud (1944) argued that this range of emotions would *not* develop between children in a normal family, where the relationship between siblings only reflects competition for the parents' love.

This absence of a real consideration of the complexity of very young children's feelings towards their siblings reflects the second assumption: That concepts such as friendship, empathy, concern, or protectiveness do not properly apply to children of this age, because such concepts presuppose a far more sophisticated ability to understand the feelings, intentions, and wishes of other people than is usually considered possible for children under three. Yet our observations of siblings at home gave us a picture of the relationship between the siblings that was very much at odds with the notion that jealousy was the only important dimension. Our observations showed that there was a wide range and a complexity of feelings expressed, and considerable pragmatic understanding of how to annoy and how to console the other. Four features of the relationship stood out from these observations and from the interviews with the mothers. The first was the *salience* of the behavior of the sibling for each child. This was evident both in the frequency of interactions between the children (the median value of the time the siblings spent interacting was 17% of the time they were together), and in the nature of this interaction—notably in the imitative sequences. At 8 months, imitations of the baby by the first-born were common, and by 14 months imitations of the first-born by the baby were also frequent (Dunn & Kendrick, 1982). These imitative sequences demonstrated both the attention paid by each child to the other and the power of the older as model for the younger. Our results here parallel those of Abramovitch et al. (1979), who note the frequency of sibling interaction at home.

The salience of the sibling was also clearly shown by the response of each child to interaction between a parent and their brother or sister. Both older and younger sibling reacted to a high proportion of the interactions between mother and sibling. In some families, for instance, the first-born reacted to as many as 78% of the interactions between mother and baby. The *nature* of this response varied very much, ranging from friendly cooperation to attack and disruption, a point to which we will return.

Finally, it was clear from the interviews with the mothers that most first-born children responded promptly to signs that the baby was upset, was in potential danger, or was being 'naughty'—approaching a forbidden object or repeating a prohibited action. Again, the ways in which the first-borns responded to these situations varied very much, but it was rare for them to ignore their sibling's actions.

A second very striking feature of the sibling relationship was the *ambivalence* apparent in the children's behavior. This was, for instance, very clear when we examined the patterning of the different aspects of the sibling's behavior towards each other. The correlations in Table 1 show that in families where the children played together frequently (peek-a-boo, hide-and-seek) the first child also was likely to help the baby and to caretake frequently and both children were likely to imitate each other frequently. A high frequency of imitations and of giving or showing toys was negatively correlated with the frequency with which the first child hit, pushed, or pinched the younger. But these negative correlations were not large, and inspection of the scatter plots revealed that although a few children were frequently warm and friendly and rarely showed aggressive behavior, others showed both friendly *and* aggressive behavior to their siblings. These results show that it would be misleading to conceptualize the sibling relationship in terms of a unitary dimension of warmth or hostility. Although there was a wide range of individual differences in the emotional quality of the relationships, there was not a simple pattern of positive and negative social behavior. It was quite

TABLE 3.1
Spearman Rank Correlations between 'Types' of
Interaction between Siblings

	Games	*Joint Physical Play*	*A giving B object*	*A helping B*	*A imitating B*	*B imitating A*
		Number of interactions (per time sibs together) which included				
Joint physical play	.28					
A give B object	.29	.14				
A helps B	.40*	.28	.48*			
A imitates B	.46**	-.30	.33*	.59***		
B imitates A	.42*	-.20	.35*	.33*	.53***	
A Prohibs B	-.18	-.08	.10	.04	.18	.01
A Neg. Touch B	-.23	-.07	-.58***	-.30	-.31*	-.38*

* p < .05
** p < .01
*** p < .001

common for a child to show both friendly and hostile behavior to his or her sibling.

The descriptions given by the mothers paralleled these findings closely. According to the mothers' reports, children who frequently comforted their siblings (22%) usually did not mind sharing toys and frequently helped their siblings when they were frustrated. However, in some of these families there was also frequent fighting between the siblings, while in others, fights were rare.[2] Some children who were 'comforters' also fought with their siblings frequently; some 'non-comforters' rarely fought. The ambivalence was also revealed when the mother scolded the younger sibling. Often the older child, although usually hostile to the baby, immediately sided with him or her against the mother. Ambivalence, hostility, comfort, and concern were all apparent in the behavior of the elder siblings. And most strikingly, some of these features were also already apparent in the behavior of the 14-month-old *younger* sibling. In those families where the first child frequently comforted the younger, the younger child also frequently approached the older for comfort, and it seemed quite appropriate to describe their relationship with their elder sibling as having the quality of an attachment, in the terms of Bowlby (1969) and Ainsworth (1973). It was clear to their mothers that they missed the elder child in his absence and used him as a source of comfort. And just as the elder child rarely ignored the interaction of mother and baby, so by 14 months most babies reacted immediately to interaction between parent and sibling.

The third feature of the relationships between the young siblings that stood out from the observations was the striking range of individual differences in the frequency and the emotional quality of the behavior of the children towards their siblings. The proportion of the elder child's socially directed behavior to the sibling that was *positive* (a category that included giving or showing objects, smiling, laughing, touching affectionately, helping, comforting, imitating, taking an active part in joint physical play, taking an active part in games [peek-a-boo, etc.], or approaching and sitting very close), ranged from 0 to 94% for the 40 first-born children (mean 55%), and from 35–100% (mean 70%) for the second-born children.

Finally, a fourth feature of the relationship between the siblings that deserves mention concerns the *difference* between the two children in the family in the ways in which they behave towards one another. In many sibling pairs, "mismatch" interactions were very frequent: for instance, exchanges where the older child behaved in a hostile fashion and the younger in a friendly way accounted for 22% of interactions for the sample as a whole (range 0–85%). Rowe and

---

[2]There was good agreement between observation and interview data on the frequency of hostile or aggressive behavior shown by children, and often the same children were *observed* to behave both in a friendly and a hostile manner towards the sibling. It is unlikely therefore that the low correlations simply reflect measurement error.

Plomin (1981), in an important theoretical discussion, argue that lack of 'mutuality' between siblings may be very important in the development of individual differences in personality, but caution that there is no evidence on whether siblings do in fact treat each other differently. Our data show that interactions between young siblings are frequently of the kind that they consider to be developmentally significant.

These results highlight the potential importance of interactions with the sibling as emotional experiences for *both* children, experiences that certainly should not be ignored by psychologists interested in social development. The observations reveal both the complexity and the ambivalence of the relationship between the children, and the great range of individual differences. But they show us much more. They give us a perspective on the child's understanding of others and his or her communicative skills that differ in important ways from the picture of the development of these skills that we gain from studying children with adults. In particular, the observations raise questions about the extent to which each child perceived and understood the other child's feelings and intentions and about the parent's role in influencing the development of this understanding. It is to these questions that we turn next.

Understanding and Communicating With the Sibling

The nature of the relationship between the siblings will be deeply influenced by the growing sensitivity of each child to the other as a person—the extent to which each child perceives the other child's feelings, understands his or her intentions, likes, and dislikes, and acts appropriately towards him or her on the basis of this understanding. The development of this sensitivity will affect not only the support, comfort, and cooperation in play offered by each child, but also the subtler forms of provocation and aggression. But how far do children of two or three recognize the emotional state of others? How far are they able to make inferences about the experiences of others and to act appropriately in response? On the one hand, it is widely held that the capacity of children under four to make such inferences, and to act appropriately in response to another emotional state are very limited (Chandler and Greenspan, 1972; Hoffman, 1975, 1981). Hoffman (1981) points out: "By two or three years of age they acquire a rudimentary sense of others as having inner states independent of their own, although they cannot yet discern the other's inner states." On the other hand, Bretherton and her colleagues (Bretherton, McNew, & Beeghly-Smith, 1981) have argued, on the basis of a systematic study of children's references to the 'inner states' of themselves and of others, that very young children do have "a fairly sophisticated model of themselves and of others as psychological beings" that is psychological beings who are *distinct* and separate. Several writers have argued that the idea of a single common process underlying the development of a unitary "perspective-taking ability" is misleading, and that we should not assume empathy is a unitary trait (Hoffman 1981). It is certainly increasingly clear that the *design* of perspective-taking tasks or tests of empathy dramatically affects the 'success' of the children who are being tested. Donaldson (1978), among others, argued convincingly that many such tasks underestimate the ability of children to perceive the perspective and intentions of others. It is still a matter of controversy as to whether or not children of this age can respond to the emotional reaction of others only by projecting their own feelings onto the situation (see Borke 1972).

The questions at the center of this controversy are clearly of great significance for our interpretation of the relationship between young siblings. How do young children respond to the emotional state of those with whom they have close relationships? Is it reasonable to infer that they can only ascribe to the sibling their *own* perspective? If they do have such difficulty in making the distinction between their own perspective and that of others, what exactly is the nature of their beliefs about the baby sibling as another being, distinct from father, mother, or themselves?

We investigated these questions with three kinds of data from the observations. First, the comments made by the children, to their mothers or to us, about the babies' wants, intentions, emotional states, capabilities, and understanding, were examined. Second, the actions of the children when the infants were upset, frustrated, or excited were studied. Third, the children's speech to the babies was analyzed to see how the first-born children responded to the difficulties of communicating with children who were linguistically and cognitively immature.

Comments About the Baby.   Comments on the wants and intentions of the baby were made by two-thirds of the children at the 14-month visits (64%) and by over half the children at the 8-month visits. These comments were just as common in the speech of the children who were under three as in the older children. Most were remarks about the immediate wishes or intentions of the baby, e.g., "Kenny wants cakey Mum." Some were comments on the expressive behavior of the baby: "Clive's happy." Others were remarks about the baby's likes or intentions in a more general sense: "Jo-Jo likes monkies." Often the child 'explained' the baby's behavior to the observer: "She wants to come to you."

The important point on the issue of perspective-taking is that the children commented on the baby's behavior in a way that certainly did not always represent a projection of their own feelings about their own situations. Sometimes the difference between the perspective of the child and the baby was made quite explicit: One boy watching his baby brother playing with a balloon, commented to the observer: "He going pop in a minute. And he going cry. And he going be frightened of me too. I *like* the pop." Comments were often made with glee about the baby's crying. The explanations offered and delight of the elder child made it clear that the children were not simply projecting their own feelings. "He crying 'cos Mummy's in garden. In't he silly? *I* don't cry for that." Such examples show clearly that these two- and three-year-olds were not confused about the situation of self and of 'other' when the 'other' was their sibling, and that they did respond to the situation of the 'other' in a way that was certainly not always a simple projection of their own feelings.

The children also commented on what the baby did or did not understand or remember, and on what he could or could not do. For instance, a two-year-old commented to the observer about her 14-month-old brother's wariness. "He doesn't know you." A three-year-old said to her sister: "You don't remember Judy. I do." They often noticed and remarked upon *new* achievements: "She called you Mum."

One of the most striking features of the discussion of the baby concerned the elder child's interest in categorization and dimensions of *self* and baby. Often in these exchanges the elder child *played* with the dimensions of age, gender, size, good-bad, as applied to themselves and to the baby, and the confidence and certainty with which they played with these notions suggested that such categories were indeed well understood in relation to the baby.

It was clear then from these comments that the baby was seen as someone with likes, dislikes, intentions, feelings, and capabilities that would develop, someone to whom social rules applied (though these social rules were seen as in many respects different from those that applied to the child). The observations give unqualified support for the arguments put forward by Bretherton and her colleagues (1981). Their systematic study of children's comments on the internal states of others and of themselves shows that as early as 20 months of age, children refer explicitly to the following states—happy, hungry, tired, mad, scared, cold—and that they refer to these states both in relation to themselves and to others. It is clear that children in their second and third year *are* interested in people's psychological states, and that they are also interested in the *cause* of these states. Hood and Bloom (1979), in a study of causal utterances by children in their second and third years, found that the majority were concerned with the internal state of people—with psychological causality rather than with physical causality.

Observations of Empathetic and Antipathetic Actions. In 63% of the families observed when the baby was 14-months old, there were incidents from which we inferred that the elder child was concerned about or understood well the other child's state. These were not incidents where the child simply *commented* on the sibling's state (as in the examples discussed above), but incidents where the child took practical action to help or comfort the other. Often these were nonverbal actions, as when a distressed whimper from a 14-month-old boy was promptly followed by the first-born boy running over to give him a bit of his biscuit. (It should be noted that the comments on the baby's capacities, feelings, or intentions that we described above were by no means always *empathetic* in the sense that they were associated with a practical attempt to help or comfort.) It is clearly important to exercise great discretion in drawing such inferences, and we were extremely conservative in making such categorizations. We included incidents where one child helped the other with a toy when he or she was frustrated by it, offered toys or food when the other was crying, asked the other if he or she wanted a drink and fetched it, or showed concern that the other should be included in games. We have discussed elsewhere the problems involved in drawing inferences from such observations, and the theoretical issues raised by apparently 'egocentric' responses to the affective states of others (Dunn & Kendrick, 1982). Here we wish simply to note three points from the observations, points that are important to consider before coming to any general conclusion about the limitations of the ability of such young children to understand the feeling state of their siblings or to act in a 'decentered' way in response to their distress, pain, or excitement.

The first point is that although the observations of the siblings do not provide direct measures of the extent to which the children understood their siblings' affective states, they do show that before the age of three, first-born children recognize some feelings and expressive behavior shown by the baby sibling, and that this recognition does not involve simply the projection of the first child's own feelings onto the baby. The children often responded to the baby's distress or pleasure in a way that was *not* the way they would expect to be treated themselves, but was appropriate for the baby's state.

The second point is that there were incidents that strongly suggest that as early as 14–15 months, some second-born children did demonstrate both powers of understanding of how to provoke the elder child and some awareness that some of their own acts could provide comfort. It should be noted that Yarrow and Waxler (1975) and Zahn-Waxler, Radke-Yarrow, and King (1979) found, in their studies of children observed at home, that children of around a year were very sensitive to the need states of others, and that they did show comfort to others in distress. They stressed that the children were not only quick to respond, but also were discriminating in their responses to the emotional state of others— showing distress at arguments between their parents, and responding to demonstrations of affection between the parents either by trying to join in or trying to separate the parents. Children aged 1½ to 2 made some sophisticated attempts at comforting others. Burlingham and Freud (1944) also provided vivid examples of consoling and comforting behavior shown by children in the second year.

The third point concerns the discrepancy between the abilities shown by the young siblings in our observations, or by the children in the studies of Yarrow and Waxler or Bretherton and her colleagues, and the abilities that would be attributed to children of this age on the basis of more formal experimental tasks (Chandler and Greenspan, 1972; Shantz, 1975). The discrepancy shows that the conclusions we draw about children's ability to respond to the feelings of others and to react appropriately depend crucially on the social situation in which we study them. If we are not to misrepresent the capabilities of children, it is clearly important to study them in situations that have real emotional meaning for them. Many of the situations in which the younger sibling shows fear, excitement, distress, or joy are situations in which the elder child feels very similar emotions. Therefore, the elder child is particularly well placed not only to recognize the emotion expressed by the younger sibling, but also to see what would constitute an adequate remedy (or indeed a further provocation!). The life world of the sibling is very close to that of the elder child—much closer than that of an adult or of the 'storybook' characters often employed in tests of empathy. It has of course been noted before that children show empathetic understanding towards *familiar* others or to people in *familiar* situations well before they show such understanding towards unfamiliar others (Shantz, 1975). It has been suggested that this discrepancy supports the view that where children are accurate in judging the emotions of those they are familiar with, yet still inaccurate about unfamiliar others, the accuracy about familiar others or about familiar situations reflects simply self-projection, and, as Shantz (1975) argued "may be no more than self description [p. 28]." But it certainly does not follow that because a child is unable to judge the emotions of a stranger in a test situation his ability to infer the emotion of his sibling is simply self-projection.

The Children's Speech to Their Baby Siblings.   The speech of the children to the siblings was analyzed with the following general questions in mind: How do 2- or 3-year-old children face the problems of communicating with their linguistically and cognitively immature baby siblings? Can they respond appropriately to the difficulties posed, when their siblings' powers of expression and understanding are so different from their own and from those of their parents?

It has been shown that 4-year-olds do adjust their speech when they address 2-year-olds (Shatz & Gelman, 1973; 1977), and indeed when they address a doll designated to be a 'baby' (Sachs & Devin, 1976). Shatz and Gelman have shown that both the simpler and the syntactically more complex utterances of the 4-year-olds reflected their selection of utterances that the younger child could be expected to understand in that particular social situation. How early does such sensitivity to the comprehension of the listener develop?

To address these questions we compared the speech of each child to his mother and his sibling, and that of his mother to the baby, looking specifically at two aspects of 'baby-talk'. First, we examined features that Brown (1977) has called 'clarification' features: Shortened utterances, repetitions, and attention-getting devices such as exhortations: *Now! Hey! Look!* (features also found in the speech of adults to foreigners, and so on). Second, features of baby-talk that Brown referred to as 'affective-expressive' features were examined: The use of endearments, diminutives, and pet names (features also found in the speech of people to pets, or between lovers.)

The results showed that all the 2- and 3-year-olds in the study did make clear adjustments in their speech when talking to the 14-month-old sibling (see Table

2). (See also Dunn & Kendrick, 1981c). They made appropriate and usually effective use of communicative devices—shortening their utterances, repeating their utterances, and drawing the baby's attention with exhortation and emphasis.

In the example that follows, the 31-month-old was trying to prevent his younger brother from licking a sweet that he had picked up off the floor. He tells him that the dog, Scottie, will eat the sweet, and tries to distract him by urging him into the kitchen. His attempts to direct his brother provide a typical example of the progressive shortening of utterances, repetitions and use of attentional devices that the children showed in speaking to their baby siblings: "No don't you eat it. Scottie will eat it. Scottie will eat it. No not you. Scottie will eat it. Not you. Scottie. Not you. Shall we go in door? Right. Come on. Come on. In door Robin. In door."

These changes in the children's speech were not a simple parallel of the adjustments their mothers made in speaking to the baby. In several respects their baby talk differed from that of the mothers. For instance, the mothers used many questions when they talked to their babies—a feature of 'motherese' that has been documented in several studies of mothers' speech to babies of this age range, and that has been plausibly linked to the 'conversational' turn-taking structure of mother-and-baby exchanges (see Snow, 1977). In contrast, the use of questions by the *siblings* was much less common. Only 17 of the 40 first-born children used questions to the baby sibling at all, and there were few of the conversational 'turn-taking' dialogues in which these questions played a central role. But the important point is that in the contexts in which the children addressed their siblings—namely prohibiting the baby or directing the baby in play—they modified their speech in a way that was appropriate.

What must be emphasized is that these very young children did adjust their speech in ways that showed that they did differentiate their siblings, in terms of their linguistic and cognitive status, from their mothers and from the others to whom they spoke. Furthermore, they did so not simply in the passive sense of the 'doll as baby' experiment (Sachs & Devin, 1976), by recognizing a different speech style as socially appropriate, but in the active sense of recognizing the

TABLE 3.2
Comparison of Child's Speech to Mother and to Sibling,
and Mother's Speech to Sibling
(Wilcoxon T test)

	Child to Sibling	Child to Mother	Mother to Sibling
MLU (median)	2.49	3.45**	3.40**
Proportion of attentional utterances (median %)	40.0	9.8**	17.5**
Proportion of repetitions (median %)	30.8	17.7**	16.3**

** p <.01, compared with child to sibling.

need to change their speech style in order to communicate effectively with their hearer. This differentiation should hardly surprise us, since, as we have seen, the children themselves frequently commented on the nature, wishes, and intentions of the baby in a way that showed they had quite a clear grasp of their capabilities, and acted towards them in an appropriate way.

Some of the children also used the 'affective-expressive' features of baby-talk, and these children were those who on the behavioral (and largely nonverbal) measures of the observations were very affectionate towards their siblings. These children were also significantly more likely to use *questions* in their speech to the baby, and this association between the use of questions and the nonverbal aspects of affectionate behavior to the baby sibling is interesting. The very frequent use of questions in the speech of mothers to their babies has been plausibly linked to the mothers' desire to communicate reciprocally with their infants (Snow, 1977). Snow argues that the frequent use of questions in mothers' speech, and the 'conversational' nature of their speech with their babies, are linked to the babies' development of turn-taking skills. This 'conversational model' was altogether less appropriate to describe the speech of our 2–3-year-olds to their siblings, but it is certainly the case that those children who did use questions were much more interested and affectionate to the baby, and the questions did apparently reflect a desire to engage the baby in reciprocal exchange. (Children who *questioned* the baby made on average 27 friendly approaches per 1000 10-sec units; those who did not made on average 17 per 1000 10-sec units).

Individual Differences and the Mutual Influence of Relationships: Mothers, Brothers, and Sisters

Individual differences between the sibling pairs in the frequency and affective tone of their interactions were striking; so too were the individual differences between the first-born children in the frequency with which they made comments on the baby's affective state, or acted towards the baby in a concerned way. It is clearly important that we should attempt to understand the development of such individual differences in the emotional intensity of interaction. One possible source of influence on the developing relationship is the mother's relationship with each of the children. Clinicians, for instance, have sometimes attributed extreme hostility between siblings to oversolicitous mothering of the first child, or to an overdependent child-mother relationship (Levy, 1937). Many parents' manuals imply that parents must take a heavy load of responsibility for the extent of jealousy between siblings (Ginnott, 1969; Calladine & Calladine, 1979). How far and in what ways were differences in the mothers' relationships with their children in our sample associated with differences in the relationship which developed between the siblings?

Although the claim that the different relationships within the family influence one another is frequently made, little is known about how precisely these influences work, or how extensive their effects may be. We examined both immediate short-term effects—the response of one individual to interaction between the other two in the family—and more long-term connections between the different family relationships. During the first three weeks after the baby was born, the immediate effects of the mother's involvement with the baby were clear. There was a significant increase in confrontation between mother and first-born, and in 'deliberate naughtiness' by the first child, when the mother was occupied in feeding or caring for the baby (Kendrick & Dunn, 1980). Time spent in confrontation increased from a median of 30 10-sec observation intervals per 1000 when the mother was *not* occupied with the baby, to a median of 63 per 1000 when she was feeding the baby. Incidents of deliberate naughtiness increased from a median of 4 to a median of 13 per 1000 10-sec units. (Interestingly, the drop in maternal attention and play which the first-born children experienced when the sibling was born was *not* due to the mother's direct involvement with the baby, but appeared instead in those periods when the baby was out of the room or asleep.) By the time the baby was 14 months, both immediate effects and more long-term patterns of association were evident.

Long-term Patterns

The quality of the relationship between mother and first-born child had differed very much in the families before the birth of the sibling, and the differences were particularly marked in two aspects of interaction: The frequency of joint play and attention between mother and first child, and the frequency of confrontation and maternal prohibition (Dunn & Kendrick, 1980). For the families with first-born *girls,* these differences were definitely associated with differences in the quality of the relationship which developed between the siblings. Where there had been a relatively high frequency of joint play and attention between mother and daughter before and immediately after the birth of the baby, the first-born girl was much less likely to behave in a friendly way to her sibling 14 months later (rs = −.63 p < .01 for joint play; rs = −.45 p < .05 for joint attention [postsibling birth visits]). In these families, the younger sibling was, by the age of 14 months, also less likely to behave in a friendly way to the older sibling (rs = −.56 p < .05) (Dunn & Kendrick, 1981a). Conversely, in families where there had been much confrontation between mother and first-born daughter in the first month after the sibling was born, the first daughters were particularly likely to engage in games (rs = 0.63) and imitation (rs = 0.46) with their sibling at the 14 month visits, and were less likely to hit (rs = −.49) prohibit, or take toys away from the 14 month old (rs = −.44).

We cannot assume from this pattern of correlations that there was a *causal* link between the earlier and later measures—that differences in the mother-first-born relationship caused the differences in sibling behavior 14 months later. Several different interpretations of these correlations are plainly possible. One such explanation lies in the mother's behavior with the baby sibling.

If mothers who had been relatively playful with their first-born child were also relatively playful with their second, then it could be that the association between the mother's behavior with the first-born and the later hostility of first child to the second arose because the first child was responding directly to this high level of play between mother and the younger sibling. When we compared the behavior of the mothers with their first- and second-born, we found that the mothers were indeed relatively consistent in their behavior. The mothers who had been most interested in playing and attending to the first children were relatively playful and attentive with the second. This consistency meant that the link between the quality of sibling interaction and the mother-first-born interaction 14 months earlier could be due to the association between each of these and the measure of mother-second-born play at 14 months. To test this possibility a Kendall's tau partial correlation was carried out holding constant the measure of mother-second-born interaction at 14 months. The results showed that the correlation between the measure of mother-first-born interaction in the period immediately after the sibling birth and the later sibling interaction was still significant. (τ xy $= -.44$ p $< .001$, τ xy.z $= -.34$ p $< .001$, where x $=$ sibling measure, y $=$ mother-first-born measure and z$=$ mother-second-born measure.) The effects of the mothers' playful behavior with their second-born children at the 14-month visits did not, therefore, wholly account for the unfriendly behavior of first-born girls to their siblings in those families where the relationship between mother and daughter had been particularly playful and attentive.

But we certainly should not assume that the quality of the relationship between mother and second-born child was not important. Analysis of the interaction between mother and baby at the 8-month visit showed that in families where mother and baby had spent much time in interaction together, and where the interaction had been especially playful, then both the first child and the sibling were particularly unfriendly to each other 6 months later. Again, we cannot make any causal inferences from the correlations. We tested the possibility that the association arose primarily because of the *other* correlations with a Kendall's tau partial correlation, and found that when the effects of these correlations were held constant, there was still a significant link between the mother-baby interaction measures at 8 months and the behavior of the first child to the baby 6 months later (τ xy $= -.28$ p $< .05$, τ xy.z $-.23$ p $< .05$, where x$=$ time mother and baby interacting at 8 months, y$=$ sibling positive measure interaction at 14 months and z$=$ time mother and baby interacting at 14 months). In families where there was an especially warm and playful involvement between mother and baby during the first year, both children were particularly hostile by the end of the first year.

There are two rather different ways in which we could interpret this pattern. We could regard the negative behavior shown towards the sibling by those girls who had been closely involved in a playful relationship with their mothers as a hostile response to displacement. But we could also focus on the frequent friendly behavior shown towards the sibling by the children whose relationship with their mothers had been characterized by much conflict and confrontation, and relatively little play. For these children, the warm and playful relationship that developed with the sibling was one that contributed very positively to their emotional life in the family. Other results from the study also fit within such a framework, for instance the finding (at first sight counter-intuitive) that in families where the mother was very tired or depressed after the sibling birth, the sibling relationship developed in a particularly friendly fashion (see Dunn & Kendrick, 1982).

It is clear, then, that to understand the differences in the relationships that developed between the young siblings, it was necessary to take into account the mothers' playful and attentive behavior with each of her children. In addition, a quite different aspect of the mothers' behavior proved to be of great importance for the development of the relationship between the siblings. This was the way in which the mother talked to the first child about the baby *as a person*, with feelings and needs, for whom they both could take responsibility.

Discussion of the Baby

During the first three weeks after the baby was born, there were marked differences among the mothers, not only in the extent of confrontation, of play and attention between mother and first child, but along an entirely separate dimension. In some families, the mother talked to the first child about the baby's wishes, likes, needs, and intentions, discussing the new baby *as a person*. These mothers also drew the first child into discussing the baby's care very much as an equal, making decisions about the interpretation of his crying, and what should be done for the baby a matter of joint responsibility of mother and child together. They explained what they thought the baby wanted, and often drew the first child's attention to the baby's interest in the elder child. Some typical examples: "He likes his bath doesn't he?" "Do you reckon he's hungry or is he just waiting for his bath?" "Shall we feed him, or just let him cry? What do you think he wants?" "Look he's calling you."

In the families where the mothers discussed the babies' feelings and intentions, the first-born children were, in the first three weeks following the birth, significantly more likely to comment on the baby as a person with wants and needs than the children in families where the mothers did not discuss the baby in this way. And, most strikingly, there were marked individual differences 14 months later in the quality of the relationship between the siblings. Both first-born and second-born siblings at this point were significantly more friendly to their siblings in families where the mother had discussed the baby's wants in the first weeks after the birth. The median frequency of friendly approaches from first-born to baby was in these families 26.7 per 1000 10-sec units, and from baby to first-born 26.8. In families where the mother had *not* discussed the baby in this way during the postpartum weeks, the comparable figures were 11.1

friendly approaches from first-born to baby, and 14.4 from baby to first-born, per 1000 10-sec units.

These differences in the discussion of the baby were not related to differences in the extent of playfulness or punitiveness of the mothers, or in the degree of confrontation between mother and first child. We also found no links between these differences in the discussion of the baby, and the degree of disturbance or negative behavior shown by the first child, or the mother's state of exhaustion after the sibling birth. Among the families where the mother made most effort to discuss the baby as a person and to encourage the first child to join in looking after the baby, were families in which the mothers were coping with extreme stress and exhaustion. The children in these families showed a wide range of different reactions to the birth. We found no links between the level of discussion of the baby and the age or the sex of the first-born.

The discussion of the baby's needs and wants was, however, more common in families where the first child was reported to show much affectionate interest in the baby—offering to help, to entertain, or to cuddle him or her. This association could of course arise in two different ways. It is possible that mothers who talked in this way did in fact encourage feelings of affection and interest in the first-born children. But it could also be that mothers who noticed that their first child was *not* interested or affectionate deliberately avoided drawing attention to the new baby as a person with wants and feelings, whereas those who noticed their first child's interest responded to this interest by discussing the baby. It seems unlikely that the differences in the mother's comments about the baby were simply responses to the behavior of the first-born children. First, the differences were not related to the differences in disturbance and negative behavior of the first-born. Second, the differences in the discussion of the baby were linked to a number of other differences in the way in which the mothers talked to their children. Those mothers who referred to the babies' wants and needs in the first visit after the baby's birth were also more likely to join verbally in their child's pretend games, to use language for relatively complex cognitive purposes (using comparisons, conditionals, generalizations, definitions, and logical inference, [see Tizard, Hughes, Pinkerton, & Carmichael]), to give justification when attempting to control the child, and to discuss motives and intentions of other people.

These differences in the use of *language* reflect, we would argue, a particular style of relating to a child, a dimension of the mother-child relationship that cuts across the playful- permissive- punitive-restrictive dimensions already mentioned. The mothers who talked to their children in this way were more likely to consider the child—at least formally—as an equal in discussing social rules and control issues, and they were more likely themselves to join in the child's pretend games in a way that reflected a close 'tuning-in' to the child's fantasies. The point to be stressed here is that there were connections between this particular style of mother-child interaction, with its focus on the discussion of the baby as a person, and the later behavior of the siblings. Even though we are not suggesting that there are simple links between any one single aspect of the 'conversational style' and the later sibling relationship, we must take seriously one implication of the pattern of associations: that the discussion of a person's wants and intentions by the mother may influence how a child—even as young as 2½ years—behaves towards and presumably feels about that individual. Such a pattern implies, that is, a far higher degree of reflection about the baby sibling as a person than many psychologists would have presumed likely in such young children. This implication is of course supported by the finding that the children whose mothers talked in this way were themselves much more likely to comment on the wants and feelings of the baby.

There were then systematic patterns of association between the marked individual differences in the quality of the sibling relationship when the second-born was 14 months, and the quality of the relationship between mother and first-born child at the time of the birth. These were by no means the *only* important variables associated with the individual differences. One key variable was the sex constellation of the sibling pair: Friendly approaches were made twice as frequently by first-born with baby siblings of the same sex (31 per 1000 10-sec units of observation, as compared with 17 per 1000 10-sec units in the different-sex sibling pairs). The second-born siblings in same-sex pairs were also far more friendly: 28 friendly approaches per 1000 10-sec units were made by the second-born with same sex siblings, compared with 15 friendly approaches per 1000 10-sec units by the second-born with different sex siblings. These results parallel those found by Whiting & Edwards (1977), who studied children in very different cultures. A second key variable was the manner in which the first child had reacted to the constellation of events surrounding the birth of the baby. But multiple regression analyses certainly suggested that the parent variables made an independent contribution to the variation in sibling behavior at 14 months.

We clearly cannot make causal inferences from the patterns of association revealed in these analyses. We can, however, look more directly at the behavior of the first child when his mother and sibling are actively involved together, and it is this behavior we examine next.

In many families, the 14-month-old second-born was a source of great pleasure and delight to the mother, and their relationship was warm and playful—full of 'conversations' and games. Such interactions between mother and baby had a marked effect on many first-born children. Once again, individual differences were marked. *Protest* was the most common response, a pattern echoing the increased demand and naughtiness shown when the mother fed or cared for the baby during the first three weeks. But attempts to join in a positive friendly fashion were also common.

Individual differences in the reaction of the first children were linked to two aspects of the mothers' relationships with the children. First, the response of the first child was related to the way in which mother and baby had behaved towards each other at the earlier visits. If mother and baby had interacted a great deal at the 8-month observation, the first-born was at the 14-month observation significantly more likely to react to a bout of interaction between mother and baby by being aggressive to the baby than the first child whose mother and sibling had spent less time in interaction at the earlier visits (a correlation of rs = 0.52). Differences in the response of the first children were also significantly related to the differences in the mothers' discussion of the baby as a person during the first three weeks. In families where the mother had discussed the baby as a person for whom both mother and first-born had responsibility, the first children joined a median of 19% of mother-baby interactions in a friendly way. In the families where the mothers had not discussed the baby in this way, the first-born children joined only 8% of mother-baby interactions in a friendly fashion.

These results thus paralleled the findings for the individual differences in the sibling interaction. Differences in the response of the first children to the interaction between their mothers and their siblings were also found to be linked to a number of other variables—to the temperament of the first child, the sex constellation of the dyad (Dunn & Kendrick, 1981(b)), and to the reaction of the first child to the birth (Dunn & Kendrick, 1982).

CONCLUSIONS

In this brief summary we have done no more than mention some of the findings in a relatively complex series of analyses. We have touched on many issues that cannot be considered here, such as the sex differences in patterns of association between different family relationships, and in continuities over time. For a full discussion of these the reader is referred to Dunn and Kendrick, 1982. In conclusion we would like to emphasize three developmental issues that stand out from the findings of the study.

The first concerns the quality of social understanding that was demonstrated by the children. The comments made by the first-born children showed that they had a good understanding of their baby siblings' likes, dislikes, wants, and intentions, and some notion of their present capabilities. The discrepancy between these findings and those based on more formal testing of children shows that if we want to understand the theories children hold about people, and to gain a picture of their abilities that is not misleading, it is important to study them in their families, in a context that has real emotional significance for them.

The second issue concerns the complex pattern of mutual influences within the family. The results that we have outlined suggest that there are important links between the mother's relationship with each child and the quality of the relationship that develops between the siblings. There are, of course, other important sources of influence on the sibling relationship. Clearly the behavior of the younger sibling is potentially of great significance. In a study of sibling pairs where the second-born was slightly older than the second-born children in our sample, Lamb (1978b) showed that the behavior of the younger sibling was ineeed of major importance, and that the social behavior of the first-born to their siblings could be predicted from the behavior of the *younger* sibling six months earlier. It is clear, from the findings of the present study, that to understand the pattern of mutual influence between the family relationships, account must be taken of the temperament of the first child, his or her reaction to the birth of the sibling, and the sex constellation of the siblings. We have here only indicated a few of the ways in which the family relationships interact. But even such a brief summary does highlight the importance of considering the mutual influence of relationships within the family—both in the immediate social context, and over the longer time span.

The third issue concerns continuities over time. Any study that focuses on the infancy or first years of children's lives must end with a query about the long-term significance of the findings it reports. How persistent were the differences in the quality of the sibling relationship between the siblings in the sample?

Consistency in the individual differences in the behavior of the first-born to the sibling was clearly evident during the first 14 months of the study. Children who were reported to show frequent friendly interest in their baby sibling in the first three weeks showed significantly more positive social behavior towards them at 14 months than the children who had not demonstrated such interest in the early weeks. Most strikingly, in these families, the second-born were, by 14 months, also showing more frequent positive social behavior to their older siblings than the babies in the other families. And the first-born who had reacted to the sibling birth by withdrawing very much showed more frequent negative behavior to the sibling at 14 months than the rest of the sample. Clearly the consistency in the first child's behavior—whether he was relatively friendly, or relatively hostile—was importantly linked to the quality of their sibling relationship by the time the second born was 14 months. What about the longer term?

The siblings were visited again, when the first children were six years old, by Robin Stilwell-Barnes (1982), as part of an interview study of friendship and family relationships in 6-year-olds. This study is not yet complete at the time of writing, but the analysis of data for the first 20 children in our sample shows some striking consistencies with the individual differences found at the 14-month stage.

The children who had shown the most frequent positive social behavior towards their younger siblings at the 14-month stage were, three years later, significantly more willing to *share* toys or sweets with their sibling and were more likely to respond to the sibling's distress by actively attempting to comfort than the first-born children who, at the earlier observations, had shown little positive social behavior to the sibling. The children's comments about their siblings were recorded by Stillwell-Barnes and she found that there was a significant positive correlation between the positive social behavior shown at the 14-month visits and the ratio of positive to negative remarks made about the sibling three years later. A rating of the quality of the sibling relationship derived from interviewing the mothers at the 6-year visits showed that children who had shown frequent friendly behavior during the observations at the 14-month visits were, three years later, much more friendly and concerned about their siblings.

Since these findings are based on only half the sample, we must be cautious about generalizing from them; nevertheless the strength of the consistencies that they reveal reinforces the significance of the findings on the first year of the sibling relationship. Not only does a study of the first year of the sibling relationship give us an illuminating perspective on the development of social understanding and communication in very young children; it also reveals to us that there are major differences in the emotional quality of the sibling relationship that will persist over several years, and that these differences are importantly linked to the mother's relationship with each child.

ACKNOWLEDGMENTS

This study was supported by the Medical Research Council. We are very grateful to the families in the sample for their generous help.

REFERENCES

Abramovitch, R., Corter, C. & Lando, B. Sibling interaction in the home. *Child Development*, 1979, *50*, 997-1003.

Abramovitch, R., Corter, C. & Pepler, D. J. Observations of mixed-sex sibling dyads. *Child Development*, 1980, *51*, 1268-1271.

Ainsworth, M. D. The development of Infant-mother attachment. In B. M. Caldwell & H. N. Ricciuti (Eds.), *Review of Child Development Research* (Vol. 3). Chicago: University of Chicago Press, 1973.

Borke, H. Interpersonal perception of young children: Egocentrism or empathy? *Developmental Psychology*, 1972, *7*, 107-109.

Bowlby, J. *Attachment and Loss* Vol. 1. London: The Hogarth Press, 1969.

Bretherton, I., McNew, S. & Beeghly-Smith, M. Early person knowledge as expressed in gestural and verbal communication: When do infants acquire a "theory of mind"? In M. E. Lamb & L. R. Sherrod (Eds.), *Infant social cognition*. Hillsdale, N.J.: Lawrence Erlbaum Associates, 1981.

Brown, R. Introduction. In C. E. Snow & C. A. Ferguson (Eds.), *Talking to Children*. Cambridge: Cambridge University Press, 1977.

Burlingham, D. & Freud, A. *Infants without families*. London: George Allen and Unwin Ltd., 1944.

Calladine, C. & Calladine, A. *Raising siblings*. New York: Delacorte Press, 1979.

Chandler, M. J. & Greenspan, S. Ersatz egocentrism: A reply to H. Borke. *Developmental Psychology*, 1972, *7*, 104-106.

Cicirelli, V. G. Sibling structure and intellectual ability. *Developmental Psychology* 1976, *12*, 369-370.

Cicirelli, V. G. Children's school grades and sibling structure. *Psychological Reports*, 1977, *41*, 1055-1058.

Donaldson, M. *Children's minds*. Glasgow: Fontana/Collins, 1978.

Dunn, J. & Kendrick, C. The arrival of a sibling: Changes in patterns of interaction between mother and first-born child. *Journal of Child Psychology and Psychiatry*, 1980, *21*, 119-132.

Dunn, J. & Kendrick, C. Interaction between young siblings: Associations with the interaction between mother and first born. *Developmental Psychology*, 1981, *17*, 336-343. (a)

Dunn, J. & Kendrick, C. Social behaviour of young siblings in the family context: Differences between same-sex and different-sex dyads. *Child Development*, 1981 (in press). (b)

Dunn, J. & Kendrick, C. The speech of two and three year olds to infant siblings: 'Baby talk' and the context of communication. *Journal of Child Language* 1981 (in press). (c)

Dunn, J. & Kendrick, C. *Siblings: Love, envy and understanding.* Cambridge: Harvard University Press, 1982 (in press).

Ginott, H. G. *Between Parent and Child.* New York: Avon Books, 1969.

Hoffman, M. L. Developmental synthesis of affect and cognition and its implications for altruistic motivation. *Developmental Psychology,* 1975, *11,* 607–622.

Hoffman, M. L. Development of prosocial motivation: empathy and guilt. In N. Eisenberg-Berg (Ed.), *Development of prosocial behavior.* New York: Academic Press, 1981.

Hood, L. & Bloom, L. What, when and how about why: A longitudinal study of early expressions of causality. *Monogr. Soc. Res. Child Develop.* 1979, *44,* No. 6.

Kendrick, C. & Dunn, J. Caring for a second baby: effects on the interaction between mother and first-born. *Developmental Psychology,* 1980, *16,* 303–311.

Lamb, M. E. Interactions between 18 month olds and their pre-school-aged siblings. *Child Development,* 1978, *49,* 51–59. (a)

Lamb, M. E. The development of sibling relationships in infancy: A short term longitudinal study. *Child Development,* 1978, *49,* 1189–1196. (b)

Levy, D. M. Studies in sibling rivalry. *American Orthopsychiatric Association Research Monograph* 1937, No. 2.

Ross, B. M. Some traits associated with sibling jealousy in problem children. *Smith College Studies in Social Work,* 1930, *1,* 364–76.

Rowe, D. C. and Plomin, R. The importance of nonshared (E_1) environmental influences in behavioral development. *Developmental Psychology* 1981, *17,* No. 5, 517–531.

Sachs, J. & Devin, J. Young children's use of age-appropriate speech styles in social interaction and role-playing. *Journal of Child Language,* 1976, *3,* 81–98.

Sewall, M. Some causes of jealousy in young children, *Smith College studies in Social Work,* 1930, *1,* 6–22.

Shantz, C. U. The development of social cognition. In E. Mavis Hetherington (Ed.), *Review of Child Development Research.* Chicago: University of Chicago Press, 1975.

Shatz, M., & Gelman, R. The development of communication skills: Modifications in the speech of young children as a function of the listener. *Monographs of the Society for Research in Child Development* 1973, *38* (No. 5. whole number).

Shatz, H. & Gelman, R. Beyond syntax: The influence of conversational constraints on speech modifications. In C. E. Snow & C. A. Ferguson (Eds.), *Talking to children,* Cambridge: Cambridge University Press, 1977.

Smalley, R. The influences of differences in age, sex, and intelligence in determining attitudes of siblings towards each other. *Smith College Studies in Social Work,* 1930, *1,* 6–20.

Snow, C. E. The development of conversation between mothers and babies. *Journal of Child Language,* 1977, *4,* 1–22.

Stilwell-Barnes, R. Social relationships in primary school children as seen by children, mothers and teachers. Unpublished Ph.D. thesis, University of Cambridge, 1982.

Sutton-Smith, B. & Rosenberg, B. G. *The Sibling.* New York: Holt, Rinehart and Winston, Inc., 1970.

Tizard, B., Hughes, M., Pinkerton, G. & Carmichael, L. Labov revisited: social class and language usage. Submitted for publication.

Whiting, B. B. & Edwards, C. P. (Eds.), The effect of age, sex and modernity on the behavior of mothers and children. Report to the Ford Foundation, January 1977.

Yarrow, M. R. & Waxler, C. Z. The emergence and functions of prosocial behavior in young children. Paper presented at the meeting of the Society for Research in Child Development, Denver Co., April 1975.

Zahn-Waxler, C., Radke-Yarrow, M., & King, R. A. Child-rearing and children's prosocial initiations toward victims of distress. *Child Development,* 1979, *50,* 319–330.

4 Patterns of Sibling Interaction Among Preschool-age Children

Rona Abramovitch
Debra Pepler
Carl Corter
University of Toronto

INTRODUCTION

There has been considerable speculation in both popular and scientific journals on the effects of sibling status. Much of the discussion has focused on the implications of being born first or second, being far apart or close in age, and having a same or opposite-sex sibling. The effects of sibling status are often described as resulting from some aspect of interaction between the siblings. For example, White (1975) argues that greater age spacing is preferable because there will be less direct competition for resources; Zajonc and Markus (1975) argue that differences in intelligence may partly reflect the opportunity older children have to teach their younger siblings. However, the speculation on the implications of sibling interaction is not matched by data on the actual behavior of siblings in their homes. In this chapter we shall summarize our attempt to provide such data. Thus the basic goal of our research has been to provide information on patterns of interaction between siblings in a natural environment. We were also interested in whether such variables as the sex and age of the individual children, the sex composition of the dyad, and the age interval between siblings would affect patterns of interaction. (See Abramovitch, Corter, & Lando, 1979; Abramovitch, Corter, & Pepler, 1980; and Pepler, Abramovitch & Corter, 1981, for more complete details.) To simplify the problem somewhat we limited our observations to families with two preschool-aged children. We observed same-sex and mixed-sex dyads in which the children were separated by either a large interval (2½ to 4 years) or a small interval (1 to 2 years). Sex of the individual, the sex composition of the dyad, and interval were included as factors in the design because it has been suggested in the literature that these factors might have effects on sibling interaction. Age of sibling within the dyad (younger and older) was also expected to affect the child's behavior because this factor includes age and birth-order differences and both might affect patterns of interaction.

It is not clear what effect birth order, apart from age, would be expected to have upon sibling interaction in the home. However, there is increasing speculation that birth-order differences among children may reflect different experiences with siblings, a view that supplements the more traditional view that birth-order effects are mediated by different parental treatment for different birth positions. For example, as mentioned above, Zajonc and Markus (1975) attempted to account for IQ differences associated with birth order, family size, and spacing, by producing a model in which both parent and sibling effects are included. Parental and sibling behaviors are assumed to combine to produce an overall level of intellectual sophistication in the family; the more siblings and the higher the birth order, the lower the intellectual level of the family and the child's IQ. It is not specified exactly how the intellectual level of the family affects IQ, though imitation might play a part. Another facet of the Zajonc and Markus model is that the opportunity to teach younger siblings is thought to increase IQ; clearly last-born siblings and only children suffer in this respect. The model is thus predicated on a significant amount of interaction between siblings, including both imitation and teaching. Zajonc and Markus, however, provide no data on sibling interaction in the home to substantiate these speculations.

Miller and Maruyama (1976) discuss the implications birth order may have for more purely social interactions among siblings. In their study, later-born children were found to be more popular among peers than early-born children. The authors state that this finding ''seems to stem from differences in the interactions of siblings within the home setting [p. 130].'' In particular, they suggest that first-borns are relatively free to act arbitrarily because of their greater power whereas later-born children must develop social skills in order to negotiate with, accommodate, and tolerate their older siblings. These skills, in turn, may account for the greater popularity of later-borns among their peers. Again, these speculations exist in the absence of data concerning sibling interaction in the home.

It seems reasonable to assume that age, apart from birth-order, would affect how siblings behave toward each other. Several studies indicate that social interactions among same-age peers vary as a function of age of the children. For example, Eckerman, Whatley, and Kutz (1975) showed that both positive and negative responses to peers increased across the second year of life. However, generalizations from studies of same-age peer interactions to different-age sibling dyads seem tenuous at best. More to the point are studies by Lamb (1978a) and Samuels (1980) that compared the behaviors of older and younger siblings in the laboratory. A striking result of these laboratory studies is a very low level of interaction between siblings. However, even in the context of relatively little interaction, age differences emerged. Lamb found that in a free-play situation, younger siblings were more likely to watch, approach, and imitate their older sibling and were more likely to take over toys abandoned by them. Samuels obtained very similar results from observations of a smaller sample of sibling dyads. Both investigators conclude that the older sibling may serve as a model for the younger child and Lamb asserts that the older child may play an important part in the infant's "mastery of the object environment [p. 57]."

These data are consistent with the only other study of sibling behavior in the home besides our own. Dunn and Kendrick (1979) reported on home observations of 20 sibling pairs in which the younger children were 14 months and their older siblings ranged from 32 to 57 months. They reported that older siblings are often imitated by the younger children.

Studies of peer dyads also suggest that interaction within same-sex and mixed-sex sibling dyads will differ. Observing the interaction of previously unacquainted 33 month-old children in same-sex and mixed-sex dyads, Jacklin and Maccoby (1978) found that more social behavior was directed to same-sex playmates. Langlois, Gottfried, and Seay (1973) reported similar results for previously acquainted 5-year olds and for 3-year-old female dyads. Jacklin and Maccoby note that the tendency for children to choose same-sex playmates and to be more sociable with same-sex peers might be explained in several ways: Children might be reinforced for same-sex choices; they might prefer same-sex playmates because they are seen as similar to themselves and therefore as more attractive; or their preference might reflect an enjoyment of similar activities, i.e., behavioral compatibility. Any of these explanations could be extended to predict a similar effect of sex composition in sibling dyads.

In fact, Dunn and Kendrick report that same-sex sibling pairs had a higher percentage of positive interactions and a lower percentage of negative interactions than mixed-sex pairs and that the frequency of imitation was higher if siblings were the same sex. However, two laboratory studies of sibling interaction, Lamb (1978a, 1978b) discovered no differences in interaction as a function of the sex composition of the dyad.

In addition to the sex composition of the dyad we expected that the sex of the individual child would be an important factor in sibling interaction. Sutton-Smith and Rosenberg (1970) reported a variety of findings that suggest sex of child may modify interaction in the home. For example, they reported questionnaire data on techniques siblings use to influence each other and found that first-born males appeared to use more physical power techniques whereas first-born females were more likely to use techniques such as explaining, asking, and taking turns. Findings compatible with the picture of older sisters as more sensitive and skillful in interaction with younger siblings are reported by Cicirelli (1975), who found that older sisters were better "teachers" for their younger siblings in a laboratory problem-solving task. Finally, data on sex differences in peer interaction (e.g.,

Maccoby & Jacklin, 1974) suggest that sex might be expected to have some parallel effect on the nature of sibling interaction—i.e., with males being more aggressive and females more prosocial.

Spacing between siblings is a variable of particular interest since parents have some control over this variable in planning their families. Advice concerning optimal spacing can be found in the research literature, and is readily available in popular magazines and various advice books. Unfortunately, little direct evidence is available for evaluating these suggestions.

One relevant notion is that the mother's relationship with her children may be affected by the spacing between them. For example, Cornoldi and Fattori (1976) found that differences in adult personality in first-borns was partly a function of whether the first-born was spaced more than three years from the second-born sibling. These differences were interpreted as resulting from a less satisfactory mother-child relationship for the first-born who must share his mother in the "crucial" first three years of life. White (1975) also claims that the mother-child relationship is adversely affected by close spacing and claims further that sibling interaction is also adversely affected. He states that the greatest source of stress for infants (and their mothers) stems from the behavior of a slightly older sibling, behavior that may be aggressive and hostile. No direct evidence is provided to support these assertions, although they presumably stem from White's extensive observations in the home.

Some evidence for the idea that greater spacing produces more prosocial interactions between siblings is provided by a laboratory study of older siblings aiding younger siblings in a sorting task (Cicirelli, 1973). It was found that younger siblings were more likely to accept help or direction from an older sibling when the interval between siblings was large. However, using data based on teachers' ratings, Koch (1956) reported more stressful relations between elementary school-aged siblings spaced two to four years apart than between those spaced less than two years apart. Thus one finds contradictory statements regarding spacing, although White's view seems to predominate.

A rough summary of the existing speculation and data concerning sibling interaction can be made in terms of a division between prosocial and agonistic acts. Based on the literature reviewed above, we expected that younger siblings would act in a more prosocial fashion than their older siblings and that the nature of prosocial acts would differ between the two ages. Prosocial behavior might also be more characteristic of female than male sibling dyads, of same-sex rather than mixed-sex dyads, and probably more characteristic of large-interval dyads than small-interval dyads. Conversely, we expected that agonistic acts would be more characteristic of older children, male dyads, mixed-sex dyads and small-interval dyads. In addition we expected to see a large amount of imitation on the part of younger siblings, especially in same-sex dyads. A longitudinal follow-up was done in order to see if the factors we were interested in would have the same effects on interaction over time and if there was stability in individual behavior.

OVERVIEW OF THE STUDIES

We observed sibling dyads two times, 18 months apart. At each point the behavior of the siblings was recorded for two one-hour periods separated by approximately one month. We were able to observe 80% of our sample at both times. The original sample consisted of 34 pairs of same-sex siblings and 36 pairs of mixed-sex siblings; the follow-up sample consisted of 28 pairs of each type.

In total, four studies were carried out—two studies of same-sex dyads and two studies of mixed-sex dyads. Data for the same-sex subjects were collected 6-8 months prior to data for the mixed-sex subjects, and it took approximately four months to complete a study. Thus data collection spanned approximately three years.

Sample

Subjects came from two-child middle-class families residing in a Toronto suburb. They were recruited by telephoning parents who had previously agreed to participate in experiments at the Infant Studies Laboratory, Erindale College,

TABLE 4.1
Average Age (and Age Range) In Months and Number
of Sibling Pairs In Each Group

Same – sex dyads		Small interval $(\bar{x} = 19.9)$	Large interval $(\bar{x} = 37.9)$
Females		N = 10	N = 6
	Younger	21.3 (19–26)	18 (13–24)
	Older	42.3 (37–49)	56.3 (48–65)
Males		N = 8	N = 10
	Younger	20.25 (15–24)	19.1 (16–22)
	Older	40 (34–46)	56.5 (52–60)

Mixed – sex dyads		Small interval $(\bar{x} = 23.7)$	Large interval $(\bar{x} = 38.2)$
Male Older, Female Younger		N = 9	N = 9
	Younger	21.1 (19–24)	20.1 (18–25)
	Older	44.8 (36–50)	58.6 (48–69)
Female Older, Male Younger		N = 10	N = 8
	Younger	19.2 (17–23)	20.3 (16–25)
	Older	42.9 (36–52)	58.3 (47–68)

University of Toronto. Almost all of the parents with children who fit the age and sex requirements of the study agreed to participate. Table 1 presents the characteristics of each of the eight types of sibling pairs. For the initial set of observations, the younger siblings were approximately $1\frac{1}{2}$ years old and the older siblings were either approximately 3 or $4\frac{1}{2}$ years old.

Thus the interval between the siblings was either small (1–2 years) or large ($2\frac{1}{2}$ to 4 years). This choice of age and interval meant that the subjects would be preschoolers and therefore in the home together much of the time. In addition, the intervals chosen were not only those most often referred to in the literature, but were also the most common, thus making subject recruitment easier. At the time of the follow-up 18 months later the younger siblings were approximately 3 years old and their older siblings either approximately $4\frac{1}{2}$ or 6 years old.

Observations

All observations were done in the homes of the subjects, usually in the family or living room. Observations were made by one of several female observers except for assessment of observer agreement when two observers were present. Visits were scheduled to correspond to times the children were likely to be playing together. The mother was told that the observer wanted to watch the ordinary activities of the children and she was asked to go about her normal routine and to ignore the observer as much as possible. The children were told that the observer had come to watch. The observer did not interact with the children, avoided eye contact, and answered all queries by briefly saying she was busy doing some work. She sat in a corner of the room from where it was possible to see both children. If one of the siblings left the room, the observer stayed with the remaining child. However, behavior was recorded only when both children were present. If the second sibling joined the first or if both left together, the observer followed. Formal observations began after a brief initial period to allow the children to become accustomed to the observer's presence.

The observer used a behavioral check list to record the children's behavior and a stopwatch to time the sessions and the number of minutes children were together in the same room. Each sibling pair was observed as a unit. Thus all relevant behaviors emitted by both siblings were recorded during the observation period. A large number of discrete behaviors were recorded, grouped into three categories: agonistic behavior, prosocial behavior, and imitation (see Table 2 for a detailed description of the particular behaviors). Each time a behavior on the check list occurred, the behavior, the initiator and the response—to agonistic or prosocial behavior—were recorded (see Table 2 for a detailed description of responses). The observer recorded only the immediate responses to agonistic and prosocial behaviors. Thus each sequence did not go beyond two steps (initiated behavior and immediate response). It should be noted that if two behaviors such as sharing and smiling or pushing and hitting occurred simultaneously, they were recorded as discrete behaviors with discrete responses.

TABLE 4.2
Behavioral Definitions

Category	Definition
Agonistic behaviors	
I *Physical*	
1. Physical aggression	Assertive physical contact, specifically: hit, push, pull, shove, kick, bite, pinch, pull hair.
II *Object-related*	
2. Object struggle	A fight over an object.
III *Verbal*	
3. Command	An order or demand stated with authority in a loud tone of voice, may be accompanied by threatening facial expressions or gestures.
4. Insult/disapproval	Teasing, name-calling, unfavorable judgements.
5. Threat	Statements of intent to harm, take toys away.
6. Tattle-tell	Telling the mother about the other sibling's "wrong-doing".
Prosocial behaviors	
1. Give/share an object	Give an object spontaneously or on request; let other sibling share an object with which child is already playing—spontaneously or on request.
2. Co-operate/help	Engaging in behaviors which require two individuals; explanations or physical aid.
3. Request	Asking for something (e.g. a toy, help) in a polite manner—low tone of voice often accompanied by positive facial expression.
4. Praise/approval	Verbal statements of approval or admiration of sibling or his behavior.
5. Comfort/reassurance	Verbal or physical consolation when sibling is in some way distressed.
6. Physical affection	Positive physical contact, specifically: hug, kiss, hold hands, pat.
7. Laugh/smile	Facial expression of laughter or smiling directed at the sibling.
8. Approach	Moving to within .5 m. of sibling with no evidence of agonistic intent.

(*continued*)

TABLE 4.2

Category	Definition
Imitation	Following sibling to another room or another area in room; performing the same behavior as sibling within 10 seconds—imitation was not recorded if an act was apparently elicited by the environment—e.g. bouncing a ball, i.e., only instances of imitating relatively "novel" behaviors were recorded.
Responses to agonistic behavior	
1. Submit	Cry, scream, whine, withdraw, request cessation, give up object, obey.
2. Counterattack	Any direct physical or verbal agonism (following agonistic categories above).
3. No response	No change occurs in ongoing behavior as a result of agonistic act.
Responses to prosocial behavior	
1. Positive	Positive acceptance (following prosocial categories above).
2. Negative	Physical or verbal rejection—hit, push, etc., "no", "go away", etc. (following agonistic categories above).
3. No response	No change occurs in ongoing behavior as a result of prosocial act.

Measures of observer agreement in each study were obtained by having two observers simultaneously record behavior during four observations periods, spaced at approximately one-month intervals. Observer agreement was assessed by dividing the number of agreements by the number of agreements plus disagreements. A disagreement was scored if there was disagreement regarding the nature of the particular behavior that had occurred, the nature of the response, or if one observer recorded an instance of a behavior that the second observer did not record. Overall observer agreement averaged across all of the studies was 77.7% (range, 71 to 90%). Agreements for the categories of agonism, prosocial behavior, and imitation were 81%, 81.2% and 77.3%, respectively.

Levels of Interaction in Same- and Mixed-Sex Sibling Dyads

In describing the pattern of results we shall talk first about the initial studies of the same- and mixed-sex dyads and then turn to the longitudinal results. Our major goal in these studies was to describe naturalistic patterns of sibling interaction. We also wanted to determine whether the surprisingly low levels of interac-

TABLE 4.3

Mean Frequencies of Agonistic, Prosocial and Imitative Behaviors and Responses to Agonistic and Prosocial Behaviors for Older and Younger Siblings in Each Group: Same – Sex Dyads

Sex Composition and Interval	*FS		FL		MS		ML	
Age	Younger	Older	Younger	Older	Younger	Older	Younger	Older
Initiations								
Agonism (total)	2.0	18.3	3.5	23.6	4.0	32.25	2.7	25.1
Physical	0.6	3.1	0.83	2.0	1.75	9.125	1.6	9.3
Object	1.1	5.6	2.0	8.5	1.625	9.5	1.0	10.6
Verbal	0.3	9.6	0.67	13.17	0.625	13.625	0.1	5.2
Prosocial	12.7	28.3	11.5	27.16	7.125	13.375	13.9	12.8
Imitation	16.8	4.7	14.0	3.3	14.25	6.25	15.5	4.7
Responses								
To agonism								
Counterattack	2.6	0.8	3.5	1.3	5.625	2.125	4.3	0.7
Submit	7.3	0.9	9.5	1.3	14.875	0.75	12.9	0.7
To prosocial								
Positive	17.2	8.0	17.8	6.3	7.5	3.25	7.2	6.4
Negative	3.1	2.0	2.1	2.5	1.375	1.125	1.4	3.1

*F = female   S = small interval

M = male   L = large interval   (FS = female, small interval)

69

TABLE 4.4

Mean Frequencies of Agonistic, Prosocial and Imitative Behaviors and Responses
to Agonistic and Prosocial Behaviors for Older and Younger Siblings in Each Group:
Mixed-Sex Dyads

Sex Composition and Interval	Small Interval				Large Interval			
	Female older, male younger		Male older, female younger		Female older, male younger		Male older, female younger	
Age	Younger	Older	Younger	Older	Younger	Older	Younger	Older
Initiations								
Agonism (total)	6.88	16.88	4.53	13.11	9.20	15.90	4.19	15.75
Physical	2.63	3.00	1.10	3.11	5.00	2.50	0.77	3.00
Object	3.38	5.88	1.88	4.44	3.60	4.90	2.20	3.55
Verbal	0.88	8.00	1.55	5.55	0.60	8.50	1.22	9.20
Prosocial	8.88	21.25	11.56	18.78	15.00	36.20	16.80	18.78
Imitation	18.63	6.63	19.89	6.56	24.60	8.10	16.00	3.78
Responses								
To agonism								
Counterattack	3.75	4.13	0.89	2.22	2.20	3.30	2.00	1.77
Submit	6.25	1.88	9.99	1.11	8.20	3.30	8.44	2.11
To prosocial								
Positive	17.38	5.25	15.10	5.67	25.80	9.10	13.00	6.57
Negative	1.88	1.13	1.89	2.56	2.50	2.00	3.33	3.33

tion and limited range of behaviors found in laboratory studies would be seen in the home. Speculation about the importance of sibling interaction suggests that it is both more pervasive and, on occasion, more hostile than laboratory observations would suggest.

The results for both same- and mixed-sex siblings were at odds with those obtained in laboratory studies. First, levels of interaction between siblings were very high. The mean frequencies of agonistic, prosocial, and imitative behaviors and responses to agonistic and prosocial behaviors for each group are presented in Tables 3 and 4.

The mean number of initiations per dyad over the two hours of observation was 79.2 for same-sex dyads and 87.3 for mixed-sex dyads. The mean number of responses was 39.6 and 44.3 for same- and mixed-sex dyads respectively. This high level of interaction held across the various types of dyads—sex, sex composition, and interval had little effect on the rate of interaction. In addition there were many behaviors not on our check list that occurred with some frequency, for example, looking, vocalizing, responding to imitation, or simply playing together. Thus, the amount of interaction is even greater than what we have recorded. These figures make it clear that the sibling pairs observed in these studies directed a large amount of behavior to one another. Second, we observed a wide range of interactions—agnostic as well as prosocial behavior (see Tables 3 & 4).

There are a number of factors in the laboratory setting that could account for these differences. The situation is unfamiliar, the sessions brief, and the large array of novel toys may distract siblings from each other. Also, the attentive audience provided by one or both parents as well as their entering and leaving between episodes may shift the children's focus from their siblings. In addition, we ranged our visits to the home during times when mothers reported that their children were likely to be together, so that the level of interaction we observed may be somewhat higher than typical or average. Lamb (1978a) has suggested that the results of cross-cultural research on siblings are consistent with the low levels of interaction he observed. However, Konner (1975) maintains that, at least for older children, sibling interaction is an important aspect of social development in hunter-gatherer societies and also among many groups of nonhuman primates. Whatever the findings from other cultures, the present results and those of Dunn and Kendrick (1979) indicate that in their own homes siblings play an important role in one another's social lives. However, the differences among the results of the various studies strengthen Lamb's argument for doing research in more than one kind of environment and especially for observing children in "natural" settings rather than in psychology laboratories.

Effects of Age, Sex, and Interval

The general findings of high levels of interaction comprising a wide range of prosocial and agonistic acts held for all sibling groups. The overall amount of interaction was unaffected by any of our variables. However, patterns of behavior differed according to age and sex, though interval was not an important factor. (All analyses were done using a mixed design ANOVA and only significant effects are reported below—for details see Abramovitch et al., 1979.)

The major effect of age was on the amount of agonism displayed. The older children initiated over 80% of agonistic behaviors. This was true of all sibling groups. On the few occasions that younger siblings initiated aggression, their older brothers and sisters often retaliated, whereas the younger siblings were more likely to submit to aggression than to counterattack.

Older siblings also initiated significantly more prosocial behavior than their younger siblings. It is interesting to note, however, that the younger siblings played a substantial role in the initiation of prosocial behavior. In contrast to agonism, which the younger children initiated only 20% of the time, they initiated 35% of all prosocial behavior. In the mixed-sex dyads the younger children also responded more positively to prosocial behavior than did their older siblings. Although the older children initiate interaction more often (probably because of their larger social repertoire), the younger children may have an important role in maintaining the interaction by responding positively to prosocial behavior and by submitting to aggressive behavior.

The pattern for imitation was quite different—younger siblings imitated their older brothers and sisters significantly more often than the reverse. This is consistent with Lamb's study. One would expect that older children would act as models and possibly as teachers for their younger siblings. (See, for example, Cicirelli, 1975.) The actual content of the imitation, however, was predominantly playful rather than behavior that might teach new skills. Some typical examples of imitative behavior were: pretending to be a monster, dancing around the room swinging arms around, blowing cake crumbs out of one's mouth, banging play dough on the table, saying "pow" and pointing a cane like a gun, and repeating various words and phrases. There were, of course, some exceptions that might have allowed the younger children to learn from the example of their older siblings—trying to cut a pattern out of a piece of paper with a pair of scissors, putting lego pieces together in a particular manner, climbing onto a chair to reach the sink, saying the "A, B, C's". Although the frequency with which younger siblings imitated their older brothers and sisters has been stressed, it should be remembered that approximately 20% of all imitation was performed by older siblings. The content of the older children's imitation was almost entirely playful, but clearly demonstrates an interest in the behavior of their younger siblings.

Sex was also an important factor in the patterning of sibling interaction. In the same-sex sibling dyads, interactions between female siblings were characterized by a greater proportion of prosocial than agonistic behaviors; the opposite was true for the males. This is consistent with the general belief that boys are more aggressive and girls more prosocial. However, we found no main effect for sex on total agonism. It was only in terms of physical aggression that males significantly exceeded females. There were no sex differences in the amount of verbal aggression or in the frequency of struggles over possessions and objects, i.e., older sisters were as likely to take things from or yell at their younger sisters as older brothers were to take things from or yell at their younger brothers. Interestingly, in the mixed-sex dyads there were no sex differences on any measure of aggression. These data contrast with the typical findings that in peer interactions boys are more aggressive than girls (cf. Maccoby & Jacklin, 1974).

Older girls in the same-sex dyads were significantly more likely than older boys to engage in positive and nurturant behavior. In the mixed-sex dyads, there was a significant interaction between sex composition and age, with the older girls being much more prosocial than younger brothers, whereas the older boys were only slightly more prosocial than their younger sisters. In other words, disregarding age, girls tended to be more prosocial than boys. However, there were no sex differences in responses to prosocial behavior. This pattern of sex differences in initiation of prosocial behaviors is consistent with Konner's (1975) observation that, among primates, alloparental behavior is typically female, and with the results of Cicirelli (1975), who found that children were more likely to receive and accept help from an older sister than from an older brother. These data are also consistent with the patterns described for peer interaction, i.e., girls are more cooperative and nurturant than boys (cf. Maccoby & Jacklin, 1974).

There were no sex differences in imitative behavior. Given our other finding that older sisters in same-sex dyads were less physically aggressive and more nurturant, it might have been expected that older sisters would be more likely to act as models than older brothers. This did not occur. Younger male siblings showed just as much interest as females in following their older siblings around and duplicating their activities. In the mixed-sex dyads, younger brothers imitated their older sisters as often as younger sisters imitated older brothers.

Interval, unlike age and sex, had almost no effect on the patterning of interactions. Despite the many theories about the importance of spacing siblings in particular ways, we were not able to find any appreciable effect of differences in spacing (1.5 to 2 years versus 2.5 to 4 years). It should be noted that, in this study, interval and age were, to a degree, confounded. That is, the oldest children were always in the large-interval groups. Future studies could examine similar intervals with different-aged children in order to assess interval effects more clearly. Our one suggestive finding regarding interval was that among the same-sex dyads the older brothers in the small interval group were the most verbally aggressive, were very likely to respond to agonism by counterattacking, and their younger brothers were least likely to initiate prosocial behaviors. (None of these differences was significant, however.) This group, therefore, seems to be characterized by somewhat more ''negative'' patterns of interaction than the other same-sex groups. This is consistent with the belief that a small interval will lead to increased sibling rivalry. However, these were the only effects that even approached significance. Differences in spacing did not affect levels of aggressive, cooperative, or imitative behavior for either same-sex or mixed-sex sibling pairs. Of course, it is possible that the age of a first child when a sibling is born might have later effects on either child's personality or other characteristics, but we found no effect on patterns of interactions.

Thus far we have not directly addressed the question of the sex composition of the dyads, (which is of course different from the issue of sex of the individual child). In neither the same-sex nor the mixed-sex studies were there any main effects for sex composition—that is, male dyads were not significantly different from female dyads on any measures, and female older, male younger dyads were not different from male older, female younger pairs. The frequencies of prosocial, agonistic, and imitative behaviors in same- versus mixed-sex dyads were very similar and showed no significant differences (by t-tests, all p's $> .10$).

These results are different from those of Dunn and Kendrick (1979), who found differences between same- and mixed-sex sibling pairs. However, subjects in that study were from British working-class families and the younger siblings were 14 months old when these patterns were described as opposed to 18 months in our studies. It is possible that any of these factors could account for the differences. Our results are more consistent with Lamb's (1978a,b) failure to find any effect of sex composition on sibling interaction in the laboratory.

Our results suggest that findings from studies of same- vs. mixed-sex peer interaction (e.g., Jacklin & Maccoby, 1978) may not extend readily to sibling interaction. There are many ways in which peer and sibling interactions differ. Siblings are obviously very familiar with one another and this might override or neutralize possible effects due to sex composition. Ordinarily, sibling dyads are also mixed-age dyads and this factor may affect interaction (see, for example, Lougee, Grueneich, & Hartup, 1977).

Although levels and patterns of interaction were generally similar across our two studies of same- and mixed-sex siblings, we did find differences consistent with the explanations suggested by Jacklin and Maccoby (1978) for differences between same- and mixed-sex peer interaction. In same-sex pairs, the older boys were more physically aggressive than the older girls. It is possible that the older boys were responding to some behaviors emitted by their younger brothers, or perhaps the older boys believed that their younger siblings, being male, were appropriate targets. Thus some aspects of behavioral matching, perceived similarity, and/or appropriate behavior might have played a role in the sex difference in frequency of aggression found in the same-sex study. Differential parental reinforcement or tolerance may also have played a role. Another difference between same- and mixed-sex sibling pairs was that it was only in the former that girls responded positively to prosocial behavior more frequently than boys. Thus sisters reinforced each other for cooperative and nurturant-acts—sex-appropriate behavior.

In conclusion, our initial studies of sibling interaction indicated high levels of interaction in the home. Older siblings initiated more agonistic and prosocial behavior and younger siblings imitated more. Older boys were the most agonistic group and older females were the most prosocial. There were no effects of sex composition of the dyad and perhaps, most surprising, no effects of age interval.

Longitudinal Follow-up

One purpose of the longitudinal follow-up was to determine if the pattern of results we found initially would replicate at a later time. We were particularly interested in our failure to find an effect for interval. It seemed that one explanation might be that when the younger siblings were only 18 months old, their older siblings had few choices regarding modes of interaction, given the rather limited social repertoire of an 18-month-old child. Perhaps by the time the younger children were three years old, the differential ages of the older siblings might play a greater role.

Another major goal of the longitudinal study was to explore changes in social interaction over time. In a laboratory study, Lamb (1978b) found that the social behavior of younger siblings increased from 12 to 18 months, whereas their older siblings showed no such increase. Similarly, Dunn and Kendrick (1979) reported that the younger member of a sibling pair joined an older sibling in a positive interaction more often at 14 months than at 8 months, even though the total amount of interaction between the two did not change. Thus the longitudinal study allowed us to look first at the consistency of the general findings regarding amount and type of social interaction and the effects of sex, age, and interval at a later point in development; and second, at longitudinal changes in sibling interaction in the home.

The results for the initial and follow-up studies for same- and mixed-sex dyads who were observed at the two points in time are presented in Tables 5 and 6.

It can readily be seen that the siblings still engaged in a great deal of social interaction. During the follow-up observations, the rate of social interaction was 85 and 84 initiations plus responses per hour for the same- and mixed-sex pairs respectively. This compared to 60 and 66 for the initial observations. The effects of age replicated the findings from the initial studies in both same- and mixed-sex dyads. As before, older siblings initiated significantly more prosocial behavior. However, the younger siblings increased their proportion of prosocial behavior from an average of 35% in the initial studies to 42% in the follow-up studies, indicating that they were becoming more equal partners in the interaction. When prosocial behavior is divided into discrete categories, older children in both same- and mixed-sex dyads engaged in significantly more cooperation and help, comfort and praise, whereas the younger siblings approached their older siblings more often. As before, younger siblings responded positively to prosocial behavior more frequently than older siblings.

The results for agonism and responses to agonism are similar to those from the initial studies for both same- and mixed-sex pairs, with one important change.

TABLE 4.5
Mean Frequencies of Prosocial, Agonistic and Imitative Behaviors of Same- and Mixed-Sex Pairs in Initial and Follow-Up Studies

Sex of older sibling and interval		FS		FL		MS		ML	
Age		Younger	Older	Younger	Older	Younger	Older	Younger	Older
Same-sex sibling pairs									
Prosocial	Initial	13.1	28.0	14.8	30.6	7.7	14.7	14.3	14.3
	Follow-up	25.0	38.4	38.4	51.8	22.8	35.2	27.5	34.0
Agonism	Initial	1.4	16.6	5.0	21.0	5.5	31.7	1.5	24.4
	Follow-up	4.4	17.7	7.4	20.8	8.2	18.3	4.8	16.4
Imitation	Initial	15.4	3.6	15.2	3.2	19.0	7.2	13.3	2.5
	Follow-up	17.1	4.8	11.0	4.6	9.7	3.8	14.1	4.8
Mixed-sex sibling pairs									
Prosocial	Initial	9.4	24.0	14.5	40.3	13.0	16.3	18.1	22.3
	Follow-up	26.3	37.8	22.8	33.2	30.8	38.8	31.9	38.3
Agonism	Initial	7.9	17.7	9.0	14.5	7.3	11.0	3.7	16.3
	Follow-up	8.6	23.3	6.8	20.0	11.3	17.5	12.1	20.6
Imitation	Initial	19.1	7.1	23.5	10.7	15.8	10.1	16.9	4.1
	Follow-up	9.0	2.1	10.5	1.5	10.2	1.9	8.1	.7

TABLE 4.6
Mean Frequencies of Responses to Prosocial and Agonistic Behaviors of Same-Sex and Mixed-Sex Pairs in Follow-Up Study

Same-sex siblings

	Sex of dyad and interval	FS		FL		MS		ML	
	Age	Younger	Older	Younger	Older	Younger	Older	Younger	Older
Responses to Prosocial	Positive	23.2	13.2	35.8	23.2	20.5	11.2	20.3	14.8
	Negative	4.8	4.2	6.2	4.6	5.7	4.8	4.9	3.5
Responses to Agonism	Counterattack	3.8	2.6	4.8	4.8	7.7	4.3	5.8	2.1
	Submit	7.1	1.3	5.8	.4	5.2	1.2	5.8	1.1

Mixed-sex siblings

	Sex of older sibling and interval	FS		FL		MS		ML	
	Age	Younger	Older	Younger	Older	Younger	Older	Younger	Older
Responses to Prosocial	Positive	25.3	11.6	20.5	10.7	24.0	13.9	23.9	12.3
	Negative	3.7	5.6	3.0	4.8	3.5	5.1	4.3	5.6
Responses to Agonism	Counterattack	6.0	5.0	4.3	4.5	4.6	4.8	7.6	7.1
	Submit	7.0	1.0	5.2	.7	3.5	2.5	4.7	1.1

Although older children initiated more agonism than younger siblings, this effect was due entirely to greater verbal agonism by the older children; the age differences in physical agonism or object struggles as seen before had disappeared. In 18 months, the younger siblings had become equal partners when it came to starting fights over possessions and other forms of physical aggression. However, the younger siblings were still more likely to submit to aggression, whereas the older siblings were more likely to counterattack.

The age differences for imitation remained the same in the follow-up studies. Younger children in both same- and mixed-sex pairs imitated their older siblings significantly more than vice versa.

The sex of the individual children was no longer an important factor. Whereas in the initial studies, girls initiated more prosocial behavior than boys, there were no significant differences in the follow-up studies. There were no sex differences in aggression or in imitation for either same- or mixed-sex sibling dyads. Nor were there any sex differences in responses to prosocial or aggressive behavior. This complete lack of sex differences was unexpected because it had seemed likely that the children would have become more sex-stereotyped as they grew older. As we have already stated, the failure to find sex differences is inconsistent with many studies of peer interaction in which boys are often found to be more aggressive and girls more prosocial (e.g., Maccoby & Jacklin, 1974).

The results for interval replicated those of the initial studies. There was no significant effect of interval in any group for the initiation of any behaviors.

Although the overall pattern of interaction between the siblings remained much the same, it is possible to ask whether there were any changes over time. To answer this question the analyses of variance were carried out again, with the additional factor of time treated as a repeated measure. The first finding was a dramatic increase in prosocial behavior from time one to time two. Almost twice as many prosocial acts were initiated during the follow-up observations. This increase was exhibited by both older and younger siblings and in both same- and mixed-sex dyads.

The changes in agonistic behavior were more complex. Among mixed-sex pairs there was a significant increase in agonism from the initial study to the follow-up study, with both younger and older siblings contributing to the increase. In contrast, there was little overall change in total agonism among same-sex pairs, but younger children showed more agonism, whereas older ones showed less. There was one major change in the pattern of imitation: For mixed-sex pairs, the frequency of imitation decreased sharply.

Another way of looking at differences between same- and mixed-sex pairs is to compare frequencies of prosocial, agonistic, and imitative behaviors directly, using T-tests. Frequencies for prosocial behavior were very similar; there were no significant differences. However, both younger and older children in same-sex dyads initiated more imitation than children in mixed-sex pairs and there was a trend, ($p < .10$) for younger children in mixed-sex dyads to be more aggressive than younger siblings in same-sex dyads. These results complement the pattern of findings in the longitudinal analysis.

Some aspects of the longitudinal data are inconsistent with those of Dunn and Kendrick (1979) and Lamb (1978b), who found that only younger siblings increased their frequency of social behavior over time. Our results indicate that both the older and the younger children initiated more behavior in the follow-up observations. This discrepancy may be accounted for by the difference in age between children in our studies and those in the other two longitudinal studies. At the time of the follow-up observations, the younger children in Lamb's study were 18 months old and in Dunn and Kendrick's study were 14 months old, whereas the younger children in our follow-up studies were approximately 36 months old. The increase in social interaction with time by the older siblings in our studies may have been in response to the growing social competence of the younger sibling. The older children might have perceived their three-year-old siblings as more interesting play partners than one-and-half-year-old siblings, and therefore also engaged in more interaction during the follow-up observations. The age difference between Lamb's subjects and ours, as well as the difference in time between initial and follow-up studies (6 months for Lamb and 18 months in our work) may also account for the fact that Lamb found stability in individual behavior, whereas our overall finding was of little individual stability over the 18-month period.

There were, however, two differences between same- and mixed-sex sibling pairs in our longitudinal analysis. Over time, the frequency of imitation for same-sex pairs remained basically the same. In contrast, the frequency of imitation for the mixed-sex pairs decreased significantly from the initial to the follow-up observations. This might be an early indication of an increase in sex-typing found around ages three and four (Kohlberg, 1966). The younger children of mixed-sex dyads may have imitated less frequently because they began to perceive their opposite-sex older siblings as different or their activities and toys as inappropriate. In addition, the frequency of aggression increased only for the mixed-sex siblings. These data are consistent with Dunn and Kendrick's (1979) finding of a higher proportion of negative behavior among mixed-sex siblings. This increase in aggression might result from fewer common interests, which become more salient as the children get older.

In conclusion, our follow-up study indicated that siblings maintained a high level of interaction. The effects of age remained the same—older siblings initiated more agonistic and prosocial behavior. However, the younger siblings were becoming more equal partners in the interaction and younger siblings still imitated more. The age interval between siblings still had no effect on the pattern of interaction, and there were no longer any effects of the sex of the individual children—i.e., girls were not more prosocial and boys were not more aggressive. However, the sex composition of the dyad affected interaction in the follow-up study. The amount of prosocial behavior increased for both same- and mixed-sex dyads. However, whereas levels of agonism and imitation remained stable for same-sex dyads, aggression increased and imitation decreased in mixed-sex dyads.

Mother-child Interaction

In addition to the sibling behaviors, we observed mother-child interactions when we did the longitudinal follow-up. The observational method did not change—we simply noted behaviors initiated by or directed to the mother, as well as the behaviors already on our list. Mother-initiated behaviors included caretaking; giving praise, comfort, and help; making requests; commanding, threatening, and punishing. Child-initiated behaviors included giving affection and help; imitating; requesting attention or information; and voicing anger or disapproval.

There are many indications in the literature (e.g., Jacobs & Moss, 1976, Kendick & Dunn, 1980) that first- and second-borns are treated differently by their parents. It also seemed likely that the age and sex of the children could have an effect on mother-child interaction. It should be noted that the situation was not ideally suited to studying mother-child interaction, since mothers were free to come and go as they pleased and, in fact, did so. However, every entrance and exit was noted and the total amount of time each mother spent with her children was recorded. Interactions were calculated as rates rather than as actual frequencies. Interestingly, for same-sex dyads, mothers spent significantly less time with female pairs than with male pairs (25% versus 50%). This was the only significant difference in amount of time spent—the average proportion of time spent with mixed-sex sibling pairs was approximately 40%.

Although there were some effects for mother-child interactions, many of them were complex and uninterpretable and there were no consistent or meaningful patterns. This was also true of child-mother interactions. This lack of clear-cut results is somewhat surprising. It is possible that mothers modified their behavior due to the presence of the observer or that we did not choose appropriate behaviors to observe. It is also possible that these results accurately reflect the situation and that mothers are more "democratic" in their treatment of younger and older and male and female children than we had supposed. It should be noted that we did not look at the specific content of behavior—mothers might have altered the content of their requests, commands, etc. depending on the age and sex of the child without altering frequency. (Assessing content might also have produced age and sex differences in child-to-mother behaviors.) Another possibility is that mothers might differentiate their behavior when interacting with just one child. However, when dealing with both siblings at once they might make an effort not to treat the children differently so as not to arouse rivalry or conflict. Clearly these possibilities deserve closer investigation.

There is some evidence in the literature of mothers being "democratic" with respect to their treatment of boys and girls. Smith and Daglish (1977) observed parent-child interaction in 32 families, each with a child between 12 and 24 months, and found almost no differences in parental behavior based on the sex of the child. Similarly Zegiob and Forehand (1975), in an investigation of the effects of race, socioeconomic status, and sex on maternal interactive behavior, reported that the sex of the child was rarely a significant factor in determining the mother's behavior.

We also compared mothers' behavior toward same- versus mixed-sex sibling dyads. Dunn and Kendrick (1981) speculate that mothers might be especially positive in their interaction with the younger child in a mixed-sex dyad, perhaps due to the novelty or the pleasure of having a different-sex child. They further speculate that this will lead to jealousy on the part of the older sibling. However, we found no differences in the frequency of positive maternal behavior toward younger or older children in same- versus mixed-sex dyads. With respect to negative behavior (commands, threats, punishments), there were no differences for older children or younger females. The one slight difference we found directly contradicted Dunn and Kendrick. There was a trend, $p < .10$, for mothers to direct more negative behavior toward younger males in mixed-sex dyads than toward younger males in same-sex dyads.

However, when we correlated mothers' behavior toward their older and younger child for negative and positive behaviors, an interesting result emerged. For negative behavior, the correlations were .52 ($p < .01$) and .38 ($p < .05$) for same- and mixed-sex dyads respectively. For positive behavior, the correlation was .85 ($p < .01$) for same-sex dyads and .39 ($p < .05$) for mixed-sex dyads. The difference between the two correlations for positive behavior is significant ($z = 2.98$, $p < .01$). Thus mothers are consistent in their treatment of younger and older siblings in both same- and mixed-sex pairs (all of the correlations are significant), but there is more consistency for same-sex dyads. The fact that mothers are significantly more consistent in their positive treatment of same-sex siblings than of mixed-sex siblings could account for the greater level of agonistic behavior among the latter. This is pure speculation, but following Dunn and Kendrick's argument mentioned earlier, it is possible that differential positive treatment in mixed-sex dyads could lead to greater jealousy and therefore greater agonism.

Another way of thinking about the role of the mother in sibling interaction is to look at the effects of her presence on the frequency of various sibling behaviors. Studying the mother's role in modifying sibling interaction is one step toward placing that interaction in the context of broader family dynamics, in keeping with Bronfenbrenner's call for an examination of "second order effects" in studies of social interaction (Bronfenbrenner, 1974). Lamb (1978a,b) provided data relevant to this issue by manipulating the presence of mother and father in laboratory observations of sibling pairs. He found less sibling interaction in the presence of two parents than in the presence of a single parent, but found no effect on the nature of that interaction. It should be noted that one parent was always present. We also conducted a laboratory study in which we examined the effects of mother's presence and absence on sibling interaction.

The subjects were 32 pairs of mixed-sex dyads—all but four of whom we had observed in the home. The laboratory study was carried out just after the initial home observations were completed and the younger siblings were all between 18 and 24 months. We observed more negative or aggressive interactions in mother's presence than in her absence on the part of both younger and older siblings. This finding is bolstered by maternal interview data (collected a little more than a year later). In response to the question, "Does whether or not you are with the children seem to affect how well they get along?", 72% of the mothers reported that their children got along better when they were absent. These findings are somewhat surprising but are compatible with some of the work done on peer interaction. Siegel (1957) reports that aggression in peer play decreased in the absence of an adult and suggested that the absence of adults places greater demands for self-control on children. Similarly, a recent study (Field, 1979) showed that older infants were more negative towards peers in a nursery school when mother was present. The interpretation advanced in this study was that the negative behavior was designed to obtain mother's attention. It should be noted that in our laboratory study, mothers were instructed not to intervene and thus did not reinforce aggression by attention (although this might be the pattern in the home and it may carry over to the lab).

We were able to look at the effects of mother's presence in our longitudinal studies because we knew exactly when each mother was present. We found no overall effect of mother's presence on frequency of aggression. However, the ratio of prosocial to agonistic behaviors fell into an interesting pattern. In many cases, mother's presence did not affect this ratio—i.e., more prosocial behavior was initiated both in her presence and in her absence (approximately 50% of the children); or less prosocial behavior was initiated both in her presence and in her absence (approximately 5% of the children). However, looking at those children for whom there was a difference, we found that in almost all instances there was more prosocial than agonistic behavior in mother's absence and either more agonistic than prosocial behavior or an equal amount of these behaviors in her presence. Thus, the tendency is for behavior to be relatively more negative in mother's presence than in her absence (in those cases where this factor has an effect). This is consistent with our laboratory study and with mothers' reports.

Another way to look at the effects of mother's presence and absence is in terms of overall levels of behavior. As noted above, Lamb (1978a) reported a reduced level of sibling interaction in the presence of one versus two parents. Similarly we found that most of our subjects engaged in lower levels of interaction in mother's presence than in her absence. An interesting exception to this was that younger males in same-sex dyads tended to initiate more aggression in mother's presence. These boys might have felt that it was safest for them to initiate aggression against their older brothers when mother was there for potential protection—this could be seen as a literal case of using mother as a "secure base".

In summary, we found no clear evidence for the patterning of mother-child interaction being affected by any of our variables i.e., age, sex, or interval. This was true for both mother-initiated and child-initiated behaviors. However, although there were few differences in the ways mothers behaved toward children in same- versus mixed-sex dyads, we did find that mothers were more consistent in their positive treatment of same-sex sibling pairs. We also found evidence for more negative behavior on the part of siblings in their mother's presence (versus her absence).

CONCLUSION

Our findings indicate that for intervals as long as three years, siblings spend a great deal of time interacting with each other, and that their interactions include a variety of behaviors. Thus, at the simplest level, these studies make it clear that siblings are deeply involved with each other. This makes it very likely that the pattern of interactions they establish affects other social interactions and the course of their socialization.

Added to this high level of interaction is the important and perhaps surprising (i.e., not predicted by some theorists) degree of prosocial behavior present in the interactions between the siblings. Not only do they treat each other in aggressive ways, but they also cooperate, help and act affectionately; and the younger siblings show a high level of imitation of the older ones. In other words, the social interactions of the two siblings at an early age represent a full range of social interactions such as would be present between older children or, for that matter, adults. One way of looking at this is that although siblings represent unique social objects for each other, their social interactions are not limited to what might be considered hallmarks of sibling interaction—they are not always and universally jealous and hostile toward each other. There is a great deal of aggressive interaction, but the relationship seems to be a full one. This makes it all the more likely that interactions with siblings are prototypical of interactions that develop later with other peers, and perhaps also with adults.

The point of this discussion is that sibling interaction should be considered a precursor to other interactions, and by studying how their patterns of interaction change over time, we may begin to understand other social interactions of children. In addition, it seems likely that the nature of early sibling interaction in a particular family may be related to how the children interact with other people outside the home. That is, children may develop patterns of interactions with siblings that carry over into other interactions. For example, children who have high levels of both aggressive and prosocial interaction with their siblings may treat peers in day care or school the same way; whereas those children who for one reason or another tend not to have aggressive interactions with siblings, may be less aggressive with peers. Alternatively, the children with siblings may learn to deal with a full range of behavior, from prosocial to aggressive, whereas children without siblings may be less accustomed to dealing with aggressive behavior from others.

All of this is, of course, highly speculative. It is mentioned merely to show the range of possibilities regarding the effects of sibling interaction on social development. The general point is that children with siblings do develop patterns of interaction, and that these patterns would be expected to influence their interaction with other children. Therefore, it seems desirable to follow siblings from the home into day care or school to investigate these relationships.

Thus far we have focused on what we found. However, perhaps the most surprising results of this series of studies are what we did *not* find, i.e., the lack of effect of the interval between the siblings, the sex of the individual, and the relatively few effects of the sex composition of the pairs. From many points of view, we would have expected interval to influence the pattern of social interaction. In the first place, interval and the age of the older sibling are confounded. We did find that the older sibling tended to be dominant, initiating most of the aggressive and prosocial interactions. Given this, it is somewhat baffling that greater age differences did not increase the degree of dominance, especially because, with the larger interval, the older child was at an older age than with the smaller interval. In addition, various writers have surmised that smaller intervals would lead to greater sibling rivalry and thus more aggressiveness. From another point of view, greater similarity in age might be expected to produce a fuller, more mutual relationship—it surely would be expected to with unrelated children.

The findings regarding sex are even more surprising. Virtually all relevant research has shown that sex affects social behavior and generally same- and mixed-sex interactions are also different. We found two instances of a familiar sex difference—older boys in same-sex dyads were more physically aggressive than older girls, and girls were more prosocial than boys—but even these effects disappeared at the second observation time.

How can we explain this? Although we do not have any explanation supported by data, one possibility is that sibling interactions are unique, that they cannot and should not be compared directly with other kinds of peer relationships. Certainly siblings tend to play unique roles in each other's lives. They are in the same household, are constantly present, are involved in continual interactions with the same set of parents, and typically share space, toys, clothes, and other such concrete objects as well as the love and attention of their parents. Added to all of this is the fact that, unlike peer friends, siblings have not chosen each other—they have a relationship by the nature of their status, and this relationship is constantly fostered and assumed by the parents as well as by society in general.

The unusual characteristics of the sibling relationship may help explain the lack of effect of such normally powerful factors as sex and age. The suggestion is that sibling relationships have something in common with each other that is different from other relationships, perhaps closer, deeper, more automatic and spontaneous. The other sibling is there forever and is always there, and is thus part of one's life, in a way that an unrelated peer is not. Perhaps the sibling relationship is unaffected by these other factors because they are irrelevant to this relationship in the sense that what really matters is the fact that they are siblings, and everything else is minor.

This is, of course, just an idea, and it is not clear yet what its implications are. It does seem to imply that the sibling relationship may be especially important in the life of a child. Thus, any disruptions in that relationships (e.g., death of a sibling; separation for any reason) may have dramatic effects. It also suggests that children without siblings may either develop their social skills quite differently, or may have to find substitutes for the relationship with a sibling. In any case, it seems clear that the sibling relationship may be in many ways special, and is therefore an important focus for future research.

Finally, let us summarize briefly the main findings of these observations of sibling interaction in the home. Siblings interact a great deal, are both prosocial and aggressive, and show a considerable amount of imitation. The interval between the siblings makes little or no difference in their social interactions. There are no consistent sex differences, though some do show up. Older children, as might be expected, are more aggressive and initiate more prosocial interaction, whereas younger siblings imitate more. However, as the children get older, all of these differences decrease and the children become more equal partners. Patterns of interaction found when the younger child is about one-and-a-half persist with very few changes for at least eighteen months, the time of our second observations. In other words, siblings in two-child families have full, continuous, and presumably important relationships with each other; and the nature of these relationships is little affected by the sex of the children, whether they are the same or different sexes and whether the age interval between them is large or small. Just how this relationship affects other relationships in the child's life remains to be discovered.

REFERENCES

Abramovitch, R., Corter, C., & Lando, B. Sibling interaction in the home. *Child Development,* 1979, *50,* 997–1003.

Abramovitch, R., Corter, C., & Pepler, D. Observations of mixed-sex sibling dyads. *Child Development,* 1980, *51,* 1268–1271.

Bronfenbrenner, U. Developmental research, public policy, and the ecology of childhood. *Child Development,* 1974, *45,* 1–5.

Cicirelli, V. Effects of sibling structure and interaction on children's categorization style. *Developmental Psychology,* 1973, *9,* 132–139.

Cicirelli, V. Effect of mother and older sibling on the problem-solving behavior of the younger child. *Developmental Psychology,* 1975, *11,* 749–756.

Cornoldi, C., & Fattori, L. Age spacing in firstborns and symbiotic dependence. *Journal of Personality and Social Psychology,* 1976, *33,* 431–434.

Dunn, J., & Kendrick, C. Interaction between young siblings in the context of family relationships. In M. Lewis & L. Rosenblum (Eds.), *The child and its family*. New York: Plenum, 1979.

Dunn, J. & Kendrick, C. Social behavior of young siblings in the family context: differences between same-sex and different-sex dyads. *Child Development*, 1981, *52*, 1265-1273.

Eckerman, C. O., Whatley, J. L., & Kutz, S. L. Growth of social play with peers during the second year of life. *Developmental Psychology*, 1975, *11*, 42-49.

Field, T. Infant behaviors directed toward peers and adults in the presence and absence of mother. *Infant Behavior and Development*, 1979, *2*, 47-54.

Jacklin, C. N., & Maccoby, E. E. Social behavior at thirty-three months in same-sex and mixed-sex dyads. *Child Development*, 1978, *49*, 557-569.

Jacobs, B. S., & Moss, H. A. Birth order and sex of siblings as determinants of mother-infant interaction. *Child Development*, 1976, *47*, 315-322.

Kendrick, C., & Dunn, J. Caring for a second baby: effects on interaction between mother and first born. *Developmental Psychology*, 1980, *18*, 303-311.

Koch, H. L. Some emotional attitudes of the young child in relation to characteristics of the sibling. *Child Development*, 1956, *27*, 393-426.

Kohlberg, L. A cognitive-developmental analysis of children's sex-role concepts and attitudes. In E. E. Maccoby (Ed.), *The development of sex differences*. Stanford: Stanford University Press, 1966.

Konner, M. Relations among infants and juveniles in comparative perspective. In M. Lewis & L. A. Rosenblum (Eds.), *Friendship and peer relations*. New York: Wiley, 1975.

Lamb, M. Interactions between 18-month-olds and their preschool-aged siblings. *Child Development*, 1978, *49*, 51-59. (a)

Lamb, M. The development of sibling relationships in infancy: a short-term longitudinal study. *Child Development*, 1978, *49*, 1189-1196. (b)

Langlois, J. H., Gottfried, N. W., & Seay, B. The influence of sex of peer on the social behavior of preschool children. *Developmental Psychology*, 1973, *8*, 93-98.

Lougee, M. D. Grueneich, R., & Hartup, W. W. Social interaction in same- and mixed-age dyads of preschool children. *Child Development*, 1977, *48*, 1353-1361.

Maccoby, E., & Jacklin, C. *The psychology of sex differences*. Stanford: Stanford University Press, 1974.

Miller, N., & Maruyama, G. Ordinal position and peer popularity. *Journal of Personality and Social Psychology*, 1976, *33*, 123-131.

Pepler, D. J., Abramovitch, R., & Corter, C. Sibling interaction in the home: A longitudinal study. *Child Development*, 1981, *52*, 1344-1347.

Samuels, H. The effect of an older sibling on infant locomotor exploration in a new environment. *Child Development*, 1980, *51*, 607-609.

Siegel, A. Aggressive behavior of young children in the absence of an adult. *Child Development*, 1957, *28*, 371-378.

Smith, P. K., & Daglish, L. Sex differences in parent and infant behavior in the home. *Child Development*, 1977, *48*, 1250-1254.

Sutton-Smith, B., & Rosenberg, B. *The Sibling*. New York: Holt, Rinehart, and Winston, 1970.

White, B. Critical influences in the origins of competence. *Merrill-Palmer Quarterly*, 1975, *21*, 243-266.

Zajonc, R. B., & Markus, G. Birth order and intellectual development. *Psychological Review*, 1975, *82*, 74-88.

Zegiob, L. E., & Forehand, R. Maternal interactive behavior as a function of race, socioeconomic status and sex of the child. *Child Development*, 1975, *46*, 564-568.

5 Sibling Relationships in Middle Childhood

Brenda K. Bryant
University of California, Davis

This chapter is concerned with research pertaining to sibling realtionships during middle childhood. It is proposed that sibling relationships during this time provide important developmental contexts. Historically, theorists first supposed that sibling relations were mediated through fundamental parent-child relations (e.g., the psychoanalytic notion that sibling rivalry is mediated by the desire for possession of the mother [Levy, 1943]) and thus that sibling influences were indirect. Thereafter, it was proposed that siblings can directly influence one another (Koch, 1956a, b, and c). Most recently it has been argued that parent-child as well as sibling-sibling interactions can mutually influence one another and thereby influence development in complex ways (Hartup, 1979). Thus, sibling relations are sometimes viewed as autonomous contexts; at other times, sibling relationships are seen as aspects of the more broadly defined family system. The importance of sibling relations in particular, as well as family relations in general, is based on the formulation that the nature of family relations is distinctly different from nonfamilial relations. Sibling and familial relations are thought to be distinguished from other peer generation and nonfamilial relations respectively, in the following ways: frequency and amount of interaction; durability of relations; existence of ascribed roles; accessibility; and, degree of common experiences (Cicirelli, 1976a). Thus, not only are sibling contexts defined by traditional sibling and family status indicators (e.g., sex of sibling, family size); the specific experiences provided by sibling relations during middle childhood define the sibling context as well. As such, the nature of sibling relationships will include sibling and family status indicators as well as actual internal and external (interpersonal interaction) experiences, both independent of and as part of the larger family system. As such, the relationship of these sibling relations to developmental concerns will be considered.

Although frequently overlooked by developmental researchers, middle child-hood can be viewed as a period of active development in which integration of social and affective phenomena are central (Bryant, 1980; Scarr, 1979; Sullivan, 1953). This integration includes dramatic advances in social understanding (Bryan, 1975), interpersonal problem solving, and transformations of the self within the context of expanding horizons (Breger, 1974). We would expect children in this developmental period to be actively engaged with their siblings, struggling to better manage sibling interaction, and attuned to social status within a variety of contexts (e.g., family, school, home neighborhood), with siblings playing important roles.

What does the existing research literature pertaining to middle childhood have to say about these matters? The lack of methodological adequacy makes it chal-lenging and difficult to evaluate the existing sibling research. Methodological limitations go beyond the more common considerations of adequate sample size and reliability and comparability of procedures. A number of sibling and family indicators are needed to adequately describe the general context in which sibling relations develop. These variables include sex of child, sex of sibling, relative ages of siblings, age spacing between siblings, family size, and socioeconomic status. The literature is replete with examples of how these sibling and family status indicators interact in complex ways to predict personality and intellectual "outcomes." For example, Rosen (1961) reported that the impact of family size on achievement motivation varied with social class. Longstreth, Longstreth, Ramirez, and Fernandez (1975), in another example, noted that certain "older-brother" effects occurred only when the age spacing between the child and the older brother was less than three years. Still other examples further document that socioeconomic status and sibling spacing factors tend to be confounded with family size (Cicirelli, 1976b, 1977; Sutton-Smith & Rosenberg, 1970). To aid the reader in considering the adequacy and comparability of studies, Table 1 presents a summary of how researchers of siblings involving children in middle childhood respond to these sampling concerns. Only studies that included chil-dren between the ages 6-12 are included in this table.

An even more selective criterion was used when choosing studies for discus-sion in the following text. These studies describe how siblings in middle child-hood directly experience and interact with each other and how this relates to children's development. The studies were also chosen because they are limited to research on sibling relations in the United States. (Weisner, in chapter 13, reviews the limited cross-cultural data base pertaining to sibling relations in other countries.)

In sum, the nature, extent, and developmental relevance of sibling relations during middle childhood are assessed in this chapter. This is done by considering both the internal experience of sibling relations and the external nature of sibling interpersonal encounters. The particular roles that siblings assume in their rela-tions with one another, independent of the larger family system, are examined. I

TABLE 5.1
Sampling Characteristics of Middle Childhood Sibling Studies

Study	n	TC Grade/Age	Sex of TC M	F	Sex of Sib. M	F	Sibling Spacing	Family Size Small	Large	SES Mid	Low	Ordinal Position 1st	Later	Race Ethnicity	Comments
Adams & Phillips (1972)	370	4th graders (5th grade follow-up)								x	x	x	x	Mexican, White, Black	Lumped 1st born w/only. Ignored sib. struc. var.
Bigner (1974a)	578	5.5-13.5 yrs. (K, 2, 4, 6, 8 gr.)	x	x	x	x	12-20 mo. 28-48 mo.			x			x	White	Both father & mother at home.
Bigner (1974b)	240	K, 2, 4, 6, 8 gr.	x	x	x	x	12-20 mo. 28-48 mo.	x (2 ch.)		x			x 2nd born	White	Both parents present at home
Bragg, Ostrowski, & Finley (1973)	54	10 yrs.	x		x		0-4 yr.	x	x (3 ch.)	x		x	x	White (Canadian)	Analysis did not consider size of family
Brim (1958) Koch (1954, '55a, b '56a-d, '57)	384	5-6 yrs.	x	x	x	x	0-2, 2-4 4-6	x (2 ch.)		(matched on father's occupation)		x	x (2nd born)	White	1. Both parents present at home. 2. Koch (1955)—subsample = 128.
Bryant, (1979, '80, '81)	168	7 & 10 yrs.	x	x	x	x	2-3 yrs. older	x (2 ch.)	x (3 ch. or more)	x (range—with no very low SES families represented)	x	x	x	White	Bryant (1979) n = 96 rather than 168. Older siblings were often 1st borns.

TABLE 5.1

Study	n	TC Grade/Age	Sex of TC		Sex of Sib.		Sibling Spacing	Family Size		S E S		Ordinal Position		Race Ethnicity	Comments
			M	F	M	F		Small	Large	Mid	Low	1st	Later		
Bryant & Crockenberg (1980)	50	4-5 gr. (older sibs)		x		x	2-3 yrs.			x (80%)	x (20%)	x	x	White	
Cicirelli (1972)	120	1 & 3 gr. (older sibs.)	x	x	x	x	2 yrs.								Sib present in one condition.
Cicirelli (1973, 1974)	160	K, 2 gr.	x	x	x	x	2 yrs. & 4 yrs.	x (2 ch.)				x	x		
Cicirelli (1975)	120	1st gr. (younger sibs.)	x	x	x	x	2-3 yr.	x (2)	x (3/more)				x	White	
Cicirelli (1976a)	80	1st gr.	x	x	x	x	2-3 yr.	x (2 ch.)	x (3/more ch.)						
Cicirelli (1976b)	603	11, 12 yrs.	x	x	x	x	(range)	x (range)		x		x	x	White	
Cicirelli (1977)	160	6th gr.	x	x	x	x		x (2 ch.)		x		x	x	White	
Gallagher & Cowen (1976)	82	K-6 gr.	x	x	x (same vs cross-sex)	x	Matched control								Control grp— non-sib pairs (n = 41)
Greenbaum (1965)	Case examples														
Grotevant, Scarr & Weinberg (1977)	319					x	(range)	(range)		x (mid. to upper-mid.)		x (range)	x	(transsocial adoptions included)	72 families

Study	N	Age					Age spacing	No. of children		Range			Race/Ethnicity	Comments
Gump, Schogen & Redl (1963)	1	9 yrs.	x	x	x	x			x	x	x	x	White	Control grp. = "only" children.
Handlon & Gross (1959)	a) 21 b) 14	Nursery, K 4, 5, 6 gr.	x	x	x					x	x			
Koch (1957, 1960)	360	5-6 yrs.	x	x	x	x	0-2, 2-4, 4-6 yrs.			range	x	x	x	
Laosa & Brophy (1972)	93	K	x	x	x					some range (not considered in analyses)		x	x		Only borns grouped with 1st borns.
Lasko (1954)	40	3, 6, 9 yrs	x	x	x	x	(range)	2 ch.	x	range	x	x	x	Age matched comparisons
Lavigueur (1976)	2	9-12 yrs.	x	x (same sex)	x	x	1-2 yrs.	(2 ch.)(3 ch.)	x	x	x	x	1 Black 1 White	Family structure variables outlined but not discussed.
Levy (1943)	1	11 yrs.	x	x	x	x	2 yrs.			x		x		
Longstreth, et al. (1975)	170	K-6 gr.	x	x	x				x	x (range)			White, M-A	
Miller & Maruyama (1976)	1,750	K-6 gr.	x	x	x	x (compared analysis of 3-4th ch. with entire sample)			x	x (range)	x (oldest, middle, youngest)	x	White, Black, M-A	
Miller & Miller (1976)	1	4 yr.	x	x	5 & 7 yrs.	x (3 ch.)				x		x		

TABLE 5.1

Study	n	TC Grade/Age	Sex of TC M	Sex of TC F	Sex of Sib. M	Sex of Sib. F	Sibling Spacing	Family Size Small	Family Size Large	SES Mid	SES Low	Ordinal Position 1st	Ordinal Position Later	Race/Ethnicity	Comments
Pfouts (1976)	50	5-14 yrs.	x		x		0-4 yrs.	x		x				White	Both parents present at home.
Rosen (1961)	1 - 427 2 - 367	8-14 yrs. 9-11 yrs.	x					x 3 categories small = 1 or 2 med. = 3 or 4 large = 5 or mr.	x	x	x	x (only, oldest, middle, youngest)	x	White Prot., Blacks, Jews, Italians, Greeks, Fr.-Canad.	Mother's age considered in study 1.
Rosenberg & Sutton-Smith (1964)	352	9-12 yrs.	x	x	x	x		x (1, 2, 3 families)		x (primarily low-mid. to mid.)		x	x		
Rosenow (1930)	1,268	1½-17½ yrs.						x (range)	x		x	x	x (range)		
Rosenow & Whyte (1930-1931)	431		x	x	x (same sex as TC)			x (2 ch.)	x (3 ch.)			x (1st, 2nd, 3rd)	x		
Rothbart (1971)	56	5 yrs.	x	x		x	2 yrs. older/younger	x				x	x		67% from professional homes
Schachter, Gilutz, Shore, & Adler (1978)	140	1 mo. to 18 yrs. (mean = 6 yrs.)						x (2 ch.)	x (3 ch.)	x		x	x		1. Both parents at home 2. Several religious groups represented

Study	n	Age							Notes
Sears (1950)	150	3-5 yrs.	x	x	x (1-2 ch.) (full range not specified)	x	x	x	1. Includes both father-present & father-absent families 2. Median level of education for parents was 12th grade. 3. Children with both younger & older sibs. not included. 4. Small n of sibs. who were older sibs.
Sells & Roff (1964)	1,013	3-6 gr.	x	x	x (embedded in sibling birth order categories)	x	x (6 categories-only; oldest; 2nd of 2; 2nd of > 2; middle; youngest)		

TABLE 5.1

Study	n	TC Grade/Age	Sex of TC M	Sex of TC F	Sex of Sib. M	Sex of Sib. F	Sibling Spacing	Family Size Small	Family Size Large	SES Mid	SES Low	Ordinal Position 1st	Ordinal Position Later	Race/Ethnicity	Comments
Sletto (1934)	1,878		x (n = 786)	x (n = 153)	x (elaborate coding)	x						x	x		Includes elaborate coding of sex of both younger & older sibs. Yields 30 categories.
Sutton-Smith & Rosenberg (1968)	95	5 & 6 gr.	x	x		x	0-4 (range)	x	x (2, 3, 4 & >4 ch.)	x		x	x	White	
Sutton-Smith & Rosenberg (1970)	140	3, 4, & 5 gr.	x	x		x		(range)		x		x	x		
Yando, Zigler, & Litzinger (1975)	144	1 & 2 gr.	x	x				x	x (0, 1, 2, 3 4 ch.)	x		x	x	White	1. Live with both biological parents. 2. Only-borns analyzed as separate groups.

Key
Blanks	= not specified	gr.	= grade level
bros.	= brothers	grp.	= group
ch.	= children	M-A	= Mexican-American
Fr.-Canad.	= French-Canadian	mid.	= middle
n	= number of sibling pairs or families involved	TC	= target children
Prot.	= Protestants	var.	= variables
sib.	= sibling	w/	= with
struct.	= structural	yrs.	= age in years

also discuss how sibling roles develop as other subsystems of the family environment interact with and differ from the sibling subsystem.

INTRAPERSONAL EXPERIENCE OF SIBLING RELATIONSHIPS IN MIDDLE CHILDHOOD

Pfouts (1976) has argued that sibling relationships are more likely to be stressful and volatile than most other human relationships because they are so firmly rooted in ambivalence; love and hate are seen as the two sides of the sibling coin. On the one side, sibling rivalry is cited as the basis for most of the negative aspects of the sibling relationships. Sibling rivalry stems from frustrated dependency needs, emotional struggles involving issues of sibling anger and identity, and competitive interference with respect to garnering parental and extrafamilial recognition and approval. On the other side, psychological closeness, supportive caretaking, direct instruction, and facilitative modeling of developmental milestones are thought to be common positive experiences of sibling relationships. Social comparison is thought to operate in both positive and negative aspects (Pfouts, 1976). The exact nature of the child's intrapersonal experience of sibling relationships may vary according to the particular developmental status of both the child and the siblings. The kinds of interpersonal exchanges within the family system experienced by the child throughout middle childhood may also affect the child's intrapersonal state. What does the existing empirical literature have to say about the foregoing formulations relevant to the intrapersonal experience of sibling relationships during middle childhood?

In this first section of the chapter, I consider the experience of and basis for ambivalence pertaining to the sibling relationship during middle childhood. Both psychoanalytic and behavioral formulations of sibling relations are considered; and both indirect and direct experiences of siblings are taken into account. Finally, the relevance of sibling structural factors (e.g., spacing between siblings; sex of siblings) are reviewed.

Sibling Rivalry and Social Comparison Processes

Sibling rivalry is thought to develop for two reasons: Competition for parental rewards, and competition while seeking to define individual identities by establishing status vis-à-vis standards set in large part by brothers and sisters (Pfouts, 1976). Thus, even when children feel equally loved and accepted by parents, Pfouts argues, the intersibling struggle for recognized competence and status includes an ever widening range of abilities and attributes. The struggle for parental rewards per se becomes less crucial. Siblings are viewed as prime targets for social comparison, not only within the family system but throughout the child's expanding extrafamilial social system. How do social comparison processes operate in sibling relations during middle childhood?

In a psychoanalytic formulation of social comparison within the family system, Schachter, Gilutz, Shore, and Adler (1978) argue that siblings come to experience themselves as different from one another ("deidentified") by the beginning of middle childhood (age six), and that experiencing themselves as different from one another is a defensive maneuver to guard against the unpleasant emotions associated with intense competition. Schachter et al. present data to support the view that siblings of the same sex who are the first two children in the family experience heightened rivalry and deidentification. Thus, one view suggests that middle childhood brings with it peaceful resolution of sibling rivalry by way of deidentification, especially when first- and second-born children are the same sex. Adler's (1924) notion that personality differences among siblings are expressions of an underlying sense of competition is congruent with this formulation, and the view that this rivalry gets fairly well resolved by age six is in keeping with a psychoanalytic timeline of development. However, additional studies are needed to document the extent to which sibling rivalry is resolved in this manner. Data to be summarized later in this chapter suggest that considerable rivalry or conflict persists throughout middle childhood.

From a behavioral perspective of social comparison processes operating in a familial context, one needs to consider aspects of family interaction that children may use as a basis for their comparisons. Parental treatment that varies from one child to another can be a dimension on which siblings compare themselves with one another. Research has shown that, as a group, mothers treat their older and younger daughters differently (Bryant & Crockenberg, 1980; Lasko, 1954). Although Lasko controlled for age effects by matching the chronological age of first- and second-born children at the time the mother's behavior toward them was rated, Bryant and Crockenberg confounded age differences with ordinal position. Bryant and Crockenberg (1980) report that mothers were both more responsive to and intrusive upon the younger children in comparison to the older siblings, even when the tasks that both children were involved in were quite challenging for both age groups. This impression was supported by an absence of difference between the number of expressed needs for help and/or attention recorded for both older and younger siblings. These results were largely congruent with the findings of Lasko (1954), which involved siblings ranging in age from 18 months to about 10 years. Lasko reported tendencies of greater maternal expression of warmth and protectiveness toward second-born relative to first-born children during home visits, although the contrast in expression of warmth was more characteristic of the preschool years than middle childhood.

Both Lasko (1954) and Bryant and Crockenberg's (1980) studies suggested more, not less, maternal attention to the younger sibling relative to the older sibling. These findings are in contrast to the findings of Rothbart (1971), who found that mothers gave more complex technical explanations to first-borns and were, overall, more intrusive in the performance of first-borns than second-borns. Rothbart interpreted this maternal stance as one providing first-borns with a more readily accessible source of support. This apparent contradiction may reflect some important contextual phenomena. Developmentally, Lasko reported systematic changes in parental treatment of first-borns, but not for second-borns, as the children studied progressed from age two to age ten. Reduced parent-child interaction was apparent only for the first-born children. In contrast to the Rothbart study, both the Lasko study and the Bryant and Crockenberg study were based on observations of parent-child interaction in situations where both siblings were present during the observation. Indeed, parent behavior may well differ in a setting in which attention to one child does not conflict with giving attention to a second child. Thus, it appears that first-born children are given preferential treatment when mothers interact with them in a private dyad but are relatively neglected when a younger sibling is present. The latter situation lends itself more readily to sibling comparison and therefore may offer the basis for the creation or maintenance of sibling rivalry during middle childhood.

These group differences in the treatment of first- and later-born siblings do not directly inform us regarding the effects of this differential treatment on the child's development, however. The one available study that does assess maternal preferential treatment of (female) children during middle childhood found that when one child had her expressed needs met to a high degree while the other sibling in the family did not, sibling discomforting of each other was high for both children in the sibling dyad (Bryant & Crockenberg, 1980). In other words, it appears that if a child's expressed needs are not met, she discomforts her sister, who responds in kind. It remains unclear whether the child whose expressed needs are not well met is motivated by either frustration of unmet expressed needs or rivalrous jealousy generated by her mother's greater responsiveness to the sibling. In sum, a child's behavior related to both the way she was treated by her mother and to the way her sister was treated. If there was discrepancy in treatment, a child showed more negative behavior toward her sister even when her own needs were well met. We can infer that children are likely to compare the extent of help and attention they get from a parent with what a sibling gets. Furthermore, ill will and emotional conflict are experienced in the sibling relationship when parents demonstrate preferential treatment to one of their children. This expression of ill will is characteristic of both siblings, not just the child who gets the short end of the parental resources.

Parents can become sources for comparative evaluation by children in middle childhood too. In addition, school and community resources of recognition can be the basis for further social comparison and continued sibling rivalry. With respect to status within the larger society, Pfouts (1976) found that when brothers in middle-class, two-boy families differed significantly in culturally valued personality or intellectual assets, the child who suffered from the comparison experienced resentment and ill will toward the brother who outshined him. Whereas the more able child in the sibling pair was not resentful of the less able sibling, the more able sibling reported feelings of discomfort and ambivalence in the sibling relationship (Pfouts, 1976).

In sum, although certain aspects of sibling rivalry may get resolved by social comparison processes that lead to sibling deidentification, social comparison processes appear to continue to operate in middle childhood. These processes can operate in the family system as well as within the larger community context in a manner that extends and perhaps elaborates the experience of sibling rivalry during middle childhood.

Direct Experience of Ambivalence, Power, and Facilitation

Not all aspects of the sibling relationship need be considered in relationship to third parties such as the parent or "society." How do children directly experience and perceive their siblings?

Bigner (1974b) asked children to describe their older sibling in terms of what their older sibling did as well as what they liked and disliked about them. Bigner found a highly significant increase with age in the mean number of constructs used to describe siblings. There was also an expected shift from the use of concrete and egocentric modes of descriptions of siblings to abstract, nonegocentric modes. In describing siblings, kindergarten and second-grade children most frequently used egocentric-concrete constructs (e.g., "He hits me when he gets mad"); nonegocentric-concrete descriptors (e.g., "She helps our mother") of older siblings prevailed at both grades four and six, with egocentric-concrete descriptors the second most common mode among the fourth graders and abstract descriptors (e.g., "He's very nice and kind") the second most common mode among the sixth graders. Finally, abstract modes were most commonly used to describe older siblings by eighth graders. Thus, children's developing sense of their siblings moves from less to more elaboration and from the egocentric to the abstract and suggests that children increasingly perceive their siblings as more elaborated individuals, differentiated from the sibling context. Parenthetically, it would appear that cognitive development in the later phase of middle childhood would enhance deidentification processes. Such a formulation suggests a more extended and elaborated developmental timeline for deidentification to occur than the one proposed by the psychoanalytic perspective.

Although increased cognitive abilities influence descriptors, Bigner (1974b) reports that lower-level constructs were used by children most commonly to describe liked qualities and higher-level constructs were used to describe disliked qualities of the older sibling across all age levels studied. This was especially true for siblings closely spaced in age (12–20 months). In other words, children are likely to perceive the positive aspects of their siblings in concrete terms that frequently involve specific interchanges (e.g., "He tells me 'neat' bedtime stories'') whereas, with age, children are more likely to distance themselves from the unliked characteristics of their sibling (e.g., ''He's a dummy'' rather than ''He finks on me to my mother''). This latter finding could also reflect that, with age, the negative characteristics of siblings get coded as ''vague'' qualities reflecting relatively pervasive ''random'' irritants as opposed to specific, habitual confrontations. The liked qualities of the closely spaced, older sibling were described in terms of psychological closeness, typically ''caretaker'' attributes, whereas the disliked qualities of the older siblings were described in terms that reflected psychological distance and were more general in nature. Thus, the ambivalence of the sibling relationship is reflected in varying levels of cognitive sophistication when describing different aspects of the sibling. The documented disparity in level of cognitive description of liked versus disliked sibling qualities suggests an arena for the future study of cognitive development in middle childhood.

Additional data demonstrate greater ambivalence among siblings who are closely spaced than for those widely spaced. Using a methodology where children discriminate sibling roles according to the relative age and sex of two siblings, Bigner (1974a) reports that females with closely spaced older sisters assigned more facilitation actions (e.g., ''You can have it'') to an older sibling role and more interference items (e.g., ''Stop doing that'') to the younger sibling role than did females with widely spaced older sisters. Thus, closely spaced same-sex female siblings appear to experience more intense ambivalence, both positive and negative, in the sibling relationship.

Power can be viewed as a dimension that tends to breed ambivalence as well. All children in middle childhood used the power dimension in discriminating sibling age roles (Bigner, 1974a). The older sibling was consistently assigned high-power attributions and the younger sibling low-power attributions. Sex of sibling is also particularly relevant here; older brothers are experienced as more powerful than older sisters. Again, age spacing appears to influence the experience of sibling power; Bigner (1974a) reports girls who were spaced 12–20 months from their older brothers assigned more high-power items to the older sibling and low-power actions to the younger sibling than did girls who were spaced 28–48 months from their older brothers. These findings are congruent with those of Sutton-Smith and Rosenberg (1968) who report that first-borns are perceived both by first-born and second-born as being bossy (i.e., powerful). Their data suggests that one reason older brothers are seen as more powerful than older sisters is because boys are more likely to use highly salient forms of physical power (e.g., hitting, wrestling, and chasing).

Not only are older siblings seen as more powerful than younger siblings; some of this power is experienced as a welcomed asset. Bigner (1974a) found that subjects as a group assigned items involving facilitation rather than interference to the older sibling. The low-power younger siblings were not viewed as resources as much as were the older siblings; yet items describing facilitation actions were assigned slightly more frequently than interference items to the younger sibling as well. The amount of power and facilitation attributed to an older sibling increased at almost each age level (ages 5, 7, 9, 11, 13). When sex of sibling and age were considered together, however, there was a curvilinear relation in the amount of power and facilitation. Male siblings are apparently viewed as increasing in their facilitation up to the age of nine, and then are experienced as becoming less facilitating with age. Girls were found to make significantly more assignments of facilitation items to the female sibling role and more interference items to the male sibling role than did boys. Those children with an older brother assigned more interference items to the male sibling role than did those who had an older sister; and, conversely, those who had an older sister assigned more facilitation items to the female sibling role than did those subjects who had an older brother. It appears, then, that older brothers are experienced as using their power to interfere, whereas older sisters are viewed as using their power in a more facilitating manner, except among boys spaced closely to older sisters. These boys with closely spaced older sisters assigned significantly more facilitation items to the male sibling role and more inter-ference items to a female sibling than did boys who were spaced widely from their older sister. Again, closely spaced sibling pairs appear prone to intense conflict. Additionally, behavioral data to be described in the following sections of this chapter document that attempts to facilitate (e.g., help) by both older brother and sister are not always experienced as welcome and facilitating to younger siblings. *In sum,* facilitation by the older sibling may easily get as-sociated with aspects of power and control over the younger sibling and form a basis for ambivalence in the sibling relationship.

Summary Regarding Intrapersonal Experience of Sibling Relationships

Ambivalence appears characteristic of sibling relationships during middle child-hood. This ambivalence considers both sibling facilitation and sibling inter-ference. With respect to sibling interference, both psychoanalytic and behavioral perspectives consider social comparison and sibling rivalry phenomena. Siblings are viewed as prime targets for social comparison not only within the family system but within the middle-childhood child's expanding extrafamilial social system as well. Social comparison processes result in sibling conflict for all siblings. But children in the sibling dyad—the one who gets the short end of important external resources in the social comparison (e.g., parental help and attention when asked for), and the other sibling—demonstrate ill will and emo-tional conflict in sibling interaction. Although certain aspects of sibling rivalry may get resolved by social comparison processes that lead to sibling deidentifica-tion, social comparison processes appear to continue to operate in middle child-hood. The data also suggest that children in middle childhood may view siblings as sources of facilitation and support. Facilitation by the older sibling appears to get easily associated with aspects of power and control over the younger sibling and form the basis for ambivalence in the sibling relationship. Perceptions regarding relative power in a sibling dyad can also be viewed as a dimension that tends to breed sibling ambivalence. Data suggest greater ambivalence among siblings who are closely spaced than for those widely spaced. These conclusions are based on research derived from perspectives that sibling relations are experienced indirectly vis-à-vis third parties such as parents, extended family members, school personnel, and other community based individuals, as well as directly experienced in fact-to-face interaction with one another.

INTERPERSONAL ENCOUNTERS BETWEEN SIBLINGS IN MIDDLE CHILDHOOD

Do these internal experiences of sibling relations have an interactional counterpart? What is the extent of sibling interaction and what are these patterns during middle childhood? In addition to considering these questions, this section of the chapter will examine the extent to which sibling roles develop during middle childhood. Are these roles characteristic of particular dimensions of the sibling context? Are they related to the relative ages and sexes of the siblings? Are they related to second-order sibling effects?

Extent of Sibling Interaction

The extent to which siblings interact in American "mainstream" culture is not well documented. In a careful case study, Gump, Schoggen, and Redl (1963) report that roughly one-half of a particular nine-year-old's interactions with children were with siblings, and that he interacted more with children than adults. The fact that he was one of a family of five children may unduly influence the findings, however. Weisner and Gallimore (1977) note that children are less likely to be "in charge" of their siblings in American culture as compared to others. Bryant (1981), in a study of later borns in the United States, found that only roughly one-third of her sample shared a room with a brother or sister, and sibling room-sharing was more common among 7–year-old children than among the 10–year-old group. On a list of 13 household/family chores and responsibilities, every child did at least one chore with a sibling on a regular (daily or weekly) basis. Less than 25% of the sample, however, performed any specific chore on the list with a brother or sister. Thus, no one chore was identified as a "sibling chore" for the group of children studied. "Cleaning the house" and "doing yardwork" were the chores most often reported performed together with siblings. It is unclear how much play children engage in with their siblings during middle childhood. Sutton-Smith and Rosenberg (1970) found that one-half their subjects reported that involvement in games was a central activity in which they had fun with siblings. Although more extensive documentation is needed, there is indication that sibling interaction is a large part of a child's social experiences, and, for American children, the social context may well be primarily recreational or non-task-oriented in nature. Nonetheless, some consistent shared responsibilities are a common feature of self-reported sibling relations in middle childhood. *In sum,* the extent to which American children interact within both recreational and task-oriented contexts needs more elaborated documentation.

Older Versus Younger Sibling Interaction Roles

Older siblings are often viewed as teachers and models to younger siblings and, as such, exert considerable influence (Cicirelli, 1975; Irish, 1964; Minuchin, Montalvo, Guerney, Rosman, & Schumer, 1967; Sutton-Smith & Rosenberg, 1970). What is the manner in which older siblings establish themselves with younger siblings?

First-borns have been found to use high-power persuasive techniques on their younger siblings, whereas last-borns used more low-power persuasion (Sutton-Smith & Rosenberg, 1968). However, Bragg, Ostrowski, and Finley (1973) found that this phenomenon had more to do with the relative age of participants in an interchange rather than the sibling ordinal position per se. Miller and Maruyama (1976) and Sells and Roff (1964) also provided data to support the view that social strategies differ for older as compared to younger siblings; they found that later-borns, especially later-born girls, were more popular with their peers than were first-born children. Miller and Maruyama (1976) found that later-born children were viewed by peers as more socially skilled than first-born children. Later-borns were described as both more sociable and friendly and less demanding and jealous. Overall, later-borns were seen as more sociable toward and accepting of friends.

These results are interpreted by Miller and Maruyama as the result of the younger sibling's position of less power within the sibling system in the home environment. The results also fit Bigner's (1974a) observation that female siblings are viewed as having less power than male siblings. First-borns (and especially first-born males), by virtue of greater power within the sibling structure, apparently do not need to rely on the development of persuasive finesse to gain compliance from the younger sibling. Miller and Maruyama (1976) suggest that younger siblings learn not to focus strictly upon the distribution of power in the situation (as they would generally "lose" when using this dimension of bargaining); they attend to other aspects of the situation, such as the needs of all the persons involved. In such a manner, then, later-born children may develop the interpersonal skills involving negotiation, accomodation, tolerance, and a capacity to accept less favorable outcomes, at least more so than first-borns.

Miller and Maruyama documented that differences in peer popularity appear as early as kindergarten and seem to persist throughout middle childhood (grade school years). What is not clear from their data is whether these modes of behavior arose in the sibling relations and were transferred directly to other child relations. Sutton-Smith and Rosenberg (1970) suggest that younger siblings have to be content with the exercise of greater power outside their own sibling context, and Gump et al. (1963) found that the child they observed was dominating toward his (younger) siblings but submissive toward neighborhood children. Thus, it is not clear how interaction patterns in sibling relations influence interaction patterns established with other children. Precise, descriptive data of the development of sibling and other peer generation relations would be of help to formulate the potential transactional nature of the development of social skills.

There do exist further data alluding to aspects of power distribution and patterns of interaction during middle childhood in sibling relationships. For example, younger siblings may well form a dependent relationship with older siblings, and older siblings may try, with varying success, to foster dependency from among the younger siblings, at least for girls (Bryant & Crockenberg, 1980; Cicirelli, 1976a; Rosenberg & Sutton-Smith, 1964). Cicirelli found that later-born girls were more quiet than later-born boys, listening to the help given them by either their older siblings or mothers, whereas later-born boys vocalized more than did girls, presumably in a show of assertiveness, reducing the stance of dependency on either older siblings or mothers. Bryant and Crockenberg (1980) found older sisters trying to foster dependency (apparently at times by force) from their younger siblings by offers of help. Younger siblings were often rewarded for signs of dependency since the older sibling's comforting/sharing and help-giving related to the younger sibling's willingness to request and to accept help. It was also evident, however, that dependency upon older sisters is not entirely accepted by younger sisters. Helping by the older sister correlated with anger expressed by the younger sister. This suggests that older sister help was not always experienced as useful or appropriate. In fact, helping was the only prosocial behavior that correlated positively with conflictual and competitive/achievement-related sibling behavior dimensions. The older sister's "help" did not always appear well-intentioned, at least from the perspective of the researchers, but rather was associated with her disparagement of the younger sister and sometimes involved more control ("bossiness") than generosity. To date, actual observations of younger siblings with older siblings do not give a picture of younger siblings being particularly accommodating and tolerant of the older siblings as suggested by Miller and Maruyama (1976). It does appear, however, that younger siblings participate in dyadic interchanges in which they experience less power and more demands for subservient behavior toward older siblings (especially girls with older sisters). This may be a situation in which skills of negotiation are learned, but behavior exhibited in interaction with older siblings does not always appear to transfer directly to situations with peers. Perhaps the patterns of interchange among children in middle childhood are more conflictual with siblings than with peers, at least for younger siblings. Conflict resolution skills may well be learned as lessons to be practiced and rehearsed, especially in problematic sibling relations, but they may be performed in more final skilled form among peers. Empirical data are needed to resolve these questions.

The view that siblings are engaged in conflictual patterns of interchanges during middle childhood is also given credence by the pattern of interrelationships of dyads of older and younger siblings observed by Bryant and Crockenberg (1980). Prosocial behaviors of helping and comforting/sharing did not intercorrelate. The negative or conflictual behaviors of older and younger siblings did related consistently. Each type of negative behavior of one sibling typically related to several other types of negative behavior in the other member of the dyad. Competitive comments by the older or younger siblings correlated with several negative behaviors in the other sibling as well; these included disparagement, refusal to help or share, anger, and discomforting.

It should also be noted that sibling structure variables such as sex of older sibling and age spacing are likely to influence the nature of patterns of interchanges established as well. Children accepted help and were comfortable in a dependency relationship more often with an older sister than with an older brother and more often with a sibling four years older than with a sibling only two years older (Cicirelli, 1973).

Finally, there is a suggestion in the research literature that throughout middle childhood older brothers challenge younger siblings to be more physically active and physically daring (Longstreth et al., 1975). At least this appears to be the case for children with brothers 0–4 years older than themselves. However, it does not seem to hold for children with older brothers more than four years their senior. Again, direct observation of older brothers with younger siblings is needed to document whether interaction patterns established with older brothers (0–4 years older) are actually directly related to their younger siblings' greater physical daring and activity.

In sum, the younger-older dimension for considering roles within sibling relations appears a relevant one for influencing the development of particular social skills (e.g., conflict resolution skills; skills related to dependency aspects of relationships). There is an urgent need for a solid body of empirical data to elaborate our minimal understanding of these developmental outcomes within the sibling context and their relationship to the development of social skills displayed in extrafamilial peer generation relations.

Cross-Sex and Same-Sex Sibling Patterns of Interaction

It has been argued that same-sex siblings, by virtue of their relatively larger common core of shared desires, will exhibit greater sibling rivalry than will opposite-sex siblings (Schachter et al., 1978). Additionally, same-sex siblings close in age are thought to engage in more extensive interaction than opposite-sex siblings (Cicirelli, 1975). Direct documentation of either of these phenomenon has not been presented. Cicirelli (1975) did find that children with an older same-sex sibling press for more rapid solution to cognitive problem-solving tasks than children working in the presence of an opposite-sex older sibling; this finding suggests greater competitiveness within the same-sex sibling dyad.

Additionally, Cicirelli (1976a) found that older siblings were more helpful, that is, gave more feedback, to an opposite-sex sibling than to a same-sex sibling. Although at first glance this would appear to yield smoother functioning and less competitive interaction among siblings, recall that help from an older sibling is not necessarily viewed with delight and equanimity. In fact, in the same study, Cicirelli found that opposite-sex second-born siblings exhibited more independence behaviors toward their older siblings than did children with older same-sex siblings. The nature of competitive patterns of interchange between same- and cross-sex siblings may vary, but competition does not seem to predominate exclusively in either pattern of sibling structure.

Finally, cross-sex siblings have been thought to offer each other the opportunity to experience and incorporate aspects of the culturally defined role of the opposite sex. Brim (1958) found cross-sex siblings had more traits of the opposite sex than did same-sex siblings, and that this was more true of younger than older siblings in cross-sex pairs. According to Brim, the younger sibling apparently assimilated the role of the other sibling more than the older sibling did. This is attributed to both the older siblings' greater power in the sibling relationship and the older siblings' relatively greater ability to differentiate themselves from their siblings' role. This phenomenon is thought to occur via role learning where the child learns how others in the group behave, how to predict what others expect, and how to behave in ways acceptable to the others (Brim, 1958). Direct empirical evidence of this process is lacking, however. If this formulation is accurate, younger siblings should be better able to predict the behavior of older siblings than vice versa, and they would behave in ways that more frequently accommodate to the wishes of the older sibling than vice versa. *In sum,* thorough and direct documentation of phenomena thought to particularly distinguish same-sex versus cross-sex sibling patterns of interaction during middle childhood remains to be done.

Second-Order Sibling Effects with Respect to Interaction Patterns

Sibling interaction may include other participants as well; these patterns of interaction are called second-order effects, where the interaction between two persons can be qualified by the presence and/or interaction of one or more of the parties with a third party. Parents, for example, who give preferential treatment to one sibling over another can, as we have seen, affect the patterns of interaction between the two siblings (Bryant & Crockenberg, 1980), and this can be an aspect of treatment in clinical work with families (Lavigueur, 1976). For example, Greenbaum (1965) has reported that siblings can reduce the inhibition of another sibling in working with adults. He noted from his clinical work that a brother or sister appeared able to reduce the inhibition of some children to engage in direct interaction or confrontation with the therapist. To date, second-order sibling effects during middle childhood have not been given adequate consideration.

Summary Regarding Interpersonal Experience of Sibling Relationships

Although there is an indication that sibling interaction is typically a large part of a middle-childhood child's social experiences, the extent to which American children interact with siblings within both recreational and task-oriented contexts needs more elaborated documentation. Not only do these children interact with siblings, the existing research literature suggests that sibling relations in middle childhood may well influence the social/emotional development in two important developmental arenas. First, issues of dependency established within the sibling relationship, including issues of how one skillfully encourages and allows others to be dependent on oneself as well as how one skillfully and comfortably accepts help, may in part be learned during middle childhood in the context of sibling relations. Second, issues regarding conflict resolution must be dealt with during middle-childhood sibling relations as well. Unequal power distribution among siblings as well as the constraints of an enduring familial relationship make the sibling context one that offers what may be a unique social context particularly conducive to the development of specific conflict resolution skills. Further research to document these two critical aspects of social/emotional development needs to be done. This research will need to consider the particular concerns and experiences of the older-younger status of siblings as well as the sex of both siblings. Finally, second order sibling effects (e.g., how parents influence the sibling interaction patterns involving issues of sibling dependency and conflict) vis-à-vis these issues deserve attention also.

SIBLINGS AS CARETAKERS

Next, let us consider the nature of sibling relations during middle childhood by considering what occurs when we consider children taking on particular roles and responsibilities in relation to their siblings. One can consider, as well, that sibling caretaking is one example of addressing issues of sibling dependency and conflict referred to in the preceding section. Additionally, sibling caretaking involves roles, responsibilities, and presumably, developmental outcomes for both the children offering and receiving the sibling caretaking.

Issues of care-giving include the consideration of circumstances under which a child learns and develops, the types and schedules of reinforcement the child is given, and the manner in which such feedback to the child is administered (McCandless, 1976). Weisner and Gallimore (1977) note that "caretaking" can refer to activities ranging from complete and independent full time care of a child by an older child to the performance of specific tasks for another child under the supervision of either adults or other children. Caretaking can include specific verbal as well as nonverbal training and supervision of a child's behavior as well as general "keeping an eye out for" younger siblings (Weisner & Gallimore, 1977). Child caretaking is widespread cross-culturally, but systematic analysis of its ethnographic incidence has been limited. So far as we know, American children seem to engage in less child caretaking than do children in most other cultures. Although Weisner and Gallimore (1977) note that American mothers are sole caretakers more often than most mothers in other cultures, they suspect that systematic observation would identify important sibling caretaking functions even in United States households. They further speculate that subcultural, class, and regional differences all influence the incidence of child caretaking. Sibling care with respect to help on homework is one likely source of sibling caretaking in the United States. Bryant (1981) in fact, documents that a majority (78%) of later-born children report that they have a sibling who would help them with their homework. This was as true for first graders as fourth graders, males as females, children from small families as well as large families, and whether the older sibling was a brother or a sister.

Although children can anticipate "academic caretaking" from both brothers and sisters, the nature of this caretaking may well differ depending on the sibling structure of the family. That structure, again, is the network of the positions in the family as defined by the number of children, birth order, sexes, ages, and age spacing.

Academic Caretaking

Cicirelli (1972) found that in middle childhood both boys and girls shifted in their approach to teaching depending on whether the child they were teaching was a sibling or nonsibling. However, the sexes differed in their style of teaching siblings. Cicirelli found that girls teaching their siblings tended to use the deductive method more often than did girls with nonsiblings or boys teaching others, whether siblings or not. Boys, on the other hand, tended to use the inductive method to teach their siblings more often than did boys teaching nonsiblings or girls teaching others, whether siblings or not. Girls teaching their siblings tended to give less feedback to the younger child's performance than did girls teaching nonsiblings or boys teaching others, whether or not they were siblings. This may in part have been because their direct, deductive approach to teaching concepts was effective with their siblings. Also of interest is Cicirelli's finding that girls tended to give more incorrect feedback to nonsiblings than did girls teaching their siblings and more than boys teaching either siblings or nonsiblings. Girls, then, appear to be more involved and deductively directive with their younger siblings than they are with nonsiblings. In comparison with sisters, older brothers in middle childhood offer their siblings more feedback and inductive modes of teaching.

Not only do older siblings vary in their teaching styles, younger siblings respond differently to an older brother or sister who teaches them. Cicirelli (1974) found that children were more likely to accept nonverbal direction from a sister than a brother. Cicirelli (1973) also found that younger siblings were more likely to work independently of an older brother than of an older sister, further suggesting that younger siblings are more willing to accept an older sister in the role of academic caretaker. As noted earlier, Cicirelli (1973) also found that children were more likely to accept help from a sibling four years older than from a sibling only two years older.

Under conditions of formal academic caretaking, then, the younger school-aged child is thought to learn more from an older sister than from an older brother (Cicirelli, 1975). The relative efficacy of older sisters in a formal learning situation is thought to be the result of two factors: First, in terms of role theory, girls are thought to be more ready to assume a teaching role because they can more easily identify with mothers and female schoolteachers (Koch, 1960; Sutton-Smith & Rosenberg, 1970) and because they tend to report more than boys that they take care of younger children (Bryant, 1981). Sisters consequently develop the role of academic teacher to younger siblings to a greater extent than do brothers, and younger siblings more readily accept the role of sister in caretaking activities (Cicirelli, 1972). Second, older sisters may be better teachers because older brothers are viewed as less effective in a formal tutoring role with a younger sibling due to the competitive attitudes the older brother brings to the situation: Koch (1960) found that boys tended to react more intensely to sibling displacement, and that the sibling displacement that occurred within the 2–4-year range was particularly intense. Indeed, Freedman (1979) argues that, across cultures, boys, more than girls, are more preoccupied with competition and are more involved both directly and vicariously in social competition. Recall also that children with older brothers assigned more interference ascriptions to the male sibling figure than did children who had an older sister (Bigner, 1974a).

Before we leave the subject of sibling academic caretakers, it is of note that older brothers do apparently stimulate the intellectual development of younger siblings (Cicirelli, 1975; Koch, 1954). The competition and rivalry of the older brother may well stimulate intellectual development in informal or incidental learning conditions. Thus, the roles of formal and informal caretaking may be worth distinguishing in more detailed investigation. However, we will see later that mothers may relate differently to later-borns if the older sibling is a boy, and that brotherly competition isn't necessarily a critical stimulant for intellectual development among children with older brothers. *In sum,* sibling academic caretaking experiences appear to be influenced by the sex of the sibling caretaker and the formal versus informal nature of caretaking context.

Siblings as Therapeutic Caretakers

Little systematic data have been collected regarding the role of siblings in clinical settings. However, with the relatively recent focus on the family systems approach to clinical intervention, siblings have begun to be seen as potential therapeutic agents. Greenbaum (1965) reports that siblings can play the very useful function of offering feedback to the identified child client regarding negative evaluations. Greenbaum reports that children's evaluations of one another seem more tolerable than the same evaluation offered from an adult. This observation deserves more systematic investigation. Second, older siblings as opposed to younger siblings are seen as more likely therapeutic agents since older children usually appear to offer greater supportive possibilities than younger siblings and because older siblings can often contribute to the verbal formulation of the child client's difficulties. And, finally, Greenbaum views closely spaced siblings as offering greater therapeutic aid than widely spaced siblings because of the presumed more frequent contact and opportunity for intimate interactions among closely spaced siblings. Indeed, research cited earlier in this chapter notes the often problematic nature of sibling relationships when siblings are closely spaced in age. The closely spaced siblings may well be viewed in the early stages of therapy as a dyad bearing enormous conflict rather than support. Rather than being a supportive influence per se, the sibling dyad rather than a particular sibling may become the focus of conflict and intervention. Unfortunately, these observations are clinical impressions rather than the result of systematic observation and, therefore, should be viewed with appropriate caution.

In the one available study that systematically documents the effectiveness of a sibling as a therapeutic caretaker, Lavigueur (1976) found that having both siblings and parents take on therapist roles was advantageous in modifying a child's disruptive behaviors at home when the disruptive behaviors had a history of sibling reinforcement. Additional studies are needed to more fully understand the criteria and conditions under which children become effective therapeutic caretakers for their siblings. *In sum*, the unique contribution of siblings as therapeutic caretakers during middle childhood has been suggested but requires more systematic documentation.

Sibling Caretaking as Different From Parental Caretaking

It has been argued that sibling caretakers may develop caretaking styles that are different from those of their parents (Cicirelli, 1976a; Weisner & Gallimore, 1977). Weisner and Gallimore posit that adults and child caretakers can have opposed caretaking styles. The caretaking child may have (frequently exaggerated) imitative ones as well. Cicirelli (1976a) suggests that older siblings may help and direct younger siblings on the basis of only partial knowledge.

Empirical data confirm the notion that sibling caretaking styles differ from adult styles. Cicirelli (1976a) found that mothers tended to give more explanations and feedback to a child than did older siblings. Bryant and Crockenberg (1980) found few relationships between mother behavior and older female child behavior when that older (fourth- or fifth-grade) child was assigned the role of helper to her younger sister, even on a task in which mother had been observed playing the role of helper: No one-to-one correlations between specific mother and older child behavior and, therefore, no clear modeling effect was found. At least at this age (fourth and fifth grades), girls do not appear to adopt the teaching/helping strategies employed by their mothers when they act as helper to a younger sister. However, a positive correlation between maternal unsolicited help, encouragement, and approval and older child unsolicited disapproval suggests that the older child may adopt the directive strategy of the mother but lack the skill to carry it off positively. The older sister may have attempted to help and encourage, but her behavior more closely approximated negative help and negative encouragement. There is, then, a suggestion that female siblings in middle childhood lack the skills, but not necessarily the intent, of mothers, in their caretaking endeavors.

Additionally, Cicirelli (1976a) found that children responded to their mothers with more help-seeking and accepting behaviors and fewer independence-seeking behaviors than they did in response to sibling caretaking. Thus, not only may older siblings bring differing styles to a situation, younger siblings receiving the caretaking may well influence the nature of the sibling caretaking by their very input in the caretaking transactions.

Bryant (1979) further considered the possible difference between parents and siblings as child caretakers. She compared how children aged seven and ten described their parents and siblings on six scales of the Cornell Parent Behavior Questionnaire (Devereaux, Bronfenbrenner, & Rodgers, 1969). The six scales were nurturance, instrumental companionship, principled discipline, demands for achievement, control, and physical punishment. Figure 1 illustrates the means of these caretaking dimensions for fathers, mothers, and siblings. Children in middle childhood differentiated caretaker roles more clearly as a function of generation than as a function of sex of caretaker. Children saw parents as more active than siblings in five of the six caretaking dimensions (nurturance, instrumental companionship, achievement demands, control, and principled discipline).

In physical punishment, however, siblings were seen as more active than parents, perhaps patterning themselves after Lucy Van Pelt, whose approach to caretaking or to socializing with peers such as Charlie Brown is ever ready to resort to the sweet reason of the mailed fist. That older siblings were seen as meting out more physical punishment than parents is congruent with Hartup's (1976) formulation that aggressive encounters are particularly relevant to child-child relations. He argues that aggressive encounters experienced in child-child

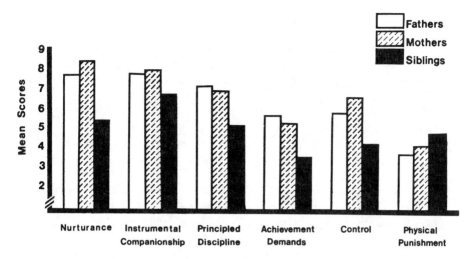

FIG. 1. Mean scores on caretaking dimensions for fathers, mothers, and siblings.

relations are more important contributors to the development of successful control of aggressive motivation than aggressive encounters experienced in parent-child relations. Although Hartup (in press,a) argues that peer (coequal) relations as opposed to cross-aged, nonpeer child-child relations offer the social context most conducive to the development of effective socialization of aggression, sibling relations may present an exception to this general formulation. Expressions of aggression among siblings in childhood rarely terminate the sibling relationship. In contrast, a relationship among peers is more easily broken. It may be that among siblings the familial constraints preventing early termination of their relationships provides a stable context in which children may learn that the expression of anger need not threaten mutual attachment and endurance of important relationships. Siblings, then, may provide an important, relatively enduring context in which siblings have the sustained opportunity to develop successful control of aggressive motivation, and sibling exchanges during middle childhood appear to reflect this issue and distinguish it from parent-child exchanges.

Also unlike the parent generation caretakers, older siblings in the Bryant (1979) study were perceived as offering nurturance and principled discipline equally to first-grade siblings and fourth-grade siblings. Among older siblings of fourth-graders, siblings with a same-sex younger sibling offered equal amounts of principled discipline as their like-sex parent. Unlike the parent generation, siblings were perceived similarly by boys and girls in achievement demands. Apparently higher levels of instrumental-companionship and physical punishment among the older siblings of the 10–year-olds as compared with 7–year-olds suggests developmental trends among sibling caretaking styles. In other words, as older siblings gain in their availability for instrumental companionship, they also apparently gain in their exercises of physical punishment. This is distinctive to the sibling generation in that parents were perceived as gaining in these two dimensions but in other support categories as well (nurturance and principled discipline). The role of physical punishment, which distinguishes parent caretaking from sibling caretaking, may again be the reflection of relatively unskilled helping strategies of older siblings in both middle childhood and early adolescence. This is congruent with the findings, reported earlier, describing the intrusive, unskilled direct helping strategies of fourth- and fifth-grade older sisters as observed by Bryant and Crockenberg (1980).

Another way to consider whether parental and sibling caretaking are distinguishable is to explore the structure of caretaking strategies employed by these groups. To do this, Bryant (1981) factor-analyzed middle childhood children's descriptions of mothers, fathers, older brothers, and older sisters using all 14 caretaker scales of the Cornell Parent Behavior Questionnaire. The four resulting factor analyses were based on a varimax rotation. In each case the number of factors retained for rotation was determined by an eigenvalue greater than 1. Three factors were obtained for the mothers and four were obtained for the fathers, brothers, and older sisters. Coefficients of congruence then were calculated between each factor in one matrix (based on descriptions of fathers, mothers, brothers, sisters, respectively) with each factor of the other matrices using the formula given by Harman (1976). A value of .90 was required to indicate factorial similarity. The caretaking factor structure for the brothers was completely congruent with the factor structure for the older sisters. The coefficients of congruence across the four factors ranged from .92 to .99, and the factors were labeled: sibling supportive nurturance; sibling supportive challenge; sibling concern and control; and punishment.

The punishment factor was similar among all four caretaker groups considered. Mothers shared a general support factor with fathers that neither parent shared with the siblings. The mother concern factor was congruent with the sibling concern and control and the father control factor was congruent with the sibling concern and control factor, but the mother concern factor was not the same as father control. Sibling control seems to overlap with expressions of concern or attempts to help. Lastly, fathers exhibited a factor of indulgence that did not overlap with any of the maternal or sibling factors.

As indicated by the factor labels, support among sibling caretaking appears to have two distinct forms, one stressing nurturance and one stressing challenge. Developmentally, this is of interest as it reflects a less integrated display of support among the sibling caretakers as compared with the more mature, integrated stance of adult caretakers. These findings also relate to differences between child-child and adult-child relations formulated by Hartup (in press,b) who argues that child-child relations are less harmonious than adult-child relations, and in particular, that nurturance plays a less dominant role in child-child relations. Supportive challenge, then, is not meshed with supportive nurturance and reflects the basis for the lack of congruence for any of the support factors among the sibling and adult caretakers.

In sum, the empirical data confirm the notion that sibling caretaking styles differ from adult styles. Additionally, children appear to respond differently to parental caretaking than they do to sibling caretaking and this, in part, may influence the documented differences in caretaking styles. Overall, children in middle childhood differentiated caretaker roles more clearly as a function of generation than as a function of sex of caretaker. The outstanding feature of the Bryant (1981) findings is that the factor structures of the older brothers and older sisters were entirely congruent with one another and only partially overlapping with parental factors. Although sex of caretaker was an important differentiator among adult caretakers, sex of caretaker did not influence the factor structure of sibling caretakers during middle childhood. Lastly, mothers (who are culturally viewed as the primary caretakers of our children) showed the most integrated underlying structure of caretaking. Fathers and siblings showed less integration, although the constituent parts were different for fathers and siblings. The results also caution us to be careful in assessing the degree to which brothers and sisters differ in the underlying structure of their caretaking.

Siblings as Second-Order Caretakers

Second-order effects suggest, in our instance, how an older sibling might affect a parent or vice versa in his/her caretaking of a younger sibling, thereby making the older sibling a "second-order" caretaker. Although there are limited data on this issue, and most of these data imply rather than describe second-order effects, the issue bears enough theoretical importance to warrant consideration.

Bryant and Crockenberg (1980) found that if mothers ignored requests for help and attention from their daughters, it was likely to stimulate prosocial interaction between the girls, simply by creating the opportunity. If a child did not get a response from her mother, she often turned to her sibling for help, and the data suggest she frequently got it. The numerous significant relationships between maternal ignoring and behavior of older children, in contrast to younger children, suggests a developmental difference in the impact of maternal distance on children at different ages. Not acknowledging request for help and attention may be picked up more often by older children as a cue to become more resourceful and nurturant toward younger siblings. Observations of several mothers who frequently ignored their children's requests for help and/or attention suggested a maternal demeanor of helplessness rather than anger or otherwise affectively negative withholding of help or attention. A display of maternal helplessness rather than anger or negative responses may induce the older child in particular to engage more actively with a sibling. It has been suggested that girls' internal locus of control orientation is facilitated at early stages of development by warm, protective, supportive maternal behaviors and at later stages of development (adolescence) by early maternal coolness (Crandell, 1973). The coolness presumably leads the adolescent to engage with others and experience her impact on others. Similarly, Whiting and Whiting (1975) have found that, when the social system required it, taking responsibility for younger siblings was related to, and presumably fostered, prosocial development. These findings are congruent with Caplow's (1968) formulation that parental unity stimulates the development of sibling coalitions.

With respect to the presence of siblings creating a different kind of parent caretaking, Cicirelli (1976a) found that the mothers' behaviors were patterned by the sex of the older sibling. Mothers gave more explanation, feedback, and more total verbalization to children with older brothers. Like Bryant and Crockenberg (1980), Cicirelli noted that this finding suggests that, within the family situation, the mother explicitly or implicitly, relinquishes some of her caretaking functions to an older sister. In another study that included boys and girls with either brothers and sisters two to three years their senior, Bryant (1979) found that, among fourth graders with an older sister, fathers were viewed as less controlling than were mothers. It is unclear whether fathers expect their older daughters to help with control issues or whether the older sisters give clues to fathers that control is not such a necessary dimension of caretaking. In other words, our notions of direct caretaking effects need to be tempered by the possibility of second order effects. Second-order effects may be the basis for previously assumed "sibling effects." For example, not only may older brothers provide greater stimulation and competitive challenge to younger siblings, mothers and fathers may respond differentially to a child who has an older brother as compared with an older sister.

In sum, as argued earlier by Cicirelli (1976a) second-order caretaking effects seem to operate with both mothers and fathers and support the position that "interactions between any two family members are influenced by the larger family interactional system, where interactions between any two family members influence and are influenced by other interaction subsystems [p. 594]."

Relevance of Sibling Caretaking for Predicting Social Development in Middle Childhood

Can the predictability of children's social development in middle childhood be enhanced by knowledge of the sibling caretaking they receive? To test this, it would be useful to have knowledge of children's maternal and paternal caretaking experiences. To date Bryant (1981) offers the only example of systematic data collection in this regard. Since sibling caretaking may not be independent of parental caretaking, Bryant considered a single simultaneous regression—a reduced or "estimation" model—involving sibling and family structural variables (e.g., sex, family size, sex of sibling, socioeconomic status), factor scores of parental support, maternal concern, and paternal control, as well as sibling supportive challenge and concern/control—all factors identified in the factor analysis described above. The control variables and parental factors were entered as a set prior to the sibling variables to determine whether, after the sibling and family structure and predictive parental factors were used to predict children's social development, knowledge of predictive sibling caretaking would still add to the predictability of social development of their younger siblings. Results indicated that older sibling caretaking experiences added to the predictability of 7-year-olds' social development but not that of 10-year-olds. Among first graders, children in small families appeared to respond to older sibling caretaking in a systematic way that was predictive of their acceptance of individual differences in peers. This was the case even after experiences with parental caretaking had been considered. The relationship obtained differed for boys as compared with girls. For boys in small families, the more their older brothers (but not sisters) showed supportive challenge, the more accepting these boys were of individual differences in peers. For girls in small families, the more older siblings showed concern and control, the more they were accepting of individual differences in peers. Additionally, 7-year-olds' attitudes toward competition with peers were predicted by their experiences with their older sibling caretakers. Girls who had siblings who showed greater concern and control were more competitive. Boys' attitudes toward competition did not bear a relationship to their siblings' concern and control. With respect to attitudes toward competition, not only was the predictability of siblings' caretaking "influences" independent of the predictability offered by parental caretaking, parental caretaking variables were not predictive of their children's attitudes toward competition.

In sum, although there are few data regarding the relative predictability of children's social development when comparing the effects of maternal, paternal, and sibling caretaking, those that do exist show promise in documenting the value of sibling relationships in predicting social development. Additionally, these data suggest that the experiences that boys and girls have with their siblings appear to lead to different outcomes. Sibling supportive challenge appears predictive of social development for boys, whereas sibling control and concern appear predictive of social development for girls. And, finally, sibling behavior appears more predictive of younger siblings' behavior when the younger sibling is in the early rather than the later stages of middle childhood. Although these must be considered tentative conclusions, additional studies in this area would seem to be potentially fruitful.

Summary Regarding Siblings as Caretakers

Children in middle childhood experienced caretaker roles as differentiated more clearly as a function of generation than as a function of sex of caretaker. The argument that children experience siblings and adults as different in the caretaking roles they assume is supported by both clinical impressions and empirical documentation. Differences in caretaking styles do not necessarily reflect, however, differences in intent of the caretakers in the two generations. Differences appear to result from at least two other factors. First, siblings of children in middle childhood appear to lack the skill of their adult counterparts, and second, middle-childhood children respond differently to caretaking attempts offered by a parent versus a sibling. To date, children have not reported experiencing older siblings in caretaking situations as differing according to the sex of the older sibling, although sex of the older sibling has been found related to the actual form of formal academic caretaking. The context of interaction needs systematic consideration when examining the roles that children assume with their siblings. Research to date suggests that this consideration of context for understanding sibling relations in middle childhood needs to include the possibility of detecting second-order effects provided by other family members. And, finally, even after parental caretaking has been considered, sibling caretaking has been found to be predictive of the social development of children, at least children in the early stages of middle childhood. These sibling factors predictive of social development also appear to vary according to the sex of the child receiving the sibling caretaking. Whereas sibling supportive challenge appears predictive of social development for boys, sibling control and concern appear predictive of social development for girls. Additional studies focused on the predictive value of understanding sibling caretaking experiences are needed. To date, there are no studies of American children to inform us about the developmental outcomes resulting from offering sibling caretaking.

PETS AS SECOND-ORDER MODIFIERS OR SIBLING SURROGATES

To end on what may seem to some as an amusing note, I would like to seriously entertain the thesis that pets are often experienced as family members and have been considered by Levenson (1972) as part of the sibling generation. That family pets are experienced as special friends by a majority of children in middle childhood has been documented in the families studied by Bryant (1981). Indeed, 83% of the children studied reported having a family pet that was a "special friend" to them; the percentage of children who reported this was also somewhat higher among the 10-year-old group than among the 7-year-old group. Additionally, children reported that they would turn to a pet to talk to about sad, angry, afraid, happy, and "secret" experiences as often as they would seek out a sibling. Moreover, reported intimate talks with pets was a reliable predictor of empathy as measured by Bryant (in press) among the 10-year-old group but not the 7-year-olds. The more the 10-year-olds talked with pets about intimate topics, the greater empathy they expressed for peers. Additionally, frequency of reported intimate talks with pets interacted statistically with family size to reli-

FIG. 2.   For better or for worse (Lynn Johnston, Universal Press Syndicate. All rights reserved. Copyright, 1981.)

ably predict attitudes toward competition: Children from large families were less likely to be competitive in attitude if they reported frequent intimate talks with pets. These findings are presented to suggest that family structure in American nonmetropolitan, "Anglo" family life has created a relevant position for pets as family-member surrogates and that their role is worth further investigation as we consider social-emotional development in middle childhood.

CONCLUSION

Several general comments can be made concerning the status of research on sibling relationships in middle childhood. First, very few sibling studies were designed to illuminate developmental changes occurring during the middle childhood years. The existing cross-sectional studies of children representing ages 6–12 yield scant suggestion of the developmental changes occurring during middle childhood, particularly for sibling relations. There is reason to believe, however, that, depending on the phase of middle childhood being experienced by one or more siblings in the family, sibling experiences result in differing outcomes. Nor are there studies that directly contrast sibling experiences in early childhood with those in middle childhood and with those in adolescence. As sibling relations increasingly begin to get defined by the specific manner in which they relate to one another, cross-sectional and longitudinal study of sibling relations may increase. Indeed, the present review calls for longitudinal consideration of sibling conflict and its pattern of resolution over time as well as developmental consideration of issues that involve sibling dependency and needs for one another.

Second, more elaborated, descriptive data detailing the sibling experience during middle childhood is needed. To what extent do American children interact within a variety of settings (e.g., recreational and task-oriented contexts)? To what extent do sibling relations differ from relations to others, including relations with parents, peers, and pets? Although it is clear that sibling relations differ from parent-child relations, continued delineation of the nature of sibling relations is warranted.

Third, more consideration is needed of the social skills and emotional response patterns developed in ongoing sibling relations. What skills and attitudes are acquired by both the younger and older sibling in a family where one sibling takes care of another? The existing data suggests that there are developmental consequences derived from such experiences for the child receiving the caretaking. The developmental consequences of caretaking for the care-giving sibling is considerably less clear.

Fourth, attention needs to be given to the role of sibling "influences" that are independent of both parental and other family "influences" but that interact with these middle childhood relationships. Existing data informs us of the value of considering that the interactions between any two family members influence and are influenced by other interaction subsystems. Furthermore, the cultural context of family experiences and the meaning of sibling relations vis-à-vis other family members and family-member surrogates warrants further understanding.

Finally, it needs to be recognized that to adequately build a viable data base for understanding sibling relationships, enormous sustained effort and commitment will be required to execute methodologically sound, informative research strategies.

ACKNOWLEDGMENTS

This chapter was written in conjunction with the Western Regional Project W-144, "Development of Social Competencies in Children," with funding in part from the Science and Education/Cooperative Research division of U.S.D.A. and the University of California, Davis, Agricultural Experiment Station. The author acknowledges the fine research assistance provided by Jeff Parker. The author also wishes to thank Curt Acredolo and Larry Harper for their thorough and critical reviews of earlier drafts of this manuscript. The author also acknowledges the perspectives offered by Victor Cicirelli and Michael Lamb that are reflected in the final version of this chapter as well.

REFERENCES

Adams, R. L., & Phillips, B. N. Motivational and achievement differences among children of various ordinal birth positions. *Child Development, 1972, 43,* 155–164.

Adler, A. *The practice and theory of individual psychology.* New York: Hartcourt, Brace, & Company, 1924.

Bigner, J. J. Second borns' discrimination of sibling role concepts. *Developmental Psychology,* 1974 *10,* 564–573. (a)

Bigner, J. A Wernerian developmental analysis of children's descriptions of siblings. *Child Development,* 1974, *45,* 317–323. (b)

Bragg, B. W. E., Ostrowski, M. V., & Finley, G. E. The effects of birth order and age of target on use of persuasive techniques. *Child Development,* 1973, *44,* 351–354.

Breger, L. *From instinct to identity: the development of personality.* Englewood Cliffs, N.J.: Prentice-Hall, 1974.

Brim, O. G., Jr. Family structure and sex role learning by children. *Sociometry,* 1958, *21,* 1-16.

Bryan, J. Children's cooperation and helping behaviors. In E. M. Hetherington (Ed.), *Review of child development research* (Vol. 4). Chicago: University of Chicago Press, 1975.

Bryant, B. *Siblings as caretakers.* Paper presented at the annual meeting of the American Psychological Association, New York, September, 1979.

Bryant, B. *Development perspective on sources of support and psychological well-being.* Final report submitted to the Foundation for Child Development, 1980.

Bryant, B. *Middle childhood experiences of stress and support.* Manuscript in preparation, 1981.

Bryant, B. An index of empathy for children and adolescents. *Child Development,* in press.

Bryant, B., & Crockenberg, S. Correlates and dimensions of prosocial behavior: A study of female siblings with their mothers. *Child Development,* 1980, *51,* 529-544.

Caplow, T. *Two against one: Coalition in triads.* Englewood Cliffs, N.J.: Prentice-Hall, 1968.

Cicirelli, V. G. Concept learning of young children as a function of sibling relationships to the teacher. *Child Development,* 1972, *43,* 282-287.

Cicirelli, V. G. Effects of sibling structure and interaction on children's categorization style. *Developmental Psychology,* 1973, *9,* 132-139.

Cicirelli, V. G. Relationship of sibling structure and interaction to younger siblings' conceptual style. *The Journal of Genetic Psychology,* 1974, *125,* 37-49.

Cicirelli, V. G. Effects of mother and older sibling on the problem-solving behavior of the younger child. *Developmental Psychology,* 1975, *11,* 749-756.

Cicirelli, V. G. Mother-child and sibling-sibling interactions on a problem-solving task. *Child Development,* 1976, *47,* 588-596. (a)

Cicirelli, V. G. Sibling structure and intellectual ability. *Developmental Psychology,* 1976, *12,* 369-370. (b)

Cicirelli, V. G. Children's school grades and sibling structure. *Psychological Reports,* 1977, *41,* 1055-1058.

Crandall, V. C. *Differences in parental antecedents of internal-external locus of control in children and in young adulthood.* Paper presented at the meeting of the American Psychological Association, Montreal, Canada, August, 1973.

Devereaux, E. C., Bronfenbrenner, U., & Rodgers, R. B. Child-rearing in England and the United States: A cross-national comparison. *Journal of Marriage and Family,* 1969, *31,* 257-270.

Freedman, D. G. *Human sociobiology.* New York: The Free Press, 1979.

Gallagher, R., & Cowen, E. L. Adjustment problems of sibling and nonsibling pairs referred to a school mental health program. *Journal of Consulting and Clinical Psychology,* 1976, *44,* 873.

Greenbaum, M. Joint sibling interview as a diagnostic procedure. *Journal of Child Psychology and Psychiatry,* 1965, *6,* 227-232.

Grotevant, H. D., Scarr, S., & Weinberg, R. A. Intellectual development in family constellations with adopted and natural children: A test of the Zajonc and Markus model. *Child Development,* 1977, *48,* 1696-1703.

Gump, P., Schoggen, P., & Redl, F. The behavior of the same child in different milieus. In R. Barker (Ed.), *The stream of behavior.* New York: Appleton-Century-Crofts, 1963.

Handlon, B. J., & Gross, P. The development of sharing behavior. *Journal of Abnormal and Social Psychology,* 1959, *59,* 425-428.

Harman, H. *Modern factor analysis.* Chicago: University of Chicago Press, 1976.

Hartup, W. W. Peer interaction and the behavioral development of the individual child. In E. Schopler & R. J. Reichler (Eds.), *Psychopathology and child development.* New York: Plenum, 1976.

Hartup, W. W. The social worlds of childhood. *American Psychologist,* 1979, *34,* 944-950.

Hartup, W. W. Children and their friends. In H. McGurk (Ed.), *Child social development.* London: Methuen, in press (a).

Hartup, W. W. Two social worlds: family relations and peer relations. In M. Rutter (Ed.), *Scientific foundations of developmental psychiatry*. London: Heinemann, in press (b).

Irish, D. P. Sibling interaction: A neglected aspect in family life research. *Social Forces*, 1964, *42*, 279–288.

Koch, H. L. The relation of primary mental abilities in five- and six-year-olds to sex of child and characteristics of his sibling. *Child Development*, 1954, *25*, 209–223.

Koch, H. L. The relation of certain family constellation characteristics and the attitudes of children toward adults. *Child Development*, 1955, *26*, 13–40. (a)

Koch, H. L Some personality correlates of sex, sibling, position, and sex of sibling among five- and six-year-old children. *Genetic Psychology Monographs*, 1955, *52*, 3–50. (b)

Koch, H. L. Attitudes of young children toward their peers as related to certain characteristics of their siblings. *Psychological Monographs: General and Applied*, 1956, *70*, Whole No. 426, 1–41. (a)

Koch, H. L. Sibling influence on children's speech. *Journal of Speech Disorders*, 1956, *21*, 322–328. (b)

Koch, H. L. Sissiness and tomboyishness in relation to sibling characteristics. *Journal of Genetic Psychology*, 1956, *88*, 231–244. (c)

Koch, H. L. Some emotional attitudes of the young child in relation to characteristics of his sibling. *Child Development*, 1956, *27*, 393–426. (d)

Koch, H. L The relation in young children between characteristics of their playmates and certain attributes of their siblings. *Child Development*, 1957, *28*, 175–201.

Koch, H. L. The relation of certain formal attributes of siblings to attitudes held toward each other and toward their parents. *Monographs of the Society for Research in Child Development*, 1960, *25*, Serial No. 78.

Laosa, L. M., & Brophy, J. E. Effects of sex and birth order on sex-role development and intelligence among kindergarten children. *Developmental Psychology*, 1972, *6*, 409–415.

Lasko, J. K. Parent behavior toward first and second children. *Genetic Psychology Monograph*, 1954, *49*, 99–137.

Lavigueur, H. The use of siblings as an adjunct to the behavioral treatment of children in the home with parents as therapists. *Behavior Therapy*, 1976, *7*, 602–613.

Levenson, B. M. *Pets and human development*. Springfield, Illinois: C. C. Thomas, 1972.

Levy, D. M. Hostility patterns in sibling rivalry experiments. *American Journal of Orthopsychiatry*, 1943, *13*, 441–461.

Longstreth, L. E., Longstreth, G. V., Ramirez, C., & Fernandez, G. The ubiquity of big brother. *Child Development*, 1975, *46*, 769–772.

McCandless, B. The socialization of the individual. In E. Schopler & R. J. Reichler (Eds.), *Psychopathology and child development: Research and treatment*. New York: Plenum, 1976.

Miller, N., & Maruyama, G. Ordinal position and peer popularity. *Journal of Personality and Social Psychology*, 1976, *33*, 123–131.

Miller, N. B., & Miller, W. H. Siblings as behavior-change agents. In J. Krumboltz & C. Thoresen (Eds.), *Counseling methods*. New York: Holt, Rinehart, & Winston, 1976.

Minuchin, S., Montalvo, B., Guerney, G. G., Jr., Rosman, B. L., & Schumer, F. *Families of the slums: An exploration of their structure and treatment*. New York: Basic Books, 1967.

Pfouts, J. H. The sibling relationship: A forgotten dimension. *Social Work*, 1976, *21*, 200–204.

Rosen, B. C. Family structure and achievement motivation. *American Sociological Review*, 1961, *26*, 574–585.

Rosenberg, B. G., & Sutton-Smith, B. Ordinal position and sex-role identification. *Genetic Psychology Monographs*, 1964, *70*, 297–328.

Rosenow, C. The incidence of first-born among problem children. *Journal of Genetic Psychology*, 1930, *37*, 145–151.

Rosenow, C., & Whyte, A. H. The ordinal position of problem children. *American Journal of Orthopsychiatry*, 1931, *1*, 430–434.

Rothbart, M. K. Birth order and mother-child interaction in an achievement situation. *Journal of Personality and Social Psychology*, 1971, *17*, 113-120.

Scarr, S. Introduction to the special issue, "Psychology and children: Current research and practice." *American Psychologist*, 1979, *34*, 809-811.

Schachter, F. F., Gilutz, G., Shore, E., & Adler, M. Sibling deidentification judged by mothers: Cross-validation and developmental studies. *Child Development*, 1978, *49*, 543-546.

Sears, R. R. Ordinal position in the family as a psychological variable. *American Sociological Review*, 1950, *15*, 397-401.

Sells, S. B., & Roff, M. Peer acceptance-rejection and birth order. *Psychology in the Schools*, 1964, *1*, 156-162.

Sletto, R. F. Sibling position and juvenile delinquency. *American Journal of Sociology*, 1934, *39*, 657-669.

Sutton-Smith, B., & Rosenberg, B. Sibling consensus on power tactics. *Journal of Genetic Psychology*, 1968, *112*, 63-72.

Sutton-Smith, B., & Rosenberg, B. G. *The sibling*. New York: Holt, Rinehart, & Winston, 1970.

Sullivan, H. S. The interpersonal theory of psychiatry. New York: W. W. Norton & Co., Inc., 1953.

Weisner, T., & Gallimore, R. My brother's keeper: Child and sibling caretaking. *Current Anthropology*, 1977, *18*, 169-190.

Whiting, B., & Whiting, J. *Children of six cultures: A psycho-cultural analysis*. Cambridge, Mass.: Harvard University Press, 1975.

Yando, R., Zigler, E., & Litzinger, S. A further investigation of the effects of birth order and number of siblings in determining children's responsiveness to social reinforcement. *The Journal of Psychology*, 1975, *89*, 95-111.

6

Sibling Deidentification and Split-Parent Identification: A Family Tetrad

Frances Fuchs Schachter
Barnard College
Columbia University

Given the general agreement that identification with one's parents plays a key role in personality development, it could considerably enhance our understanding of this process if we knew the rules governing the choice of the main parental identification figure, mother or father. The dominant rule to date has been the same-same-parent rule, that children identify with the parent of the same sex. It is a rule that derives from each of the three major theories of identification—psychoanalytic, modeling (Bandura, 1977) and cognitive-developmental (Kohlberg, 1966). The evidence for this rule, however, has been weak. A large number of investigators have failed to demonstrate that children resemble their same-sex parent any more than their opposite-sex parent (Hetherington, 1965; Hoffeditz, 1934; Lazowick, 1955; Mussen & Rutherford, 1963; Newcomb & Svehla, 1937; Peterson, 1936; Rosenberg & Sutton-Smith, 1968; Sward & Friedman, 1935–36; Troll, Neugarten & Kraines, 1969). Two recent studies report a larger number of significant correlations with same-sex parents than with opposite-sex, but the average correlations for the same-sex-parent samples rarely reach .30 (Grotevant, Scarr, & Weinberg, 1977; Munsinger & Rabin, 1978).

Is there perhaps another rule that governs the choice of the main parental identification figure? Might some alternative rule operate in interaction with the same-sex-parent rule so as to limit its range of applicability?

An alternative rule was suggested by a commonplace observation. Acquaintances, when asked to describe their siblings, or parents, when asked to describe their "other child," often produced the following kinds of comments: "My sister is entirely different from me; she takes after my father and I take after my mother." "My two children are as different as day and night; this one is just like my side of the family; the other one is just like my husband's folks." These kinds of remarks occurred often enough to warrant serious investigation. We called the phenomenon of being "different" from one's sibling *sibling deidentification* (Schachter, Gilutz, Shore, & Adler, 1978; Schachter, Shore, Feldman-Rotman, Marquis, & Campbell, 1976), and the phenomenon of each sibling in a pair identifying with a different parent *split-parent identification*. We then proceeded to study these phenomena systematically. Split-parent identification appeared to offer a new rule for the choice of parental identification figure, namely, when one sibling in a pair identifies with one parent, the other sibling identifies with the other parent.

Note that the process of split-parent identification, unlike that of same-sex-parent identification, implies that the choice of the main parental identification figure depends on the entire family constellation, not simply on the child-parent dyad. Indeed, the everyday remarks that prompted our research suggested a new kind of family structure, a *family tetrad,* with two siblings different from each other and each identified with a different parent. And in this tetrad, the intra-familial unit is the sibling pair, not the individual child.

Before embarking on the study of resemblances between members of sibling pairs and their parents, it seemed essential to examine similarities and differences between and within these sibling pairs themselves. We thus began our research with an investigation of the phenomenon of sibling deidentification (Schachter et al, 1978; Schachter et al, 1976). This research forms the basis of our studies of split-parent identification as follows:

As our research was prompted by an everyday empirical observation, the main thrust of our previous studies of sibling deidentification was to generate a theoretical framework to account for the phenomenon. To this end, we studied whether the phenomenon was associated with any special pattern of sibling constellation. We focused on variations in the incidence of deidentification between and within sibling pairs in two- and three-child families. In comparing variations between pairs, we studied whether deidentification is more likely to occur in the *first pair* of children in a family (the first two children) than in the *second pair* (the second and third children) or the *jump pair* (the first and third children). In comparing variations within pairs, we asked: Is the later-born in the sibling pair more apt to deidentify than the prior-born? Do same-sex pairs deidentify more often than opposite-sex? Is spacing, sex of subject, or sex of sibling related to the incidence of deidentification?

Data on these comparisons between and within sibling pairs were intended to shed light on the determinants of sibling deidentification. In conjunction with these data, a number of theories promised to be useful in generating hypotheses to account for deidentification: a) the three major theories of identification-psychoanalytic, modeling, and cognitive-developmental; b) the theory of Bossard and Boll (1956) on personality-role differentiation among siblings in large families; and c) the social comparison theory of Leon Festinger (1954; Suls & Miller, 1977). As we searched for an explanation of our findings on sibling deidentification, we drew upon these theories. The psychoanalytic theory of conflict and defense, supported by research on social comparison theory, generated the hypothesis that sibling deidentification is a defense against sibling rivalry, mitigating its disruptive effects on family life. In the first section of this report, we will review the findings of our studies in sibling deidentification and present the evidence that generated this rivalry-defense hypothesis.

These studies on sibling deidentification laid the groundwork for our studies of split-parent identification in two respects. First, the findings on variations in sibling deidentification between and within sibling pairs generated predictions concerning the intrafamilial domain of split-parent identification, i.e., its variations between and within sibling pairs. Data on these predictions are presented in the second section of this chapter, as well as data comparing the range of applicability of the split-parent rule with that of the same-sex-parent rule. Second, the rivalry-defense hypothesis, developed to account for sibling deidentification, provided a theoretical framework to account for split-parent identification and the family tetrad. These theoretical issues are discussed in a concluding section on the family tetrad, its structure and function.

STUDIES IN SIBLING DEIDENTIFICATION

Sibling deidentification was studied from two perspectives—that of undergraduates judging their own siblings and that of mothers judging their own children. A complete report of the undergraduate study can be found in Schachter et al., 1976 and the mother study in Schachter et al., 1978. A summary of these reports is presented here, together with an expanded theoretical discussion.

Undergraduate Study

Questionnaires were distributed to 383 Columbia University students,[1] 203 from three-child families and 180 from the two-child families, all families intact. The larger families provided judgments on first, second, and jump pairs; the two-child families provided an additional sample of first pair judgments to be compared with the second and jump pairs of the three-child families. At the same time, the two-child families provide data on what has become the national modal family size, given the advent of zero population growth. Altogether, these subjects generated data on 585 sibling pairs.

For each sibling, subjects were asked to judge whether they were alike or different in personality. The answer "different" to this global question was adopted as our index of deidentification, because the everyday remarks that

---

[1]Females of Barnard College; males of Columbia College; other undergraduates in engineering etc.; and a handful of graduates attending college courses.

prompted our research took the form of a global judgment of this kind. To shed light on what people mean when they judge siblings as globally "different," the questionnaire included a set of semantic differential scales (Osgood, Suci, & Tannenbaum, 1957) soliciting personality ratings for each member of the family. The scales consisted of 13 bipolar items, including three personality traits representing each of Osgood's three major factors and four items based on a pilot study of sibling descriptions: good-bad, pleasant-unpleasant, and cheerful-depressed (Osgood's evaluation factor); active-passive, fast-slow, and hot-cold (Osgood's activity factor); strong-weak, rugged-delicate, and deep-shallow (Osgood's potency factor); tense-relaxed, introverted-extroverted, conventional-unconventional, and achieving-nonachieving.

Everyday remarks suggested that when people say they are different from their siblings they mean that they tend to polarize on personality attributes. For example, if one sibling is described as extroverted, the other is described as introverted; one as active, the other as passive. On this basis, a Sibling Polarization score was developed based on the number of bipolar items where siblings were rated as polarized (i.e., rated on opposite sides of the neutral midpoint for the item). To clarify the meaning of global deidentification judgments, the relationship between these judgments and the Sibling Polarization scores was examined.

Between-Pair Comparisons in Deidentification.   Table 1 shows the percentage of deidentification judgments for each type of sibling pair. It can be seen that the highest percentage occurs in first pairs in both two- and three-child families, the lowest percentage in jump pairs. The percentage of deidentification is higher for second pairs than for jump pairs, but the increment is not statistically significant. Compared to the other pairs, it is only the first pairs that show a significantly higher incidence of deidentification. Nor is this first-pair increment effected by variations in within-pair characteristics such as birth order, spacing, etc.

Within-Pair Comparisons in Deidentification.   Table 1 shows that the later-born within each pair was no more likely to deidentify than the prior-born. In fact, birth order had no significant effect on deidentification whether we compared the percentage of prior- and later-borns for each pair or the percentage for first-, second-, and third-borns in the family. Nor did spacing or sex of subject or sex of sibling have any significant effect on the incidence of deidentification within pairs. The only variable that significantly affected the percentage of deidentification within pairs was whether the siblings were of the same or opposite sex, and the effect of this variable was significant for only one pair, the first pair of the three-child family. For this pair, same-sex siblings deidentified significantly more often than opposite-sex.

TABLE 6.1
Percentage Sibling Deidentification for Pairs and for
Prior- and Later-born Members Within Pairs
(Undergraduate Sample)

Pairs and members	Percentage	n^a
Two-child first pairs		
S1Sb2 (Prior)	60.0	100
S2Sb1 (Later)	65.0	80
Total	62.2*	180
Three-child pairs		
First pair		
S1Sb2 (Prior)	79.0	90
S2Sb1 (Later)	70.3	64
Total	75.3*	154
Second pair		
S2Sb3 (Prior)	52.4	63
S3Sb2 (Later)	53.1	49
Total	52.7	112
Jump pair		
S1Sb3 (Prior)	42.2	90
S3Sb1 (Later)	51.0	49
Total	45.3	139

Note. S1, S2, S3 = first-, second-, and third-born subjects, respectively; Sb1, Sb2, Sb3 = first-, second-, and third-born siblings, respectively.

[a]N = 585 pairs. Missing one second-born judgment of third-born sibling.

* Significant increment for three-child first pairs vs. second and jump pairs and for two-child first pairs vs. jump pairs. No significant effects of birth order within pairs.

The Meaning of Global Sibling Deidentification Judgments. Data on Sibling Polarization scores of the semantic differential scales indicated that when subjects judge siblings as different they mean that they polarize on a significantly greater number of personality attributes than when they judge siblings as alike. The selection of polarized traits was similar for same- and opposite-sex siblings and for male and female subjects.

Mother Study

Before proceeding with our studies of split-parent identification, it seemed essential to cross-validate our findings on a different population of judges and at a different age level. Because the undergraduates judged their own siblings, it seemed particularly important to see if the findings would be replicated by judges who were not themselves members of the sibling pair yet were equally familiar with both siblings. For this reason, we studied mothers judging pairs of their own children: 140 mothers, 45 with three children, 95 with two (all with intact families). The mean age of the children was 6.4 years, the standard deviation 3.7. As in the undergraduate study, mothers were asked to judge whether the members of each sibling pair—i.e., each pair of their children—were alike or different in personality, and semantic-differential ratings were solicited for each member of the family. In addition, mothers were asked whether the members of each pair were the same or opposite in personality. The answer "opposite" provided another global index of deidentification. Unlike the relatively ambiguous term "different," the term "opposite" implies polarization. If results proved to be similar for both indices of deidentification, the meaning of siblings being described as "different" would be further elucidated.

The data on mothers' perceptions of their own children replicated all the main findings based on undergraduates' perceptions of their own siblings. Table 2 shows the mothers' percentages for both indices of deidentification for each type of sibling pair. Relative to the undergraduate percentages of Table 1, the mothers' percentages are somewhat higher, but they follow the same pattern. Comparison between pairs shows deidentification highest in first pairs, lowest in jump pairs, and at intermediate levels in second pairs. Additionally, the only

TABLE 6.2
Percentage Sibling Deidentification for Pairs
-Different and Opposite Judgments-
(Mother Sample)

Pairs and judgments	Percentage	n
Two-child first pairs		
Different	80.0*	95
Opposite	69.9*	93
Three-child pairs		
First pair		
Different	90.9*	44
Opposite	84.1*	44
Second pair		
Different	65.9	44
Opposite	60.0	40
Jump pair		
Different	57.8	45
Opposite	40.0	40

Note. N mothers = 95 with two children, 45 with three children; a few judgments missing.
*Significant increment for three-child first pairs vs. second and jump pairs and for two-child first pairs vs. jump pairs.

variable that significantly affected the percentage of deidentification within pairs was again whether the siblings were of the same or opposite sex. Again, only one of the pairs showed this effect, and again, deidentification was more common among same-sex siblings. In the mother sample, it was the first pair in two-child families that showed this increment for same-sex pairs; in the undergraduate sample, it was the first pair in the three-child family.

Finally, as in the undergraduate study, data on the Sibling Polarization score[2] of the semantic differential indicated that when siblings are described as different they are perceived as polarized on more personality attributes than when they are described as alike. The mother study provided additional evidence that sibling deidentification implies sibling polarization in that findings based on opposite judgments were similar to those based on different judgments, as can be seen in Table 2. Although percentage deidentification was consistently lower for the opposite judgments, the differences failed to reach significance for any of the four pairs.

The Rivalry-Defense Hypothesis: Cain Complex

It was these results that suggested the psychoanalytic hypothesis that sibling deidentification is a defense against sibling rivalry. Evidence for this rivalry-defense hypothesis includes the following:

1. Variations in sibling deidentification between sibling pairs correspond to expected variation in sibling rivalry. First pairs, who deidentify the most, are likely to be the most rivalrous, since competition is undiluted by the inevitable delay in the arrival of the third born. Jump pairs, who deidentify the least, are likely to be least rivalrous, since competition would probably be mitigated by the intervening sibling. The rivalry of second pairs, like their level of deidentification, would likely be at intermediate levels, unmitigated by an intervening sibling as in the jump pair, yet somewhat diluted by the perpetual presence of a third sibling.

2. Variations within sibling pairs also correspond with expected variations in sibling rivalry. Same-sex siblings—who deidentify more than opposite-sex—are likely to rival more often than the latter because of a common core of shared desires and attributes.

3. The evidence of sibling polarization also suggests that deidentification may be a defensive, somewhat muted, social acceptable form of expressing polar opposition or rivalrous feelings between siblings. For example, by polarizing,

---

[2]Only the semantic differentials for two-child families could be used for this analysis, because these scales were presented in random order across children (Schachter et al. 1978; 1976) and a number of the mothers mistakenly rated them in order of the birth of their children. Since the questionaires were anonymous there was no way of identifying which mothers used which order.

the "unconventional" sibling can feel superior to the other in originality or spontaneity, secretly viewing the other as banal or rigid, whereas the "conventional" sibling can feel superior in responsibility or dependability, secretly viewing the other as wild or explosive. Ross and Milgram (1980) point out that few siblings are willing to admit openly to sibling rivalry. Do any of us need to be reminded of how reluctant we are to acknowledge wanting to remove or replace our everyday rivals, whether in the family, on the job, or among friends? Deidentification seems like a plausible defense against these socially unacceptable impulses.

The parallel between deidentification as a defense against sibling rivalry and identification as a defense against child-parent (oedipal) rivalry suggested that the term *Cain Complex* be applied to the sibling phenomenon, by analogy with the Oedipus Complex. It is important to note, however, that whereas the Oedipus Complex generates the same-sex-parent rule for the choice of the main parental identification figure, the Cain Complex suggests an alternative rule, the split-parent rule. Nevertheless, the two complexes share in common the most fundamental tenet of psychoanalysis, the concept of conflict and defenses. As Holtzman (1970) points out, psychoanalysis is above all a theory of the universality of intrapsychic conflict. We desire and we fear our desires; we always hate the ones we love. Deidentification helps make these conflicts manageable among siblings, fostering peace and harmony in the family. By expressing themselves in different ways and in different spheres, siblings are spared the necessity of constantly defending their turf against incursions from each other. Negative feelings abate, strengthening the bonds of love between them.

Alternative Explanatory Theories

The data are inconsistent with Bandura's (1977) behavioristic modeling theory of identification. Modeling theory would predict that identification with the sibling model increases as the similarity, power, and nurturance of the model increases. Yet results on similarity in the sex of the sibling show that same-sex siblings (in some pairs) deidentify more—that is, they identify less—than do opposite-sex siblings, contrary to the prediction from modeling theory. With regard to power, one would expect younger siblings to identify more with older siblings, especially when spacing is wide, since a much older sibling should be viewed as more powerful. Yet the data show no significant effects of birth order and/or spacing within sibling pairs. Nor does nurturance of the sibling model seem to affect modeling or identification. One might expect older sisters to be the most nurturant siblings, but deidentification was no less common in pairs with older sisters than those with older brothers.

Kohlberg's (1966) Piagetian cognitive-developmental theory of identification may contribute to our understanding of the developmental course of sibling deidentification. It may be that deidentification cannot be fully realized until 6–8, when logical classes such as male versus female or alike versus different are cognitively organized. (See Schachter et al., 1978, for a developmental study of sibling deidentification.) Kohlberg's cognitive approach to identification, however, offers little help in explaining why siblings are viewed as different in the first place, especially when they are the first two children in the family.

Nor is Bossard and Boll's (1956) sibling theory useful in accounting for our findings. These investigators have suggested that siblings in large families assume different personalities in search of a distinctive ego-identity; the larger the family the greater the likelihood of role differentiation. The finding of more deidentification in two-child family pairs than in the second and jump pairs of the larger three-child family fails to support their thesis. Even more detrimental to Bossard and Boll's thesis is that members of first pairs in three-child families seem to strive for distinction from each other significantly more often than do members of second and jump pairs. Their theory would predict that all children in the family would be equally different from each other.

We have always assumed that a fundamental human need for self-definition, what social comparison theorists call a drive for self-evaluation (Festinger, 1954; Suls & Miller, 1977), lies at the heart of any identification or deidentification process (we will elaborate on this point later); but it cannot in itself account for the differences we have obtained between and within sibling pairs. It would appear that Bossard and Boll's theory fails because it is a theory of family dynamics that ignores family structure; it does not take into account the organization of family units like sibling pairs.

The rivalry-defense hypothesis seems to account for more of the data than do the other theories so far considered. Moreover, the hypothesis is consistent with related research on sex-role identity in same-sex siblings and with research on social comparison theory.

Related Research

Sex-Role Identity.   Both Grotevant (1978) and Leventhal (1970) take issue with the earlier position of Sutton-Smith and Rosenberg (1965) and Brim (1958) that siblings tend to serve as models for each other in developing their sex-role identity; that, for example, boys with older brothers tend to be more masculine than boys with older sisters. Leventhal (1970) finds that boys with older brothers are more feminine, not more masculine, and Grotevant (1978) finds that girls with older sisters are more masculine. Both of these investigators argue that sibling contrast is more often the rule than sibling modeling or identification.

Grotevant notes that his findings on sibling contrast are consistent with our theory of sibling deidentification as well as with Bossard and Boll's theory of personality role differentiation, but he supplies no data comparing first pairs with other pairs, so that there is no discussion of the relative merits of the rivalry-defense hypothesis as against Bossard and Boll's hypothesis on personality-role differentiation in large families. On the other hand, Leventhal proposes a hypothesis very similar to our rivalry-defense hypothesis. He suggests that the feminine younger brother "adopts a comparison-prevention strategy . . . behavior patterns opposite those of his older brother to prevent himself from being evaluated unfavorably [p. 463]."

The similarity between Leventhal's hypothesis that siblings become opposite to prevent comparison and our hypothesis that siblings deidentify or polarize to minimize rivalry is striking. Indeed, it would seem that a rivalry-defense hypothesis would subsume a comparison-prevention strategy. Rivalry itself seems to consist of two basis components, *competition,* looking outward toward winning a desired object or goal, to gain what psychoanalysts call the gratification of the object, and *comparison,* looking inward toward subjective satisfaction, ego-enhancement or self-esteem, to gain what psychoanalysts call the gratification of the ego or narcissistic gratification (Kernberg, 1975; Kohut, 1971). The rivalry-defense hypothesis is intended to encompass both sibling competition and sibling comparison. The deidentification defense is viewed as mitigating the frustrations that arise when siblings compete for the same object, and as softening the blow to the ego that comes when the other sibling makes one look worse by comparison. Thus Leventhal's evidence in support of a comparison-prevention strategy supports the validity of the rivalry-defense hypothesis.

Social Comparison Theory.   If rivalry can be viewed as a process of social comparison as well as social competition, then we have a rare opportunity of linking experimental social psychology, specifically the large body of laboratory research on social comparison, with a hypothesis derived from clinical theory, our rivalry-defense hypothesis. Since such a synthesis between experimental and clinical work is more often honored than attempted, it seems important to devote careful attention to this matter. For this reason, relevant research on social comparison is reviewed at this point. It can be seen that this research provides experimental support for the rivalry-defense hypothesis. Because this issue is tangential to the focus of this chapter, however, it is printed in smaller type.

Traditional research on Festinger's (1954) social comparison theory focuses on whom one chooses to be compared with, the *comparison other.* Is it someone similar? Is it someone better than oneself? In the typical experimental paradigm, undergraduates are tested and then asked to choose a comparison other from among a homogenous group of their peers at one point in time. Typically, the subjects do not interact socially with the comparison other—they are merely told their own test score and the other's score—so that the pair never needs to deal with the costs of the comparison to ongoing social interaction. By contrast, in the comparison and competition that exists between siblings, they do not choose the comparison other; nature chooses, although after a third child arrives some element of choice is introduced. Siblings are of different ages and, if there is more than one, only one is available for comparison to begin with. Moreover, siblings constantly interact with each other so that they must confront the continual costs of social comparison to the relationship and to themselves.

In view of the disparity between the conditions of research on traditional social comparison theory and the condition of social comparison in family life, one might question any attempt to relate the two. The attempt is worthwhile, however, for two reasons. First, recent work on social comparison has begun to investigate its costs in ongoing social interaction (Brickman & Bulman 1977). Second, traditional social comparison theory, in addition to its concern with the choice of the comparison other, provides a framework for considering the benefits of social comparison (Festinger 1954; Suls & Miller 1977). Before discussing these costs and benefits, we will note the limited relationship between our sibling data and the traditional work on the choice of the comparison other.

The findings based on within-pair comparisons, that in some pairs same-sex siblings are more likely to deidentify then opposite-sex, can be viewed as consistent with the 'similarity hypothesis' of social comparison theory, namely, that subjects tend to compare themselves with similar others in order to obtain accurate and stable self-evaluation information (Festinger 1954). The increase in defensive deidentification among same-sex siblings would be accounted for by the greater tendency for similar-sex siblings to compare themselves and to be compared, just as they are more likely to compete with each other for the same goals. On the other hand, the findings based on between-pair comparisons do not support the similarity hypothesis. Second-borns are significantly more likely to deidentify with first-borns than with third-borns although they resemble both in age, whereas third-borns are not significantly more likely to deidentify with second-borns than with first-borns, although nature makes the third-born far more similar in age to the second-born.

The problem with the similarity hypothesis of traditional social comparison theory appears to be that, like Bossard and Boll's theory of personality-role differentiation, it fails to take into account the structural characteristics of the group of comparison others. Processes influencing undergraduates in choosing a comparison other from a homogenous group of their peers are not likely to be the same as those influencing siblings, who seem to organize into distinct structural units, distinct sibling pairs. Our data on between-pair variations in percent deidentification suggest that members of these sibling pairs are under varying pressures to compete and compare. The highest pressure is likely to confront the first pair, given the inevitable delay in the arrival of the third-born. This increased pressure is likely to increase the costs of comparison and competition, and therefore increase the need for defensive deidentification.

In contrast to traditional social comparison theory, recent work on social comparison theory addresses itself to these costs (Brickman & Bulman 1977; Mettee & Smith 1977). The formulations of Brickman & Bulman (1977) relate directly to the validity of Leventhal's (1970) comparison-prevention strategy, so that they have a direct bearing on the validity of our rivalry-defense hypothesis which subsumes Leventhal's strategy.

Brickman and Bulman propose that: a) people strive to avoid social comparison; that b) if comparison can not be avoided, they prefer comparison with dissimilar rather than similar others; and that c) they prefer to compare upward (with their superiors) rather than downward (with their inferiors) only when they can identify with the other's success, so that it does not make them feel worse by comparison. These propositions are unusual in that they are the opposite of the postulates of traditional social comparison theory (Festinger 1954; Suls & Miller 1977), namely, that people desire to engage in social comparison because of a drive for self-evaluation, that they prefer comparison with similar others (the similarity hypothesis), and that they prefer upward comparison to downward.

Although Brickman and Bulman (1977) acknowledge that these traditional postulates have been substantiated by considerable research, they argue that "the interesting problem of social comparison begins at the point where past research on social comparison has typically seen the problem as ending: When an individual knows both his or her own position and the general distribution of positions in the group [p. 149]." They argue that in the context of ongoing social interaction, in contrast to the cost-free anonymous experimental setting, it is at this juncture in the relationship that the costs of social comparison begin to be felt. In the natural course of events, social comparison is likely to demonstrate that one party is superior and the other inferior. Since this information is likely to breed resentment, envy, and a loss of self-esteem on the part of the inferior one, and guilt, fear of loss of love, and the need to hide one's delight on the part of the superior one, both parties must be prepared to cope with a flood of negative feelings if they do not wish to jeopardize their ongoing relationship. It is to this problem of coping with the affective costs of social comparison in real life settings that Brickman and Bulman's propositions are designed to apply.

Brickman and Bulman's propositions if supported could serve to affirm the validity of the rivalry-defense hypothesis as follows:

(a). The need for a defense against sibling rivalry, competition and comparison, is predicated on the assumption that people find these experiences painful and wish to avoid them. Brickman and Bulman (1977), in support of their first proposition on avoiding comparison, provide experimental evidence substantiating this assumption. A study of the amount of enjoyment anticipated in social interaction with a comparison other, following a situation in which pairs of subjects disclose their scores on an ability test to each other, shows that they anticipate significantly less enjoyment after mutual disclosure than unilateral disclosure. The results indicate that people prefer to avoid the unpleasant feeling that social comparison information introduces into a social relationship. It thus seems plausible that siblings would set up a defense to avoid the negative feelings that come with social comparison or competition.

(b). If deidentification is to be viewed as an effective means of minimizing the costs of sibling rivalry, then it must be shown to minimize these costs. Brickman and Bulman, in support of their second proposition on the advantages of comparing to dissimilar others (when comparison cannot be avoided), cite evidence indicating that deidentification can indeed diminish these costs. They cite a key study of Mettee and Riskind (1974) showing that subjects feel more favorably toward a superior-performing other when the latter is promoted to a higher ability level, a level that is so different that it places the other in a noncomparable category. Making the other dissimilar and noncomparable also makes him or her less threatening to the subject. Similarly, Nadler, Jazwinski and Lau (1976) found that males who were rejected by females in favor of another male felt better about themselves, and disliked the other male less, if they thought the other male was dissimilar to themselves. These studies (plus a related study of Martens & White, 1975), demonstrate that deidentification, becoming different from one's sibling, can serve to diminish the costs of social comparison, the costs to the relationship itself (i.e., siblings are apt to like each other better), and the costs to themselves (i.e., their self-esteem is less likely to be threatened).

(c). As psychoanalytic theory suggests that identification can serve as a defense against rivalry between child and parent (the Oedipus complex), why does it not serve as a useful defense against sibling rivalry (the Cain complex)? Brickman and Bulman (1977), in support of their third proposition on comparing upward, present data to show that undergraduates, upon hearing about successful older alumni who are similar to themselves, feel better about themselves than when hearing about successful oldsters that are dissimilar, whereas these same students, upon hearing about recent successful graduates who are similar feel less happy about themselves than when hearing about recent successful graduates who are dissimilar. Brickman and Bulman suggest that the similarity of an older successful person can increase one's self-esteem because it may enhance one's estimate of future success, whereas the similarity of a successful person of one's own generation carries the ever present threat of looking worse by comparison. These findings help to explain why siblings might identify with their parents and fail to identify with their siblings. The former can be gratifying, the latter might be threatening.

It can be seen that recent research on avoiding social comparison provides experimental support for the hypothesis that deidentification can serve as an effective mechanism for minimizing the negative feelings that accompany sibling rivalry. But psychoanalytic defenses are no mere avoidance responses. They presumably serve as compromises, effecting a stable equilibrium between two conflicting forces. They are designed to provide pleasure as well as avoid pain. Our data on sibling polarization—that siblings are viewed not merely as different, but as opposite—has suggested that deidentification may be a muted way of maintaining the pleasures of sibling opposition (i.e. competition, and comparison) while at the same time minimizing the pain. Recall our example of this polarization, the "unconventional" sibling who can feel superior to the other in originality or spontaneity, and the "conventional" sibling who can feel superior in responsibility or dependability. Deidentification can maintain the benefits of sibling rivalry at the same time that it minimizes the costs.

The benefits of social comparison are well substantiated by traditional research in this area. In Festinger's (1954) original formulation, social comparison is viewed as serving a universal drive for self-evaluation, a basic need for accurate self-appraisal that is essential for effective survival. Since 1954, evidence has accumulated suggesting that social comparison serves a second need as well, that of self-validation, the distinction between self-evaluation and self-validation corresponding to the distinction between self-concept and self-esteem (Suls & Miller 1977). As Goethals and Darley (1977) put it in their recent attributional analysis of social comparison: "While people may have a need to find out whether they are correct or good, they also need to discover that they are correct or good [p. 263]." It is the gratification of these needs for self-evaluation and self-validation that supplies the pleasures of social comparison, even if the pleasures are derived at the expense of the comparison other—even if being good means being better than the comparison other.

That social comparison yields these benefits has been demonstrated by more than 25 years of experimental research on traditional social comparison theory (Festinger 1954; Suls & Miller 1977). That it incurs costs has been demonstrated by the recent work of Brickman and Bulman (1977). This evidence that social comparison may induce conflict, together with our data on sibling polarization—indicating that deidentification can maintain the pleasures of social comparison while reducing its costs—suggests that our defense against sibling rivalry fulfills the requirements of a classic psychoanalytic defense. It seems to serve as a compromise between two conflicting needs, the desire to compare or compete with one's sibling and the desire to avoid the inevitable costs. It can thus be seen that our theoretical framework derived from clinical psychoanalytic theory is supported by experimental research on social comparison.

STUDIES OF SPLIT-PARENT IDENTIFICATION

The everyday remarks that prompted our research suggested that sibling deidentification was part of a broader pattern of intrafamilial similarities and differences, one that encompasses the choice of the main parental identification figure. As noted earlier, these remarks suggested a new kind of family structure, a family tetrad, with each sibling in a pair different from the other in personality, i.e., sibling deidentification, and each identified with a different parent, i.e., split-parent identification. Based on this everyday formulation, it was possible to generate the following predictions about the domain of applicability of the split-parent rule:

1. Sibling deidentification and split-parent identification covary, i.e., sibling pairs that deidentify tend to split-parent identify.
2. Just as sibling deidentification occurs mainly in first pairs, so does split-parent identification.
3. Just as sibling deidentification occurs more often in same-sex siblings than in opposite-sex in some sibling pairs, so does split-parent identification.

Our first task was to test these predictions concerning the intrafamilial domain of the split-parent rule. If the predictions proved valid, we planned to compare the intrafamilial domain of the split-parent rule with that of the same-sex-parent rule. Because of the long and respected history of the same-sex-parent rule, we are compelled to devote considerable attention to an analysis of its range of applicability. For this reason, a discussion of the theoretical implication of our findings on split-parent identification will be delayed until the following final section of the chapter.

Methods

Four samples were studied with systematic variations in procedure.

Sibling Deidentification and Parent Identification Judgments Solicited: Under-graduates. The first sample was derived from our previous undergraduate sample (Schachter et al., 1976) and consisted of 366 undergraduates, 197 from three-child families and 169 from two-child families. Omitted from the original sample were sibling pairs with missing parent identification choices for the self (11 missing) and/or for siblings (22 missing), or missing sibling deidentification judgments (1 missing).

When we distributed the questionnaires for our sibling deidentification studies (Schachter et al., 1978; 1976), we anticipated a future study of split-parent identification, so that we elicited global judgments of the choice of the main parental identification figure in addition to global sibling deidentification judgments. For each subject's personality, we asked, "In general, are you more like your mother or your father?", and for each sibling's personality, "In general, is your sibling more like your mother or your father?". The order of the sibling deidentification questions and the parental identification questions was randomized across subjects; subsequent analysis revealed no significant order effects.

To gain some insight into what people mean when they say they identify more with one parent than the other, a Parent Identification score was developed based on the 13 personality traits of the semantic differential scales, just as a Sibling Polarization score had been developed to clarify the meaning of global judgments of sibling deidentification. The Parent Identification score consisted of the number of traits shared in common by child and parent, defined as the number where scores for both child and parent fell on the same side of the neutral midpoint for a given item (e.g., for the active-passive item, child and parent both scored active). Parent Identification scores were developed for each parent for each child in the family and compared with the global judgments of parent identification.

Sibling Deidentification and Parent Identification Judgments Solicited: Mothers. The second sample was derived from our previous sample of mothers. The sample consisted of 126 mothers, 42 from three-child families and 84 from two-child families. Omitted from the original sample were sibling pairs with missing parent identification choices for one (12 missing) or more (7 missing) children in the family.

The procedure was the same as in the undergraduate study except that mothers were asked to judge the main parental identification figure for each of their children, and to rate the semantic differential scales for each of their children, themselves, and their spouses. Again, the mother sample provided data to cross-validate the findings of the undergraduate study on a different population of judges and at a different age level.

Only Parent Identification Judgments Solicited: Forced Choice. The third sample was drawn from the same undergraduate population as the previous undergraduate sample. It consisted of 525 subjects, 281 from three-child families and 244 from two-child families. Criteria for inclusion in the sample and matching procedures were the same as in the previous undergraduate sample (Schachter et al., 1976), as follows: Subjects from nonintact families, those with half-siblings or with siblings already in the sample, and twins were excluded from the sample. In addition, sibling pairs with missing parent identification choices for the self (12 missing) and/or for siblings (19 missing) were omitted. All four types of pairs, first pairs in two-child families and first, second, and jump pairs in three-child families, were matched in social class, ethnicity, and years at the university.

The procedure was the same as in the previous undergraduate study except for eliminating the question soliciting global sibling deidentification judgments. Subjects who judged their sibling as different might think it inconsistent to answer that they both identified with the same parent. If so, split-parent identification might conform to the same intrafamilial pattern as sibling deidentification merely because of the subject's need to appear consistent in responding to a questionnaire. It was to eliminate the influence of this need that only the split-parent identification judgments were solicited from the present sample.

Only Parent Identification Judgments Solicited: Free Choice. In eliciting global judgments for all of the other samples, we used the method of forced choice, asking if the child was more like the mother or the father without suggesting that the answer might be "neither" or "both." Under these conditions, few subjects failed to make a choice, as can be noted above. We favored the forced choice method because it conformed to the everyday remarks that prompted our research—people commonly refer to being more like their mother or their father—and also because free choice methods tend to produce socially desirable or conventional answers. In research like ours that is vulnerable to sexual stereotypes, anxiety about socially unacceptable responses can lead to serious distorting sets.[3] For example, reluctance to admit to cross-sex-parent identification could spuriously inflate the number of noncommittal "both-parent" or "neither-parent" responses. Since males are more often censured for sexually inappropriate behavior (Maccoby & Jacklin, 1974), such answers might be especially common among sons. It seemed that where forced choice might underestimate the incidence of neither or both parent responses, free choice might overestimate it.

Given this dilemma, we conducted an exploratory study using free choice methods on a sample of 60 Columbia undergraduates, 30 of each sex. For this

---

[3]Spence, Helmreich and Stapp (1975) have demonstrated that measures related to sexual stereotypes are vulnerable to these sets. As they put it, "It all depends on how you ask [p. 93]."

sample, the global identification question for subjects read as follows—the question(s) for the subject's sibling(s) substitute(s) the words "is your sibling" for the words "are you":

In general, are *you* like your mother, father, neither, or both? Indicate your answer by circling each of the following scales:

LIKE MOTHER   0   1   2   3   4
              not at all   somewhat   very much
                alike   alike   alike

LIKE FATHER   0   1   2   3   4
              not at all   somewhat   very much
                alike   alike   alike

This formulation allows for free choice and permits us to operationally define being *more like mother,* higher rating for her than for father; *more like father,* higher rating for him; *neither,* zero rating for both parents; and *both,* same rating for both parents.[4]

Results of this exploratory study showed that only one of the 60 subjects (a male) answered that he identified with neither parent. The percentage of subjects answering that they were equally like both parents was 31.7, but there was a significant sex difference—46.7% for males and 16.7% for females.

The finding that identifying with neither parent was so rare suggests that the forced choice method does not significantly underestimate its occurrence. Forced choice, however, appears to underestimate identifying equally with both parents, since it occurred in 31.7% of this free choice sample. Yet, that it was mainly males that gave these noncommittal "both-parents" answers suggests that the free choice method probably overestimates their incidence. It is, after all, girls rather than boys who have consistently been found to be more androgenous (both masculine and feminine) in studies of sex typing (Maccoby & Jacklin, 1974). Contrary to this well-established finding, it was mainly boys who tended to say that they identified equally with both their mothers' and their fathers' personalities. It seems that boys more than girls tended to use the free choice method defensively to avoid making sexually inappropriate choices. It thus appears that we can no more rely on the free choice method than on the force choice to provide the true incidence of identifying equally with both parents.

What are the implications of these findings for the study of split-parent identification? If neither forced nor free choice methods provides the true estimate of

---

[4]The use of relative rather than absolute ratings to define the main identification figure makes it possible to eliminate the effects of what Bronfenbrenner (1958) calls "expressivity," the generalized tendency of some people to use extreme ends of rating scales, others to use only the middle range. For the former, the absolute difference between the parents would be spuriously exaggerated; for the latter spuriously minimized.

identifying equally with both parents, then neither method can yield the true estimate of the incidence of split-parent identification since the latter is based on identifying more with one parent than the other. At this time, it seems reasonable to assume that the incidence of split-parent identification lies somewhere between estimates based on force and free choice methods.

More important than the question of the overall incidence of split-parent identification—which will always depend on the precise measure used and also on the particular sample studied—is the question of whether variations between and within sibling pairs follow the same pattern no matter which method is used, forced or free choice. In using the free choice method, sibling pairs with both-parent or neither-parent ratings for either the subject or the sibling must be omitted from the analyses of these intrafamilial variations in split-parent identification. Does the omission of these pairs affect the results of these analyses, i.e., that split-parent identification occurs mainly in first pairs and that, for some pairs, it occurs more often in same-sex siblings than opposite sex?

To answer these questions, a fourth major sample was studied using the free choice rating scales described above. This sample was drawn from the same undergraduate population as the other undergraduate samples and selected on the same basis.[5] It consisted of 682 subjects, 336 from three-child families, 346 from two-child. In this sample, neither-parent judgments were rare as in the exploratory study. Again they occurred only among male subjects, five in all. Males again showed a higher proportion of noncommittal answers (both or neither) than did females, 30.3% (N = 300) versus 24.9% (N = 382), although the difference was smaller than in the exploratory study.

Altogether, both-parent or neither-parent ratings occurred for 27.3% of subjects and 28.5% of siblings, so that 45.7% of the sibling pairs (309 subjects) could not be used in the analyses of between- and within-pair variations in split-parent identification. The remaining subsample available for these analyses—because parent choices were provided for both members of sibling pairs—consisted of 373 subjects, 178 from three-child families and 195 from two-child.

For all three forced choice samples and for these 373 subjects of the free choice sample, sibling pairs were classified as either *uni-parent* or *split-parent* identified, depending on whether parent identification choices indicated that the siblings identified with the same or different parents. On this basis, the percentage of split-parent identification per pair was derived.

The Intrafamilial Domain of Split-Parent Identification

The concept of a family tetrad based on sibling deidentification, on the one hand, and split-parent identification, on the other, is supported by the data. Sibling pairs that deidentify also tend to split-parent identify rather than uni-parent iden-

---

[5]In addition, all undergraduate samples were checked to make sure that no subject appeared in more than one sample.

tify. This covariation was significant for both of the samples that provided data on global sibling and parent judgments—the original undergraduate sample and the mother sample. And the covariation was significant for both two- and three-child families.

Given this covariation, one would expect split-parent identification, like sibling deidentification, to occur mainly in first pairs. This proved to be the case. Table 3 shows the percentage of split-parent identification for the three samples using the forced choice method—the undergraduate and mother samples with both sibling and parent judgments and the undergraduate sample with parent judgments only. It can be seen that in all these samples, first pairs, and only first pairs, show a significant percentage of split-parent identification, i.e., exceeding chance levels. These percentages ranged from 65.7 to 89.3 in two- and three-child families.

Moreover, these percentages were not spuriously inflated by having subjects judge their own siblings. Mothers judging pairs of their own children show even higher percentages of split-parent identification for these first pairs than students judging their own siblings. The mothers' data also demonstrate that this phenomenon is not limited to college-age students. The average age of the children judged by their mothers was six years. Table 3 also shows that percentages of split-parent identification were not inflated by asking subjects whether their siblings are alike or different. Undergraduates asked only for parent identification judgments show the same or slightly higher percentages of split-parent identification than those asked for sibling and parent judgments.

Results for the free choice sample are summarized in Table 4. It can be seen that, for the subsample with parent choices for both members of sibling pairs, the findings for split-parent identification—as against uni-parent identification—follow the same pattern as those for the forced choice samples. First pairs, and only first pairs, in both two- and three-child families show a significant percentage of split-parent identification. Percentages of split-parent identification for each pair of this subsample are almost identical to those of the comparable forced

TABLE 6.3
Percentage Split-parent Identification for Pairs
of Forced-choice Samples

Pairs	Sibling & Parent Judgments Undergraduates	Mothers	Parent Judgment Only Undergraduates
Two-child first pairs	65.7*	89.3*	72.9*
Three-child pairs			
First pair	65.8*	80.0*	66.5*
Second pair	52.8	56.4	57.6
Jump pair	46.9	35.1	46.7
Number of pairs	551	200	796

*Significantly greater than chance.

choice sample of Table 3, the sample asked only for parent judgments (see column 3, Table 3).

Table 4 also shows the number of pairs with no-parent choice for one or both siblings in a pair (because of neither- or both-parent ratings). Taking the size of this no-choice subsample into account, split-parent identification occurs in about one-third of first pairs in the total free choice sample. By contrast, the percentages of Table 3, based on forced choice, show split-parent identification to occur in about two-thirds of first pairs. Since the latter is probably an overestimate because of forcing a choice, whereas the former is probably an underestimate because of evading socially undesirable choices, the true incidence of split-parent identification in first pairs is likely to be about 50%. The remaining 50% probably show either uni-parent identification or both-parent identification given the rarity of neither-parent identification. When we consider that first pairs include two-child families and that these families have become the national mode, split-parent identification proves to be a common phenomenon.

Finally, comparisons within pairs indicate that, like sibling deidentification, split-parent identification tends to be more common in same-sex siblings. Recall that in our studies of sibling deidentification, whenever significant differences were found between same- and opposite-sex siblings, it was the same-sex siblings who showed more deidentification. These increments were found in one of the pairs in each of the samples studied: the three-child-family first pair of the undergraduate sample and the two-child-family first pair of the mother sample.

For split-parent identification, again it is the same-sex siblings that show significant increments within pairs. These increments reached significance in two of the samples studied, and again for one pair in each sample: the three-child-family first pair of the new forced choice sample and the jump pair of the free choice subsample with parent choices.

TABLE 6.4
Results for Pairs of Free-Choice Subsamples

Subsamples	2-child pair First	3-child pair First	Second	Jump
Parent choices for both siblings				
Number of pairs	195	123	107	126
Split-parent percentage	73.8*	64.2*	57.3	51.6
Uni-parent percentage	26.2	35.8	42.7	48.4
No choice for one or both siblings				
Number of pairs	151	93	106	116

*Significantly greater than chance.

Apparently this increment for same-sex-siblings, although it is characteristic of both sibling deidentification and split-parent identification, does not occur in every sample or in every pair within a sample. Nor is the increment associated with any single type of pair since it appeared in first and jump pairs.[6] That it occurs at all is, in fact, surprising, because it defies ordinary expectations. Ordinarily, we would expect two brothers or two sisters to be viewed as more alike than a brother and a sister, and we would also expect opposite-sex siblings to identify with different parents more often than same-sex siblings. We will have more to say about this issue in the following section.

To sum up our results on the intrafamilial domain of split-parent identification, the evidence from all sources seems to support the validity of the tetradic structure. Sibling deidentification and split-parent identification seem to co-occur, generating a structure of family similarities and differences that we call the family tetrad. The family tetrad is mainly a first pair phenomenon and there is a tendency for it to occur more often in same-sex than in opposite-sex siblings. Our theoretical framework to account for these findings will be presented in the final section of this chapter, as noted above. At this point, we must turn our attention to a comparison of the range of applicability of the split-parent and the same-sex-parent rules.

Split-Parent and Same-Sex-Parent Identification

The same-sex-parent rule for identification generates the prediction that split-parent identification is more common in opposite-sex sibling pairs than in same-sex, since each sibling in the opposite-sex pair is expected to identify with a different parent—boys with their fathers and girls with their mothers—whereas siblings in same-sex pairs are expected to show uni-parent identification, both identifying with the same-sex-parent. As we have seen, this prediction is not confirmed. None of the pairs in any of the four samples showed significantly more split-parent identification among opposite-sex siblings. On the contrary, when significant differences were found between opposite- and same-sex siblings, it was the latter and not the former that showed more split-parent identification.

Do these results mean that the same-sex-parent rule has little or no validity as previous research would suggest? Or might the same- sex-parent rule apply under certain limited conditions? The condition that interested us most bears on the relationship between the split-parent rule and the same-sex-parent rule.

Clearly, these two rules conflict in the case of same-sex siblings, the split-parent rule generating the prediction that two sisters or two brothers will identify

---

[6]It should be noted that the percentage of split-parent identification for these same-sex jump pairs, although it was significantly higher than for opposite-sex jump pairs, did not exceed chance levels as did the percentage for same-sex first pairs.

with different parents, the same-sex-parent rule that they will identify with the same parent. When two rules conflict, each may obscure the effects of the other. For example, if split-parent identification tends to occur more often in same-sex siblings than in opposite-sex, this effect may be obscured at times by the same-sex rule which has the effect of increasing uni-parent identification among opposite-sex siblings. Indeed, these conflicting effects may account for the finding that not all pairs showed significantly more split-parent identification among same-sex siblings. That some pairs did show this increment, while none showed significant increments for opposite-sex siblings, suggests that the split-parent rule is dominant relative to the same-sex rule, i.e., more likely to obscure the effects of the latter.

These considerations concerning the interactions between two conflicting rules for identification suggested that the same-sex rule might apply under conditions where the split-parent rule does not predominate. Since the split-parent rule predominates among first pairs, it might well obscure the effects of the same-sex rule for members of these first pairs, namely, for first- and second-borns. On the other hand, for other ordinal positions such as the third-born, the same-sex rule might become salient. To study this possibility, the percentage of same-sex-parent identification was calculated for each ordinal position for all four samples. Percentages were based on all subjects with parent identification choices, whether or not the choice was missing for a sibling. Table 5 shows these percentages.

It can be seen that of the eight percentage figures given for first-borns (in two- and three-child families), only one shows a significant degree of same-sex-parent identification-60.1% for three-child first-borns in the free choice sample. Results

TABLE 6.5
Percentage Same-Sex-Parent Identification
First-, Second-, and Third-Born Subjects in Each Sample
(Number in Parentheses)

| | Sibling & Parent Judgments | | Parent Judgments Only | |
| | Undergraduates | Mothers | Undergraduates | |
Birth Order	Forced-choice	Forced-choice	Forced-choice	Free-choice
Two-child pairs				
First Born	50.5 (95)	52.2 (90)	51.4 (140)	60.1* (138)
Second Born	51.8 (81)	62.4* (85)	48.1 (106)	41.7 (120)
Three-child pairs				
First Born	47.7 (88)	61.0 (41)	54.7 (106)	52.3 (86)
Second Born	51.6 (62)	52.4 (42)	60.0 (85)	60.6 (66)
Third Born	67.4* (46)	82.1* (39)	52.2 (92)	67.0* (85)

Note. Percentages were based on all subjects with parent identification choices, whether or not the choice was missing for a sibling.
*Significantly greater than chance.

for second-borns were similar; only one of the eight percentages exceeded chance levels-62.4% for two-child second-borns in the mother sample. By contrast, three of the four percentages for third-borns show a significant degree of same-sex parent identification-67.4% for the original undergraduate sample, 82.1% for the mother sample, and 67.0% for the first choice sample.

These findings on birth order, like the findings comparing same- and opposite-sex siblings, suggest that the split-parent rule is dominant relative to the same-sex rule in that it can overwhelm the effects of the same-sex-rule. Where the split-parent rule does not apply, as is the case for third-borns, the effects of the same-sex rule becomes clearly evident.

It seemed worthwhile to examine the data further in search of other specific conditions that might be associated with same-sex-parent identification. Two such conditions were identified. Because it would take us too far afield to report these findings in detail, they will be summarized as follows:

1. Salience of the child's sexual identity: In three-child families, same-sex-parent identification exceeded chance levels for sons born after one or two daughters (percentages were 69.0 and 66.7, respectively, for all samples combined) and for daughters born after two sons (67.8%). Since parents who have children of one sex often yearn for a child of the other sex, when their "dream comes true" the child's sex is apt to be a salient feature of his or her identity, and hence likely to form the basis for identification choices. That boys show significant same-sex-parent identification with only one older sister, whereas girls do so only when there are two older brothers, probably reflects the more intense longing for a son on the part of parents in our culture. In support of this explanation is the additional finding that sons who are the only boy in three-child families tend to identify significantly with their fathers (67.8%), no matter what their birth order, whereas daughters in comparable circumstances identify as often with their fathers as their mothers.

In two-child families, the sex of the other sibling had no effect on the percentage of same-sex-parent identification. And in three-child families, chance levels of same-sex-identification were obtained when earlier-born siblings were of the same sex. It should be added that the effect of having older opposite-sex siblings in itself cannot account for the finding that third-borns tend to identify with their same-sex parents. When third-borns with two older opposite-sex siblings were excluded from the samples, the results for the other third-borns remained the same.

2. Specific personality attributes: to see if the same-sex rule applied to specific attributes rather than global resemblances, the items of the semantic differential scales were examined. Most of these items showed a halo effect, with subjects viewing themselves and their parents in a positive light. To study the application of the same-sex rule to specific attributes, only the items with disparate ratings for each parent were examined (e.g., mother rated extrovert vs. father rated introvert.

For the two undergraduate samples available for study,[7] one tested in the early seventies and the other in 1979 and 1980, the results for these items were very different. The early sample showed considerable sex-typing. Boys viewing their mother as weak, delicate, and shallow identified significantly with their strong, rugged, and deep fathers. Girls viewing their mothers as nonachieving identified significantly with their achieving fathers. By the late seventies, this sex-typed pattern was replaced by an androgynous one. Boys viewing their fathers as unpleasant and cold identified with their pleasant, warm mothers, and they also identified with their strong, rugged, deep, and achieving fathers. Girls viewing their mothers as weak identified with their strong fathers, and they also identified with their warm mothers.

The shift to androgyny probably reflects the growing influence of the women's movement. Yet it is important to note that both the early and the later samples show the boys identifying with the potency attributes of their fathers, as measured by the items strong-weak, rugged-delicate, and deep-shallow. For these potency attributes, the same-sex-parent rule seems to apply for boys, even when we consider changing trends in the social desirability of sex-typing. These findings on specific attributes for one specific sex suggest that research using total scores on masculinity and femininity scales may obscure some of the effects of the same-sex rule.

In sum, the same-sex-parent rule for identification seems to apply under several conditions: (a) in the case of third-borns, where the split-parent rule does not apply; (b) when the sex of the child is a salient feature of his or her identity, e.g., for only sons in large families; and (c) for potency attributes of males.

The Meaning of Global Parent Identification Judgments

The semantic differential scales were also examined to shed light on the meaning of global parent identification judgments. Recall that siblings who were judged as different obtained higher Sibling Polarization scores on the semantic differential scales than siblings who were judged alike, i.e., they polarized on significantly more of the personality attributes. Similarly, we found that the parent chosen as the main identification figure showed significantly higher Parent Identification scores on the semantic differential than did the other parent. It seems that when people say that a child is more like one parent than another, they mean the child shares more personality traits with the former.

Apart from this general finding, the semantic differential was of limited use in further clarifying the meaning of global parent identification judgments because of the extensive halo effects. Subjects tended to rate themselves and their parents

---

[7]Note that the semantic differential was not administered to the free-choice sample. It was administered to all other samples but the mother data could not be used for this parent-identification analysis because mothers departed from our instructions for the order of rating their chidlren. See footnote 2.

as good, cheerful, pleasant, active, fast, strong, deep, and achieving in at least 70% of cases. It was these halo effects, together with other methodological problems, that prompted Bronfrenbrenner's (1958) critique of the use of the semantic differential Difference score (D) as an index of parent identification, a common practice in previous research. Bronfrenbrenner pointed out that halo effects and other response sets would tend to exaggerate or distort the extent of child-parent similarity. With the benefit of hindsight, we did not use the D score as our index of identification. We used global judgments, relying on the semantic differential merely to elucidate the meaning of these judgments. In the event, pervasive halo effects rendered the semantic differential of limited use even in this modest role.

Perhaps a more promising tool for investigating the meaning of global parent identification judgments would be Kelly's (1955) Construct Repertory Test, adapted so as to elicit the repertory of personal constructs within the family. Kelly (1955) assumes that individuals apply a unique set of core personality constructs in their perceptions of themselves and others, and his test is designed to elicit these constructs. Everyday conversations with families suggest that families too use a unique set of core constructs in their perceptions of themselves, and that they apply them in their attributions of identification. For example, one mother might say, "My son is a go-getter like his father, my daughter is lazy like me", whereas another might describe her two daughters as follows: "This one let's everything hang out like I do, but that one keeps her feelings to herself like my husband." There may even be group variations in family constructs, ethnic or social class differences, and/or differences between dysfunctional and well-functioning families. Overall, a family-construct approach is consistent with recent research on cognition and personality and stands to benefit from advances in this field.

Whatever the outcome of further investigation on the widespread view that siblings identify with different parents, it seems clear from the prevalence of this view and from the consistent pattern of its occurrence that it plays a significant role in personality development. With diverse samples and diverse procedures, global judgments of the main parental identification figure show that split-parent identification occurs consistently in the first pair of children in the family and in close association with sibling deidentification, generating the new structure that we call the family tetrad.

FAMILY TETRAD: STRUCTURE AND FUNCTION

In view of the covariation of sibling deidentification and split-parent identification, the theoretical framework developed to account for the former can be extended to apply to the latter, giving us some insight into the structure and function of the family tetrad—a four-person grouping with two siblings different from each other and each identified with a different parent.

Family Structure

The family tetrad, although it consists of two child-parent dyads, does not appear to be constructed in accordance with the same-sex-parent rule. That is, it is not limited to son-father and daughter-mother dyads. Tetrads based on son-father, son-mother dyads or daughter-mother, daughter-father dyads occur just as often or more often, and those based on son-mother, daughter-father dyads are also common. The tetrad also differs from the family structure that has been the major concern of family systems theory, the pathological or "perverse" triad (Haley, 1975; Minuchin, 1974). This triad, consisting of a cross-generational dyad—a parent and the child who is the identified patient forming a coalition against another member—the other parent—has been the main focus of intervention among family therapists. The tetradic structure we have described has been virtually ignored. Further, this triad is described as pathological, whereas our tetradic structure, though it might serve some pathological function in some families, appears to be prevalent in normal samples. Finally, in defining the pathological triad, structure and function are inseparable. The pathological triad is an unhealthy alliance of two against one. By contrast, our tetradic structure is defined in terms of personality similarities and differences, so that questions about its function can be debated without affecting the validity of the finding that the structure appears to be a prevalent one. Given the shrinking size of the American family, the tetrad may well become the predominant family structure.

Of added significance is the pivotal role assigned to siblings in the family tetrad. Cicirelli (1979) reminds us that the relationship between siblings is the most enduring of all human ties, spanning a lifetime. Yet siblings have been generally neglected in personality research, and in studies of identification they have been entirely ignored. Apart from the Oedipal triad of psychoanalytic theory, identification theory has focused on the single child-parent dyad, disregarding the other members of the family. Our findings indicate that to understand the development of identification, we need to move beyond the child-parent dyad and the Oedipal triad and take into account the entire family constellation.

Family Dynamics

The data suggest that split-parent identification, like sibling deidentification, is a defense against sibling rivalry. Variations in the incidence of both of these phenomena correspond with variations in expected levels of sibling rivalry, as both occur mainly in first pairs and more often in same-sex siblings than opposite. With each sibling in the pair identified with a different parent, neither child need feel that the other is favored by a special relationship to the parents. Both can feel that they have a special niche in the family, even if it is a different niche. Split-parent identification may even be a secondary defense, secondary to the need for siblings to defend themselves against competition and comparison by being different or deidentifying. In any case, sibling deidentification and split-parent identification operating jointly to mitigate rivalry would together generate the family tetrad.

It also seems probable that a complementary *split-the-children* defense on the part of parents serves to further consolidate the tetradic structure. Only the most egalitarian married couple, who complement each other perfectly, can be completely free of competition and comparison. If this idyllic picture were to exist in the early phases of marriage, it would surely be shattered with the arrival of children. Is there a parent who does not wonder occasionally if his or her child prefers the other parent (viz., competition)? Is there a parent who might not wonder occasionally if he or she provides a superior model for the child to emulate (viz., comparison)?

The arrival of the second child could provide a perfect means of muting these disruptive feelings. Each parent can have one child who seems consistently to prefer him or her when competition arises, one who seems to attest to the superiority of his or her approach by consistently adopting it. That is, a defense of splitting-the-children could serve to maintain the benefits and minimize the costs of the competition and comparison between parents that comes with rearing children. In the form of the family tetrad, these complementary defenses of parents and children could maintain family equilibrium, stability, and harmony in the face of our all too human disruptive feelings.

ACKNOWLEDGMENTS

This research was supported in part by a grant from the William T. Grant Foundation and by a Barnard College mini-grant. We would like to thank Lourdes Ochoa, Jane Polich, Phyllis Kolling, and Katherine Monroe for their invaluable assistance in carrying out the project.

REFERENCES

Bandura, A. L. *Social learning theory*. Englewood Cliffs, N.J.: Prentice Hall, 1977.

Bossard, J. H. & Boll, E. S. *The large family system*. Philadelphia: University of Pennsylvania Press, 1956.

Brickman, P. & Bulman, R. J. Pleasure and pain in social comparison. In J. Suls & R. Miller (Eds.), *Social comparison processes*. Washington: Hemisphere Publishing Corporation, 1977.

Brim, O. G. Family structure and sex role learning by children: A further anlaysis of Helen Koch's data. *Sociometry*, 1958, *21*, 1–16.

Bronfenbrenner, U. The study of identification through interpersonal perception. In R. Tagiuri & L. Petrullo (Eds.), *Person, perception and interpersonal behavior*. Standford, Calif.: Stanford University Press, 1958.

Cicirelli, V. G. Sibling influence throughout the life span. In B. Sutton-Smith (Chair), *Life-span perspectives on sibling socialization*. Symposium presented at the meeting of the American Psychological Association, New York, 1979.

Festinger, L. A theory of social comparison processes. *Human Relations*, 1954, *7*, 117–140.

Goethals, G. R. & Darley, J. M. Social comparison theory: An attributional approach. In J. Suls & R. Miller (Eds.), *Social comparison processes*. Washington: Hemisphere Publishing Corporation, 1977.

Grotevant, H. D. Sibling constellations and sex typing of interests in adolescence. *Child Development*, 1978, *49*, 540–542.

Grotevant, H. D., Scarr, S., & Weinberg, R. A. Patterns of interest similarity in adoptive and biological families. *Journal of Personality and Social Psychology*, 1977, *35*, 667–676.

Haley, J. Toward a theory of pathological systems. In G. H. Zuk & I. Boszormenyi-Nagy (Eds.), *Family therapy and disturbed families*. Palo Alto Calif.: Science and Behavior, 1975.

Hetherington, E. M. A developmental study of the effects of sex of the dominant parent on sex-role preference, identification, and imitation in children. *Journal of Personality and Social Psychology*, 1965, *2*, 188–194.

Hoffeditz, E. L. Family resemblances in personality traits. *Journal of Social Psychology*, 1934, *5*, 214–227.

Holtzman, P. S. *Psychoanalysis and psychopathology*. New York: McGraw-Hill, 1970.

Kelly, G. S. *The psychology of personal constructs*. New York: W. W. Norton, 1955.

Kernberg, O. F. *Borderline conditions & pathological narcissim*. New York: J. Aronson, 1975.

Kohlberg, L. A. A cognitive-developmental analysis of children's sex-role concepts and attitudes. In E. E. Maccoby (Ed.), *The development of sex differences*. Stanford, Calif.: Stanford University Press, 1966.

Kohut, H. *The analysis of self*. New York: International Universities Press, 1971.

Lazowick, L. M. On the nature of identification. *Journal of Abnormal and Social Psychology*, 1955, *51*, 175–183.

Leventhal, G. S. Influence of brothers and sisters on sex-role behavior. *Journal of Personality and Social Psychology*, 1970, *16*, 452–465.

Maccoby, E. E. & Jacklin, C. N. *The psychology of sex differences*. Stanford, Calif.: Stanford University Press, 1974.

Martens, R. & White, V. Influence of win-loss ratio on performance, satisfaction, and preference for opponents. *Journal of Experimental Social Psychology*, 1975, *11*, 343–362.

Mettee, D. R. & Riskind, J. Size of defeat and liking for superior and similar ability competitors. *Journal of Experimental Social Psychology*, 1974, *10*, 333–351.

Mettee, D. R. & Smith, G. Social comparison and interpersonal attraction: The case for dissimilarity. In J. Suls & R. Miller (Eds.), *Social comparison processes*. Washington: Hemisphere Publishing Corporation, 1977.

Minuchin, S. *Families and family therapy*. London: Tavistock Publications, 1974.

Munsinger, H. & Rabin, A. A family study of gender identification. *Child Development*, 1978, *49*, 537–539.

Mussen, P. H. & Rutherford, E. Parent-child relations and parental personality in relation to young children's sex-role preferences. *Child Development*, 1963, *34*, 589–607.

Nadler, A., Jazwinski, C., & Lau, S. The cold glow of success: Effects of the interpersonal success of a similar and dissimilar other on observer's self and other perceptions. Unpublished manuscript, Purdue University, 1976.

Newcomb, T. & Svehla, G. Intra-family relationships in attitude. *Sociometry*, 1937, *1*, 271–283.

Osgood, C. E., Suci, G. J., & Tannenbaum, P. H. *The measurement of meaning*. Urbana, Ill.: University of Illinois Press, 1957.

Peterson, T. D. The relationship between certain attitudes of parents and children. *Purdue University Studies in Higher Education*, 1936, *No. 31*, 127–144.

Rosenberg, B. G. & Sutton-Smith, B. Family interaction effects on masculinity-feminity. *Journal of Personality and Social Psychology*, 1968, *8*, 117–120.

Ross, H. G. & Milgram, J. I. *Rivalry in adult sibling relationships: Its antecedents and dynamics.* Poster session presented at the meeting of the American Psychological Association, Montreal, 1980.

Schachter, F. F., Gilutz, G., Shore, E., & Adler, M. Sibling deidentification judged by mothers: cross-validation and developmental studies. *Child Development,* 1978, *49,* 543-546.

Schachter, F. F., Shore, E., Feldman-Rotman, S., Marquis, R. E., & Campbell, S., Sibling deidentification. *Development Psychology,* 1976, *12,* 418-427.

Spence, J. T., Helmreich, R. & Stapp, J. Likability, sex-role congruence of interest, and competence: It all depends on how you ask. *Journal of Applied Social Psychology,* 1975, *5,* 93-109.

Suls, J. M., & Miller, R. L. (Eds.), *Social comparison processes.* Washington: Hemisphere Publishing Corporation, 1977.

Sutton-Smith, B. & Rosenberg, B. G. Age changes in the effects of ordinal position on sex-role identification. *Journal of Genetic Psychology,* 1965, *107,* 61-73.

Sward, K., & Friedman, M. B. The family resemblance in temperament. *Journal of Abnormal and Social Psychology,* 1935-36, *30,* 256-261.

Troll, L. E., Neugarten, B. L., & Kraines, R. J. Similarities in values and other personality characteristics in college students and their parents. *Merrill-Palmer Quarterly,* 1969, *15,* 323-336.

7 Birth Order and Sibling Status Effects

Brian Sutton-Smith
University of Pennsylvania

It would not be misleading to argue that the most consistent theme in birth-order studies from the last century to the present has been the special eminence of first-born children. From Galton's speculations of 1874 to Zajonc's Confluence Model of 1975 there has been a 100-year preoccupation with the "psychological" primogeniture of the first-born. In our book, *The sibling* (1970), Ben Rosenberg and I suggested that it was time for a shift in emphasis.[1] Together with Alfred Adler, another nonfirst-born, we argued for greater attention to the other siblings. In particular we sought to draw attention to those interactions that took place between siblings that might help to explain the unique characteristics of each sibling position.

In this chapter, I first review the continuing history of the study of the first-borns, showing, paradoxically, that recent evidence now interprets their particular eminence partly in sibling interactive terms; and second, the data on sibling status effects.

PSYCHOLOGICAL PRIMOGENITURE

Given that birth order effects, with a few notable exceptions (Belmont & Marolla, 1973; Berbaum & Moreland, 1980), have relatively little power in accounting for psychological outcomes, it remains a puzzle that so many thousands of studies have been devoted to such minimal ends. (See, for example,

---

[1]In general, citations in this chapter are confined to references after the appearance of this book in 1970.

153

the bibliographies of Jones, 1933; Murphy, Murphy, & Newcomb, 1937; Sutton-Smith & Rosenberg, 1970.) One sometimes wonders whether this interest itself has been a vestige of earlier primogenitural habits of thought or yet another instance of that tropistic pursuit of inexorable and trivial laws that has sometimes characterized psychology as an infant science.

Nineteenth century notions that first-born children were inherently more *intelligent* were originally dealt a blow by a series of careful reviews apparently indicating that most of the claimed advantages in intelligence were actually reducible to uncontrolled variances arising from family size, socioeconomic status, incomplete families in the sample, defects in test standardization thresholds, or varying nativity statistics for different birth cohorts. After Jones' review of 1933, little of substance was heard of first-born intelligence (Altus, 1966; Jones, 1933; Murphy, Murphy, & Newcomb, 1937; Sampson, 1965; Schooler, 1972; Strodtbeck & Creelan, 1968; Warren, 1966), until 1973, when Belmont and Marolla, in an analysis of the entire male population of Dutch males reaching the age of 19 years between 1963 and 1969 (over 300,000), discovered a strong linear relationship between birth order and scores on the Ravens Progressive Matrices. Furthermore, with controls for family size and socioeconomic status, these differences were quite considerable, amounting to about two-thirds of one standard deviation between the first-born of two siblings and the last-born of nine siblings. Parallel to this finding, an impressive number of large-scale studies with adequate controls reached similar results (Berbaum & Moreland, 1980; Breland, 1972, 1973, 1974; Markus & Zajonc, 1977; Nuttall & Nuttall, 1975; Zajonc & Bargh, 1980a; Zajonc & Markus, 1975) although sometimes with minimal differences (Grotevant, Scarr & Weinberg, 1977) or with cross-cultural complications (Davis, Cahan & Bashi, 1977), and in a few cases with no such differences (Circirelli, 1976; McCall, 1971).

On grounds of *eminence* rather than intelligence, there has been in general a greater consensus on first-born superiority. Their overrepresentation amongst eminent persons, national merit scholars and Ph.D.'s has received widespread confirmation (Altus, 1966; Bayer, 1967). Some have suggested that this eminence derives from their overrepresentation amongst college students (Altus, 1966; Epstein & Bronzaft, 1971; Schachter, 1963) and that, in turn, they are at college in the first place because of their higher academic aspirations and achievement (Chittenden, Foan, Zweill, & Smith, 1968; Elder, 1962; Elliot & Elliot, 1970; Falbo, 1980; Konig, 1963; Oberlander & Jenkins, 1967; Rosen, 1964). They have been shown to fail at school to a lesser extent than later-born children (Belmont, Stein & Wittes, 1976). When achievement is measured by projective tests, however, the results are quite inconsistent, which is probably more a comment on those tests than on the issue of achievement (Adams & Sutton-Smith & Rosenberg, 1972; 1970). Bayer has argued that the superiority of first-borns is less striking than the underachievement of the middle-born children (1967), and that many positive findings in this area still have their basis in lack of control for the vitality statistics of the birth cohorts being assessed; still even he finds such differences favoring the first-born.

Whereas Galton (1874) believed that the first-born are favored because of the greater responsibility conferred upon them by the laws of primogeniture, psychologists of the 1960s were seized by a thesis more consistent with the infant deterministic assumptions prevalent at that time. This thesis developed out of Stanley Schachter's work on the psychology of affiliation (1959) in which he showed that in states of anxiety induced by experimental procedures, first-born females were more likely to seek the company and evaluation of others than were later-born females who would be more likely to seek isolation in similar circumstances. Speculating on the origins of these differences, Schachter suggested that because of greater attention and reinforcement by their mothers, first-borns had been taught to associate the reduction of pain with her presence and generalized this expectancy to others in subsequent anxiety-inducing situations. A series of investigations with adult subjects indeed seemed to show that first-borns more often showed affiliative responses to anxiety-provoking experimental situations. By our count, up to 1970, 15 studies supported this thesis and four did not (10:3 females: 5:1 males). A second large group of experimental studies similar to the others and also derived from social comparison theory, focused on the allied thesis that in conditions of uncertainty first-borns would be more likely to conform to the opinions of others. In this case the results were less striking, eleven favoring the thesis and seven not supporting it (females 2:5 and males 9:2). As a corollary of these approaches, there were other studies focused on whether first-borns were more anxious in general (Weiss, 1970), more anxious in test situations, or more anxious as young children. Studies also sought to discover with whom the first-born preferred to compare themselves (inferiors, equals, or superiors). More tantalizing were the fragments of real life data suggesting first-borns more often used psychotherapy (an affiliative technique) and later-borns more often favored isolated or dangerous avocations such as sports, fighter piloting, or the use of alcohol (Blane & Barry, 1973). Without exception, none of these studies, despite their experimental or real life character, exerted any control or showed any assessment of the demographic sources of their subjects birth orders. We cannot, in consequence, feel very reassured about the evidence they yielded.

Another more observational line of research, partly associated with the Schachter thesis but also growing out of the general preoccupation of developmental psychologists with mother-infant relationships, sought to discover if, in fact, mothers did treat infants differently as a function of birth order. Here the results seemed more consistent. Mothers appeared to expect more of first-born infants (Cushna, 1966; Lasko, 1954), to be more inconsistent and intrusive with them

(Hilton, 1967; Rothbart, 1967) and to interact with them more (Cohen & Beckwith, 1977; Gewirtz & Gewirtz, 1965; Jacobs & Moss, 1976; Lewis & Kreitzberg, 1979).

In consequence, it was argued, first-borns, even as infants, showed superior motor development (Bayley, 1965; Cohen & Beckwith, 1977; Solomon & Solomon, 1964). Studies of birth order during childhood also showed that first-borns more often reach out for the help of others or have some kind of "special" relationship with their parents. Somewhat more tenuously connected with the anxiety-affiliation thesis were studies giving fragmentary support to the ideas that the first-born child, being more adult-like, would be more conservative, responsible, dominant, have a harsher superego, show a preference for verbal over nonverbal forms of inference, perceive themselves as more orderly, nurturant, and self-controlling, and have a great preference for working in hierarchical rather than egalitarian role relationships (Exner and Sutton-Smith, 1970).

In the 1970s, the most interesting attempt to explain first-born differences (by contrast to Galton's (1874) Responsibility Model and Schachter's (1959) Anxiety Affiliation model), was the Confluence Model offered by Robert Zajonc and coworkers (1975). Unlike Schachter's Affiliation Model, which took only the parents and the child's infant experience into account, the confluence model made use also of the number of siblings in the family, their ages, the spacing between siblings, and the opportunities available to older siblings to teach those younger than themselves. This new model was in tune with a general move in developmental psychology away from infant determinism and towards more interactive models of socialization. Specifically, the Confluence Model was a mathematical one that sought to assign weights to parent and child intellectual levels in order to match the achieved parameters of birth order variance. It is described by Zajonc in 1975 as follows:

> We began by arbitrarily setting the parent's intellectual level at 100, and the newborn's at near zero. Then we used theoretical growth curves to estimate the intellect of a child at a given time, and to describe the intellectual level of any family. I want to emphasize here that these figures are not IQ scores. An IQ score shows a person's intelligence corrected for his age, whereas our estimates are absolute and vary with age. They refer to the total absolute "quantity" of intellect at the person's disposal: his knowledge, wisdom, skills and abilities.
>
> For example, a couple without children has an average intellectual environment of 100 $\left(\dfrac{100 + 100}{2} \right)$ When they have their first child the family's average environment changes. Now there are two adults, each contributing their maximum to the intellectual environment, and one child whose intellect is near zero. The average of the three is 200/3, or .67. The family environment—the pool of intellectual capacity—is now about 67 percent of what it was before the child arrived. If a second child is born to our hypothetical parents after two years, the family intellect drops again. After two years the first child has about four percent of his adult

intellect, so the second child enters an environment of 100 plus 100 plus four plus zero, for an average level of 51. The second child enters a less intelligent atmosphere.

If a third child is born in another two years, the family level sinks still further. The eldest child is four years old and up to a whopping 15 percent of adult intelligence, while the second child is at four percent, the family average falls to 44. Note that we consider that the individual's intellectual environment consists not only of the intellectual levels of those around him, but of his own level as well.

With each additional child, the family's intellectual environment depreciates, because a child's intellectual growth is partly controlled by the overall intellectual climate of his household. Children who grow up surrounded by people with higher intellectual levels have a better chance to achieve their maximum intellectual powers than children who develop in intellectually impoverished milieus. Thus, children from large families, who spent more time in a world of child-sized minds, should develop more slowly and therefore attain lower IQs than children from small families, who have more contacts with grown-up minds.

According to our model of sibling influence, another variable that ought to affect intelligence is the length of time between the births of the children. The longer the gaps, the more time the older children have to develop, hence to raise the family's intellectual level [pp. 38–39].

The model predicts that because only children and last-born children do not have the opportunity to teach others, their scores will be lower than expected on grounds such as the spacing between siblings and the number of siblings in the family (Falbo, 1978). In general this mathematical model has had considerable predictive success in dealing with a variety of large size samples from Holland, France, Scotland, the USA and Israel (Zajonc & Bargh, 1980a), and in dealing also with apparent exceptions to the data. For example, with Oriental Israeli children large-size families are associated with increasing (not decreasing) IQ scores as a function of birth order: That is, later-born children do better. Whereas this appears to contradict the Confluence Model, the cultural data suggest that it does not. Here the very low academic level of the parents, together with the relatively greater schooling experience of their own first-born children, leads to an upward improvement of the scores in their later-born children (Davis, Cahan & Bashi, 1977). More impressively, in a study involving actual sibling and parental scores rather than ordinal position data and assumed parental scores, Berbaum & Moreland (1980) found they could use a version of the model to predict 51% of the variance in the observed mental ages of their subjects. They argued: "The confluence model suggests elements of a psychological theory of mental development that explicitly includes family structure and mutual influences of family members on one another's intellectual growth [p. 511]."

The results from this study are sufficiently striking to suggest that much of the variability in birth-order data must indeed arise from failure to deal with the actual siblings and actual parents being studied. Furthermore, the usual kind of birth-order data often include many uncontrolled variances from other sources such as the nativity statistics mentioned earlier. It might be wise to recommend that editors of journals stop publishing material on birth order when the basic presupposition so often adopted, that the birth-order position can be abstracted from its actual family context, seems not to have been satisfied by so many years of inconsistent findings. And even when there is some, though not entirely consistent, accumulation of data about first-borns being more eminent, scoring more highly on intelligence or achievement measures and responding in a more affiliative or socially comparative ways to situations of anxiety and uncertainty, we should not treat this as a vindication of our knowledge about birth-order positions in the abstract, but as a measure of our ignorance of how strong this effect might be if we were comparing the actual siblings from the same families.

SIBLING STATUS AND SEX ROLE EFFECTS

One important significance of the Confluence Model is that for the first time it brings under one conceptual umbrella the issues of first-born eminence and sibling interaction. It deals not only with the child-parent relationships but also with the child-child relationships. Helen Koch, in a series of studies between 1954 and 1960 (1954, 1955a, & b, 1956, a,b,c,d,e, 1957, 1958) was the first to demonstrate, however, that contrasts between first- and nonfirst-born obscure many differences that are actually the result of much more specific patterns of sibling status. Her studies of the four kinds of two-child sibling families (older and younger brothers; older and younger sisters; older brother and younger sister; older sister and younger brother) revealed important distinctions between these dyads in the differences produced in each dyad member's primary mental abilities, work and emotional attitudes, personality correlates, speech patterns, sissiness and tomboyishness, playmates, etc. In general, she and subsequent workers found that each sibling heightened his or her own characteristics (preferences, interests, and abilities) in the other sibling, although the older siblings had a stronger impact on the younger ones than vice versa and boys had a stronger effect than girls. These effects seem to have been of a more obviously modelled kind in the case of the same-sex siblings and of a more complex, sometimes counter-intuitive kind in the opposite-sex siblings. Although Koch had some interesting statements to make about the effects of spacing between siblings, the literature on spacing has been a particularly inconsistent one (Belmont, Stein & Zybert, 1978). A useful sidelight from Koch is that her data suggest reasons for some of the contradictions in the affiliation-conformity studies presented earlier. It would seem that not all kinds of first-born are to be distinguished similarly from all kinds of second-born. For example, second-born males and females appear to be the most stereotypically sex-typed, particularly the boy with an older brother (MM2) and the girl with an older sister (FF2), and this leads these males to fit the expectations that they will be unaffiliative and nonconforming (confirming Schachter), but has the opposite effects for these girls (not confirming Schachter). In Rosenberg's study, these sex-role stereotypic birth orders (MM2 and FF2) also show the greatest stability in personality traits over three decades.

The impact of sibling status on sex role development was a central focus of research during the 1950s and 1960s but has not been salient in the 1970s. In general, in that earlier research, males in all-male families were higher on interests, recreations, and occupations regarded as stereotypically "masculine" and females in all-female families were higher on the stereotypically "feminine." Children in opposite-sex families showed much more complex profiles, being less stereotyped and more "androgynous," to use a more recent term. But the picture was always complex as is well indicated in Brim's (1958) quite thorough reanalysis of the Koch (1955) data on her 384 six-year-olds, which is quoted here from Sutton-Smith and Rosenberg (1970).

TABLE 3.8
The Variables in Brim's Reanalysis

High Masculine Rating	Low Masculine Rating	High Feminine Rating	Low Feminine Rating
1. Tenacity	1. Dawdling and	1. Affectionate	1. Anger
2. Aggressiveness	procrastinating	2. Obedience (responds	2. Quarrelsom
3. Curiosity	2. Wavering in	to sympathy	3. Revengefulness
4. Ambition	decision	3. Approval from adults	4. Teasing
5. Planfulness		4. Speedy recovery from	5. Insistence on
6. Responsibility		emotional upset	rights
7. Originality		5. Cheerfulness	6. Exhibitionism
8. Competitiveness		6. Kindness	7. Uncooperative
9. Self-confidence		7. Friendliness to adults	with group
		8. Children	8. Upset by defeat
			9. Jealousy
			10. Negativism
			11. Tattling

	Number of Ratings on Which Each Group Was Superior		
F1F	5	15	33	16
FF2	7	18	36	14
	(12)	(33)	(69)	(30)
F1M	20	3	33	7
MF2	20	0	48	0
	(40)	(3)	(81)	(7)
M1M	9	12	0	41
MM2	12	13	10	33
	(21)	(25)	(10)	(33)
M1F	6	14	12	42
FM2	0	19	23	15
	(6)	(33)	(35)	(57)

Brim adopted the Parsonian distinctions between instrumental task roles (masculine) and expressive, socioemotional roles (feminine). Brim's judges were able to assign 30 of Koch's ratings to either the instrumental or expressive role category on theoretical grounds. "Some of the traits were stated in a negative way which made them, while pertinent to the role, incongruent with the role conception. Thus, 'uncooperativeness with the group' seemed clearly relevant to the expressive role but as an incongruent trait" (p. 7). Role traits were said to be either highly masculine if congruent (aggressiveness) and low masculine if incongruent (dawdling), or highly feminine if congruent (affectionateness), or low feminine if incongruent (anger). Koch's results were scored so that each group was compared with every other group on all 30 traits and scored as superior or inferior on each trait. The sibling group was then assigned a high or low rating on this trait, but only if this group was superior or inferior to all other same-sex groups on this comparison. Table 3.8 adapted from Brim (1958) shows the traits judged as fitting each category and the number of times each sex group was found to be extreme on that category. It is clear that the opposite-sex sibling overlaps the other sex traits to a greater extent than the same-sex siblings. The differences are most noticeable for the girls with male siblings [pp. 27–29].

There are interesting hints in this earlier research that on some occasions the siblings affect each other in ways that are the inverse of their own characteristics rather than consonant with them, an effect that we termed the counteractive sex effect (1970). Thus we discovered that boys with an older sister, when compared with boys with an older brother, more often showed feminine preferences on inventories and interacted more with girls in the classroom. However, boys with two older sisters showed an opposite effect-less preferences for feminine items and less interaction with opposite sex members in the classroom. Furthermore, the Berkeley Longitudinal data showed that the boy with one older sister begins to move towards the norm of masculine interests as he gets older and may in some cases, as in Leventhal's data, show excessive "masculinity" in his college years (1970). In a similar vein, we found that fathers in families with all male children scored higher on femininity scales than fathers who only had daughters.

More recent work on sex role effects has enlarged upon these kinds of inversions of effect between siblings and has discussed the ways in which they "disidentify" with each other. Thus Schachter (this volume) has found that adjacent siblings usually judge themselves as different from each other, though this is more true of the first two siblings in a family than of latter close pairs, and more true of same than of opposite sex siblings. She advances the view that these counteractions are a defense against sibling rivalry, which is more extreme amongst the earlier born and those of the same sex role. Grotevant (1978) has also presented data on sex-role interests that are consonant with those results, particularly for females. He finds that the more sisters in the family, the greater the masculinity of the girls. In addition, in two-child families, boys with older sisters were more masculine than those with younger sisters, and girls with older brothers were more feminine than those with younger sisters. These data so clearly contradict earlier findings that they require some attention. The differences might lie in the different measuring instruments used (Schachter), the use of actual siblings rather than sibling positions (Grotevant), or in the use of older rather than child subjects (Schachter and Grotevant). What might be implied, however, is some dialectical and diachronic process whereby older siblings reinforce their own characteristics in younger siblings (as in Koch's six-year-old subjects), which is responded to by negative identification as the years go by, leading to the kind of disidentification that Schachter finds in college-aged subjects. Such age changes in sibling characteristics have been found in the longitudinal literature, as Rosenberg shows in his chapter of this volume. Alternatively, the counteraction discovered by Schachter and Grotevant might be prefigured in variables other than sex role at the earlier age. For example, although at six years of age it might be difficult for children to tamper with sex role stereotypes, even at those earlier years, they can show differences in their power struggles and power tactics. They can already struggle against the dominance of their older siblings. As Bragg, Ostrowski, & Finley (1973) have shown, the age of one's target, not the birth order as such, is the critical variable in power struggles. In sum, there is the possibility of reconciling these findings in terms of age differences and in terms of the kinds of personality variables being studied.

The most important way in which recent studies of sibling status effects have improved upon earlier work, however, is through the use of direct experimental or observational studies of actual sibling relationships. Thus in a series of experimental studies, Cicirelli has shown the impact of older siblings when they act as teachers of their younger siblings (1972, 1973, 1975, 1978). Older female siblings are usually more effective than older male siblings and, like the males, they do better with wider age spacing. They do better with their siblings, whereas the males do better with strangers. (See the chapter by Bryant in this volume). Cicirelli concludes, as has Zajonc, that sibling interaction is an independent source of variance in child development.

Again, other recent studies have been of an observational nature and have focused on sibling interactions in the first several years of life. These studies, carried out in both laboratory and home settings, have focused on the interaction of preschoolers and their infant siblings in same-sex or mixed-sex dyads with or without the presence of parents nearby. Different rates of aggression, prosocial, imitative, and other behaviors have been derived. As most of this data is summarized in the chapters by Abramovitch, Corter & Pepler; Dunn & Kendrick; and Bryant they will not be reviewed here. Suffice to say that this work for the first time begins to broaden the consideration of child development beyond either parent-child interaction or sibling-sibling interaction alone to the intersection of both of these role sectors. Along with the Confluence Model, therefore, we have for the first time in the study of sibling development very real efforts to take under the same empirical umbrella these multiple interactional characteristics of child growth.

The history of this subject matter, then, shows a shift from its earlier (100-year) dominant concern with first-borns and with parent-first-born relationships alone. This is the period from Galton through Schachter. In this past decade there has been increasing attention to sibling-sibling interactions. More importantly, much significant work has dealt with *real* sibling relationships and interactions (not assumed ones), and has now begun to take up the task of considering the mutual influences of sibling-sibling-parent interactions together. Once again, we doubt whether journal editors should be satisfied with less.

REFERENCES

Abramovitch, R., Corter, C. & Lando, B. Sibling interaction in the home. *Child Development,* 1979, *50*(4), 997–1003.

Abramovitch, R., Corter, C. & Pepler, D. J. Observations of mixed-sex sibling dyads. *Child Development,* 1980, *51*(4), 1268–1271.

Adams, R. L. & Beeman, N. Phillips. Motivational and achievement differences among children of various ordinal birth positions. *Child Development,* 1972, *43,* 155–164.

Altus, W. D. Birth order and its sequelae. *Science,* 1966, *151,* 44–49.

Bayer, A. E. Birth order and attainment of the doctorate: A test of an economic hypothesis. *American Journal of Sociology,* 1967, *72,* 540–550.

Bayley, N. Comparisons of mental and motor test scores for ages 1–15 months by sex, birth order, race, geographical location, and education of parents. *Child Development,* 1965, *36,* 379–411.

Belmont, L. & Marolla, F. A. Birth order, family size and intelligence. *Science,* 1973, *182,* 1096–1101.

Belmont, L., Stein, Z. A. & Zybert, P. Child spacing and birth order: Effect on intellectual ability in two-child families. *Science,* 1978, *202,* 995–996.

Belmont, L., Stein, Z. A. & Wittes, J. T. Birth order, family size and school failure. *Develop. Med. Child Neurol.* 1976, *18,* 421–430.

Berbaum, M. L., & Moreland, R. L. Intellectual development within the family: A new application of the confluence model. *Developmental Psychology,* 1980, *16,* 506–515.

Blane, H. T. & Barry III, H. Birth order and alcoholism. *Quarterly Journal of Studies on Alcohol,* 1973, *34,* 837–852.

Bragg, W. E., Ostrowski, M. V. & Finley, G. E. The effects of birth order and age of target on use of persuasive techniques. *Child Development,* 1973, *44,* 351–354.

Breland, H. M. Birth order and intelligence. Ph.D. Dissertation, State University of New York at Buffalo, 1972 (microfilm, Ann Arbor, 72-27, 238).

Breland, H. M. Birth order effects: a reply to Schooler. *Psychology Bulletin,* 1973, *80,* 210–212.

Breland, H. M. Birth order, family configuration, and mental achievement. *Child Development,* 1974, *45,* 1011–1019.

Brim, O. G. Family structure and sex role learning by children: A further analysis of Helen Koch's data. *Sociometry,* 1958, *21,* 1–16.

Chittenden, E. A., Foan, W., Zweil, D. M. & Smith, J. R. School achievement of first and second born children. *Child Development,* 1968, *39,* 1123–1129.

Cicirelli, V. G. The effect of sibling relationship on concept learning of young children taught by child teachers. *Child Development,* 1972, *43,* 282–287.

Cicirelli, V. G. Effects of sibling structure and interaction on children's categorization style. *Developmental Psychology,* 1973, *9,* 132–139.

Cicirelli, V. G. Siblings teach siblings. In L. V. Allen (Ed.), *Interage interaction in children: Theory and research on the helping relationship.* Madison: University of Wisconsin Press, 1975.

Cicirelli, V. G. Sibling structure and intellectual ability. *Developmental Psychology,* 1976, *12,* 369–370.

Cicirelli, V. G. Effect of sibling presence on mother-child interaction. *Developmental Psychology,* 1978, *14,* 315–316.

Cohen, S. E. & Beckwith, L. Caregiving behaviors and early cognitive development as related to ordinal position in preterm infants. *Child Development,* 1977, *48,* 152–157.

Cushna, B. *Agency and birth order differences in very early childhood.* Paper presented at the meeting of the American Psychological Association, New York, September 1966.

Davis, D., Cahan, S. & Bashi, J. Birth order and intellectual development: the confluence model in the light of cross-cultural evidence. *Science,* 1977, *196,* 1470–1472.

Dunn, J. & Kendrick, C. Interactions between young siblings in the context of family relationships. In M. Lewis & L. Rosenblum (Eds.), *The child and its family: The genesis of behavior* (Vol. 2). New York: Plenum Press, 1979.

Elder, G. H. *Adolescent achievement and mobility aspirations.* Chapel Hill, N.C.: Institute for Research in Social Science, 1962.

Elliot, J. L. & Elliot, D. H. Effects of birth order and age gap on aspiration level. Proceedings of the 78th Annual Convention, American Psychological Association, 1970.

Epstein, G. F. & Bronzaft, A. L. Academic primogeniture revisited. Unpublished manuscript, 1971.

Exner, J. & Sutton-Smith, B. Birth order and hierarchical vs. innovative role requirements. Journal of Personality, 1970, *38,* 581–587.

Falbo, T. Sibling tutoring and other explanations for intelligence discontinues of only and last borns. *Journal of Population,* 1978, *1,* 349–363.

Falbo, T. Only children, achievement and interpersonal orientation. Paper presented at 88th Convention American Psychological Association, Montreal, 1980.

Feiring, C. & Lewis, M. Children, parents and siblings: Possible sources of variation in the behavior of first born and only children. Symposium Paper, American Psychological Association, Montreal, September 1980.

Galton, F. *English men of science: Their nature and nurture.* London: MacMillan, 1874.

Gewirtz, J. L. & Gewirtz, H. B. Stimulus conditions, infant behaviors and social learning in four Israeli child rearing environments: In B. M. Foss (Ed.) *Determinants of Infant Behavior* III, London, Methuen, 1965, 161–184.

Glass, D. C., Neulinger, J. & Brian, O. G. Birth order, verbal intelligence and educational aspiration. *Child Development,* 1974, *45,* 807–811.

Grotevant, H. D. Sibling constellations and sex typing of interests in adolescents. *Child Development,* 1978, *49,* 540–542.

Grotevant, H. D., Scarr, S. & Weinberg, R. A. Intellectual development in family constellations with adopted and natural children. *Child Development,* 1977, *48,* 1699–1703.

Hilton, I. Differences in the behavior of mothers toward first and later born children. *Journal of Personality and Social Psychology,* 1967, *7,* 282–290.

Jacobs, B. S. & Moss, H. A. Birth order and sex of siblings as determinants of mother-infant interaction. *Child Development,* 1976, *47,* 315–322.

Jones, H. E. Order of birth in relation to the development of the child. In C. Murchison (Ed.), *A handbook of child psychology.* Worcester, Mass.: Clark University Press, 1933.

Koch, H. L. The relation of "primary mental abilities" in five- and six-year-olds to sex of child and characteristics of his sibling. *Child Development,* 1954, *25,* 209–223.

Koch, H. L. The relation of certain family constellation characteristics and the attitudes of children toward adults. *Child Development,* 1955, *26,* 13–40. (a)

Koch, H. L. Some personality correlates of sex, sibling position, and sex of sibling among five and six year old children. *Genetic Psychological Monographs,* 1955, *52,* 3–50. (b)

Koch, H. L. Attitudes of young children toward their peers as related to certain characteristics of their siblings. *Psychological Monographs,* 1956, *70* (Whole No. 425). (e)

Koch, H. L. Children's work attitudes and sibling characteristics. *Child Development*, 1956, *27*, 289–310. (b)

Koch, H. L. Sibling influence on children's speech. *Journal of Speech Disorders*, 1956, *21*, 322–328. (c)

Koch, H. L. Sissiness and tomboyishness in relation to sibling characteristics. *Journal of Genetic Psychology*, 1956, *88*, 231–244. (d)

Koch, H. L. Some emotional attitudes of the young child in relation to characteristics of his sibling. *Child Development*, 1956, *27*, 393–426. (e)

Koch, H. L. The relation in young children between characteristics of their playmates and certain attributes of their siblings. *Child Development*, 1957, *28*, 175–202.

Koch, H. L. The influence of siblings on the personality development of younger boys. *Journal of Psychology and Psychotherapy*, 1958, *5*, 211–225.

Konig, K. *Brothers and sisters: A study in child psychology.* New York: St. George Books, Blauvelt, 1963.

Lamb, M. E. Interactions between eighteen-month-olds and preschool-aged siblings. *Child Development*, 1978, *49*(1), 51–59.

Lamb, M. E. The Development of sibling relationships in infancy: A short-term longitudinal study. *Child Development*, 1978, *49*(4), 1189–1197(b).

Lasko, J. K. Parent behavior towards first and second children. *Genetic Psychological Monographs*, 1954, *49*, 96–137.

Leventhal, G. S. Influence of brothers and sisters on sex role behavior. *Journal of Personality and Social Psychology*, 1970, *16*, 452–465.

McCall, J. N. The relation of family size, birth order, and socioeconomic status to the abilities of high school students. Final Report Project No. O-E-022. Southern Illinois University at Edwardsville, U.S. Department of Health, Education, and Welfare, 1971.

Markus, G. B. & Zajonc, R. B. Family configuration and intellectual development: a simulation. *Behavioral Science*, 1977, *22*, 137–142.

Murphy, L. B., Murphy, G. & Newcomb, T. *Experimental social psychology.* New York: Harper and Brothers, 1937, 348–363.

Nuttall, R. L. & Nuttall, E. V. *Family size and spacing in the USA and Puerto Rico.* Final Report, National Institute of Child Health and Human Development, 1975, 72–2033.

Oberlander, M. & Jenkins, N. Birth order and academic achievement. *Journal of Individual Psychology*, 1967, *23*, 103–109.

Pierce, J. V. *The educational motivation of superior children who do and do not achieve in high school.* Washington, D.C.: U.S. Office of Education, Department of Health, Education, and Welfare, November 1959.

Rosen, B. C. Family structure and achievement motivation. *American Sociological Review*, 1961, *26*, 574–585.

Rosen, B. C. Family structure and value transmission. *Merrill-Palmer Quarterly*, 1964, *10*, 59–76.

Rothbart, M. L. K. Birth order and mother child interaction. Dissertation, Stanford Univ. 1967. Microfilms #67-7961, Ann Arbor, Mich.

Samuels, H. R. The effect of an older sibling on infant locomotive exploration of a new environment. *Child Development*, 1980, *51*(2), 607–609.

Sampson, E. E. The study of ordinal position: Antecedents and outcomes. In B. Maher (Ed.), *Progress in experimental personality research.* New York: Academic Press, 1965.

Schachter, S. *The psychology of affiliation.* Stanford, Calif.: Stanford University Press, 1959.

Schachter, S. Birth order, eminence and higher education. *American Sociological Review*, 1963, *28*, 757–767.

Schooler, C. Birth order effects: Not here, not now. *Psychological Bulletin*, 1972, *78*, 161–175.

Solomon, G., & Solomon, H. C. Factors affecting motor performances in four-month-old infants. *Child Development*, 1964, *35*, 1283–1296.

Strodtbeck, F. L., & Creelan, P. Interaction, linkage between family size, intelligence, and sex role identity. *Journal of Marriage and Family,* 1968, *30,* 301-307.

Sutton-Smith, B., & Rosenberg, B. G. *The sibling.* New York: Holt, Rinehart and Winston, 1970.

Svanum, S. & Bringle, R. G. Evaluation of confluence model variables on I.Q. and achievement test scores in a sample of 6 to 11 year old children. *Journal of Educational Psychology,* 1980, *72,* 427-436.

Thomas, E. B., Leiderman, P. H. & Olson, J. P. Neonate-motives interaction during breast feeding. *Developmental Psychology,* 1972, *6,* 110-118.

Warren, J. R. Birth order and social behavior. *Psychological Bulletin,* 1966, *65,* 38-49.

Weiss, J. H. Birth order and physiological stress response. *Child Development,* 1970, *41,* 461-470.

Zajonc, R. B. & Markus, G. B. Birth order and intellectual development. *Psychological Review,* 1975, *82,* 74-88.

Zajonc, R. B. Dumber by the dozen. *Psychology Today,* 1975, *8,* 37-43.

Zajonc, R. B. Family configuration and intelligence. *Science,* 1976, *192,* 227-236.

Zajonc, R. B., Markus, H. & Markus, G. B. The birth order puzzle. *Journal of Personality and Social Psychology,* 1979, *37,* 1325-1341.

Zajonc, R. B. & Bargh, J. Birth order, family size and decline in SAT scores. *American Psychologist,* 1980, *35,* 662-668. (a)

Zajonc, R. B. & Bargh, J. The confluence model: parameter estimation for six divergent data sets on family factors and intelligence. *Intelligence,* 1980, *4,* 349-361. (b)

8

Life Span Personality Stability in Sibling Status

B. G. Rosenberg
Antioch University
Institute of Human Development
University of California, Berkeley

One of the most formidable "givens" in the study of human development is the impact of the formative years on all subsequent development. The notions of dependency and malleability in the young have appeared so self-evident that every major theory of man in modern times has accepted them as premises. As a result, the outcomes in human development continue to appear understandable in social learning terms. For example, Sears, Maccoby and Levin (1957) showed that the dispensing of rewards and punishments (reinforcement contingencies) by a caretaker (adult) presumably resulted in predictable outcomes. Knowingly or otherwise, this model employed the psychoanalytic concept of the family as a four-person group, critical in socialization, varied only by generation and sex (Parsons, 1964). Suffice it to say in retrospect that Freud's (1949) categories, the basis for a supposedly dynamic analysis, may be seen today as highly subjective products of the time, rather than parts of a truly dynamic theory. Freud's approach has been called infant-determinism, in which most major life outcomes presumably are preset in the early formative years through the shaping influence of the parent.

Recent research and theoretical innovations have expanded the boundaries and suggested the limitations of this model. Neonatal research (Lipsitt, 1976; Korner, 1971) suggests the active role played by inherited biological factors in the disposition and capacity to respond to contingencies. Again, what might be called reciprocal action models (Bell, 1968; Lewis & Rosenblum, 1974; Moss, 1967; Price, 1977; Rosenberg & Sutton-Smith, 1968) invalidate the view that socialization is one way, as postulated by earlier learning theories. Proponents of reciprocal action models argue instead for reciprocals and mutual shaping. Finally, the cognitive-developmental approach (Kohlberg, 1966, 1969) provided evidence of active participation (self-selection) in acquisitions on the part of the heretofore presumably passive child.

Such events did not provide the death knell for the infant deterministic thesis so much as they suggested its limitations. Implicit in these formulations and outcomes were two central changes: univariate to multivariate analysis, and isolated to contextual models. The first emphasizes the multiplicity of sources accounting for socialization; the latter places great import on analysis in the context of interaction during socialization. Grudgingly, we moved closer to a representative design (Brunswik, 1956) in psychological theory and research.

In summary, then, the infant deterministic model that has occupied such a firm niche in most Western theories argues that the early, formative years preset the organism in many ways for the remainder of its life. The present approach argues for the continuing capacity for change and modification throughout the developmental span of the individual and allocates theoretical space for the continuing influence of a sibling and other encounters well beyond the usual period of parental impact and presumed fixity of many psychological processes. Such concepts are embraced in the theories of Erikson (1950, 1959), Brim and Kagan (1980), Havighurst (1973), Neugarten (1968), and others. Human beings, notwithstanding the importance of early, formative experiences, remain, in measure, an open system, capable of modifications and transformations throughout life. As Mussen, Eichorn, Honzik, Becker, and Meridith (1980) suggest: "... it seems reasonable to hypothesize that some characteristics are more stable over time and situations than others [p. 333]." The assumption seriously questions a model predicated on parental impacts alone as the major or only influence in development. It further assigns to the individual the capability of varying behavior as a result of continuing influence, justifying the use of a contextual model over time. In effect, we are arguing for change rather than constancy (Kagan, 1978; Mischel, 1969) as the generative condition in humans over the life span.

How, then, do such methodological and theoretical changes benefit our understanding? One major breakthrough is in the attempt to systematically dimensionalize the family as an instrument of socialization (Aldous, 1977; Koch, 1955; Lewis & Rosenblum, 1974; Nye & Berardo, 1973; Sutton-Smith & Rosenberg, 1970; Tesser, 1980). If the nuclear family has the utility and relevance assigned to it, what configuration of factors regarding the family can be studied with a degree of precision? And what has finally catalyzed our willingness for such an undertaking? Certainly, the innovations we have presented (multivariate, contextual, reciprocal, open-system) have made such an attempt more probable. Adler (1959) further acknowledged aspects of the family (sibling rivalry) to account for passions and conflicts in the family disposing to personologic outcomes. In addition, though a century has passed since Galton (1874) piqued interest with a predictive outcome associated with a family parameter (primogeniture/borness), recent emphases in psychiatry on therapy with families of schizophrenics (Speck, 1967) and on the sociology of the family

(Bossard & Boll, 1955, 1956; Toman, 1976) have had an effect. During the last decade or so, systematic study of the entire family as a representative model of socialization has been undertaken.

As more recent investigations of the family have shifted from a focus on the parent effects, in particular the mother, who was assumed to have greater impact on the young due to time and proximity (Belsky, 1981), to the manner in which children interact and affect one another, a host of outcomes have suggested new structures and dynamics associated with the family that were not previously conceptualized. Interestingly, some of the questions raised by the data suggest equal weight to parents and children in some aspects of socialization (Landy, Rosenberg & Sutton-Smith, 1969; Sutton-Smith, Rosenberg, & Landy, 1968), a suggestion considered heretical not too many years ago.

As a result of the foregoing, a proliferation of studies of children's impact on children and parents has appeared in the scientific literature (cf., Sutton-Smith & Rosenberg, 1970). Significant inroads into the body politic of the family, the context in which learning does occur, have been made. Where ordinal position was formerly viewed as a sufficient variable to account for outcomes in personality (Jones, 1931), study has revealed that even a modest outcome prediction from the family matrix must involve consideration of the covariation in ordinal position, sex of the subject, sex of sibling, age spacing, and family size in order to increase the precision in prediction and understanding of complicated outcomes (cf., Koch, 1954, 1955, 1960; Sutton-Smith, Roberts, & Rosenberg, 1964). As a result, the literature reveals a host of psychological dispositions and behaviors (social, emotional, intellectual, and personologic) that are now better understood, such as achievement motive, conscience development, sex role identity and its acquisition, cognitive abilities, role-taking behavior, creativity, and socialization effectiveness. The theoretical thrust has been to uncover in some systematic way the elements of family structure and interaction that provide the primary influence in early socialization; to take into account the context in which these elements occur; and to understand outcomes in the developing organism.

Children learn from children as surely as they learn from parents. In addition, parents are not insulated from learning from their own children, thus altering the nature of the configuration of contingencies they intentionally provide as models. Such reciprocal, contextual approaches do decrease the variance in those phenomena (socialization) we would understand. Importantly, such learning continues well beyond childhood for all members of the nuclear family, such that sustained associations (e.g., life long sibling relationships) continue to influence the individual throughout long periods of the life span (Cicirelli, 1979). And finally, we reaffirm the active participation that must be accorded all learners—that is, their selective responses to stimuli based on biological-genetic factors; inborn dispositions; and learned dispositions to respond (Kohlberg, 1966).

For purposes of the present chapter, then, the model for analysis of the family comes from the following theoretical perspectives: Learning occurs in the matrix of reciprocal interaction; learning is contextual; and learning continues well beyond the early formative years, with the subject actively selecting, in part, what will be learned that is appropriate to its status.

(As an aside, Brim and Kagan (1980) may be correct in their interesting arguments regarding the possible limits of the scientific model embraced by our culture in which antecedent-consequent chains presumably explain what heretofore has been inexplicable. Such "explanations," under the aegis of developmental transformations or epigenesis, never have been totally palatable. Nevertheless, one might suggest that the pursuit of variance sources in a contextual model that was previously ignored and poorly understood may well provide some renewed faith in the utility of the scientific model that has prevailed.)

Objectivity rather than modesty prompts us to acknowledge the multiplicity of variance sources and their differing levels of impact in the family. We also acknowledge that our set of structural factors (ordinal position, sex of subject, sex of sibling, age spacing, family size) only begin to offer full explanations. Thus, for example, numerous variations in intellectual and personological qualities of parents and children that are causal and critical are not taken into account by the present methodology. Notwithstanding these limitations, predictive outcomes are rather impressive.

Much of the remainder of this chapter is devoted to a life span evaluation of sibling impacts. It seems reasonable to assume that differential effects of such associations, with all their importance, will occur over time in definable areas of human psychological make up (Sutton-Smith & Rosenberg, 1970).

THE STUDY

In a body of some 800 studies of ordinal position and sibling sex status influences, none has addressed itself to the same sibling subjects throughout the life span. None discuss the changing influences of borness, sex, sex of sibling, age spacing, and family size in terms of developmental status. The present study examines the personologic concomitants of change in sibling influences from early adolescence through middle age. It is assumed that the results reported here will provide some means of determining the validity to be assigned the multitude of studies of sibling association impacts gathered through cross-sectional methods (cf., summary in Sutton-Smith & Rosenberg, 1970; Sampson, 1965). The results, in addition, will provide some evidence regarding personality stability and changes in sibling status with the same subjects over long periods of time.

Subjects and Procedures

The subjects comprising the sample were 33 male and 34 female members of the one- and two-child families in the Oakland Growth and Berkeley Guidance studies at the Institute of Human Development, University of California, Berkeley. The studies, initiated in the 1920s and still going on (Macfarlane, 1938; Jones, Bayley, Macfarlane, & Honzik, 1971; Block, 1971), provide a remarkable array of physical, social, and psychological measures on the same subjects over the course of a lifetime. With such a vast array of data, the present results focus on an examination of Q-sort data obtained on the same sibling subjects at early adolescence (A), late adolescence (B), early adulthood (C), and middle adulthood (D). Two independent clinical assessors employed at each stage for each subject had available the subject and all the data (measures, interviews, etc.) for that subject at the point in time in which the Q-sort was used (Block, 1961; 1971). Correlational analyses of the overall configurations and individual items over the four time periods by subject and by group were conducted.

A word of caution: Extensive use of the Q-sort at the Institute of Human Development yielded 90 common items over the life span that were usable. Of those 90, only 67 were found to be sufficiently reliable to be employed in analysis of the study. In addition, the rate of attrition in longitudinal ventures tends to be high; thus, caution should be observed in interpreting the results of some single sibling categories.

Results

Table 1 addresses the question of personality stability over time. It presents the correlations of Q-sort profiles at early adolescence (A), late adolescence (B), early adulthood (C), and middle adulthood (D) by sibling status group, borness, and same-sex and opposite-sex siblings. This does not reflect personality attribution, merely consistency of those qualities differentially assigned over the four life periods.

Personality Profiles Over Time

As is evident from Table 1:

(1) Greatest consistency in personality for all groups obtains for early and late adolescence (AB); then early and middle adulthood (CD). Least consistency obtains for late adolescence and early adulthood (BC).

(2) Generally, only-child males show greater personality stability over time than males with siblings.

(3) Though *sex differences* do not coincide with other significant differences, females appear to be somewhat more consistent at BC than males.

(4) Regarding the question of sibling *presence-absence* and *borness*, there is a tendency for first-born males (with or without siblings) to be more stable in profile than second-borns at adolescence (AB).

There are no significant differences between onlies and second-born males at BC or CD, both showing more stable profiles than first-born males with siblings.

TABLE 8.1
Q-sorts Over Time: Four Periods, Sibling Groups.
Correlation Coefficients of Q-sort Profiles for Borness and Sex

Group	N	AB	AC	AD	BC	BD	CD
M	9	.54	.35	.37	.47	.41	.62
SEX							
M1M	5	.60	.16	.13	.04	.10	.43
MM2	4	.43	.23	.45	.42	.31	.46
M1F	9	.60	.27	.34	.33	.34	.31
FM2	6	.56	.31	.37	.43	.39	.56
BORNESS							
M1M	5	.60	.16	.13	.04	.10	.43
M1F	9	.60	.27	.34	.33	.34	.30
MM2	4	.43	.23	.45	.42	.31	.46
FM2	6	.56	.31	.37	.43	.39	.56
F	12	.60	.54	.31	.47	.24	.44
SEX							
F1F	6	.58	.37	.29	.37	.26	.45
FF2	3	.51	.28	.15	.17	.37	.51
F1M	3	.64	.60	.45	.68	.52	.65
MF2	10	.57	.41	.32	.33	.30	.49
BORNESS							
F1F	6	.58	.37	.29	.37	.26	.46
F1M	3	.64	.60	.45	.68	.52	.65
FF2	3	.51	.28	.15	.17	.37	.51
MF2	10	.57	.41	.32	.33	.30	.49

Regarding the influence of sex of sibling, the presence or absence of a sibling regardless of sex appears not to influence personality stability at AB; like-sex dyads are the least stable profiles at BC; and onlies are more stable than males with siblings at CD. In summary, for males, no significant differences obtain at adolescence (AB), but first-borns are significantly less stable in personality profile at BC and CD. Again, for sex of sibling, onlies tend to be more stable across life span in contrast to males with brothers, who are the least stable in late adolescence-early adulthood (BC).

For females, there are no significant differences for sibling-nonsibling at AB; at BC, second-born females show the least stable profiles; and finally, there are no differences for sibling presence-absence at CD. Interestingly, like-sex dyads are the least stable at BC, a result that parallels that obtained with males.

From this preliminary analysis of personality stability in sibling statuses, onlies appear to be more stable throughout the life span than those subjects with siblings; secondly, like-sex dyads appear to be less stable for both sexes at late adolescence-early adulthood. One might wonder after reviewing the demonstrated relevance of siblings and their particular sex in early life why a like-sex sibling appears to be associated with disadvantage in late adolescence and early adulthood. It is possible we see here magnified the advantage posed by the presence of an opposite-sex sibling (cf., Koch, 1954; Sutton-Smith, Roberts, and Rosenberg, 1964) in role-modeling and role-taking in adulthood, when the awareness of the role of the significant other involves an awareness or understanding of both sex roles rather than the excessive emphasis on the appropriate acquisition of one's own sex role in childhood and early adolescence.

Item Stability Over Time

In addition to correlations of personality profiles over time, another aspect of personality stability may be seen in the numbers of individual items as they correlate over time. The question asked, then, is: How many individual items receive similar ratings for the same subject over time? Table 2 presents the results of an analysis of *item-stability* assigned by two independent raters over time. All items included showed a correlation coefficient significant at the $P = .05$ or less in order to be included. Thus, for example, if the item "dependable" correlated $+.68$ for the M1M (first-born boy with younger brother) sibling group at AB, this indicated that "dependable" was assigned a similar rating for members of the M1M sample at A and later again at B. Such a finding does not address the question of personality characterization, only the consistency of such assignation over time (whether high or low).

Judging from the results of Table 2, for males, greater personality consistency occurs during adolescence. For females, the results are more equivocal, with a tendency for personality stability to be greater at adolescence. It is clear that only boys and only girls manifest greater stability in personality than boys and girls with siblings. First-born males with siblings are more consistent than second-

TABLE 8.2
Number of Stable Q-sort Items (P=.05) Over Three Periods
Ordinal and LS/OS

Period	M_9	$M1_{14}$	$M2_{10}$	MM_9	MF_{15}	$\bar{x}$
AB	28	39	24	31	32	18
BC	20	14	15	13	16	10
CD	31	15	16	12	19	12
	26	23	18	19	22	

Period	F_{12}	FI_9	$F2_{13}$	FF_9	FM_{13}	$\bar{x}$
AB	35	21	29	20	30	17
BC	24	20	15	16	19	12
CD	10	29	32	22	39	14
	23	23	25	19	29	

born males with siblings. There is a tendency for males with sisters to be more consistent than males with brothers. For females, girls with brothers tend to greater profile stability than girls with sisters.

Sibling Statuses, Personality Ascription, and Time

The focus of this study addresses itself to the personologic characteristics of the various sibling groups over time. One analysis examines the apparent changes of sibling status over time; another, how sibling statuses compare with one another at each of the four life stages. This analysis may strike the reader as laborious, comparing each sibship with all others at each of four life periods and, in addition, with itself over four life periods, but it is necessary in order to answer the questions we posed.

Tables 3 through 10 present the results based on personality ascription (scores of 7, 8, 9 on a nine-point scale) for each subject. If, in fact, the majority of the sibling group was so characterized, the item was deemed to be characteristic of that sibling grouping. Thus, for example, the majority (7 to 9) members of the only males (M) were assigned the item "productive" by both raters in the "certainty" categories 7, 8, 9 on the nine-point scale of the Q-sort. In general, we will examine borness and sibling sex effects.

Males: Adolescence. As can be seen in Table 3, first-borns are characterized as high in intellectual capacity; as being masculine, gregarious, fantasizing, and repressive, a characterization in concert with much prior literature (cf., Sutton-Smith & Rosenberg, 1970). In turn, second-borns appear intelligent (whether they are or not) and aloof. Interestingly, at this stage, boys with sisters and only boys (noted for a larger feminine component in sex role identity) are both viewed as dependable, thin skinned, valuing intellectual matters, ambitious, etc. The characterization "overcontrolled" might well be the result of the interaction of first-borness and feminine influence. Certainly this limited evidence suggests a profound personologic impact of sister presence at adolescence. Again worthy of note, only males and first-born males with brothers are alike in fantasizing, concern with appearance, bodily concerns, and repressive tendencies, suggesting some of the negative pressures associated with being a first-born male.

Late Adolescence. From Table 4 we see a confirmation years later of the cohering personality characteristics noted earlier: First-borns are characterized as having high intellectual capacity, valuing independence, being masculine, and exhibiting repressive tendencies, whereas second-borns are intelligent-appearing. Most interesting, it would appear, are the sex effects at this stage. Now somewhat confirmed in their life-long characteristics, boys with sisters are alike in reflecting that association: Concerned with appearance, dependable, productive, valuing intellectual matters, overcontrolled, and ambitious. It may well be that ambitious and productive are *reactive* rather than *assimilative* qualities of feminine influence (Sutton-Smith & Rosenberg, 1969; Brim, 1958).

TABLE 8.3
Q-sort: 7, 8, 9 Group Ascriptions Over Time
Early Adolescence

M_9	$M1M_5$	$M1F_9$	$MM2_4$	$FM2_6$
dependable		dependable		dependable
		hi intellectual capacity	appears intelligent	appears intelligent
	hi intellectual capacity			
masculine	masculine	masculine		
productive		productive		
			aloof	aloof
gregarious	gregarious			
ambitious				ambitious
values intellectual matters				values intellectual matters
overcontrolled		overcontrolled		
		thin skinned		thin skinned
fantasizing	fantasizing			
concerned with appearance	concerned with appearance			
has bodily concerns	has bodily concerns			
repressive	repressive			
	self defensive			
values independence		verbally fluent		feels guilty
arouses liking		talkative		rapid tempo
straightforward		compares self with others		proffers advice
cheerful				
		calm		
		poised		

175

TABLE 8.4
Q-sort: 7, 8, 9 Group Ascriptions Over Time
Late Adolescence

M_9	$M1M_5$	$M1F_9$	$MM2_4$	$FM2_6$
				concerned with appearance
hi intellectual capacity	hi intellectual capacity	hi intellectual capacity		
values independence	values independence	values independence		
repressive	repressive		repressive	
	concerned with appearance	concerned with appearance		
masculine		masculine		
gregarious		gregarious		
responds to humor	responds to humor			dependable
		dependable		productive
		productive		values intellectual matters
		values intellectual matters		ambitious
		ambitious		
gregarious		gregarious		
			appears intelligent	appears intelligent
	has bodily concerns			has bodily concerns
		overcontrolled		overcontrolled
	communicates nonverbally	straightforward		verbally fluent
		arouses liking		feels guilty
		sympathetic		fantasizing
power oriented		assertive		compares self with others
prides self on objectivity		cheerful		
skeptical				
talkative				
self-indulgent				

TABLE 8.5
Q-sort: 7, 8, 9 Group Ascriptions Over Time
Early Adulthood

M_9	$M1M_5$	$M1F_9$	$MM2_4$	$FM2_6$
dependable		dependable		dependable
productive			productive	productive
concerned with adequacy	concerned with adequacy	concerned with adequacy	verbally fluent	
		verbally fluent		verbally fluent
values independence				values independence
ambitious				ambitious
values intellectual matters				values intellectual matters
overcontrolled				overcontrolled
poised				poised
other-directed	repressive	other-directed	distrustful	appears intelligent
power-oriented	giving	self-defensive		conservative
hi intellectual capacity	thin skinned	feels guilty		ethically consistent
status quo	basically anxious			straightforward
basic hostility				fastidious
				arouses liking

177

Early Adulthood. Table 5 demonstrates that adulthood predictably brings a diminution in the relevance of sibling effect variables (borness and sex of sibling). Except for only males (M) and second-born males with older sisters (FM2), the other three male sibling statuses show less conspicuous similarities based on variables relevant to sibling sex status. First-borns tend to be concerned with adequacy, whereas second-born males are productive and verbally fluent, but generally the similarities are, at best, meager. Sex of sibling appears somewhat relevant, with boys with sisters or less masculine sex role identity (onlies) assigned dependable. Most interesting are the similarities in only males and younger males with older sisters (FM2), described as valuing independence, ambitious, valuing intellectual matters, overcontrolled, and poised. These categories reflect, we believe, assimilative (Brim, 1958) or reactive (Sutton-Smith & Rosenberg, 1969) qualities due to sibling absence or female presence.

Middle Adulthood. As can be seen from Table 6, general characteristics of the adult male role rather than those unique to sibling status tend to predominate: productive; values independence; dependable; ambitious. There is little illumination of the impact of one's borness or sex of one's sibling. A case might be made for the sister-effect resulting in "prides self on objectivity" and "ethically consistent," but the data, after all, is a bit modest.

Females: Adolescence. In Table 7 we see characterization of the female role appearing to override sibling differences. Thus, feminine, fastidious, concerned with appearance, and dependable are characteristics of the traditional female sex role for which coercive pressures occur in sex role acquisition at adolescence, not female sibling categories. Probably one of the most interesting outcomes is the impact of brother-presence on sisters. Such subjects are described as feminine, fastidious, repressive, poised, and productive. Borness seems not to be a paramount factor. The end result of the pressures of reactive modeling appear focused and clear.

Late Adolescence. At this point, Table 8 reveals that first-born females tend to be concerned with appearance; they appear intelligent; they conform to adult standards, are power oriented, fastidious, and compare themselves to others. Females with brothers show qualities of gregariousness and dependability. They also are overcontrolled, and they arouse liking. It is as though the presence of a brother, older or younger, disposes a girl to emphasize traditional female sex role characteristics rather profoundly.

Early Adulthood. Again, as we saw with males, adulthood obscures sibling status similarities and differences (see Table 5). First-born females are characterized as arousing liking, productive, fastidious, seeking reassurance (shades of Stanley Schachter, 1959), whereas second-born females are hostile, concerned

TABLE 8.6
Q-sort: 7, 8, 9 Group Ascriptions Over Time
Middle Adulthood

M_9	MIM_5	MIF_9	$MM2_4$	$FM2_6$
productive	productive	productive	productive	productive
values independence	values independence		values independence	values independence
dependable		dependable	dependable	dependable
ambitious			ambitious	ambitious
values intellectual matters		values intellectual matters	values intellectual matters	
prides self on objectivity		prides self on objectivity		prides self on objectivity
masculine	masculine			
giving	giving			
assertive	assertive			
satisfied with self		satisfied with self		
straightforward				straightforward
other-directed			other-directed	
power oriented	gregarious			ethically consistent
hi intellectual capacity	wide interests	ethically consistent		verbally fluent
status quo	initiates humor	talkative	has bodily concerns	conservative
aloof		philosophically concerned		uncomfortable with uncertainty

179

TABLE 8.7
Q-sort: 7, 8, 9 Group Ascriptions Over Time
Early Adolescence

F_{12}	FIF_6	FIM_3	$FF2_3$	$MF2_{10}$
feminine	feminine	feminine		feminine
fastidious	fastidious	fastidious		fastidious
concerned with appearance	concerned with appearance		concerned with appearance	concerned with appearance
	dependable	dependable	dependable	dependable
gregarious	gregarious			gregarious
conforms to adult standards	conforms to adult standards			conforms to adult standards
repressive		repressive		repressive
poised		poised		poised
productive		productive		productive
	appears intelligent	appears intelligent		appears intelligent
	overcontrolled	overcontrolled	overcontrolled	
talkative			talkative	
	arouses liking			arouses liking
		sympathetic		sympathetic
		protective		verbally fluent
self indulgent	compares self to others	giving		cheerful
interested in opposite sex		feels guilty	values independence	status quo
	physically attractive		skeptical	uncomfortable with uncertainty
fantasizing				emotionally involved with same sex

TABLE 8.8
Q-sort: 7, 8, 9 Group Ascriptions Over Time
Late Adolescence

$F1_2$	$F1F_6$	$F1M_3$	$FF2_3$	$MF2_{10}$
gregarious	gregarious	gregarious	gregarious	gregarious
repressive	repressive		repressive	repressive
feminine	feminine		feminine	
concerned with appearance	concerned with appearance	concerned with appearance		
thin skinned	thin skinned			thin skinned
	appears intelligent	appears intelligent		appears intelligent
conforms to adult standards	conforms to adult standards			
power-oriented	power-oriented			
emotionally involved with same sex	emotionally involved with same sex			
moralistic			moralistic	
talkative			talkative	
	fastidious	fastidious		interested in opposite sex
	interested in opposite sex	dependable		dependable
		overcontrolled		overcontrolled
		arouses liking		arouses liking
compares self to others	compares self to others	submissive	cheerful	productive
self-indulgent	poised	has bodily concerns	undercontrolled	feels guilty
extropunitive	fantasizing	dependent	bothered by demands	
self-dramatizing	uncomfortable with uncertainty			
projective				

TABLE 8.9
Q-sort: 7, 8, 9 Group Ascriptions Over Time
Early Adulthood

$F1_2$	$F1F_6$	$F1M_3$	$FF2_3$	$MF2_{10}$
feels guilty	dependable	dependable	dependable	dependable
arouses liking	feels guilty			feels guilty
productive	arouses liking	productive		
fastidious		fastidious		
seeks reassurance	seeks reassurance			
repressive				repressive
poised				poised
somatizes				somatizes
	basically anxious			basically anxious
		overcontrolled	overcontrolled	
		verbally fluent		verbally fluent
			concerned with adequacy	concerned with adequacy
			introspective	introspective
			basic hostility	basic hostility
gregarious	submissive	ethically consistent	values independence	sympathetic
power-oriented	expressive	ambitious	assertive	giving
has bodily concerns		conservative	fearful	
cheerful			values intellectual matters	
			compares self to others	

with adequacy, and introspective. Borness effects are not salient. Interestingly, only females (F) are the exception. Their male counterparts are described as ''dependable'' at early adolescence and early adulthood, a finding to be dealt with later.

Middle Adulthood. Table 10 finally provides evidence that first-born females are feminine, sympathetic, poised; they arouse liking; they are protective, warm, straightforward, giving, socially perceptive—certainly more traditional sex role attributes than sibling effects. Girls with brothers differ from girls with sisters in being protective, and dependable. They also evaluate the motives of others. Notably, second-born girls continue (through early and middle adulthood) to be concerned with adequacy and assertiveness, suggesting some long-term sibling threads from their less powerful position throughout childhood and adolescence.

Sibling Statuses: Life Span Changes

Tables 11 through 15 present the personality ascriptions over time by individual sibling category. The question addressed in this analysis refers to how the individual sibling category alters with time: What are the consistencies? What are the changes?

Males: M (Only Males). From Table 11, only males present a core characterization over the life span such as valuing independence; being dependable, masculine, productive, and ambitious; valuing intellectual matters; being power oriented; and possessing high intellectual capacity—a rather remarkable consistency. In adolescence they are overcontrolled, gregarious, repressive, and straightforward. In adulthood, additionally, they are characterized as status quo, other-directed, and priding themselves on objectivity. Interestingly, the lower portion of Table 11 provides some idea of how only males differ over time. From a fantasizing, inner concern (repressive, has bodily concerns) at adolescence, we see the emergence of skepticism and self-indulgence in late adolescence. This, then, potentiates in basic hostility and concern with adequacy in early adulthood, and is followed in middle adulthood by aloofness and assertiveness.

MIM. From Table 12, first-born boys with younger brothers tend to be most homogeneous as a group during adolescence. Interestingly, they are characterized as repressive, possessed of high intellectual capacity, concerned with appearance, having bodily concerns, and somewhat masculine and gregarious. (Note the somewhat negative cast to the descriptions.) Fewer consistencies across time obtain. For example, where they are characterized as repressive and having bodily concerns, a thread of anxiety appears to pervade the life span qualities: defensive at early adolescence; thin skinned; anxious; and concerned with adequacy at early adulthood. In contrast to their peers with siblings, they

TABLE 8.10
Q-sort: 7, 8, 9 Group Ascriptions Over Time
Middle Adulthood

$F1_2$	FIF_6	FIM_3	$FF2_3$	$MF2_{10}$
productive	productive	productive	productive	productive
cheerful	cheerful	cheerful	cheerful	
ethically consistent	ethically consistent	ethically consistent		ethically consistent
sympathetic	sympathetic	sympathetic		sympathetic
feminine	feminine	feminine		
poised	poised	poised		
arouses liking	arouses liking	arouses liking		
protective		protective		protective
warm	warm	warm		
straightforward	straightforward	straightforward		
dependable		dependable		dependable
	giving	giving		giving
	evaluates others' motives	evaluates others' motives		evaluates others' motives
	concerned with adequacy		concerned with adequacy	concerned with adequacy
fastidious	fastidious			
talkative			talkative	
rapid tempo			rapid tempo	
	wide interests	wide interests		
	socially perceptive	socially perceptive		
	initiates humor	initiates humor		
	values independence			values independence
has bodily concerns	feels guilty	introspective	assertive	assertive
expressive		insightful	somatizes	repressive
submissive			self-dramatizing	overcontrolled
satisfied with self				basically anxious
				fearful

184

TABLE 8.11
Q-sort: Category 7, 8, 9 Ascriptions
M
(N = 9)

Early Adolescence	Late Adolescence	Early Adulthood	Middle Adulthood
values independence	values independence	values independence	values independence
dependable		dependable	dependable
masculine	masculine		masculine
productive		productive	productive
ambitious		ambitious	ambitious
values intellectual matters		values intellectual matters	values intellectual matters
	power-oriented	power-oriented	power-oriented
	hi intellectual capacity	hi intellectual capacity	hi intellectual capacity
overcontrolled		overcontrolled	
gregarious	gregarious		
repressive	repressive		
straightforward			straightforward
		status quo	status quo
		other-directed	other-directed
	prides self on objectivity		prides self on objectivity
arouses liking	responds to humor	basic hostility	giving
fantasizing	skeptical	poised	aloof
has bodily concerns	talkative	concerned with adequacy	assertive
cheerful	self-indulgent		satisfied with self
concerned with appearance			

185

TABLE 8.12

Q-sort: Category 7, 8, 9 Ascriptions

MIM

(N = 5)

Early Adolescence	Late Adolescence	Early Adulthood	Middle Adulthood
repressive	repressive	repressive	
hi intellectual capacity	hi intellectual capacity		
concerned with appearance	concerned with appearance		
has bodily concerns	has bodily concerns		
	values independence		values independence
gregarious			gregarious
masculine			masculine
		giving	giving
		thin skinned	productive
fantasizing	responds to humor	basically anxious	wide interests
self-defensive	communicates nonverbally	concerned with adequacy	assertive
			initiates humor

appear to achieve a less coherent core personality over time than only males. Worth noting: though they are seen as anxious and concerned in early adulthood, in middle adulthood they are mature, productive, and apparently well adjusted.

M1F. There appear a number of consistent life long attributes of first-born males with younger sisters, namely, dependability and productivity. Consistency at adolescence obtains. First-born males with younger sisters are seen as masculine, overcontrolled, and as having high intellectual interests. The borness (first) effects continue to show through, as was the case with only males and first born males with younger brothers (overcontrolled, productive, high intellectual capacity). Sex effects also remain evident (verbal fluency, talkative, overcontrolled, valuing intellectual matters). Worth noting is the rather coherent, well-adjusted characterization during adolescence; the somewhat painful sensitivities of early adulthood (defensive, concerned with adequacy, feels guilty), which may well have their roots in sister-presence; and the positive internal consistencies found in middle age (philosophically concerned, ethically consistent, objectivity).

MM2. The small number of subjects for this category precludes much generalization, but one is struck by the absence of high intellectual capacity, overcontrol, etc.; and the presence of "appears to be intelligent" rather than *is* intelligent.

FM2. Again, the presence of an older sister for this second born male is accompanied by seemingly greater consistency over the life span, as can be seen in Table 15. This sibling group is seen as appearing intelligent, ambitious, dependable, valuing intellectual matters, productive, and verbally fluent. Most interestingly, this is the second-born male apparently most affected by an older sister, and the characterization appears to "hold": dependable, verbally fluent, feels guilty, overcontrolled. Indeed, one is impressed with the greater consistency in personality during adulthood than in adolescence, an outcome compatible with the several studies of MF2s in childhood and adolescence (see summary in Sutton-Smith & Rosenberg, 1970). The ascriptions of guilt, overcontrol, and verbal fluency reinforce the profound effects of older sister presence, it is believed. In addition, Table 15 indicates that the FM2 at middle age is independent, conservative, straightforward, ethically consistent, and dependable—a status quo life style emerges with a second-born with an older sister, as contrasted with the MM2. Again, the unique characterizations at developmental points emphasize the anxiety present in identity formation with an older, more powerful female sibling—thin skinned, concern with appearance and bodily functions, fantasizing, fastidious, uncomfortable with uncertainty—a consistency surprising with so small a sample and a measuring instrument of only a fair degree of precision.

A brief note or observation of this multiple coverage: sex effects are clear and consistent well into adulthood. Important to point out is the first-borns' uniform

TABLE 8.13
Q-sort: Category 7, 8, 9 Ascriptions
M1F
(N = 9)

Early Adolescence	Late Adolescence	Early Adulthood	Middle Adulthood
dependable	dependable	dependable	dependable
productive	productive		productive
masculine	masculine		
overcontrolled	overcontrolled		
hi intellectual capacity	hi intellectual capacity		
verbally fluent		verbally fluent	
talkative			talkative
	values intellectual matters		values intellectual matters
compares self with others	straightforward	concerned with adequacy	philosophically concerned
thin skinned	arouses liking	self-defensive	ethically consistent
calm	ambitious	feels guilty	prides self on objectivity
poised	values independence	other-directed	satisfied with self
	sympathetic		
	gregarious		
	assertive		
	cheerful		
	concerned with appearance		

TABLE 8.14
Q-sort: Category 7, 8, 9 Ascriptions
MM2
(N = 4)

Early Adolescence	Late Adolescence	Early Adulthood	Middle Adulthood
appears intelligent	appears intelligent		appears intelligent
aloof	repressive	productive	productive
		distrustful	dependable
		verbally fluent	values intellectual matters
			has bodily concerns
			ambitious
			values independence
			other-directed

TABLE 8.15
Q-sort: Category 7, 8, 9 Ascriptions
FM2
(N = 6)

Early Adolescence	Late Adolescence	Early Adulthood	Middle Adulthood
appears intelligent	appears intelligent	appears intelligent	appears intelligent
ambitious	ambitious	ambitious	ambitious
dependable	dependable	dependable	dependable
values intellectual matters	values intellectual matters	values intellectual matters	
	productive	productive	productive
	verbally fluent	verbally fluent	verbally fluent
feels guilty	feels guilty		
	over controlled	overcontrolled	
		values independence	values independence
		conservative	conservative
		ethically consistent	ethically consistent
		straightforward	straightforward
thin skinned	has bodily concerns	poised	prides self on objectivity
rapid tempo	fantasizing	fastidious	uncomfortable with uncertainty
aloof	compares self with others	arouses liking	
proffers advice	concerned with appearance		

"concern with adequacy" in late adolescence and early adulthood—a coercive quality which, in a sense, "umbrellas" many of the characteristics uniformly assigned to first-borns in numerous studies in childhood and adolescence (Rosenberg & Sutton-Smith, 1973; Bossard & Boll, 1956; Sampson, 1965).

Females: F (Only Females). From Table 16, one is impressed with the structural similarity and consistencies of only males and females. As was noted with the only males, there is a great deal of consistency in personality across the life span, much like a core structure. Uniform ascriptions are: feminine, gregarious, repressive, poised, fastidious, productive, and talkative. At early and late adolescence only females are commonly characterized as conforming to adult standards, concerned with appearance, and self-indulgent. Rather notably, the only boys and only girls appear to be power-oriented at late adolescence and early adulthood, a yet-to-be explained phenomena. Is sibling absence a critical factor here in the realm of adapting to the external world without sibling models? Examining the characterizations unique to each developmental stage, one is impressed with the apparent stress of late adolescence for the only girl: extropunitive, thin skinned, moralistic, projective, etc. Other characteristics suggesting stress are also present, to a lesser degree: somatizes, seeks reassurance, feels guilty in early adulthood. Again, is the absence of a sibling in this drama of transition not a critical element?

F1F. The female counterpart of the M1M strikes one as far more consistent or stable across life, as can be seen from Table 17. First-born girls appear more consistent and homogeneous during adolescence than they are later on; they are marked by conformance and concern with appearance; they are gregarious, intelligent appearing, and compare themselves to others. Like only females, they are uniformly seen as feminine and fastidious. Though late adolescence appears somewhat less stressful for this female with a younger sister, early adulthood shows characteristics highly similar to only females: anxious, seeks reassurance, and exhibits submissiveness. The pressure to conform on young first-born women, would appear to be profound.

F1M. The small sample precludes much generalization here, though members of this group appear to be dependable, overcontrolled, fastidious, and productive—a rather definite first-born set of qualities. Interestingly, early adolescence and middle adulthood yield highly similar descriptions, such as protective, giving, sympathetic, poised, and feminine. One might speculate regarding the presence of a younger brother, the mother-surrogate flavor of personality description, and the positive, feminine qualities assigned.

FF2. Within the limits of sample size, this second-born girl does reflect expected qualities of independence, assertiveness, and concern with adequacy,

TABLE 8.16

Q-sort: Category 7, 8, 9 Ascriptions

F

(N = 12)

Early Adolescence	Late Adolescence	Early Adulthood	Middle Adulthood
feminine	feminine		feminine
gregarious	gregarious	gregarious	
repressive	repressive	repressive	
poised		poised	poised
talkative	talkative		talkative
productive		productive	productive
fastidious		fastidious	fastidious
conforms to adult standards	conforms to adult standards		
concerned with appearance	concerned with appearance		
self-indulgent	self-indulgent		
		arouses liking	arouses liking
	power-oriented	power-oriented	
		has bodily concerns	has bodily concerns
		cheerful	cheerful
interested in opposite sex	extropunitive	somatizes	dependable
fantasizing	compares self to others	seeks reassurance	protective
	emotionally involved with same sex	feels guilty	sympathetic
	thin skinned		warm
	moralistic		expressive
	projective		straightforward
	self-dramatizing		submissive
			rapid tempo
			ethically consistent
			satisfied with self

TABLE 8.17

Q-sort: Category 7, 8, 9 Ascriptions

F1F

(N = 6)

Early Adolescence	Late Adolescence	Early Adulthood	Middle Adulthood
fastidious	fastidious		fastidious
feminine	feminine		feminine
arouses liking		arouses liking	arouses liking
Conforms to adult standards	conforms to adult standards		
concerned with appearance	concerned with appearance		
gregarious	gregarious		
appears intelligent	appears intelligent		
compares self to others	compares self to others		
dependable		dependable	poised
	poised		feels guilty
		feels guilty	
			giving
overcontrolled	repressive	basically anxious	sympathetic
physically attractive	fantasizing	submissive	productive
	interested in opposite sex	seeks reassurance	warm
	emotionally involved with same sex	expressive	evaluates others' motives
	uncomfortable with uncertainty		wide interests
	thin skinned		socially perceptive
	power-oriented		straightforward
			cheerful
			values independence
			initiates humor
			ethically consistent
			concerned with adequacy

193

TABLE 8.18

Q-sort: Category 7, 8, 9 Ascriptions

F1M

(N = 3)

Early Adolescence	Late Adolescence	Early Adulthood	Middle Adulthood
dependable	dependable	dependable	dependable
fastidious	fastidious	fastidious	
overcontrolled	overcontrolled	overcontrolled	
productive		productive	productive
appears intelligent	appears intelligent		
protective			protective
giving			giving
sympathetic			sympathetic
poised			poised
feminine			feminine
	arouses liking		arouses liking
		ethically consistent	ethically consistent
feels guilty	concerned with appearance	ambitious	warm
repressive	submissive	verbally fluent	wide interests
	gregarious	conservative	introspective
	has bodily concerns		insightful
	dependent		evaluates others' motives
			socially perceptive
			straightforward
			cheerful
			initiates humor

TABLE 8.19

Q-sort: Category 7, 8, 9 Ascriptions

FF2

(N = 3)

Early Adolescence	Late Adolescence	Early Adulthood	Middle Adulthood
dependable		dependable	
overcontrolled		overcontrolled	
values independence		values independence	
	talkative		talkative
	cheerful		cheerful
		assertive	assertive
		concerned with adequacy	concerned with adequacy
skeptical	repressive	introspective	rapid tempo
concerned with appearance	moralistic	basic hostility	somatizes
	undercontrolled	fearful	productive
	gregarious	values intellectual matters	self-dramatizing
	bothered by demands	compares self to others	
	feminine		

TABLE 8.20

Q-sort: Category 7, 8, 9 Ascriptions

MF2

(N = 10)

Early Adolescence	Late Adolescence	Early Adulthood	Middle Adulthood
dependable	dependable	dependable	dependable
repressive	repressive	repressive	repressive
productive	productive		productive
sympathetic		sympathetic	sympathetic
arouses liking	arouses liking		
gregarious	gregarious		
appears intelligent	appears intelligent		
verbally fluent		verbally fluent	
poised		poised	
	feels guilty	feels guilty	
	overcontrolled		overcontrolled
		basically anxious	basically anxious
		giving	giving
		concerned with adequacy	concerned with adequacy
uncomfortable with uncertainty	interested in opposite sex	introspective	protective
feminine	thin skinned	basic hostility	ethically consistent
cheerful		somatizes	evaluates other's motives
emotionally involved with same sex			fearful
talkative			assertive
fastidious			values independence
conforms to adult standards			
status quo			

findings in concert with earlier research on FF2s. Again, with caution regarding the small sample, we find, for the first time, qualities of a negative cast—undercontrolled, bothered by demands, basic hostility, fearful, and so on—rare in the personality of the first-borns we have examined.

MF2. The girl with an older brother manifests some rather confirmed stereotyped feminine qualities (dependable, repressive, sympathetic, gregarious, verbally fluent; feels guilty; is overcontrolled, anxious, giving, and poised). She seems not to suffer from the presence of the older, opposite-sex sibling in adolescence. During this time, she is pictured as someone who arouses liking, is gregarious, and appears intelligent. Opposite-sex effects of the brother may be seen in other characteristics: productive, appears intelligent, and so on. Of interest for both FF2 and MF2—the quality "feminine" is absent. (It was present in the characterization of all three first-born girl categories.) Finally, the girl with an older brother is described in terms more frequently employed to characterize males in adulthood: concerned with adequacy, assertive, and valuing independence. This, we believe, is confirmation of the weighty impact of an older, opposite-sex sibling, as well as a second-born effect.

DISCUSSION

The investigation concerned itself with the persisting influences over time of the early formative years, especially the impact of siblings on subsequent personality development over the life span. The assessment material was multivariate in personality content. The concern was multiple: How stable are varied sibling statuses over time? What do various sibling positions accrue in qualitative evaluation? How do they compare with other sibling positions? How do they uniquely change or remain consistent within the category over time? How well or poorly do such outcomes confirm the host of earlier, non-longitudinal studies on sibling characteristics?

With all the acknowledged limitations of longitudinal studies (cf. Baltes & Schaie, 1973; Block, 1971; Moss & Susman, 1980), it should be emphasized that the subjects of this study were first assessed in the 1920s, and, as such, traditional roles and personality characterizations would be far more likely than might be the case if the same study were initiated today. One must temper the present outcomes in that context.

Personality Stability

A summary of these outcomes reveals: a) personality stability in males and females is greatest at adolescence, less stable at middle adulthood, and least stable at late adolescence-early adulthood; b) only males are more consistent in personality than males with siblings; c) females tend to greater stability than males, especially at the transition point of late adolescence-early adulthood; d) generally, only and second-born males are more stable at this transition point than first-born males; e) opposite-sex males are more stable than like-sex males over the life span; and f) opposite-sex females are more stable than like-sex females at late adolescence-early adulthood.

Comparison of Sibling Statuses at Four Life Stages: Males

Early Adolescence.

1. Like-sex dyads are least stable at BC for both males and females. This is a transition period, one of some stress. The desirability of an opposite-sex sibling may be due to the fact that it provides role models of the opposite sex such that transition in late adolescence is facilitated. The stress of adolescence appears to be mediated by learning the role of the other.

2. First-borns are uniformly described as of high intellectual capacity whereas second-borns *appear* intelligent. This finding is consistent over numbers of studies since the 1930s (Jones, 1931) that have predominantly found first-borns to rank higher on intelligence and achievement.

3. Only boys are found to be more consistent in personality over time as contrasted with boys with siblings. (Keep in mind that there is a generational difference in the sample.) Certainly the absence of a sibling at some stages in development should be propitious for greater ease in defining role and identity without competition (sex or power) produced by sibling presence (and rivalry).

4. Sex effects are quite evident at this time. Boys with a sister or onlies (noted for a greater feminine component in sex roles) are seen as dependable, thin skinned, valuing intellectual matters, and overcontrolled, as contrasted with males with brothers. The notion of role assimilation (Brim, 1958) appears apt here, to account for the sensitivity and dependability found in boys with sisters, somewhat dissonant from the masculine sex-role emphases at this time.

5. Strong socialization pressures on first-borns is revealed in the characterizations of fantasizing, repressive behavior, and concern with appearance. This is in concert with the growing literature emphasizing the pressures on first-borns for early conscience development, responsibility, and parental surrogation.

Late Adolescence.   From a socialization perspective, this appears to be a period of transition and stress. Nevertheless, there appears a measure of continuity with the previous period, with first-born males continuing to be described as possessing high intellectual capacity, valuing independence, and demonstrating masculine and repressive behaviors. Second borns are, again, intelligent appearing. In addition, sex effects are reflected in a continuing manner with boys, with sisters characterized as concerned with appearance, dependable, valuing intellectual matters, and overcontrolled, as contrasted with boys with brothers.

Early Adulthood.

1. With adulthood, we might expect an attenuation of sibling influences, and, in large measure, that is what we see. Interestingly, first-borns heretofore seen as of high intellectual capacity and striving are now characterized somewhat uniformly as concerned with adequacy. It is as though the bright, achieving first-born is role-modeling the parent, continually doubting his level of achievement.

2. Sex effects are still perceptible, with only males and males with sisters continuing to be described as valuing independence, valuing intellectual matters, poised, and overcontrolled. It is not at all unlikely that the dynamics for independence-striving are quite different (modeling vs. reactive modeling) for onlies and males with sisters, but the consistency of the continuing influence from adolescence is clear.

Middle Adulthood. It should not be surprising that this period reflects fewer notable sibling influences. Most descriptive material on the several sibling dyads is dominated by generalized concepts of the male sex role.

Comparison of Sibling Statuses at Four Life Stages: Females

Early Adolescence.

1. As we know from the results, the firm establishment of the sex role appears to carry greater impact for girls at adolescence than sibling influences. For whatever reasons—precocity in growth, accelerated language development, greater learning ability—society appears to place a premium on sex role adoption for females at this time, and other influences are somewhat obscured. There are few discriminable effects from borness at this time.

2. Girls with brothers are described as repressive, sympathetic (taking the role of the other), and productive, as contrasted with girls with sisters.

Late Adolescence. By late adolescence, sibling influences become less obscure. Sex and borness effects obtain a degree of prominence.

1. A second-born girl with an older sister is described as cheerful, undercontrolled, and bothered by demands, much as second-born girls appear in the

literature. A second-born girl with an older brother is described as feeling guilty and productive.

2. Borness effects congruent with the literature become increasingly clear. First-borns are described as concerned with appearance, conforming, and fastidious, as compared with second-borns.

3. One gets the impression of greater clarity in sex role identity and less stress on girls than boys at this period.

Early Adulthood.   This period, somewhat akin to our findings with males, reveals the impact of great emphasis on sex role into early adulthood. Nevertheless, there are some conspicious threads of earlier sibling influences. First-born females seek reassurance (Schacter, 1959) and appeal to others. Second-born females continue to show less conformance and less stable self (hostile, concerned with adequacy, introspective).

Middle Adulthood.   In early and middle adulthood, first-born females reflect almost stereotypic mature feminine role (feminine, sympathetic, protective, warm, giving, socially perceptive). That is to say, socialization impact on first-borns throughout development appears to have "taken." One gets the sense of psychological primogeniture (or a first-born as a culture carrier), with first-borns moving into and occupying former surrogate roles. Second-born females continue to reflect the threads of the developmental past in continuing to be described as assertive and concerned with adequacy.

Cicirelli (1979) and others have pointed to this role absorption in the relations between elderly women and their brothers, i.e., they are nurturant, providers of concern and care, and protective of the once-dominant male sibling.

Changes in Individual Sibling Statuses Over Time

In the course of separately examining the array of outcomes for each sibling status over the four life stages, it became apparent that there was a natural "grouping" or "clustering" of the descriptive materials on five dimensions: dominance, achievement, conformance-conservation, sociability, and a collage best termed "personal attitude." It is believed that the reader will find that these five collectivities make the descriptive data more meaingful (See Tables 11A through 20A).

The question asked here is simply: How does each sibling category change over time? The following is a summary of each of the 10 categories.

1. *M*: Only males show continuity throughout life on dominance, independence, and masculine behavior, and are seen as assertive and power-oriented. One might speculate that these outcomes are a result of adult proximity and

TABLE 8.11A
Q-sort: Category 7, 8, 9 Ascriptions
M
(N = 9)

Early Adolescence	Late Adolescence	Early Adulthood	Middle Adulthood
values independence	values independence	values independence	values independence
masculine	masculine		masculine
	power-oriented	power-oriented	power-oriented
straightforward			straightforward
			assertive
DOMINANCE			
productive		productive	productive
ambitious		ambitious	ambitious
values intellectual matters		values intellectual matters	values intellectual matters
	high intellectual capacity	high intellectual capacity	high intellectual capacity
	prides self on objectivity		prides self on objectivity
		concerned with adequacy	
ACHIEVEMENT			
dependable		dependable	dependable
overcontrolled		overcontrolled	
concerned with appearance		status quo	status quo
CONFORMANCE-CONSERVATION			
gregarious	gregarious		
arouses liking		other-directed	other-directed
cheerful	talkative		giving
	responds to humor	poised	satisfied with self
SOCIABILITY			
repressive	repressive	basis hostility	
fantasizing	skeptical		
has bodily concerns	self-indulgent		aloof
PERSONAL ATTITUDE			

201

TABLE 8.12A
Q-sort Category 7, 8, 9 Ascriptions
M1M
(N = 5)

	Early Adolescence	Late Adolescence	Early Adulthood	Middle Adulthood
DOMINANCE	masculine values independence			masculine values independence assertive
ACHIEVEMENT	high intellectual capacity	high intellectual capacity	concerned with adequacy	productive wide interests
CONFORMANCE-CONSERVATION	concerned with appearance	concerned with appearance		
SOCIABILITY	gregarious	responds to humor communicates nonverbally	giving	gregarious giving initiates humor
PERSONAL ATTITUDE	repressive has bodily concerns fantasizing self defensive	repressive has bodily concerns	repressive thin-skinned basically anxious	

TABLE 8.10A

Q-sort: Category 7, 8, 9 Ascriptions

M1F

(N = 9)

	Early Adolescence	Late Adolescence	Early Adulthood	Middle Adulthood
DOMINANCE	masculine	masculine straightforward values independence assertive		productive values intellectual matters
ACHIEVEMENT	productive high intellectual capacity verbally fluent	productive high intellectual capacity values intellectual matters ambitious	verbally fluent concerned with adequacy	dependable
CONFORMANCE-CONSERVATION	dependable overcontrolled concerned with appearance	dependable overcontrolled concerned with appearance	dependable	talkative
SOCIABILITY	talkative poised	arouses liking sympathetic gregarious	other-directed	
PERSONAL ATTITUDE	thin-skinned calm	cheerful	self defensive feels guilty	philosophically concerned ethically consistent prides self on objectivity satisfied with self

TABLE 8.14A
Q-sort Category 7, 8, 9 Ascriptions
MM2
(N = 4)

Early Adolescence	Late Adolescence	Early Adulthood	Middle Adulthood
DOMINANCE			
			values independence
appears intelligent	appears intelligent	productive verbally fluent	appears intelligent productive values intellectual matters ambitious
ACHIEVEMENT			
			dependable
CONFORMANCE-CONSERVATION			
aloof			other-oriented
SOCIABILITY			
repressive		distrustful	has bodily concerns
PERSONAL ATTITUDE			

TABLE 8.15A
Q-sort: Category 7, 8, 9 Ascriptions
FM2
(N = 6)

Early Adolescence	Late Adolescence	Early Adulthood	Middle Adulthood
DOMINANCE			
proffers advice		values independence straightforward	values independence straightforward
ACHIEVEMENT			
appears intelligent ambitious values intellectual matters	appears intelligent ambitious values intellectual matters productive verbally fluent	appears intelligent ambitious values intellectual matters productive verbally fluent	appears intelligent ambitious productive verbally fluent
CONFORMANCE-CONSERVATION			
dependable	dependable overcontrolled fastidious	dependable overcontrolled conservative fastidious	dependable conservative
SOCIABILITY			
aloof		poised arouses liking	
PERSONAL ATTITUDE			
feels guilty thin-skinned rapid tempo has bodily concerns	feels guilty has bodily concerns	ethically consistent	ethically consistent prides self on objectivity uncomfortable with uncertainty

TABLE 8.16A

Q-sort: Category 7, 8, 9 Ascriptions

F

(N = 12)

Early Adolescence	Late Adolescence	Early Adulthood	Middle Adulthood
feminine	feminine		feminine
DOMINANCE	power-oriented	power-oriented	straightforward
productive		productive	productive
ACHIEVEMENT			
fastidious		fastidious	fastidious
conforms to adult standards	conforms to adult standards		
concerned with appearance	concerned with appearance		
	compares self to others		
	moralistic		
CONFORMANCE-CONSERVATION			dependable

gregarious, poised, talkative	gregarious, talkative	gregarious, poised	poised, talkative, arouses liking, cheerful, protective, sympathetic, warm
		arouses liking, cheerful	
SOCIABILITY			
repressive, self-indulgent	repressive, self-indulgent	repressive	has bodily concerns
		has bodily concerns	
interested in opposite sex, fantasizing			
emotionally involved with same sex, thin-skinned, projective, self-dramatizing	emotionally involved with same sex, thin-skinned, projective, self-dramatizing	somatizes, seeks reassurance, feels guilty	submissive, rapid tempo, ethically consistent, satisfied with self, expressive
PERSONAL ATTITUDE			

TABLE 8.17A
Q-sort: Category 7, 8, 9 Ascriptions
F1F
(N = 6)

Early Adolescence	Late Adolescence	Early Adulthood	Middle Adulthood
feminine	feminine		feminine
DOMINANCE	power-oriented	straightforward	values independence
appears intelligent	appears intelligent		productive
			evaluates other's motives
ACHIEVEMENT			wide interests
fastidious	fastidious		fastidious
conforms to adult standards	conforms to adult standards		
concerned with appearance	concerned with appearance		
compares self to others	compares self to others		
dependable		dependable	straightforward
overcontrolled			
CONFORMANCE-CONSERVATION			

208

arouses liking		arouses liking	arouses liking
gregarious	gregarious		
physically attractive	poised		poised
			cheerful
			giving
			sympathetic
			warm
			socially perceptive
			initiates humor
SOCIABILITY			
	repressive	feels guilty	feels guilty
	fantasizing	basically anxious	concerned with adequacy
	interested in opposite sex	submissive	
	emotionally involved with same sex	seeks reassurance	
	uncomfortable with uncertainty	expressive	
	thin-skinned		
PERSONAL ATTITUDE			

TABLE 8.18A
Q-sort: Category 7, 8, 9 Ascriptions
F1M
(N = 3)

Early Adolescence	Late Adolescence	Early Adulthood	Middle Adulthood
feminine			feminine
DOMINANCE			straightforward
productive		productive	productive
appears intelligent	appears intelligent	ambitious	wide interests
		verbally fluent	insightful
			evaluates other's motives
ACHIEVEMENT			
dependable	dependable	dependable	dependable
fastidious	fastidious	fastidious	
over-controlled	over-controlled	over-controlled	
	concerned with appearance	conservative	
CONFORMANCE-CONSERVATION			
protective			protective
giving			giving
sympathetic			sympathetic
poised			poised
	arouses liking		arouses liking
	gregarious		socially perceptive
			initiates humor
			cheerful
SOCIABILITY			
feels guilty	submissive	ethically consistent	warm
repressive	has bodily concerns	ethically consistent	introspective
	dependent		ethically consistent
PERSONAL ATTITUDE			

TABLE 8.19A

Q-sort: Category 7, 8, 9 Ascriptions

FF2

(N = 3)

	Early Adolescence	Late Adolescence	Early Adulthood	Middle Adulthood
DOMINANCE	values independence	undercontrolled feminine	values independence assertive basic hostility	assertive
ACHIEVEMENT	dependable overcontrolled concerned with appearance	moralistic	values intellectual matters dependable overcontrolled compares self to others	productive
CONFORMANCE-CONSERVATION	talkative cheerful gregarious			talkative cheerful
SOCIABILITY	skeptical	repressive bothered by demands	concerned with adequacy introspective	concerned with adequacy
PERSONAL ATTITUDE				rapid tempo somatizes self-dramatizing

TABLE 8.20A

Q-sort: Category 7, 8, 9 Ascriptions

MF2

(N = 10)

Early Adolescence	Late Adolescence	Early Adulthood	Middle Adulthood
feminine		basic hostility	assertive
			values independence
DOMINANCE			
productive	productive		productive
appears intelligent	appears intelligent		
verbally fluent		verbally fluent	evaluates other's motives
ACHIEVEMENT			
dependable	dependable	dependable	dependable
	overcontrolled		overcontrolled
fastidious			
conforms to adult standards			
status quo			ethically consistent
CONFORMANCE-CONSERVATION			

SOCIABILITY	sympathetic arouses liking gregarious poised cheerful talkative	arouses liking gregarious	sympathetic poised giving	sympathetic giving protective
PERSONAL ATTITUDE	repressive uncomfortable with uncertainty emotionally involved with same sex	repressive feels guilty thin-skinned interested in opposite sex	repressive feels guilty concerned with adequacy basically anxious somatizes	repressive concerned with adequacy basically anxious fearful ethically consistent

availability, sibling absence, and role-modeling parents. Again, high intellectual capacity, ambition, and productiveness in all probability result from the role-modeling found in a predominantly adult milieu. Adolescence is accompanied by much conformance, but this is diluted with time. Only males are moderate on sociability (possibly due to the absence of sibling socialization), and manifest relatively few personal problems in adulthood.

2. *M1M*: Here we find an interesting absence of dominance in late adolescence and early adulthood. Achievement (high intellectual capacity) is noted early and retained throughout life. Sociability is a somewhat lesser dimension, along with indices of conformance. Personal attitude is repressive, fantasizing, possessed of bodily concerns throughout adolescence and early adulthood, along with a basically anxious character structure. The latter may well result from early pressure to emulate adult roles and behavior resulting in an early marked inhibition of age-appropriate expressiveness.

3. *M1F*: Less dominance-masculinity exhibited than other males, except at late adolescence. The latter may be a reaction to peer expectations and compensation for sister-presence, to reassure or assert appropriate sex role identity. Achievement-intelligence is noted early and remains high for much of the life span. Here we find a greater degree of consistency in conformance-conservative. Personal attitude is less negative than was noted with the M1M, possibly due in measure to a less threatening younger sibling.

4. *MM2*: The findings here are relatively few, due in large part to the small sample. Unlike much of the literature on second-borns, our study shows little evidence of reactive dominance-independent behavior. The achievement dimension is low, sociability and conformance are low, and we saw more distrustful behavior, not unlike those in less powerful positions.

5. *FM2*: Interestingly, we find dominance low until adulthood, where valuing independence is clear and central (possibly indicating an attempt to escape from the feminine dominance of youth). The achievement orientation is rich and continuous throughout life (possibly due to the effect of the older sister); and it is more comprehensive (ambitious, fluent, productive) than other categories of male sibships. The FM2 is conservative, dependable, and careful; he is somewhat less socially adept; he shows guilt and discomfort. Uncertainty obtains through much of life. One might speculate that here we find a most apt example of the impact of an older, more powerful sister as a model to be emulated, to be rebelled against, but never to be overcome (Koch, 1960; Sutton-Smith & Rosenberg, 1970).

6. *F*: Only females are found to be rather consistently feminine and power-oriented (tryadic roles, father impact). It is as though the female only child is saying, "I am like mother, having her all to myself; but, in part, I am like father, strong and powerful." Achievement-intelligence is not a cornerstone of this category, with accompanying conformance-conservativeness quite high (the

probable impact of two older, more powerful adults, and the lack of sibling socialization). Sociability is high and a relevant personologic dimension. Personal attitude reflects a rather brittle self-assurance (self-dramatizing, self-indulgent) in adolescence, and questionable stability as an adult (repressive, seeks reassurance, feels guilty, submissive).

7. *F1F:* The primary characterizations of the F1Fs is feminine, productive in adulthood, with greatest emphasis on conforming behavior in adolescence. Interestingly, where conformance dilutes as a broad factor in adulthood, its prominence is replaced by extensive, confirmed, positive sex role qualities of the adult female (warm, sympathetic, kind, giving). From late adolescence on through life, though, personal attitudes representing inner turmoil (guilt, anxiety, seeking reassurance, repressiveness) predominate, suggesting a sacrifice of self for the acquisition of much-heralded adult, feminine qualities so socially approved in society.

8. *F1M*: The limited sample precludes much generality. Though seen as intelligent in adolescence and productive in adulthood, the greatest emphasis would appear to be on the responsible, dependable nature of this category throughout life. Prosocial characteristics predominate in early adolescence and adulthood. One might assign adult ambition and competence, in some measure, to the presence of a male sibling and role assimilation.

9. *FF2:* Generality based on sample size is questionable. Despite this, FF2s are uniformly characterized as independent, undercontrolled, and assertive throughout the life span, a finding in consonance with early findings on second-borns in the literature. Adulthood is accompanied by a predictable concern with adequacy, emerging from a parent and parent-surrogate (older sibling) dominated early life.

10. *MF2:* Here, where we might expect greatest impact of an older male, we find it. MF2s are assertive and independent in adulthood, as well as productive, intelligent, and verbally fluent (the best of all worlds!). Lower power status reflects itself in life long dependability, excessive control, and conformance. Rather broadly socialized, they evidence taking the role of the other in adulthood (sympathetic, protective). The "costs" of living a low-power status become clear, though, as anxiety, repression, guilt, and concern with adequacy are rather continuous throughout life.

In summary, the results of this life span examination lend credence to numerous studies emphasizing the critical impact of one's sibling throughout the course of development. It has been possible to document greater stability in personality at adolescence, then middle adulthood, and finally in late adolescence-early adulthood.

Again, stress in adjustment seems greatest at late adolescence-early adulthood. And finally, females show less stress than males.

First-Borns and Parent Proximity

Regarding direct sibling influences, the results are revealing. Borness carries great impact. As can be seen with first-borns, proximity to parents leads to pressures for early adoption of adult behaviors. This is differentially effective, but generally occurs. Such impact leads to an inhibition of some early developmental needs in first-borns that remain unexpressed or unconsummated. The positive aspect of this premature resolution of childhood is accompanied by early and greater intellectual focus, ambition, and achievement in life (Altus, 1962, 1966; Jones, 1931; Rosenberg & Sutton-Smith, 1966). The process appears rather similar for males and females, but in a male-valuing society, the outcomes (achievement, status) are seen more clearly with males. Socialization in terms of learning theory appears sufficient to account for such phenomena.

Since personality development may well appear to involve a series of developmental crises and resolutions (Erikson, 1950, 1959), timing becomes a relevant factor. For the only child, the tryadic relationship has an impact different from that felt by a child who subsequently greets a sibling. Where both first-borns occupy a central position in the family structure, the latter must relinquish this role, in part, and accept the divided resources of the parents. As a result, a different focus is accompanied by new pressures to conform to an adult caretaker role regarding the sibling. Such pressures likely inhibit aspects of the childhood experience and result in early development of conscience, responsibility, and the concepts of time.

The parent, in turn, doubly burdened by the newcomer, having experienced one child, is less anxious and more learned regarding the new responsibility. Expectations are commonly held that the first-born should have already had some reasonable resolution of the needs of childhood when the second child arrives. Some measure of parent surrogation is expected in the first-born towards the new sibling.

Family Dynamics and Outcomes

Interestingly, the one-child family contains a dynamic best described in terms of power. The child has been the powerless one with two parental figures (Sutton-Smith & Rosenberg, 1968). Assimilation rather than reaction to the role of parent occurs. With the arrival of the newborn, the dynamics of family structure (as is the case in small groups) shift. The pressures on the first-born to surrogation have their obvious liability. At the same time, the first-born finally acquires a form of power.

When looking at such early pressures and outcomes, one cannot help but be struck with the parallels in the first-born—second-born comparison with Freud's (1933, p. 129) analogous pronouncements on oedipal resolution and superego formation with males and females. In a sense, "The superego is never so clear and focussed in the second born as in the first born [p. 129]." Where Freud's underlying premise was the presence or absence of external genitalia and threat, the borness premise has to do with position, timing, and the evocation of socialization stimuli. In a sense it is saying structurally that, like women, the superego of the second-born is more differentiated and less resolved than is the case in the first-born.

Family and the Group

Again, to the differences in first-borns. The tryadic relationships in the one-child family strike one as inclusive of more intense and continuing effect than is the case in the four-person family. Emotional use and manipulation of one another continues in the tryad. The multireciprocals change with time, developmental status, and satisfactions obtained by each member. In the four-person (two-child) family, a steadying group structure, of necessity, takes place, and role definition, change, and divided resources are more readily likened to a nonfamilial small group, in order to sustain the family balance. Greater clarity in roles, functions, and responsibilities is required and occurs—the parents' differential in the treatment of the children, with the first-born primarily involved in a more formalized relationship to the parents and the younger sibling. Maturity (in the adult sense) and responsibility in the first-born is requisite; not so the case of changing status of the first-born in the one-child family. The only child continues identification with one parent, then the other, absorbing elements of both sex roles. Not surprisingly, only boys are less masculine and only girls less feminine than expected. In the four-person family, the first-born (attended to less, by necessity) is pressured not only into accelerated development, but into the appropriate sex role.

What of the younger sibling? This child, by definition, is born into a less anxious world, one in which several persons exist, all of greater power than himself. Born into this world, the second-born enjoys the previously divided spotlight of attention in a transient manner, and thus, he can never so traumatically lose sole center of attention as did his older sibling. Again, limited resources are present from the start, leading inevitably to a realistic shared existence, the likes of which his older sibling had to learn forcibly.

Born with a deficit in power by dint of his order and position, he does have multiple models with whom to relate and identify; and most importantly, he has one model residing in a similar development status (behavior, language, intellect, socialization) with whom to relate, as his older sibling never did. The pressures to perform, then, can never be viewed as being as alien and coercive as they were for the first-born. Contextually, though the second-born's power is low, the context is actually most benign for living out childhood needs and aspirations. The fact that powerlessness leads to the development of excess strategies to achieve ends leads to greater psychological differentiation (empathy, role-taking) than is probable in the older sibling. The less anxious, tense environment reflects itself in a less anxious perception of the self (Rosenberg & Sutton-Smith, 1964). He is therefore a more relaxed learner, less pressured to attain premature closure than the first-born.

The inconsistencies in the parents in dealing with the first-born (Hilton, 1967) and the newness and concern surrounding the first-born occur far less often with the second-born, leading to the prediction of a slower, more surely obtained identity on the part of the latter. The first-born, forcibly catalyzed into premature identification is, as we have seen, conforming, responsive to adults, and like them. A clear, but premature, identity is so acquired, with the threads of unresolved wants and impulses long since ignored or bypassed. One might assume from this that first-borns are culture-carriers, even today in Western culture, where the concept of primogeniture has seemingly lost its relevance.

Power? Borness and power *are* related. No doubt an examination of most outcomes confirm that older siblings have greater impact on the younger ones than vice versa. Again, in a male-valuing society, masculine values have more impact on the sibling than female values. It is interesting to note that when one covaries the influence of borness and sex with sibling influences, time and again the cultural myth of the desirability of a first-born son and a second-born daughter yields most positive results. Here, as in some of our earlier work, the sex-ordinal position axis confirms in research what folklore has led us to expect (Sutton-Smith, Roberts, & Rosenberg, 1964).

In summary, boys have more impact on their sisters than the reverse; first-borns have more impact on second-borns than the reverse. Nevertheless, sex effects are real and predictable among all siblings. Generally, one tends to *assimilate* (Brim, 1958) the qualities of the other. For example, boys with sisters are more verbally fluent, value intellectual matters more, and are less masculine than boys with brothers. *Reactive modeling* (Sutton-Smith & Rosenberg, 1969) does occur in predictable fashion with other combinations of sex and ordinal position. For example, the younger brother with an older, more powerful sister emulates her to some extent, but basically he *reacts* more, ending up as more masculine, independent, and dominant than one might be led to expect. Still, the presence of an older sister will be reflected in the younger brother. He is described as more sensitive, verbally fluent, and conforming than a boy with an older brother.

It is worth noting that the premature acquisition of self-schemata found in the first-born is accompanied by questions of adequacy in adulthood, no matter how achieving they may be. As we have noted elsewhere, the models set for first-borns are idealized, never really to be achieved. Such is not the case with the second-borns. Whatever their level of achievement, their drive seems not so intense, their achievements less often questioned.

Socialization and the Condition of Effectiveness

One can certainly draw the conclusion that socialization within a sibling context is a more representative (Brunswik, 1956) design, i.e., more natural and thus effective, than socialization without siblings. The only child gives the impression of an adult with a precarious identity and belief in himself, as though his inner self isn't real. One need not reach beyond the efforts of Harlow (1979) to find some notion of a phylogenetic basis for the effectiveness of sibling socialization.

It seems critical to remind ourselves of the history of socialization theory at this point. We began with the premise that the outcome of socialization was primarily due to the parent controlling the reinforcement contingencies that presumably shape the malleable child. Subsequently, we (belatedly) glimpsed that the shapeable (tabula rasa) child was, in fact, a contributor to what contingencies not only were offered, but what, in fact, "took"; i.e., there were reciprocals built into the acquisition process (Bell, 1968; Moss, 1967). In our terms, child control of contingencies did exist. In addition, it was discovered that a different structural dynamic was achieved with each change in family size (Rosenberg & Sutton-Smith, 1964). Thus, the timing, sex, and number of children each provide *different conditions* in which the elements of socialization occur. The major influences on socialization processes have to do with the individual personality of the contributors, the interaction among them, the consistencies (tuitioned learning) and inconsistencies (nontuitioned learning) that occurred, and the feedback mechanisms between the object of socialization and the models. Critical here, too, is the *developmental status* and sex of the models. Generational differences provide different models of differing power, i.e., effectiveness, contingent upon their clarity and availability. Models more proximal on the developmental scale provide more readily comprehended and imitated models. These latter models provide a less veridical version of adult role models, with a uniqueness and quality of their own. The outcome of such shaping (socialization) is a more plurisignificant variant than the earlier, more simplistic notions guiding us—and, if you will, a more *representative* design of socialization—i.e., *socialization in person context.*

Nonsibling Socialization

It is worth pursuing some general notions regarding the socialization milieu in which the only child develops. As we have noted, the first child is greeted by a level of anxiety appropriate to the newness of the role of the parent. This anxiety, though decreasing with time, remains at a higher level than is the case in multichild families. The tryadic relations alter constantly, parent-parent and child-parent dynamics changing with time, developmental status of the child, and the contingencies of daily life. Embrace it or not, much of the interaction is based on a re-creation or recapitulation of the individual parent's own socialization. Depending on the sex of the child, different values and behaviors are differentially promulgated by one parent or the other. Where they find unity, we note consistency in the offspring. Where they diverge, differential behaviors or inconsistencies in the offspring are notable. In a way, the three-person family represents a cul-de-sac in which the "trying out" and change of contingencies is clearly present.

For the child, on the other hand, there is simply no recourse to a nonadult world with the absence of siblings. Adult ways, behaviors, and values are models for development, many inappropriate to the capacities and needs of the developing child (an exuberant father providing a baseball bat for his newborn son; an elated mother providing a doll for the newborn daughter). On one hand, then, there is great tolerance for infancy and childhood; on the other, the constant expectation for adult behaviors that are dominant in the milieu—and most readily recognized and rewarded. It is no surprise, then, that the only child, modeling after well-defined adult roles (sex roles included) reflects in early behavior, certainly by adolescence, achievement, ambition, power, conscience, guilt, and all those behaviors appropriate to adults, at the cost of behaviors indigenous to an earlier developmental phase.

The first major encounter with a child-oriented world occurs with entrance into school. Here one would have to predict that achievement should more readily obtain, whereas the socialization deficits (as contrasted with children who possess a sibling) should require efforts at coping that are new and problematic. The impact of early and prolonged adult-oriented socialization probably retains its influence, and the intellectual adjustment of the only should be minimal as a problem, the personal, peer-oriented adjustment should be somewhat great. Well into adolescence, the learning of a new socialization should be reflected in the only's behavior: excess narcissism, difficulty in cooperative or sharing behavior, and so on. They learn too well the elements of socially appropriate behavior in an adult-oriented world, inevitably giving rise to acquiescence to forms of behavior pleasing to adults and authority, but dissonant with peer expectations in adolescence, early and late.

In marked contrast, after the initial "trauma" of the coming of the second-born, all later children are born into a condition of parents with divided resources and multiple children as the generative condition. This provides a quasi-small group condition in which cooperativeness, sharing, some degree of selflessness is requisite and normal. In essence, this is socialization in a model reflecting socialization in the greater society, where adaptation, adjustment, and give-and-take are part of development. Power orientation and narcissism are far less likely concerns as a result. There is no trauma of loss of the center stage as with the first-born, who learned to value it and then lost it. In addition, the assets of multichild families are large: No adult dominated milieu; linguistic models of relevant and similar developmental status; multimodels for child-appropriate behaviors, needs, and expressions; lowered anxiety in parent and child; more and appropriate identificatory models; and so on. Additionally, shared power is the constant in a multichild family, to be used as occasion allows, not to be over-valued, as would appear to be the case with the only child.

Such thinking might lead to the view that the only child and the first-born child with siblings (contingent on age-spacing in the latter case) are spurred into achievement not only because of the need to resolve identificatory problems, socialization in an adult world, and competition with the other elements of the family (the parents), but as a searching after power (authority, knowledge, economic sufficiency), so as to equalize the power statuses inherited in the family. That is to say, separation, autonomy, and self definition are achieved by striving for and acquiring power. By this line of thinking, then, achievement, in itself, is a by-product of the primary drive to make up for the inherited, low-power status of first-borns in the family. This is not so readily explained away as another example of role modeling and imitation learning.

Another implication of this sort of thinking that may well strike one as unlikely, or at least obscure, is that the child in the three-person family in measure deals with the parents as though they were siblings; that is to say that despite the generational axis and the parent control of resources, rather than envying and emulating them, the child perceives them as ''equal'' rivals in day-to-day interaction, now siding with one, then the other, in order to establish role equality (a la sibling rivalry) in the relationships. Before dismissing such a notion out of hand, it may be well to reckon with the fact that such a perception rather facilitates understanding oft-noted behaviors described as cliques, ''siding'' with one or another against a third family member, instances in which the generational axis (Parsons, 1964) seems absent.

In summary, the results of this brief discourse give impressive evidence of the multiple influences dominating the psychological life of the individual in the nuclear family. It pays homage to the continuing, enriched role played by one's siblings throughout the life span. It credits appropriate numbers and kinds of influences in psychological development that make the complex outcomes of socialization more understandable.

ACKNOWLEDGMENTS

I am grateful to Paul Mussen and Marjorie Honzik for making this study possible. The data for this study was made possible by USPHS Grant HD 03617 to the Institute of Human Development, University of California, Berkeley.

REFERENCES

Adler, A. *Understanding human nature*. New York: Premier Books, Fawcett Publications, 1959.
Aldous, J. Family interaction patterns. *American Review of Sociology,* 1977, *3,* 105–135.
Altus, W. D. Sibling order and scholastic aptitude. *American Psychologist,* 1962, *17,* 304.
Altus, W. D. Birth order and its sequelae. *Science,* 1966, *151,* 44–49.

Baltes, P. B., & Schaie, K. W. (Eds.). *Life-span developmental psychology: Personality and socialization.* New York: Academic Press, 1973.

Bell, R. Q. A reinterpretation of the direction of effects in studies of socialization. *Psychological Review,* 1968, *75,* 81–95.

Belsky, J. Early human experience: A family perspective. *Developmental Psychology,* 1981, *17,* 3–23.

Block, J. *The Q-sort method in personality assessment and psychiatric research.* Springfield, Ill.: C. C. Thomas, 1961.

Block, J. *Lives through time* (In collaboration with N. Haan). Berkeley, Calif.: Bancroft Books, 1971.

Bossard, J. H. S., & Boll, E. Personality roles in the large family. *Child Development,* 1955, *26,* 71–78.

Bossard, J. H. S., & Boll, E. *The large family system.* Philadelphia: University of Pennsylvania Press, 1956.

Brim, O. G. Family structure and sex role learning by children. A further analysis of Helen Koch's data. *Sociometry,* 1958, 1–16.

Brim, O. G., & Kagan, J. (Eds.). *Constancy and change in human development.* Cambridge, Mass.: Harvard University Press, 1980.

Brunswik, E. *Perception and the representative design of psychological experiments.* Berkeley, Calif.: University of California Press, 1956.

Cicirelli, V. Sibling influences throughout the life span. Paper read at *American Psychological Association* Meetings, New York, Sept. 1979.

Diamond, M. A critical evaluation of the ontogeny of sexual behavior. *Quarterly Review of Biology,* 1965, *40,* 147–175.

Erikson, E. *Childhood and society.* New York: W. W. Norton, 1950.

Erikson, E. Identity and the life cycle: Selected papers. *Psychological Issues,* 1959, *1,* 1–171.

Freud, S. *New introductory lectures in psychoanalysis.* New York: W. W. Norton, 1933.

Freud, S. *An outline of psychoanalysis.* New York: W. W. Norton, 1949.

Galton, F. *English men of science: Their nature and nurture.* London: Macmillan, 1874.

Harlow, H. F. *The human model: Primate perspectives.* New York: Halstead, 1979.

Havighurst, R. J. History of developmental psychology: Socialization and personality development through the life-span. In Baltes, P. B., & Schaie, K. W. (Eds.), *Life span developmental psychology.* New York: Academic Press, 1973.

Hilton, I. Differences in the behavior of mothers towards first and later born children. *Journal of Personality and Social Psychology,* 1967, *7,* 282–290.

Jones, H. E. Order of birth in relation to the development of the child. In Murchison, C., (Ed.), *A handbook of child psychology.* Worcester, Mass.: Clark University Press, 1931, 204–241.

Jones, M. C., Bayley, N., Macfarlane, J. W., & Honzik, M. P. (Eds.). *The course of human development.* Waltham, Mass.: Zerox College Publishers, 1971.

Kagan, J. Continuity and stage in human development. In Bateson, P. G., & Klopfer, P. H. (Eds.), *Perspectives in ethology* (Vol. 3). New York: Plenum, 1978.

Koch, H. The relations of "primary mental abilities" in five- and six-year olds to sex of child and characteristics of his sibling. *Child Development,* 1954, *25,* 209–223.

Koch, H. The relation of certain family constellation characteristics and the attitudes of children towards adults. *Child Development,* 1955, *26,* 13–40.

Koch, H. The relation of certain formal attributes of siblings to attitudes held toward each other and toward their parents. *Monographs for the Society for Research in Child Development,* 1960, *25* (4, Serial No. 78).

Kohlberg, L. A cognitive-developmental analysis of children's sex-role concepts and attitudes. In Maccoby, E. E. (Ed.), *The development of sex differences.* Stanford, Calif.: Stanford University Press, 1966.

Kohlberg, L. Stage and sequence: The cognitive-developmental approach to socialization. In Goslin, D. A. (Ed.), *Handbook of socialization theory and research*. Chicago: Rand-McNally, 1969, 347–480.

Korner, A. F. Individual differences at birth: Implications for early experience and later development. *American Journal of Orthopsychiatry*, 1971, *41*, 605–619.

Landy, F. S., Rosenberg, B. G., & Sutton-Smith, B. The effects of limited father absence on cognitive development. *Child Development*, 1969, *40*, 941–944.

Lewis, M., & Rosenblum, L. (Eds.). *The effect of the infant on its caregiver*. New York: Wiley, 1974.

Lipsitt, L. P. *Developmental psychobiology: The significance of infancy*. Hillsdale, N.J.: Lawrence Erlbaum Associates, 1976.

Macfarlane, J. W. Studies in child guidance: I. Methodology of data collection and organization. *Monographs of the Society for Research in Child Development*, 1938, *3* (6, Whole No. 19).

Mischel, W. On continuity and change in personality. Presentation at *Society for Research in Child Development Meetings*, Santa Monica, Calif., March, 1969.

Moss, H. A. Sex, age and state as determinants of mother-infant interaction. *Merrill Palmer Quarterly*, 1967, *13*, 19–36.

Moss, H. A., & Susman, E. J. Constancy and change in personality development. In Brim, O. G., & Kagan, J. (Eds.), *Constancy and change in human development*. Cambridge, Mass.: Harvard University Press, 1980.

Mussen, P., Eichorn, D. H., Honzik, M. P., Becker, S. L., & Meridith, W. M. Continuity and change in women's characteristics over four decades. *International Journal of Behavior Development*, 1980, *3*, 333–347.

Neugarten, B. L. Adult personality: Toward a psychology of the life cycle. In Neugarten, B. L. (Ed.), *Middle age and aging*. Chicago: University of Chicago Press, 1968.

Nye, F., & Berardo, F. *The family: Its structure and interaction*. New York: Macmillan, 1973.

Parsons, T. *Social structure and personality*. New York: Free Press, 1964.

Price, G. Factors influencing reciprocity in early mother-infant interaction. Presented at *Society for Research in Child Development* Meetings, New Orleans, March, 1977.

Rosenberg, B. G., & Sutton-Smith, B. Ordinal position and sex role identification. *Genetic Psychology Monographs*, 1964, *70*, 297–328.

Rosenberg, B. G., & Sutton-Smith, B. Sibling association, family size, and cognitive abilities. *Journal of Genetic Psychology*, 1966, *109*, 271–209.

Rosenberg, B. G., & Sutton-Smith, B. Family interaction effects on masculinity-feminity. *Journal of Personality & Social Psychology*, 1968, *8*, 117–120.

Rosenberg, B. G., & Sutton-Smith, B. Family structure and sex-role variations. In Coles, J., & Dienstbier, R. (Eds.), *Nebraska symposium on motivation*. Lincoln, Neb.: University of Nebraska Press, 1973.

Sampson, E. E. The study of ordinal position: Antecedents and outcomes. In Maher, B. (Ed.), *Progress in experimental personality research*. Vol. II, New York: Academic Press, 1965, 115–228.

Schachter, S. *The psychology of affiliation*. Stanford, Calif.: Stanford University Press, 1959.

Sears, R. R., Maccoby, E. E., & Levin, H. *Patterns of child rearing*. Evanston, Ill.: Row, Peterson & Co., 1957.

Speck, R. V. Psychotherapy of the social network of a schizophrenic family. *Family Process*, 1967, *6*, 208–214.

Sutton-Smith, B., Roberts, J. R., & Rosenberg, B. G. Sibling associations and role involvement. *Merrill Palmer Quarterly*, 1964, *10*, 25–38.

Sutton-Smith, B., & Rosenberg, B. G. Sibling consensus on power tactics. *Journal of Genetic Psychology*, 1968, *112*, 63–72.

Sutton-Smith, B., & Rosenberg, B. G. Modeling and reactive components of sibling modeling. In

Hill, J. P. (Ed.), *Minnesota Symposium on Child Psychology*, Minneapolis: University of Minnesota Press, 1969.

Sutton-Smith, B., & Rosenberg, B. G. *The sibling*. New York: Holt, Rinehart & Winston, 1970.

Sutton-Smith, B., Rosenberg, B. G., & Landy, F. S. Father absence effects in families of different sibling composition. *Child Development*, 1968, *39*, 1213–1221.

Tesser, A. Self-esteem maintenance in family dynamics. *Journal of Personality & Social Psychology*, 1980, *39*, 77–91.

Toman, W. *Family constellation: Its effects on personality and social behavior*. (2nd ed.) New York: Springer, 1976.

9 Important Variables in Adult Sibling Relationships: A Qualitative Study

Helgola G. Ross
Joel I. Milgram
University of Cincinnati

In our study of adult sibling relationships we explored three specific areas: perceptions of closeness, sibling rivalry, and critical incidents and their consequences to the relationships. We wanted to know what it means to be close to a brother or sister, and what brings closeness about. Why are some siblings closer than others? Why are they closer at particular times in their lives? Do feelings of closeness change through the life span in identifiable patterns? How does sibling rivalry affect these relationships? Who starts it? How long does it last? Is it always detrimental to the siblings, or the relationships, or can it also be beneficial? If so, under what circumstances? How do critical incidents, both anticipated and unexpected, change feelings of closeness, sibling rivalry, and sibling relationships in general? We wanted to know what these incidents are, and we wanted to find out about their short-term and long-term consequences. Do they affect all siblings alike?

These questions seemed important to us. They became more so when we realized that we could not find the answers in the literature. For the most part, the questions had been unexplored and, thus, remained unanswered.

To find answers we worked with 75 volunteer participants recruited from a large university community, two urban senior citizen centers, and a suburban retirement home. We tried to bridge as much of the adult lifespan as possible, and we succeeded, for our participants' ages ranged from 22 to 93 years. Participants were selected for their willingness to join our discussion groups and to reflect on their sibling relationships. Participants were all white and middle-class; their education ranged from two years of high school to the doctorate. The cultural backgrounds represented were Anglo-Saxon, Jewish, German, and Italian. Table 1 shows the age range, sex breakdown, and number of siblings.

TABLE 9.1
Age, Sex, and Number of Siblings of Participants

Variable	Frequency
Age (in years)	
20 – 29	8
30 – 39	21
40 – 54	16
55 – 69	8
70 – 93	22
Total	75
Sex	
Males	28
Females	47
Total	75
Number of Siblings	
1	17
2 – 3	31
4 – 5	13
6 – 9	11
10 – 17	3
Total	75

Participants met in 13 small groups, each consisting of four to six individuals. Two groups each were composed of individuals in their twenties, thirties, forties, and fifties. Five groups of participants were sixty years or older. The group sessions lasted 2 to 2½ hours, and were led by two investigators. The sessions were semistructured, with the investigators focusing the discussions, probing issues, and occasionally contributing their own experiences to model openness and to stimulate the participants' reflections. Ultimately, all sessions explored the participants' sense of closeness to their siblings, feelings of rivalry and perceptions of favoritism, critical incidents and their consequences, and changes of feelings and perceptions over time. Ten individual follow-up interviews were conducted to investigate sibling rivalry in greater depth, another ten to study critical incidents in more detail. All sessions were tape-recorded with the permission of the participants. Participants also completed questionnaires asking for demographic information about themselves and their siblings. The group sessions were chosen to help participants stimulate each others' reflections. This allowed us to keep the sessions relatively unstructured and to let important variables emerge spontaneously.

Tapes were transcribed and their content analyzed. The focus of the qualitative analyses was to identify recurrent regularities in topics, patterns, and dynamics (Bogdan & Taylor, 1975), and in particularly salient events (Guba,

1978). Specifically, the aim was not to determine the frequencies but to ascertain the patterns, events, and dynamics that seemed to have the greatest impact on adult sibling relationships. The identified variables and their dynamics are, of course, also descriptive of the group of participants studied and may well be equally important in the sibling relationships of similar groups. More importantly, however, the findings serve as the source of hypotheses and as a set of directions in which future studies might proceed.

PERCEIVED CLOSENESS

By far the most complex, elusive, and somewhat abstract concept to emerge from our study of adult sibling relationships was that of closeness. Closeness was perceived both as an attribute of the family as well as a descriptor of the relationships between siblings. We focused on how individuals perceived the lifespan patterns of family and sibling closeness, as well as the factors contributing to the origins and maintenance of closeness.

Perceived Lifespan Patterns of Closeness

Three lifespan patterns of family and sibling closeness were identified. Closeness, *as a family,* was more frequently reported than closeness to siblings, despite the relatively large number of siblings to which participants could have felt close (see Table 1). Family closeness was also described as more stable than closeness in specific relationships with siblings. Feelings of closeness to the family increased or decreased over time in only a few cases. In sibling relationships, however, increases and decreases of closeness were the predominant lifespan patterns (Ross, Dalton & Milgram, 1981). There was a suggestion that closeness to the family was particularly prominent during childhood and old age. Not surprisingly, during young and middle adulthood participants seemed to focus more on their spouses and children, and on relationships to one or a few particular siblings. These patterns are documented in Table 2.

Few families were perceived as never having been close. And, although in absolute terms such complete lack of closeness to siblings was relatively rare, it was mentioned twice as often as never having been close to the family. Furthermore, many siblings, especially those that were part of large families, were not mentioned at all during the interviews; we only know about their existence from the demographic data collected. Older individuals (55 to 93 years) perceived themselves as never having been close to siblings less frequently than the younger participants (22 to 54 years). In general, older participants appeared to have a stronger sense of family unity. They also tended to view siblings as kin rather than friends, models, advisors, or peers. In fact, older participants used kinship terms more than three times as often as all other role terms com-

TABLE 9.2
Perceived Life Span Patterns of Closeness

Life Span Patterns of Closeness to Family*	Frequencies Reported
Family has always been close	26
Closeness to family changed over lifetime	5
Family has never been close	8
Total Number of Subjects Reporting on Family Closeness	39
*Life Span Patterns of Closeness to Siblings***	
Sibling has always been close	21
Closeness to sibling changed over lifetime	72
Sibling has never been close	16
Total Instances of Closeness to Siblings Reported	109

*Closeness ratings to family are based on one family for each of the 55 participants.
**Closeness ratings to siblings are based on the 55 participants' total number of siblings.

bined. In contrast, the younger participants referred to kinship and other role terms equally. Friendship was somewhat more important in their sibling relationships than in those of older participants.

Origins of Closeness

The most powerful contributor to feelings of closeness between individual siblings was the framework of the family in which siblings grew up. The sense of belonging to the family, and of being close to particular siblings, was, for most subjects, permanently affected by experiences shared in childhood.

Certain conditions may prevent such closeness from developing. If siblings are far apart in age, or become separated during childhood, they may not have the opportunity to grow close while young. In rare instances, family interaction patterns may discourage the development of closeness among siblings. For example, a woman whose parents had always preferred their older sons to their daughter rebelled against the brothers' control as her guardians when her parents died while she was still young. She never developed close feelings for them. Another family, torn apart by divorce, did not value family unity. Siblings were expected to care for their own needs, and did. The sense of brother- or sisterhood characterizing close family relationships never developed between them. The diversity of reactions to similar conditions is apparent from a number of participant reports of surrogate parenting as a means of developing closeness in sibling pairs who were relatively far apart in age. Why surrogate parenting in some cases becomes the basis for special life long bonds and in others becomes the source of resentment and long-standing conflicts between siblings is not clear. It certainly is worth further investigation. The diversity of reactions to similar incidents is also illustrated by the fact that divorce, death of a parent, or other major disruptions of family life do not have to result in lack of closeness between brothers and sisters. As the discussion of critical incidents appearing later in this chapter shows, closeness, lack of closeness, and conflict in sibling relationships are all possible outcomes of such events. Bank & Kahn (see chapter 10) found that such incidents can even foster intense loyalties among siblings.

Generally, however, childhood experiences shared as families—such common activities as having meals together as well as family games, church attendance, enjoyment of special events and sharing of fear, pain, and grief when a major illness or death occurred—were the context in which family values and traditions were taught and expectations developed. Participants who felt close to their families and to their siblings recalled an emphasis on family unity and believed that democratic child rearing practices further encouraged its development. Especially important among these recollections were practices which stressed expectations for harmony, absence of favoritism, recognition of individual talents and accomplishments and—less frequently—the teaching of strategies for getting along and using conflict constructively.

Aside from these family experiences, experiences shared with particular siblings while siblings still lived at home—study, work, recreational activities, events arising out of common or complementary interests—were the most often cited instances originating feelings of closeness in childhood. These feelings were enhanced if siblings also shared close physical proximity, such as bedrooms, walks to and from school; or if they lived in geographically isolated areas. (See Table 3 for relative frequencies.)

Closeness also developed when children shared significant amounts of time in groups. Grouping was affected by age spacing ("the older kids," "the little sisters"), by gender ("the girls," "the boys"), by personality characteristics or interests ("the intellectuals," "the athletes"), and by the number of children in the family. Larger families provided more opportunities for grouping; indeed, they might have made grouping necessary. Some play groups became so close that they resembled exclusive clubs. In a few, parental preferences conferred rights and obligations on certain groups that resulted in alliances against other groups of children and/or the parents. A male participant reported the positive effects of such childhood cliques. The closeness in his group bonded the brothers so firmly that it became the source of an absolute reliance on each other in any kind of emergency in adulthood. A female participant reported the negative effects of childhood grouping by gender. Emphasizing the frustrations she experienced when her brothers were encouraged to play while she and her sisters were babysitting and doing household chores, she perceives being grouped by gender as the origin of conflicts still existing in the relationship with her parents.

The factors contributing to closeness in childhood remained important as long as siblings lived in the parents' home. As they grew older, however, the growing

TABLE 9.3
Factors Contributing to the Origins and Maintenance
of Perceived Closeness

Origin Descriptors	Percentage of All Instances Reported
Experiences shared with family	26
Experiences shared with groups of siblings	16
Experiences shared with particular siblings	23
Shared family values	17
Shared personal values	8
Shared physical space	10
Total Percentage of Origin Descriptors	100
Maintenance Descriptors	
Shared personal values	9
Shared goals and interests	18
Shared family traditions	15
Personal commitments to:	
family values	23
family traditions	13
communication with family members	22
Total Percentage of Maintenance Descriptors	100

differentiation of sibling personalities was reflected in increased numbers of references to shared personal values, shared and complementary interests, and activities arising from them. Adolescence was also a time in which siblings grew together, forging their identities by similarity and contrast. Inspiring and teaching each other, modeling (much of it cross-sex [c.f. Milgram & Ross, 1982; Ross, Dalton, & Milgram, 1981]); exploring issues through intense discussion, even providing dates for each other, were all relatively frequent. Through these interactions close personal relationships between siblings developed. Some even became good friends.

Rarely did closeness originate in adulthood. Some participants whose ages were quite disparate were able to build personal relationships when circumstances brought them geographically close in adulthood. In one case, siblings united against a common foe, a stepfather, for the first time in their lives, and stayed close from then on. More frequent were quantitative changes in closeness as siblings became more tolerant and understanding, resolved some of their earlier differences, or discovered that they had grown in opposite directions.

Maintenance of Closeness

Leaving the parental home was an incident that many siblings regarded as loosening ties and reducing closeness—geographical distance developed into psychological distance.[1] However, the family continued to provide a framework within which most relationships between siblings existed. In fact, these special qualities of the family became particularly evident at this time. Asked why they did not discontinue those relationships with siblings that had never been close, our participants were stunned. Most seemed to assume that sibling relationships are permanent. Some tried to explain, but did not get far beyond blood ties and family bonds. Very few, almost wistfully, realized that the question implied a choice—but the reality did not. When referring to "the family" the participants' voices sounded as if they described an invisible space that enveloped siblings, a space that protected but also confined. That this space is not impermeable is shown by reports of participants who felt that their siblings' marriages enhanced sibling relationships. They attributed this to their respect and liking for the siblings' spouses, and in general to the spouses' ability to fit into the family in terms of values, goals, and interests. Conversely, participants who felt that marriages detracted from sibling relationships attributed this to the siblings' spouses' different religion, ethnic background, socioeconomic status, and/or educational level. And some of the most difficult and conflicted family situations described by our participants arose when some siblings in a family changed values, life styles, and even socioeconomic status while other members did not. This conservative influence of the family was conceptualized by Ross & Dalton (1981a) as the family life space. Borrowing the concept of life space from Lewin (1936), they extended it from the individual to the family level. Incorporating psychologically salient aspects of life from past, present, and future, the concept explains why the family values, traditions, and interaction patterns remained the single most important factor in maintaining closeness among siblings. The content of the personal values and shared goals and interests mentioned as important in adulthood matched closely the religious affiliations, professional aspirations, interpersonal expectations, and beliefs in family solidarity that appeared as family values in childhood. It is difficult to avoid the conclusion that family values instilled in childhood reappeared in adulthood as internalized personal values whose sharing maintained continuity and closeness among siblings. This was especially true if siblings made conscious personal commitments to such family values and traditions, and to maintaining regular contact with siblings.

Memories were another essential factor for the maintenance of closeness among siblings. Memories of events perceived as originating closeness in childhood served to maintain it in later years. The older the participants were, the more these memories were cherished. Family rituals, regular reunions, such as joint vacations, holidays, especially significant birthdays or celebrations of major accomplishments, did much to maintain family unity and, within it, sibling closeness. These get-togethers allowed siblings to reminisce, to keep traditions

---

[1]See the critical incident section of this chapter.

alive, to add further common experiences, and to incorporate the siblings' spouses and children into the families. Perhaps these reunions were most important during the middle years, when they provided a major source of renewal and updating of sibling relationships.

But reunions were only one means for sharing experiences with siblings during adulthood. When siblings lived geographically close, sharing of daily events, the joys and frustrations of raising children, the maintenance of marriage relationships, occupational pressures, and adjustments to different life stages maintained closeness. These events were also shared with siblings who did not live close but who were chosen as especially significant others in the participants' lives. Further, siblings maintained contact through the sharing of responsibilities with respect to the physical, emotional, and financial needs of ailing or aging parents. As described later in this section, similar events again elicited divergent reactions and different consequences in sibling relationships.

In old age, family reunions lost a good deal of their importance in the maintenance of closeness for a number of reasons. Many siblings were no longer able to attend such meetings because of ill health or frailty. Further, such reunions by then were uniting the children and grandchildren rather than the elderly participants' brothers and sisters. Instead, regularity and frequency of contact seemed more valued than it had been since childhood, and appeared to subsume the functions family reunions served earlier in life. But the memories of family reunions remained important throughout old age.

A possible explanation for the importance of regular and frequent contact in old age is provided by a number of studies. As Lowenthal (1964) and Rosow (1970) have shown, the number of social contacts decreases with advancing age. Thus, siblings may become relatively more important members of each others' social networks (Cicirelli, 1979; Clark & Anderson, 1967). Several aspects of the elderly siblings' special status in each others' lives emerged from the data, fitting into social network functions described by Pilisuk and Minkler (1980). One social network function has to do with an individual's continual sense of contribution to life's tasks. Another has to do with a person's status as an object of affection. In old age, supporting each other appeared to be a major task for siblings and must have fed into the function of affirming each other as objects of affection and care. Elderly siblings provided a good deal more support for each other than younger siblings. Physical, emotional, psychological, and if necessary, financial support was provided. Physical care ranged from fixing a faucet to nursing a sibling for an extended period of time. Emotional and psychological care was inherent in the frequency and meaningfulness of writing, calling, and visiting each other. Numerous references were made to waiting for such communications as highlights of the day. Such forms of communication were considerably more frequent than between younger adults. Communications included almost all siblings still alive, even those who could no longer write or read. Others saw to it that information was disseminated to and about them. Almost all siblings appeared to have the sense of being part of communication networks that kept them in touch with each other's state of well-being and affairs. A third function of social networks, possibly specific to old-age sibling relationships, was suggested by Ross, Dalton & Milgram (1981). This function has to do with an elderly person's need for validation of perceptions of self and reality. Such perceptions, it was argued, may have become tenuous because of the direct effects of the stereotypes this society holds about its aged (Rodin & Langer, 1980) and because of the indirect effects of helplessness brought about by decreases in control over one's life (Schulz & Hanusa, 1980). Since sibling relationships appear to be among the most stable of all interpersonal relationships (Cicirelli, 1979; Ross & Dalton, 1981b), and since siblings function within the framework of common family values, interaction patterns, and perceptions of reality inherent in the family life space, they may be in a unique position to validate each others' perceptions of self and the world around them.

Memories were at least as important in maintaining closeness as social network functions. Sharing recollections of happy childhood experiences and cooperative and rewarding interactions in adulthood appeared to be a major source of comfort and pride. Being able to do so seemed to confer a sense of integrity—one had lived one's life in harmony with the family and one's own values. Not being able to do so appeared to be a cause for discomfort, anguish, and even despair. The quality of these reports was so descriptive of Erikson's (1963) last stage of life that Ross, Dalton and Milgram (1981) suggested dealing with memories may be a way of addressing a late developmental task. The notion deserves further attention.

PERCEIVED SIBLING RIVALRY

While the concept of closeness was difficult to deal with for our participants because of its abstract quality, sibling rivalry was hard to discuss because of the social stigma associated with it. Sibling rivalry was perceived as originated and maintained by parents and/or siblings. We will focus on the structural factors and dynamics involved in the origins and maintenance of sibling rivalry.

Origins of Sibling Rivalry

Seventy-one percent of the 55 participants in the group interviews experienced rivalrous feelings toward their brothers or sisters. Among them, rivalry was as often perceived as initiated by adults as it was remembered as an outcome of sibling interactions (see Table 4 for frequencies). *Adult-initiated rivalry* usually begins in childhood. Most commonly, one or both parents were mentioned. Other adults living in the same household—grandparents in particular—contributed. Initiation of rivalry by adults involves adults preferring one sibling over another (or a group of siblings over another group). Two dynamics were clear. One of these is based on *overt comparison*. These can be expressed positively, with the apparent intent of providing models of positive behavior for all children. In such cases, adults ask one child to model himself after another child in a variety of ways. Overt comparisons can also be expressed negatively, by denouncing one child for not living up to the superior qualities of another. In either case, it seemed clear to the young perceiver that the comparison child was more acceptable to the adult, and possibly more worthy of love. The second dynamic is based on *covert comparison*. One child observes an adult's preferential treatment of another child, again perceiving that greater value is placed on the comparison child by the adult. Both types of comparison can involve one or more adults.

Although in most cases these dynamics started in childhood, they were not limited to that period. One participant presented a clear case in which a parent started overt comparisons in later life. Our subject qualified his remarks by the observation that his siblings had been well matched on important dimensions until one obtained a graduate degree and a professional job, and his "maturity" significantly exceeded his siblings'. Once his father found a basis for comparison, he promptly seized it.

Sibling-generated rivalry is perceived most frequently as initiated by a brother, less frequently by a sister, and least often by the self. Some participants from larger families felt that groups of siblings started the rivalry. This kind of rivalry was much more frequently recalled as occurring first in adolescence or adulthood than in earlier years. When rivalry among children was reported, it seemed to be a vying for the parents' attention, recognition, and love, but also a more general juggling for power and position among siblings. Issues of control arose when siblings tried, or were set up by their parents, to act as substitute mothers or fathers. In several cases the precipitating factor was an older or, in the eyes of the parents, more mature sibling, who was asked to babysit for her or his brothers or sisters. Other instances arose out of the death of one parent and the surviving parent's transfer of the other's powers to one of the older siblings.

Another dynamic involved younger siblings seeing an older brother or sister as a mentor and extending this special relationship into adolescence and adulthood. An important aspect of this dynamic is the mentor's recognition of the younger sibling's accomplishments. Rivalry ensued when mentors, instead of providing the required recognition, compared their younger siblings unfavorably against their own greater accomplishments on the same dimension of growth. Direct comparisons between siblings on valued physical or psychological dimensions or achievements also led to rivalry. Many of these dynamics may be extensions of early learned interaction patterns into adulthood. Possibly, adult-initiated or condoned rivalry in childhood becomes a model for sibling-generated rivalry in adolescence and adulthood.

TABLE 9.4
Origin, Maintenance, and Structural Factors of
Perceived Sibling Rivalry

Origins		Instances Mentioned
Adult-initiated rivalry		40
Overt comparisons	17	
Covert comparisons	23	
Sibling-generated rivalry		39
Brother	19	
Sister	12	
Group of Siblings	4	
Self	4	
Maintenance		
Continued parental favoritism		22
Competitive behaviors between siblings		13
Feeling excluded from family interactions		8
Maintaining family-assigned roles/labels		9
Never mentioning rivalrous feelings to siblings involved		9
Structural Factors		
Dimensions		
Achievement		19
Physical attractiveness		12
Intelligence		11
Interpersonal competence		8
Maturity		6
Types of sibling rivalry		
Simple		59
Reciprocal		11
Sex-linked		6

Maintenance of Sibling Rivalry

Table 4 shows frequencies for various maintenance dynamics. The most frequently mentioned maintenance behaviors were the parents' continued favoritism, expressed in preferential treatment and overt comparisons. Next in
frequency were competitive behaviors between the siblings themselves. These
ranged from all-out conflict over power and control to more or less subtle and
creative ways of reminding siblings of their status. Some of these interactions
seemed harmless. They irritated, annoyed, even upset siblings; but they could
also be fun, helping all to sharpen their wits. Others created or maintained more
deep-seated hurts. Many siblings felt excluded from valued sibling or family
interactions and the sense of belongingness they can provide. Some dissociated

themselves psychologically and geographically from particular siblings or the family on a semipermanent basis. Two broke relations completely.

Sibling rivalry can extend beyond the relationship between two siblings and involve parts or the whole nuclear and even extended families. A frequently found mechanism in such cases is the assignment of a label to a sibling. When the sibling internalizes the label—i.e., acts in the role assigned to him or her—family thoughts, communications, and interpersonal behaviors become structured to accommodate the role. Such pervasive family involvement tends to lock a person permanently into the assigned role. Intelligent and stupid are two favorite labels. The first is generally positive, but it can generate considerable pressure if a family expects a child to carry on its intellectual tradition or, worse, to become the first who has ever obtained a college degree. Being labeled stupid and acting accordingly has equally or more far-reaching consequences. A participant described how by all objective standards her brother is quite successful in life, but he finds it difficult to take credit for or value his accomplishments.

Another maintenance dynamic is an apparent tacit agreement between siblings not to talk about their rivalries. In fact, the comparison sibling may well be unaware of the rivalry. Generally, only the self-perspective was associated with feelings of inferiority, rivalry, and competition, and few subjects ever discussed these feelings with their brothers or sisters. Conversely, siblings whose strengths served as standards of comparison did not realize their role as the stimulus in their sibling's feelings of rivalry, and had no affective reactions. Several participants *derived* their status as comparison children and/or adults once other participants described the opposite perspective. But recognition did not generate rivalrous feelings, and the contribution of the comparison sibling was frequently perceived as completely passive, made for him or her by others. In a few especially severe and long-lasting cases, the two siblings involved in the rivalry engaged in power games. One seemed to prefer the role of victim, the other the role of victor, repeating the process with regularity. In these cases parents preferred the sibling playing the victor, and both players knew it. A curious approach-avoidance tendency noted as a reaction to critical incidents involving reactivated parental favoritism (Ross, 1981) alludes to a need for recognition not only from the parents but also from the sibling perceived as the more valuable person. All but one of the siblings involved in these interactions kept their feelings to themselves.

Why do siblings keep their rivalrous feelings secret from each other? We do not know. However, a number of studies linking severe sibling rivalry to various problems of mental health (Cavenar & Butts, 1977; Frank, 1979; Robbins, 1964; Steele & Pollock, 1968) may provide a clue. Admitting sibling rivalry may be threatening and experienced as equivalent to admitting maladjustment. Furthermore, to reveal feelings of rivalry to a brother or sister who is perceived as being stronger or as having the upper hand in the relationship increases one's vulnerability in an already unsafe situation. The more intense these feelings, the less safe it is. And if the sibling experiencing rivalrous feelings essentially likes the rival and has a need to be accepted by him or her, he or she may fear that self-disclosure could permanently damage the relationships (c.f. Barrell & Jourard, 1976). Certainly this is a topic worth further investigation.

Structural Factors in Sibling Rivalry

Although competition for recognition, approval, acceptance, and love are assumed to underlie expressions of sibling rivalry (Adler, 1959), they were rarely mentioned directly by our participants. However, the need for them may well have provided the foundation for early rivalries, and seemed to remain a basic motivating force in cases where adult rivalries were intense. These underlying dynamics are not at all understood. They seem to be largely unconscious, as if a taboo operates to keep them repressed. Much more indepth work, probably in clinical settings, needs to be done to unravel these mysteries.

Much more frequent than vying for parental recognition were dynamics based on dimensions (traits, competencies, preferences, behaviors) on which siblings could be compared. Comparisons, whether made by others or self, were not merely descriptive but evaluative—they translated quantitative statements into value judgments. Simply having more or less success does not generate sibling rivalry. When more becomes better rivalry ensues. "Better" may be defined by the standards of a significant other or those internalized by the self.

Yet, sibling rivalry can be constructive. When it occurs on dimensions over which the compared sibling has control, it may be a motivator. For example, if siblings have the ability to live up to high standards, comparative expectations are not necessarily debilitating. Numerous siblings of the famous (Milgram & Ross, 1982) have described their famous brothers and sisters as inspirations. There was competition and rivalry, especially during late adolescent and early adult years when the establishment of a professional identity was a high priority. But once they found their own areas of expertise, rivalry disappeared, giving way to pride in each others' accomplishments. If siblings are devalued, however, because they are less intelligent, less attractive, or female, i.e., they fall short on a dimension over which they have no control, rivalry becomes destructive. Constructive rivalry was much less frequently reported than destructive rivalry. Perhaps, phenomenologically, sibling rivalry is of the destructive kind.

Dimensions.   The dimensions on which sibling rivalry are experienced clearly express the values of our society. They differ in terms of their frequency, intensity, and duration. By far the most frequently mentioned dimensions centered around achievement, intelligence, physical attractiveness, social competence, and maturity (See Table 4). From childhood to old age, achievement is the dimension of rivalry *par excellence*. It engenders more intense feelings, and feelings of longer duration, than any other. Occasionally, it involves entire families and spans lifetimes. It does so perhaps because it can take on many forms—from the toddler's first attempts to walk and talk, to grades in elementary, high school and college, to professional, academic, and financial success, material and cultural possessions, skills, social prestige, and even fame. And—above all—achievement is valued in this society to a degree to which many people do not perceive themselves as being valued without it (Beery, 1975).

Physical attractiveness proceeds from cuteness in childhood to what is generally accepted as attractive in males and females. It derives its power from this culture's preoccupation with youth and young looks. The dimension disappears largely from the rivalry repertoire during middle age. Occasionally, it is replaced by physical fitness and, in later years, by health and longevity. However, the power it exerts in younger years vanishes with its youthful expression.

Another dimension is maturity. It is most salient at the time siblings should establish their professional and married lives, but can remain an active issue if a sibling does not do so.

Interpersonal competence, a further comparison dimension, was often juxtaposed as a comparison strength to another sibling's accomplishments, although it is recognized as a dimension of sibling rivalry in its own right. Several brothers and sisters of famous persons saw their own major strength in this area (Milgram & Ross, 1982).

Types of Sibling Rivalry.   Types of sibling rivalry vary in complexity and generality. *Simple sibling rivalry* is by far the most common. It involves a sibling's weakness on a dimension and the rival's greater strength on the same dimension, along with a comparison in terms of a value judgment by a significant other or the self. The dimension may be relatively unimportant and time bound (e.g., tidiness during adolescence), or it may be highly valued by the sibling's family and culture, and continuous throughout life (e.g., academic achievement). A sibling may be actively engaged in several simple rivalries at the same time, involving the same or different brothers and sisters.

Reciprocal Sibling Rivalry.   This involves two siblings, each of whom has a strength and a weakness that serve as the stimuli for sibling comparisons. In one example the dimensions were academic achievement and physical attractiveness, in another achievement and social competence. Each sibling excelled on the dimension on which the other was perceived of as weak. Again, a sibling may be involved in more than one reciprocal rivalry, or in simple and reciprocal rivalries at the same time.

Sex-Linked Sibling Rivalry.   This affects individuals in a more general way than either of the above. Several female participants identified their rivalrous feelings as being tied to their brothers' greater privileges. Such privileges allowed the males in the family stereotypic male freedoms while confining the females to stereotypic female tasks. Sometimes the preferred treatment received by the male siblings from the parents generated alliances that split siblings into male and female groups. Particularly in larger families, this type of rivalry may be an individual/group or group/group phenomenon, with a woman or group of women expressing feelings of rivalry toward a group of brothers or a generalized brother. When both father and mother support this stereotype, feelings of conflict, frustration, helplessness, and rebellion can become directed toward the whole family. How powerful this type of rivalry can be was clearly established by the bitterness with which one woman in her eighties denounced her brother and *his* mother and father.

Intensity.   Sibling rivalry exists to varying degrees of intensity. For some participants it was essentially a matter of vying, almost affectionately, for supremacy on the same dimension of growth. For others, it was serious competition, sometimes with the apparent intent not only to surpass the other but to make her or him appear as the less valuable person. The greatest degree of intensity was observed in only three cases. In each, the entire family became involved. The dimension was academic achievement, which all three families valued highly. In each case, parents initiated the rivalry, and all siblings picked up the theme. In one case, it lasted until the sibling's death at the age of 75; in another, it continues today in middle age. In the third, one of the siblings left the country, thereby removing herself as the comparison stimulus. Although the move eliminated opportunities for reactivation of rivalries, it did not expurgate memories that continue to take their toll.

CRITICAL INCIDENTS

In contrast to closeness and sibling rivalry, most critical incidents and their consequences were easily identified. Critical incidents were defined as relatively specific events that brought about changes in sibling relationships. Differences in emotional reactions accompanying the incidents and the duration of their consequences also emerged from the study.

Types of Critical Incidents

Our study revealed several kinds of incidents. Most of them could be classified into two major categories: *normative* and *idiosyncratic* events (Lowenthal, Thurnher, Chiriboga & Associates 1975). Normative events are developmental—

they can be expected to occur at certain stages of life. Examples are marriage of a sibling during young adulthood or death of a parent during middle age. If normative events occur at such expected times in life, they are *on-time*; if they occur at unexpected times (death of a parent while siblings are still children) they are *off-time* (Neugarten, 1977). Idiosyncratic events are events that cannot be expected. Examples are divorces, car accidents, and arguments over values.

Eighty-five percent of the 55 participants involved in group interviews reported one or more critical incidents. The percentages of occurrences of particular types of incidents and their long-term consequences are shown in Table 5.

Normative Incidents and Their Consequences

The normative incidents identified in our study include geographical moves away from home and siblings, marriage of siblings, sickness of parents, loss of parents through death, sickness and death of siblings, and loss of spouses.

TABLE 9.5
Percentages of Types of Critical Incidents and
Their Long-Term Consequences

Type of Incident	Percentage*	Pos.	Neg.	No Change	Conflicted
Geographical Moves					
Away from siblings	12		100		
Closer to siblings	7	100			
Marriage of sibling	12	31	69		
Sickness of parent	6	44	56		
Loss of parent					
Through death	12	31	69		
Through divorce	2		33	33	33
Sickness of sibling	4	60	40		
Death of sibling	6	80		20	
Loss of spouse					
Through death	3	100			
Through divorce	3	50	25		25
Aid to siblings	6	75	25		
Employment/educational					
discrepancy	8	18	64		18
Value differences	8		100		
Violations of expectations	6		78	22	
Parental favoritism	5		100		
	100				

*Percentages are based on the 55 participants involved in group interviews plus ten participants involved in the individual interviews.

Geographical Moves.   The most frequently mentioned normative event was a geographical move. Moves away from siblings were more frequently reported than moves closer to siblings. Most moves away were on-time normative events, a move out of the parental home during late adolescence or early adulthood. Geographical distance, which varied from moving to the next city to moving half way across the world, was perceived as reducing contact and feelings of closeness, if the distance was maintained over long periods of time. An example are three sisters who had spent childhood and adolescence being "together all the time." Upon their marriages they moved to different towns. Because of the distance, contact and closeness diminished. Of three other sisters only one moved away. Sharing daily events and also major happenings maintained closeness with the sister in town, whereas geographical distance reduced contact and closeness to the other. That geographical distance can be used to legitimize desired dissociation from the family was revealed by several participants. If close family ties mean confinement or inability to grow, moves provide acceptable ways out. For others, geographical distance made it difficult or impossible to work out conflicts in their relationships. Seeing each other only briefly on occasional visits did not provide opportunities for resolution—or such visits were in fact set up to prevent them. Age spacing also affected geographical moves. Several participants, considerably older than some of their siblings, left home before they had a chance to develop close relationships.

Thus, on-time moves away from each other reduced contact and often ultimately reduced closeness in sibling relationships. Such loosening of ties seems to be a developmental progression as siblings prepare for closer emotional bonds to spouses and children. For some, geographical moves meant more than taking developmental steps. Leaving interpersonal conflicts with siblings was one such reason. Leaving family traditions and siblings closely tied to them to pursue other values, professional aspirations, and life styles was another. Interestingly, little emotion accompanied the reports of these moves, verifying Neugarten's (1977) suggestion that on-time normative incidents do not result in emotional crises. Rather, participants seemed to realize that moves presented major transition points whose consequences were long term, changing their lives as well as the quality of their relationships.

Moves closer to siblings invariably resulted in more frequent communication and increased feelings of closeness. It did not matter if siblings were young, middle aged, or elderly. Some attended college together. Several, prevented from getting to know each other in the parental home by age spacing, had that chance in mid-life. Value differences keeping siblings psychologically as well as geographically apart in young adulthood were treated with more tolerance in later years, and old age recreated bonds that had been latent since childhood.

Marriage of Siblings.   Two-thirds of the marriages reported detracted from sibling relationships; one-third enhanced them. Over half of the siblings involved in marriages detracting from sibling relationships were of the same sex, more often males than females. Several dynamics became evident. One shows how intense sibling relationships were disrupted when one sibling got married. Feelings of resentment and being rejected were strong. The remaining incidents involved siblings marrying persons of different religions, ethnic backgrounds, socioeconomic status, or educational levels. Mostly, dislike and lack of common interests resulted from siblings "marrying down." Perceptions of wives competing with each other or not liking each other sometimes accompanied these reports. A few participants reported simply that they did not like a sibling's spouse or were not liked by them. The duration of these consequences varied. In some cases, it lasted lifetimes; in others, marriages dissolved, giving the siblings another chance; in a few, adjustments were made.

In contrast, marriages enhancing sibling relationships were almost uniformly reported by females and involved male and female siblings alike. Emotional involvement accompanying these reports were less high than for marriages detracting from relationships; and the consequences were positive and long term. Liking and respecting the siblings' spouses was important. Spouses who enhanced sibling relationships fit into the family, sharing its values and interests. For these cases, already close ties were enhanced.

Sickness of Parents. Most of the reported incidents were on-time normative events, with the parents' illness occurring in old age. The incidents split almost evenly into sets having negative or positive consequences. In two instances, sisters criticized their younger brothers' behaviors toward their ailing parents, comparing them explicitly to their own superior—but unpracticed—abilities. A younger sister whose elderly mother could not manage her home any more complained bitterly that her older sister took control and advantage of the situation by moving in with mother. Other very similar situations had strikingly different effects. Younger sisters felt appreciative and grateful toward older brothers who helped ailing fathers. Illness of the father brought all siblings in one family into closer contact than they had had in years, rekindling feelings of "operating as a unit" that had been strong in childhood. These opposite reactions to similar events may be explained by the nature of pre-existing relationships. Negative reactions occurred in relationships characterized by strong sibling rivalry and conflict; positive reactions occurred in those that had been close since childhood.

Loss of Parents. Parents were lost through divorce and death. The three divorces mentioned are, by definition, idiosyncratic events. Two were traumatic, resulting in long-term disruption of the siblings' lives and relationships. In one family, close relationships never developed; in the other, relationships are very conflicted. Emotions still run high. The third divorce also had disrupting effects, but they were confined to the time surrounding the incident. In the long run, sibling relationships remained close, as they had been before the family's breakup.

Loss of parents by death was five times as frequent as by divorce. Only one-third of the deaths were on-time normative events; most occurred at unexpected times, many in the siblings' childhood. It is quite remarkable that so few on-time deaths of parents were reported, given that 30 of the participants were over 55 years of age and undoubtedly had lived through the experience once, if not twice. On-time deaths brought siblings closer together. Shared grief and the recollection of happy experiences and family closeness was one theme. "Mom is not there any more to keep us together, so we have to do it ourselves," is another.

Off-time events were reacted to quite differently. Participants who were children or adolescents when their parents died reported complex reactions. Short-term consequences increased closeness as pain, confusion, and memories were shared. Long-term consequences were more diverse. Some older brothers, taking on the role of "the man in the house," were resented by their younger brothers and sisters. In other cases, surrogate parenting was successful.

Sickness or Death of Siblings.   All but one of the reported incidents were off-time events, when illness and death occurred at times other than old age. Most consequences were positive for sibling relationships. When an oldest brother developed polio as a child the entire family rallied around him. Ultimately, he became the family counselor for a large group of siblings who trusted him with their problems and secrets. A late pregnancy drew two sisters close, setting up reciprocal support patterns for each others' major illnesses. Such periods of drawing close were recalled with special fondness.

Consequences of siblings' deaths were unequivocal. They enhanced the remaining siblings' feelings of closeness as they dealt with a common tragedy.

Loss of Spouses.   A few elderly women reported loss of spouses through deaths. They had relatively little to say about these on-time normative incidents, except that the consequences were long term and uniformly positive for sibling relationships. They brought both sisters and brothers closer to the bereaved.

Spouses lost through divorce elicited more mixed reactions, all characterized by intense emotionality, as expected for idiosyncratic events (Fiske, 1978). One woman became "closer to her brother than ever before in her whole life" when he helped her through this crisis. Another woman, feeling that she had violated family law, cut herself off from the family, feeling rejected. It took years before her siblings could convince her of their love. Another woman lost the respect of her sister, who felt that the divorcee should have tried harder to maintain a home for her five children. As noted before, previously conflicted relationships seemed to generate negative reactions, whereas positive relationships generated support.

Idiosyncratic Incidents and Their Consequences

Idiosyncratic incidents, like normative ones, were easily classified into the major category. Subcategories became more subjective. The most intuitively compelling subcategories were chosen. They include aid to siblings, employment and educational discrepancies, value differences, violations of expectations, and reactions to parental favoritism and sibling competition.

Aid to Siblings.   Different kinds of aid were given or received by participants. Some incidents involved money. Putting a younger sister or a brother's child through college generated gratitude and appreciation in already positive relationships. When money was lent and returned late, generally good relationships suffered temporarily. Not returning money deteriorated previously conflicted relationships. Another group of incidents involved personal counsel. Older sisters helped younger brothers or their children, always with very positive consequences for the relationships. Almost as if to prove that helping in difficult situations is not the prerogative of older sisters, two younger brothers helped older siblings work on interpersonal conflicts. That, too, enhanced positive relationships.

Employment and Educational Discrepancies.   Discrepancies in employment status and/or disparaties in educational levels were mostly reported by male participants. At least among our participants, males were more prone than females to make such comparisons. The reports were accompanied by moderate to intense emotions, possibly because most consequences were negative. Disappointment, lack of respect, absence of common values and interests led to reduced closeness and contact between siblings. Some consequences were mixed. In these cases professional discrepancies fed into competition based on parental favoritism. Becoming aware of a wide employment discrepancy reduced competition—but not necessarily jealousy—in two relationships: Competition was obviously futile. At the same time, increased admiration enhanced the ties. Unqualifiedly positive reactions came from an admiring elderly lady whose brother far surpassed the family's hopes for him. And two brothers in business together shared goals and interests and became even closer than they had been before.

Value Differences.   Incidents related to value differences fell into two clearly distinguishable groups. The larger involved incidents in which personal values were at odds with family values. Twice as many participants disagreed with family values as supported them. In one case, the oldest brother was expected to financially support his many brothers and sisters; family plans conflicted with personal plans for achievement and marriage. Other incidents involved disagreements over funeral expenses: family-oriented siblings demanded a lavish outlay that others considered a waste. Diverse other issues arose when family values were in conflict with acquired personal values.

The second major group of incidents related to value differences concerned personal value conflicts. These centered around issues of life styles and morals.

These disagreements and arguments between siblings generated especially long-term feelings of resentment and strong emotions. In all cases the consequences decreased closeness in sibling relationships, often involving several members of the family. For some of the older participants in whose families adherence to values seemed strongest, value conflicts virtually terminated relationships.

Violations of Expectations.   Violations of expectations for certain kinds of behavior, either by participants or, more frequently, by a participant's sibling, are similar to incidents arising out of value differences; however, they focus on behaviors rather than the values themselves. The behavior expected was clearly defined by family interaction traditions and/or by norms that siblings had acquired through new reference groups.

Most incidents were reported by women whose younger brothers did not behave as anticipated. One female participant reported several situations in which her brother had made her feel foolish, stupid, and ugly, or had taken advantage of her generosity. Another incident consisted of adolescent pranks. One involved a younger brother not being supported by an older sibling. Several incidents illustrate forms of rejecting a sibling. An interesting perspective was provided by two participants who consciously blocked family interaction patterns they considered detrimental to themselves and their siblings. Both generated feelings of rejection in their siblings that resulted in lessened social interactions and weaker emotional ties. The effects of these incidents were generally negative and involved strong emotions. These effects did not last very long when they occurred in essentially sound relationships. Many of them, however, maintained—like favoritism, on which they might have been based—open wounds in conflicted relationships. Some generated an approach-avoidance tendency. Others led to much reduced closeness.

Parental Favoritism and Sibling Competition.   Most incidents in this category were reported by older sisters whose younger brothers were preferred by one or both parents. For instance, a father, engaged in conversation with his daughter, dropped it in mid-sentence when her brother appeared at the door. Several incidents consisted of sisters finding out that their younger brothers had taken money from parents who really could not afford to give it. The older sisters were upset because brothers were still preferred by their parents, because brothers acted immaturely (they should not have asked for the money, knowing the parental circumstances), and because they were not recognized for their own more mature attitudes and behaviors. Another participant was told, on different occasions, that her older sister—or younger brother—would inherit the parental home. One elderly man's mother repeatedly made it clear who was the preferred child—by feeding him choice bits of meat and bigger pieces of cake than anyone else. The continued favoritism expressed by parents in these incidents reactivated jealousies, pains, and frustrations that participants had experienced since childhood and, in some cases, had tried hard to overcome.

A few incidents did not involve parents. One sister envied another her husband's wealth. Penned up feelings of inferiority surfaced between two other sisters.

All these incidents were accompanied by intense emotions despite the time passed since their occurrence. Consequences were uniformly negative, generating or reactivating deep resentments, pain, and frustrations. These incidents, arising in already conflicted relationships, resulted in more conflict, continual and increased approach-avoidance, and a lessening of positive feelings for each other.

CONCLUDING REMARKS

Our study was exploratory. Its primary purpose was to identify events, trends, and dynamics that we hoped would provide the basis for further studies. We got quite a bit more than we bargained for: a description of the study participants' perceptions of closeness, sibling rivalry, and the effects of critical incidents that in many cases amounted to an insider's view of the quality of their sibling relationships. Not only were the participants open in the group discussions; many returned to us, some several times, to give us additional information they felt we needed, or to go into deeper explanations of points they had made. Others wanted to share new realizations they had become aware of since the meeting. With a few, we still have ongoing discussions of ourselves and our siblings.

Equally fascinating was the process of seeing the findings emerge. As taped conversations turned into frequency tables and then into patterns, as dynamics and special events came into focus, we felt like detectives hunting concepts that furnished their own cues for being caught. It was, without doubt, the most interesting research we have ever done. We learned a great deal. But, despite a sense of closure at finishing this chapter, we now also have more questions than we started with. Let us share some with you.

We wonder to what extent the volunteer status of the study participants has affected the patterns, dynamics, and frequencies reported here. It is possible that persons for whom sibling relationships were not salient would not have volunteered. Considering the overwhelmingly positive response we got, however, we do not believe that the way subjects were identified had much of an effect on the qualitative aspects of the study. Given our observations, we believe that the dynamics that give rise to and maintain closeness and sibling rivalry are qualitatively less affected by subject selection methods, the norms of the setting in which data are collected, and possibly the cultural contexts in which siblings were raised and the reference group norms with which they identify as adults than the quantitative frequencies with which patterns and dynamics are reported. An extension of this type of study to randomly selected samples of subjects with different cultural and socioeconomic backgrounds, using a variety of data collection and analysis methods, should, of course, answer these questions.

Aside from these methodological considerations, we have a number of substantive questions. Not infrequently, practically identical critical events elicited different reactions and consequences from participants. These differences appeared to us to be related to the quality of sibling relationships existing prior to the incident. Essentially good relationships seemed to survive minor and, given enough time, even major incidents. In conflicted relationships such incidents seemed to maintain or increase conflict. In other words, positive or negative reactions to certain events seemed as much a matter of interpretation of these events, within the framework of existing bonds, as it seemed a result of the events themselves. Does the quality of existing relationships structure perceptions leading to interpretations of events commensurate with pre-existing relationships? Do these, in turn, structure the incidents' consequences? If the answer is yes, how can this be squared with the changes that we know to occur in some sibling relationships?

Could such differences be accounted for in terms of perceptual shifts? We wondered about the importance older adults attached to cherished childhood memories, and their emphasis on family unity and sibling solidarity. Is this a generational difference, a sample difference, or have events been reinterpreted over time? Many of the perceptions involved memories of times long passed. Perceptual shifts may have accommodated changing needs. Events may have been forgotten, and forgetting may not have been random. Some may have been repressed. In particular, we would like to know why on-time normative events such as deaths of parents, spouses, and siblings were not mentioned more often. Perceptual shifts, systematic forgetting, and repression are not actually necessary for a study of perceptions that determine the quality of sibling relationships at any given time. However, their study could contribute greatly to an understanding of differences in meaning and quality of closeness and other variables in sibling relationships at various stages of life. And the dynamics bringing about such shifts themselves are of interest. If we understood them, could we use the knowledge to improve our sibling relationships?

We have questions about the role proximity plays in sibling relationships, too. It was clear that close physical proximity is important for the development of closeness. But what about its maintenance? As siblings stated their preferences, both physical closeness and distance emerged as contributing to feelings of closeness. Of course, there are individual differences in affiliation needs. But are some of these preferences attributable to varying degrees of conflict in the relationships? When sibling relationships are marked by rivalry, it may be preferable to avoid being too close too often. Conflicts cannot erupt and rivalry cannot be reactivated when siblings are not around each other. Of course, neither can anything be resolved. Such avoidance may, nevertheless, allow siblings to find strengths, even identities, that will allow them at later dates to re-enter relationships that earlier were too dangerous to deal with. We would like to know under what conditions avoidance behaviors may be beneficial. When should they stop? And how?

Related are questions concerning the preponderance of older sisters reporting violations of expectations and parental favoritism involving younger brothers. How can these be explained? How can they be reconciled with the findings that most aid to siblings was also extended by older sisters to younger brothers? Findings of childhood studies showing that females are more affected by males than vice versa (Sutton-Smith & Rosenberg, 1970) echo the greater sensitivity of sisters to brothers illustrated here. But what are the specific dynamics?

Further, why do older sisters allow younger brothers to perpetuate patterns that appear to be so painful and frustrating to them? More generally, given the amount of negative affect accompanying these critical incidents and severe sibling rivalry, the question arises why siblings do not even consider severing ties. In this and another study (Ross & Dalton, 1981b) we have found only four persons who had broken ties with a brother or sister. Although each had excellent reasons for doing so, only one felt comfortable with the break. There were strong feelings, recurrent questions, and, in one case, attempts to contact a sibling late in life. Is it psychologically impossible to dissociate oneself from one's siblings in the way one can forget old friends or even former mates? If it is, the continual search for answers, even if questions beget questions, seems especially worthwhile.

ACKNOWLEDGMENTS

We wish to thank our research assistants, Mary Jo Dalton and Harriet Grood, for their help in analyzing the data and their insightful contributions to the analyses.

This study was in part supported by a grant from the University of Cincinnati Research Council.

REFERENCES

Adler, A. *Understanding human nature.* New York: Premier Books, 1959.

Barrell, J. & Jourard, S. Being honest with persons we like. *Journal of Individual Psychology,* 1976, *32,* 185–193.

Beery, R. G. Fear of failure in the student experience. *Personnel and Guidance Journal,* 1975, *54,* 190–203.

Bogdan, R. & Taylor, S. J. *Introduction to qualitative research methods: A phenomenological approach to the social sciences.* New York: Wiley & Sons, 1975.

Cavenar, J. O. Jr. & Butts, N. T. Fatherhood and emotional illness. *American Journal of Psychiatry.* 1977, *134,* 429–431.

Cicirelli, V. G. Sibling influence throughout the life span. *Paper presented at the 87th Annual Convention of the American Psychological Association,* New York, September, 1979.

Clark, M. & Anderson, B. *Culture and aging.* Springfield, Ill: Charles C. Thomas, 1967.

Erikson, E. H. *Childhood and society.* (2nd ed.). New York: W. W. Norton, 1963.

Fiske, M. Adult transitions: Theory and research from a longitudinal perspective. *Paper presented at the meeting of the Gerontological Society,* Dallas, Tex., November, 1978.

Frank, H. Psychodynamic conflicts in female law students. *American Journal of Psychoanalysis.* 1979, *39,* 65–69.

Guba, E. G. *Toward a methodology of naturalistic inquiry in educational evaluation.* Los Angeles, Calif.: Center for the Study of Evaluation, UCLA Graduate School of Education, 1978.

Lewin, K. *Principles of topological psychology.* New York: McGraw Hill, 1936.

Lowenthal, M. F., Social isolation and mental illness in old age. *American Sociological Review,* 1964, *29,* 54–70.

Lowenthal, M. F. Thurnher, M., Chiriboga, D. & Associates. *Four stages of life: A comparative study of women and men facing transitions.* San Francisco, Calif.: Jossey-Bass, 1975.

Milgram, J. I. & Ross, H. G. Effects of fame on adult sibling relationships. *Journal of Individual Psychology,* 1982, *38,* in press.

Neugarten, B. L. Adaptation and the life cycle. In N. K. Schlossberg & A. D. Entine (Eds.), *Counseling adults.* Monterey, Calif.: Brooks/Cole, 1977.

Pilisuk, M. & Minkler, M. Supportive networks: Life ties for the elderly. *Journal of Social Issues,* 1980, *36,* 95–116.

Robbins, S. D. 1000 Stutterers: A personal report of clinical experiences and research with recommendations for therapy. *Journal of Speech and Hearing Disorders,* 1964, *29,* 178–186.

Rodin, J. & Langer, E. Aging labels: The decline of control and the fall of self-esteem. *Journal of Social Issues,* 1980, *36,* 12–29.

Rosow, I. Old people: Their friends and neighbors. *American Behavioral Scientist,* 1970, *14,* 59–69.

Ross, H. G. Critical incidents and their perceived consequences in adult sibling relationships. *Paper presented at the American Psychological Association Convention,* Los Angeles, Calif., August 1981.

Ross, H. G. & Dalton, M. J. Perceived determinants of closeness in adult sibling relationships. *Paper presented at the American Psychological Association Convention,* Los Angeles, Calif., August 1981. (a)

Ross, H. G. & Dalton, M. J. *Similarities and differences in perceptions of closeness toward mates, friends, and siblings through the adult life span.* In preparation. 1981. (b)

Ross, H. G., Dalton, M. J., & Milgram, J. I. Older adults' perceptions of closeness in sibling relationships. ERIC/CAPS, Document Service: Document ED201903, 1981.

Schulz, R. & Hanusa, B. H. Experimental social gerontology: A social psychological perspective. *Journal of Social Issues,* 1980, *36,* 30–46.

Steele, B. F. & Pollock, C. B. A psychiatric study of parents who abuse infants and small children. In R. Helfer (Ed.), *The battered child.* Chicago: University of Chicago Press, 1968.

Sutton-Smith, B. & Rosenberg, B. G. *The sibling.* New York: Holt, Rinehart & Winston, 1970.

10 Intense Sibling Loyalties

Stephen Bank
Wesleyan University

Michael D. Kahn
University of Hartford

Like Hansel and Gretel, some siblings form intensely positive relationships with one another. These relationships rest on a foundation of mutually agreed upon principles that we have termed "intense sibling loyalties." We have been studying (Bank & Kahn, 1982) videotaped interviews of groups of intensely loyal and caring siblings who have much in common with Hansel and Gretel.[1] Like Grimm's fairy tale siblings, many of them suffered severe parental losses and grew up together under emotionally trying conditions.Loyalty, attachment, and devotion to one another seemed to be the outstanding themes of their interaction with each other.

In other publications (Bank & Kahn, 1975; Bank & Kahn, 1980–81; Kahn & Bank, 1980; Kahn & Bank, 1981) we have noted that both clinical and academic psychologists have emphasized rivalry, strife, and dominance in sibling relationships, but the word "loyalty" rarely appears. We suggest that loyalty is a major theme or dimension of sibling relationships, that it can coexist with rivalry, conflict, and competition. We felt that loyalty was a topic worthy of study in its own right. As Boszormenyi-Nagy and Spark have observed (1973), loyalty is a dynamic that operates in a powerful manner throughout family systems, dictating the pattern and cycle of intimate relationships.

---

[1]In the present discussion we will confine our focus to reciprocal sibling loyalties. Those loyalties in which one sibling cares intensely for one or more siblings without necessarily having the caring reciprocated are a separate topic and are described in: Bank and Kahn (1982).

LOYALTY DEFINED

We are interested in intense loyalties, not in temporary or convenient coalitions. Intense loyalty is not based on a simple strategic alliance that can easily be broken, changed, or forgotten about. Unlike a momentary alliance, loyalty between siblings takes years to develop and affects the loyal sibling's identity over much of his lifetime. Loyalty should not be confused with what some sociologists refer to as "sibling solidarity" (Cummings & Schneider, 1961). Most siblings will *say* that they have enduring relationships that involve staying in touch with one another, recognizing each other's birthdays, and meeting occasionally on the common turf of their parents' home. Sibling solidarity describes siblings who participate in a friendly and companionable network; but such a network may not be intensely loyal. Loyalty goes deeper. It has powerful emotional accompaniments. Loyalty refers to what Josiah Royce (1908) called "the willing and practical and thoroughgoing devotion of a person to a cause [p. 17]." Loyalty involves feeling and identification with the other person; it also requires tangible action and sacrifice.

We recruited for our project families in which there were known parental losses. We had reason to believe that loyalty between siblings would be most likely to form in a vacuum of adequate parental care and attention. As we reviewed the literature of the last 40 years, we came across evidence that supported the idea that parental unavailability can promote intense loyalties among the children. In a study of sibling rivalry among children aged 3 and 4 who had younger brothers and sisters, Levy (1937) found an inverse relationship between rivalry and size of family. More children appear to dilute the relationship with parents; this in turn appears to intensify the childrens' rapport with one another. Sewall and Smalley, in *Two Studies in Sibling Rivalry* (1930), illustrate the same point in another group of younger children, noting that "maternal oversolicitude" seemed to be a major factor in preventing the formation of warm sibling relationships. In large families "oversolicitude" is sharply limited by parental considerations of time, energy, and fairness. Bossard and Boll (1956) interviewed adults who had grown up amidst many brothers and sisters. For the most part they acknowledged that there were warm and enduring bonds with brothers and sisters. Furthermore, they attributed these bonds in part to the difficulty of getting enough attention from parents: They were forced to cooperate with one another, knowing that they could not turn to parents to solve sibling conflicts.

Anna Freud and Sophie Dann (1951) studied a unique group of children whose parents had been murdered by the Nazis. They were reared together in the Ward for Motherless Children at the Terezin concentration camp. Four of these children had lost their mothers immediately after birth; the other two probably had lost their mothers before 12 months of age. "After the loss of their mothers all the children wandered for some time from one place to another, with several complete changes of adult evironment. . . . they were ignorant of the meaning of a 'family' [p. 129]." Once they were placed in the concentration camp nursery, only their basic biological needs were met by adults. Lacking toys, their social activity apparently consisted entirely of play with one another. They never knew or attached themselves to adults. When the Allies finally liberated Terezin in 1945, the children were flown as a group to a therapeutic nursery where Freud and Dann studied them. Striking was the total absence of rivalry and aggression amongst this sibling-like group and their lack of trust for all adults.

> The children's positive feelings were centered exclusively in their own group. It was evident that they cared greatly for each other and not at all for anybody or anything else. . . . They had no other wish than to be together and became upset when they were separated from each other even for short moments. . . . This insistence on being inseparable made it impossible in the beginning to treat the children as individuals or to vary their lives according to their special needs [p. 131].

> The children's unusual emotional dependence on each other was borne out further by the almost complete absence of jealousy, rivalry and competition. . . . Since the adults played no part in their emotional lives at the time, they did not compete with each other for favors or recognition. . . . They did not grudge each other their possessions. . . . When one of them received a present from a shopkeeper, they demanded the same for each of the other children, even in their absence. . . . At mealtimes handing food to the neighbor was of greater importance than eating oneself [p. 134].

Other studies that suggest that intense sibling involvements was promoted by parents' unavailability have focused on twins. National attention was recently given to a set of twins who developed "idioglossia"—a private language which was understood only by one another and had to be decoded by linguists (O'Brien, 1978). The parents of these twins were overburdened by outside responsibilities and spent little "quality time" with them. They were reared primarily by a non-English-speaking caretaker who gave them routine custodial service. Like the twins about whom Burlingham wrote (1952), their access to each others' conscious and unconscious lives was nearly complete. And like the twins in Burlingham's studies, their parents' influence on their development was seriously dilluted by their involvement.

In our discussions with the families in our project, we have been interested in the following questions:

1. What *is* loyalty among siblings, and how is loyalty demonstrated?
2. How do brothers and sisters develop such intense attachments to one another?
3. What are the benefits and the burdens for each sibling who participates in such a loyal relationship?

We have selected three groups of siblings for detailed description. Representative of three different points in the life cycle, they include:

1. Four brothers in mid-life, aged 36–45, three of whom were married. All four were college graduates and successfully established in business and professional careers.
2. Two brothers, aged 20 and 22, attending the same university.
3. A brother aged 6, and his 9-year-old sister living together in a foster home, awaiting adoption.

These siblings were referred to us by colleagues who knew we were conducting a project on sibling loyalties. They were selected for the present study because they represent extreme instances of intense loyalty, and therefore provide an opportunity to study sibling loyalty in its strongest form. By studying extreme cases of sibling loyalty, we hope to learn something about why loyalty might not develop and how weaker loyalties develop among siblings. All of our subjects were willing and eager to discuss their experiences.

We proceeded by interviewing each group of siblings together as a natural group. The interviews lasted approximately three hours. As the siblings discussed their relationships, we questioned them. We focused particularly on the reciprocal influences of the siblings upon one another. The siblings were bright, articulate, and able to reflect upon their relationship as it had developed over time. Although we recognize that there are certain limitations to this interview method, one unique advantage has been that siblings could validate or disagree with one anothers' memories of events. Furthermore, their feelings about their relationship were shown by their actions toward one another as they answered our questions, or reacted to each others' comments. In-depth interviewing of this nature yields much richer information than that gathered by standard questionnaire methods. The interview method therefore allowed us to verify important facts and experiences and to observe the siblings as part of an ongoing, living, social system. Our findings are based on the contents, major themes, and interpersonal processes as recorded on videotapes of these interviews. In the material that follows, we will utilize concepts that are derived from social psychology, communications theory, family systems theory, and ego psychology. It is our view that describing the relationships between siblings requires an eclectic perspective, which affords us a rich descriptive language, rather than a narrow, theoretically-bound orientation with concomitantly limited technical vocabulary.

HOW LOYALTY IS DEMONSTRATED

Among the families we have studied, their commitment to one another was, to put it simply, fierce. There was a sense, subscribed to by the families we interviewed, that their relationships with each other would come before all others in importance. Their relationships seemed governed by an unwritten "law" that ordained that first and foremost—"we will stick together." These were not temporary alliances. They were, rather, relationship agreements or contacts with a long history that the siblings expected to continue in the future. As two of the four brothers in our mid-life group put it:

Youngest Brother: There's four brothers, going through life. Instead of falling apart, as many would do at a crisis—like the death of our mother or the crumbling of our father as a 'figurehead' of the family, we didn't. We complement each other. If one is down, the others are up. At *no* time would all four of us be down, because whoever might be down at a particular time, it will be recognized by the others, and they would help to get him up.

Second Oldest
Brother: Whether that be financially or spiritually.

Youngest Brother: Right! Regardless of what it is. For example, I know as I sit right here, if I ever got in any trouble—the *first* ones I go to is my brothers. I don't call my father. I don't call my in-laws. I don't *call my wife*. I call my brothers.

All three families communicated a sense that the siblings would always be available, that problems could be shared immediately and without embarrassment, that common values were shared, and that they could *count* on each other for honesty and understanding.

Sibling loyalties, as demonstrated in our research families, are similar to what Hartup (1975) has termed "the unique qualities of a friendship." We have selected four of the qualities of friendship that Hartup described as conditions that also constitute sibling loyalty. These include: a) actively trying to be with each other; negative reactions to being separated; b) cooperation, sympathy, and mutual helpfulness; c) a special language, not usually shared by outsiders; and d) defense of one another against outsiders. A fifth quality, *not* mentioned by Hartup involves conflict resolution and rituals of forgiveness.

1. Loyal Siblings Actively Try to Be With Each Other and Have Negative Reactions to Being Separated.   For example, the middle-aged brothers saw each other frequently or spoke often on the phone. Two of the brothers who lived one hundred miles apart saw each other at least every two months. The uncle-status of one of these brothers to his three nieces and nephew was celebrated by the entire family. The children's birthdays were occasions for get-togethers among these brothers. Even if one brother had not visited the others in recent months, an informal network of phone calling always served to relay his whereabouts to the others. When one brother's wife gave birth to twins, his oldest brother was in Europe at a conference. He immediately placed a transatlantic call (rather than sending a telegram) and insisted that the operator hold the line until his brother could be located.

The urgency of that phone call was paralleled by an instance of the older of these two brothers' reactions to separation, many years earlier. He recalled:

Older brother to younger: The low point for me was when you were four years old and you had a hernia operation. I mean, this, to me, was terrible! You know... four years old, my kid brother went to the hospital. That was *terrible* for me.

Interviewer: Do you remember your reaction?

Older brother: You know, 'THEY'RE CUTTING HIM OPEN! WHAT ARE THEY DOING *THAT* TO HIM FOR?' And the next day I went down there.

The two college-age brothers we studied reported a similar experience. As the older brother remembered:

Older brother: He had to encounter a lot of things that I didn't when I was growing up. A couple of things happened to him when he was younger. (His voice begins to tremble and he suddenly weeps, remembering.) He was in the hospital. I was upset. And it was like... (his voice breaks, unable to speak for a moment)—*I* was going through it. I felt that it was the worst thing that could happen to me. It was like sympathy, I felt pain for him. When he has an operation or goes into any adverse situation—it, it makes me cry.

In addition these young men, ages 20 and 22, chose the same small Eastern college many miles from their home in the Midwest. They spent most major holidays together. And they shared a fantasy that after each had married they would buy a vacation spot together—a homestead where their wives and children could blend with them into a big, happy household.

The nine-year-old girl and her brother sought to be with each other so frequently that their social worker became worried that neither would learn to function without the other.

Interviewer: What have you observed of their relationship?

Social Worker: Len (the little boy) makes no independent decisions without consulting her, even over a matter about what they are going to have for lunch or buy at the store, or anything that he has a question on, he will turn to her to get reassurance, a nod, approval or whatever. He would rather turn to her than to the foster mother.

These same children shared the worry that, if separated, the little boy might collapse or get into serious trouble. When, in the interview, the idea of separate adoptions (separate homes) was introduced, he became visibly anxious, ran around the room and hid his head under the pillow. The little girl who, since the age of three, had considered herself his caretaker, worried constantly about this hyperactive youngster, *especially* when they couldn't be near one another.

Older sister: Sometimes, when I'm away from him, and he is somewhere else, I
(age 9)   think about him.
Interviewer: Oh, well, what do you think about him when you are away from
                each other?
Older sister: That . . . I wish he was with me so that I could see him more and talk
                to him more.

This girl lived with the daily apprehension that her brother would act "bad" if
not supervised closely by her. In restaurants, when he would go to the bathroom,
she would worry about his getting lost on the way back to the table. Upon hearing
that he had, once again, gotten into trouble, she would monitor him even more
closely and assume even greater responsibility for his activities and whereabouts.

   *2. Cooperation, Sympathy, and Mutual Helpfulness Is Another Aspect of
Sibling Loyalty.* All members of the three sibling groups maintained a positive
and helpful attitude towards one another. Often this included a willingness to
sacrifice their immediate interests on behalf of siblings. For example, the nine-
year-old girl, speaking about her hyperactive, unstable younger brother, proudly
informed us that she frequently left her third grade classroom to discuss her
brother's progress with his first grade teacher. She requested information on his
grades, behavior, and attitude with the thoroughness that might characterize a
"concerned parent." She chose to play with him and frequently missed opportunities to join her own peers.
   This same attitude of "willingness to sacrifice" appeared among the brothers
in their 40s:

Second oldest brother: If you came to me with any difficulty, you know, if it's
                         financial, academic, or whatever, I'd give you my last
                         buck. And I *mean* that, sincerely, in *spite* of my respon-
                         sibilities to my children and wife. You know, I've got a
                         lifetime to live, and I got a lifetime to make it back. I
                         would give him my last buck.

   One of these brothers, the oldest, became the mentor to the other four. When
he became the chairman of an academic department at a high school in his early
twenties, he learned that one of his younger brothers was in serious academic
difficulty. He coached him for his examinations and made sure that he didn't
neglect his homework. His role as cultural and academic leader of the brothers
was further established when he tutored his next youngest brother, after that
brother had transferred from a high school in the ghetto with lower academic
standards to a more academically demanding high school. The transition had
been so abrupt, the younger brother was in danger of flunking out. The older
brother therefore encouraged him, set an example of concern, and took the time
to tutor him. Years later the younger brother attributed his own successful com-

pletion of a college and architectural degree largely to the helpful relationship he had experienced with his brother.

The reciprocity of helping and sacrifice that permeated their relationship was indicated when the older brother described what the younger had done for him when their mother had died. Her death placed the older brother at the helm of the group of four. He organized the group and monitored them. He chastized them for smoking, monitored their grades, set a good example for them. But his efforts were made possible by his next younger brother who helped to calm him in moments of crisis, who shared the burden of teaching the two youngest to get along, who put himself at risk in breaking up the fights of the two youngest and even taught one of the boys to cook. The older brother considered him an ally, a backup, an extra resource whom he could fall back upon.

3. Loyal Siblings Share a Special Language Not Always Understood by Outsiders. Each of the sibling groups we interviewed had a special "code" that bound them together in a privately shared world, *and* served to warn outsiders (in this case, the interviewer) that understanding this, their private communication system, was a key to understanding their sibling relationship. For example: the four brothers repeatedly broke into raucous laughter after one member had made, what to the interviewer, seemed a perfectly neutral comment. They sarcastically "apologized" to the interviewer for the "silly" behavior of their brother, as if to say, "This is our sense of humor: *you'll* never understand it since you didn't grow up with us."

Speaking their "language" became a major issue for others who wished to penetrate into their exclusive "club." One of their wives was almost completely accepted because she could "be one of the boys." She understood their special language, never challenged their relationships, went along with their male humor, participated in sports with them, and related to them in a down-to-earth way. She knew that in order to be accepted by her husband she had to appreciate and participate in her husband's appreciation of his brothers. On the other hand, failure to accept or understand their special communication system led to the exclusion of the youngest brother's wife. Although a part of this "family" for four years, she had never understood the brothers' humor and seemed shocked and offended by their occasional expressions of machismo and vulgarity. She became the object of their humor and was treated by the three brothers-in-law with forebearance at best, but more often with scorn and exclusion.

Another example: The little boy became nervous and overactive during the televised interview and, at one point it looked as if he might knock over the lights. The interviewer helplessly commanded and cajoled him. His sister then squinted furiously at him. He abruptly stopped jumping and, after one more piercing look, stayed angelically in his chair for the rest of the interview.

Another example: The colege brothers, even though they were sensitive and cooperative with our interview, frequently used names of special places and persons that were obviously known only to them and not to the interviewer. It became necessary to ask repeatedly about who and what they were talking.

4. Loyal Siblings Defend One Another Against Outside Threats. When threatened by an outside force, loyal siblings will close ranks and protect each other. This can occur even under conditions of great risk or potential personal sacrifice. For example, the college-age brothers spent their pubertal and adolescent years with a foster mother who was manifestly disturbed and who treated them sadistically. Like Hansel and Gretel in the witch's house, each maintained a conspiracy of silence on each other's behalf when the foster mother would pump one for personal information about the other. They both recognized early in their stay with her that she was quite troubled. Each could reassure and verify for the other that her actions were irrational and each provided the other with emotional protection. As boys (and later as young adults) they would swap stories about her vicious attacks; the story-swapping united them against their common enemy.

Both foster parents continued to abuse them, implying that the eldest was a homosexual and that the youngest was academically inferior. They also made up lies about the boys' biological parents in order to hurt them. In an attempt to separate the boys so they couldn't speak to each other at night, the foster parents assigned them separate bedrooms. They flatly refused and, rather than live in comfortably separated second floor bedrooms, they chose to live together in a tiny attic room where their two beds could only be accommodated with great difficulty. By refusing to be separated, they were able to defend each other and their relationship from these hostile outsiders.

The little girl hovered protectively over her little brother and frequently became angry with him when she learned that he was embarrassing himself in public by his "silly" behavior. One of her central fears was that he would be ridiculed by other children. She was forever teaching him how to behave better lest he bring down the wrath of teachers; friends, and other outsiders. She occasionally interceded with foster parents when her sibling misbehaved, getting him "off the hook" by promising to speak sternly with him.

The middle-aged brothers grew up in a ghetto neighborhood in a large city where racial conflicts and gang fights were not uncommon. Although each might venture outside sensing danger, an attack on one member was remembered and quickly retaliated by the joint action of two or more of the brothers.

Second oldest brother: I remember a time Bob (4th brother) was getting beat up by this kid. Next day Ed (3rd brother) and I sent him out to fight the kid again. Sure enough, the kid smashes Bob right in the mouth and he gushes blood. Then we got the guy. I held him down and Ed whacked him while he was on the ground. (As 2nd brother told this story the other three nodded, smiled and enjoyed remembering the incident.)

The Three Musketeers' "One for all and all for one" could easily have served as their motto. Their defense of one another had been learned at home. Their father, a physically abusive man, beat them all down in varying degrees. They tipped each other off about their father's moods and quietly showed support for each other when he was angry. The third brother "enjoyed" showing his other three brothers that he could take the father's beatings without reacting emotionally in any visible way. They felt terrified by what had happened to him and yet encouraged that if he could stand up to this man, so could they.

5. Loyal Siblings Can Contain and Resolve Conflicts Openly and Rapidly. This fifth quality, (although Hartup has not noted it as a "quality of friendship") seems to us to be an important mechanism in maintaining any close relationship between relative equals, and was found in the three groups of siblings in our study. In all three groups, siblings argued, disagreed, and fought. Striking, however, was the quality of forgiving and forgetting any hurt or grievance. Differences were never magnified; neither were they "swept under the carpet."

For example, the eldest of the four brothers was a patron of the arts and lived a very fashionable and culturally sophisticated life. This difference from his equally successful but less "culturally fashionable" brothers had become a point for caustic humor.

3rd oldest Brother: (an athletic, traditionally masculine type—pointing to his oldest brother) Now, his high falutenness till today still bugs me. He calls me up and gives me what I refer to as 'high class bull shit.' I sit there and say to myself, 'Why is he still trying to impress me?' Really! And I can *tell* it to Tom, too! There is no doubt in my mind that he'll call me up and try to impress me about some star he's met.

Or as a birthday gift 2 or 3 years ago he sent me a silk scarf. His giving me a silk scarf is like me giving him a baseball glove. *I* will never use the silk scarf, *he* will never use the baseball glove. (All four brothers break into raucous laughter.)

Interviewer: You mean he still tries to improve your 'class?'

3rd oldest brother: Sure he does. The negative thing from Tom is, he's always trying to impress me. I humor him. I can enjoy it at this point. But while I was growing up, it used to bother me.

Youngest brother: Look, if you don't like it, send it to me!

Oldest brother: Wait! You *already took* it! (More uproarious laughter.)

Annoyances could be worked out in the open, and made light of, as a way of detoxifying conflicting opinions. More serious differences could be discussed objectively. These brothers acknowledged that they had had serious differences of opinion yet they maintained their affection for one another. When the youngest decided to marry a girl of a different ethnic background, he first checked with his brothers, knowing that this might offend them.

Youngest Brother: (to his older brothers: I said to Ed, 'Look, I've been dating this girl for 2½ years and I'm gonna marry her, do you see any problems?'

Third oldest: (to brother 4): Bob, I told you, when you told me about getting married, I tried to talk you out of it.

Youngest: That's right.

Third oldest: I said, Bob I think you're making a mistake. I was speaking to him as seriously as I could. Number one, the girl was much younger than him. Number two, I really didn't believe Bob was ready for marriage, . . . and I said 'Bob, I think you're crazy.' And he says, 'Okay, but I just want to know, would you *not* talk to me if I marry her? Would you *not* talk to me? Does that end our relationship?' And I said, 'No, it's no big deal.' But I did after *that,* and he evaluated what I had to say and still got married.

Not only are differences like the above dealt with openly, but aggressive behavior seems to be understood and forgiven as a necessary part of a loyal sibling relationship. All three groups of siblings recalled physical fights that they overlooked, or that even added an exciting and challenging dimention to the relationship. Grudges, if held for too long, could erupt into useful, cathartic (sometimes even physical) confrontations that were followed by calmer discussions and better understanding.

The college student siblings once had a violent physical confrontation that resulted in a black eye for one and a bloodied nose for the other, only a month before their participation in the project. The brawl, triggered by a "bossy" comment by the elder brother, continued as a verbal argument for a full day spent alone at a winter cottage. The altercation led them to discuss hurt feelings that each had harbored for several years, including the older brother's rage about an incident in which the younger brother had left unchallenged a rumor that his sibling was mentally ill. At the end of the argument the younger brother admitted he had slandered his older brother: "I know you felt betrayed, Nick. I didn't know whether or not you were going to hit me again, so all I could do was cry on your shoulder and say, 'I love you and I didn't mean to say that.' . . . I loved you and respected you for what you felt, but I didn't feel you were right. . . . That's how I still feel, we both did things we regretted. Nick has a very dynamic temper and sometimes he doesn't have control over it and neither do I . . . . I've always considered that temper as advantage, you know, you could *really* get upset about things, and it was okay."

Experiences and Events That Predispose Siblings to Intense Loyalties

These three sibling groups, though of different ethnic backgrounds, ages, sexual compositions, family sizes, and lifestyles, had had strikingly similar experiences with parents. In each of these families, the parents had been weak, absent, hostile, or had actually died during the siblings' formative years. This put the siblings in need of reorganization, guidance, and protection. With other support systems relatively unpredictable or unavailable, and confronted with neutral or hostile substitute parents, they clung together as the only steady and constant people in each others' lives.

Their enormous accessibility to each other (see Kahn & Bank, 1980) made it possible for them to spend a great deal of time together, to know what the others were doing and where they were going. They lived in close physical proximity, ate at the same table, exchanged clothes, food, and valued possessions and were close enough in age to enjoy play activities with one another. This "access" partly made up for the inaccessibility of parents, and made clinging to one another a natural option.

In Table 1 (following) are indicated the kinds of parental losses and over-whelming external threats and instabilities that seemed to drive these siblings we have studied to forge powerful and intense personal bonds.

SIBLING LOYALTY: BENEFITS AND BURDENS

Each of the siblings in our study felt it was advantageous to participate in such close sibling relationships. Having a sense that one was never entirely alone—in ways unmatched by friends who had *other* loyalties—was one such advantage. Learning skills from each other, learning to be "in tune" as only age-similar people can be, practicing being a parent, learning to receive as well as to give, to reciprocate and to have a shared sense of humor, knowing that someone else was in the same mess as oneself - - - these were all mentioned as pluses.

Yet there often were distinct disadvantages to being a loyal sibling. For example, the nine-year-old girl was becoming an old lady before her time, and although able to relate sensitively as an "adult," she seemed unaware of the world of play. At nine, she had found herself burdened with the care of her little brother and she appeared well on her way to a life of serious overresponsible behavior and grim perfection. Even though there was reciprocity in the relationship, and he verbalized his love for his sister, her sleeping and waking life was so preoccupied with worry about him that she often withdrew from contact with other people. In order to forget her worries about her brother she would (to quote her), "read a good book so I can get my mind off of him!" Although she loved

TABLE 1
Sources of Intense Sibling Loyalties

	Type of Parental Loss	*Threats From Outside*
Four Brothers (mid-life)	Mother died when boys were 23, 17, 13, and 12. Father exhausted, occasionally abusive, emotionally unavailable.	Slum-ghetto conditions. Physical danger. Financial difficulties. Father and boys isolated and rejected by the extended family, except for maternal grandmother nearby.
Two Brothers (college age)	Father died when boys were 9 and 11. Their mother died two years later when boys were 11 and 13.	No support whatever from extended family of deceased parents. Both boys seriously abused by psychotic foster mother and foster father.
Brother and Sister (middle childhood)	Father abandoned family after birth of second child (girl then age 3). Mother voluntarily placed children in foster care when they were age 5 and 2.	Several different foster homes and schools; very little continuity of care.

him, and he could be loving to her, she frequently verbalized frustration and rage about his behavior. She seemed to feel that his obnoxiousness and immaturity were a lifelong burden that she would willingly but resentfully carry for a lifetime. In her case, the loyalty appeared to be lopsided. Although they were attached to one another, it was up to *her* to make certain that the other conditions of loyalty (such as cooperation, sacrifice, quick conflict resolution) were maintained. In short, by giving, she was becoming depleted. She appeared relieved when she learned that she and her brother would be adopted by separate families.

Keeping loyalty "alive" requires energy, and some loyal siblings expend more energy than others. Thus among the four brothers at mid-life, the second oldest acted, in the presence of the interviewer, as a watchdog over the conflicts in the group, never allowing differences to become serious, changing the topic just enough to make it "discussable," and reminding his brothers of their common interest. This had, interestingly, been his role years before, when his two youngest brothers had daily pummeled each other. He was the buffer, peacemaker, and emotional leader of the group. Although he appeared to enjoy this role and was respected for it, he appeared less free to "take" from his brothers than they were to take from him.

The younger of the college-age brothers experienced a different hardship. study was periodically restricted when they honored their loyal commitments to one another. For example, when women began to enter their lives, three of the mid-life brothers acted almost as a censorship board when two of them married.

Their collective view that women would have to enter their lives cautiously, always respecting the brothers' previous relationship with one another, upset one wife, and later on, visits between this wife and her husband with the other brothers became infrequent because she had become a point of criticism and teasing. He had married a woman "who doesn't fit in with us." His contacts with his brothers were still warm but he had to be careful not to let his wife's presence in the family become divisive.

The younger of the college-age brothers experienced a different hardship. Although he expressed great admiration for his older brother, he said he felt like a "nobody," living only as an extension of this competent older brother's personality. Despite the warmth they felt for each other, the younger brother stated that he knew he had to get away from his older brother for a few years so that he would find out who he, uniquely, was. He felt he had leaned too heavily on his older brother and related this to a feeling of emptiness and "not having really gone out and experienced life." He knew that the brotherly relationship, although providing security, could disable him if he continued to rely upon it. For him, as for the other siblings we have studied, the benefits of intense loyalty were periodically outweighed by the personal "enmeshment" (Minuchin, 1974) that loyalty often demands.

Parental Abandonment: A Sufficient Condition For the Development of Loyalty

Is abandonment or deficiency of care by parents the only condition necessary for the development of intense sibling loyalties? We would have to answer this question with "No — but." Unavailability of parents can promote loyalty to siblings, but many other factors can intensify the effect that abandonment might have upon loyalty. In the three families that were the subject of our research, the siblings' positive relationships had been "launched" or stimulated by factors that preceded parental abandonment.

1. They had all *had at least one nurturing parent* who set an early example of caring for others.

2. In none of these three sibling groups had the children been played actively against one another by their natural parents. Parental monitoring of their relationships early in their lives had been sufficient to allow *relatively harmonious and equitable interactions* (Ihinger, 1975).

3. The children *had been reared together rather than being separated.* Their access to one another was ample enough to allow them to know each other and to become dependent upon one another. (Bank & Kahn, 1982)

4. There existed a factor of compatibility among the siblings that involved *closeness in age.* Because they shared common life issues, and thus could readily

identify with one anothers' concerns, they could honor the relationship agreements that involved loyalty to each other.

More difficult to validate, although empirically observable, was the "fit" of personalities, roles, styles and interests with one another in a lock-and-key fashion. Thus the overresponsible style fashioned by the nine-year-old girl fit perfectly with the impulsive and underorganized style of her younger brother; the artistic interests of one older brother complemented and played a unique and amusing counterpoint to his younger brother's aggressively macho orientation. This "fit" of their identities and their subidentities with one another (see Miller, 1963) allowed each to play a distinct role and permitted each to benefit from the role that was played by his or her siblings. Whether this complementarity existed initially or was fostered by the loyal relationship is difficult to verify. But since these siblings had depended on one another for proportionately long periods in their life cycle, it seems safe to conclude this "fit" flourished rather than withered because of the siblings' reciprocal needs.

We have discovered other sibling constellations where parents have abandoned children, where some of the factors just mentioned are absent and where the siblings display little loyalty to one another. When parents have never nurtured their children, when the parents' model of a marital relationship is conflicted and is internalized by the children at vulnerable ages, when the children are separated by a large age span or are physically taken away from one another, loyalty appears more difficult to attain. If other supportive people, such as uncles, aunts, grandparents, teachers, mentors of all kinds, as well as peers, are available and powerful enough, the sibling system becomes comparatively less influential. We can also imagine that intense loyalty can be instilled by parents who are emotionally available to children, but who refuse to become involved in settling their differences. It is entirely possible that sibling loyalty, as an ethic of conduct, can be deliberately modeled, taught, and reinforced by thoughful parents who have not abandoned their children. Abandonment does not necessarily cause the phenomenon of sibling loyalty but rather endows it with an intense and powerful quality.

REFERENCES

Bank, S., & Kahn, M. D. Sisterhood-brotherhood is powerful: Sibling subsystems and family therapy. *Family Process,* 1975 *14*(3), 311–337.
Bank, S., & Kahn, M. D. Freudian siblings. *The Psychoanalytic Review, 1980–81, 6*(4), 493–504.
Bank, S., & Kahn, M. D. *The sibling bond.* New York: Basic Books, 1982.
Bossard, J. H. S. & Boll, E. S. *The large family system.* Philadelphia: University of Pennsylvania Press, 1956.

Boszormenyi-Nagy, I., & Spark, G. *Invisible loyalties: Reciprocity in intergenerational family therapy*. New York: Harper & Row, 1973.

Burlingham, D. T. *Twins*. New York: International University Press, 1952.

Cummings, E. & Schneider, D. Sibling solidarity: a property of American kinship. *American Anthropologist*, 1961, *63*, 498–507.

Freud, A. & Dann, S. An experiment in group upbringing. In R. Eisler, (Eds.), [Freud, A., Hartmann, H., Kris E. International Universities Press, New York] *The psychoanalytic study of the child* (Vol. 6), 1951.

Hartup, W. W. The origins of friendship. In M. Lewis & L. A. Rosenblum (Eds.), *Friendship and peer relations*. New York: Wiley, 1975.

Ihinger, M. The referee role and norms of equity: A contribution toward a theory of sibling conflict. *Journal of Marriage and Family*, 1975, *37*(3) 515–524.

Kahn, M. D., & Bank, S., Discussion: Therapy with siblings in reorganizing families., *International Journal of Family Therapy*, 1980, *3*(2), 155–158.

Kahn, M. D., & Bank, S. In pursuit of sisterhood: Adult siblings as a resource for combined individual and family therapy. *Family Process*, 1981, *20*(1), 85–95.

Levy, D. M. Sibling rivalry. *American Orthopsychiatric* Association Research Monographs, NO. 2, 1937.

O'Brien, D. O. The twins who made their own language. *Family Health*, 1978, *10*, 32:35.

Miller, D. R. The study of social interaction. In S. Koch (Ed.), *Psychology: A study of a science* (Vol. 5). New York McGraw Hill, 1963.

Minuchin, S. *Families and family therapy*. Cambridge, Mass.: Harvard University Press, 1974.

Royce, J. The philosophy of loyalty. New York: Macmillan, 1936.

Sewall, N., & Smalley, R. *Two studies in sibling rivalry*. Smith College Studies in Social Work, 1930.

11
Sibling Influence Throughout the Lifespan

Victor G. Cicirelli
Purdue University

The influence of siblings on a child's early development is recognized by social scientists and the lay public alike. From birth on, an infant may be treated differently by parents and others depending on its position in the sibling structure of the family. Thus, a first-born boy may receive qualitatively different parenting than a later-born girl, and so on. Soon the infant grows old enough to begin interacting directly with any siblings who have already been born into the family. Through the preschool years, the young child is likely to share most waking hours with whatever brothers and sisters there may be. Behavior patterns of an older sibling may be imitated, play activities may be dictated by a sibling, and so on. Gradually, the child's intellectual and personality characteristics are shaped by the combination of differential parental treatment and the interactions with siblings.

During middle childhood, each child clearly establishes certain roles within the family that are determined by the positions and characteristics of the various siblings. An older sister may become a caretaker of a younger child; a middle child may become the family clown: and so on. As the children go off to school, in most cases they will enter different classrooms and associate with different peer groups. Nevertheless, they still have many home experiences in common. Above all, they must deal with the same parents. They may form alliances or coalitions with one or more siblings in order to negotiate more effectively with parents, or one sibling may act as a pioneer into new activities, making it easier or more acceptable for others to do the same.

Through the years of adolescence, siblings can become very close as they help one another face the changes of emerging sexuality, dating, and other adolescent activities. Later, as they leave home to go to college, to assume a new job, or simply to live away from the parental home, they may separate from each other as well.

From this period and through the adult years, contact with siblings becomes more volitional and dependent on external circumstances. At one extreme, siblings may move to different cities and never see each other again. At the other, they may live together or go into business together, and maintain a close daily relationship. Most adult sibling relationships fall somewhere between these extremes. Some only see each other on holidays and other family occasions, but keep up with the other's activities and achievements by letter or telephone or indirectly through parents. Others may plan much of their social and recreational activities together, help each other with the rearing of children and household tasks, and serve as close confidants.

When children are grown, adult siblings often share the care of elderly parents when they become dependent, and later participate together in the dismantling of the parental home and division of the parents' property and possessions after the parents' deaths.

Later, in their own old age, brothers and sisters help each other in reviewing events of their early lives together and conveying family history to their descendents.

The relationship between siblings begins with birth and ends only with the death of one of the siblings. It is unique among human relationships by virtue of its very duration. Secondly, the sibling relationship is unique in that the participants share a common genetic heritage, common cultural milieu, and common early experiences within the family. Thirdly, the relationship between siblings is highly egalitarian, with the siblings of approximately equal power in the relationship. Each sibling feels free to say or do as he or she pleases in the relationship. Finally, to be a sibling is an ascribed rather than an earned role, so that an individual remains a brother or a sister regardless of achievements or circumstances. The nature of the sibling relationship is such that intimacy between siblings is immediately restored even after long absences. Siblings often go to great lengths to locate a brother or sister who has been separated by adoption or other circumstances, and when reunited, a uniquely close relationship develops almost immediately, even when none existed before.

This brief informal overview of the course of the sibling relationship over the lifespan indicates the importance of siblings for many individuals. Yet, as suggested, the course of the relationship proceeds from inevitable daily contact in childhood to occasional volitional meetings in adulthood and old age. Also, the nature of the sibling relationship varies with the particular individuals involved, ranging from extreme closeness to extreme rivalry and hostility and, in some cases, total apathy.

The purpose of this paper is to examine some of the evidence for the continuation of the sibling relationship across the lifespan and for sibling influence from childhood to old age. (Although the paper will focus on the period from early adulthood to old age, the period from childhood to adolescence will be considered where pertinent.) Four major questions will be addressed:

1. Do siblings continue to interact over the lifespan and, if so, to what extent?
2. What kind of relationship do siblings have with each other over the lifespan?
3. Do siblings have a demonstrable influence on each other's behavior in adulthood and old age? If so, is this influence contemporaneous or merely an extension of behavior patterns shaped early in life?
4. Do sibling interaction and influence depend on such sibling structure variables as sex and birth order of the siblings and the age spacing between them? (Sibling structure effects will be considered in conjunction with the other questions.)

EXISTENCE OF THE SIBLING RELATIONSHIP

The question of whether an individual continues to interact with siblings over the life span depends on three factors: (a) whether the individual has living siblings: (b) whether geographic distance is near enough to permit interaction: and (c) whether there is actual contact between siblings through visiting, telephoning, and/or letter writing. Without a living sibling who resides at an accessible distance and without some form of contact with the sibling, there is clearly no ongoing sibling relationship.

Living Siblings

The great majority of children have at least one sibling, with only about 10% having no siblings at all. Mortality rates in the United States are low in childhood and adolescence, so it is to be expected that the family size is affected little in these years. Studies in adulthood find approximately the same percentage. Adams (1968), in his study of the kinship relationships of young to middle-aged adults, found that 88% had at least one living sibling. The median age of his sample was 33 years. In a study recently completed for the Andrus Foundation, Cicirelli (1980b) found that 85% of a sample of middle-aged adults (mean age 46.4 years) had at least one living sibling: 88% had one sibling or more at birth. The number of elderly with at least one living sibling has been reported variously as 85% by Shanas, Townsend, Wedderburn, Friis, Milhoj, and Stehouwer (1968): 93% by Clark and Anderson (1967): and 78% by Cicirelli (1979). The Cicirelli sample represented the older portions of the age range more heavily than did the others, which accounts for the somewhat lower percentage of subjects with siblings than in the other samples. Obviously, each of the cohorts involved in the studies mentioned here reflects the childbearing trends of the period in which the subjects were born as well as mortality trends. However, one can conclude that the majority of individuals have a living sibling even into old age.

Looking at these data in terms of the number of living siblings reported by each person, Adams (1968) found young adults to have a mean of 3.9 living siblings. Cicirelli (1980b) found middle-aged adults to have a mean of 2.2 living siblings. Among the elderly, Cicirelli (1979) found that those in the 60–69 age range had a mean of 2.88 living siblings, those in the 70–79 range had 2.18 living siblings, and those aged 80 and over had only 1.08 living siblings. These three groups originally had 4.6, 4.9, and 4.2 siblings in the family, respectively. The decline in the mean number of living siblings with age is mainly due to sibling mortality and not differences in childbearing trends for the different cohorts. What emerges from consideration of these data is that most people are likely to have a sibling available to them throughout their adult life until they are into their eighties or beyond.

Geographic Distance

In childhood and adolescence, siblings almost always live together in the parental home. Later, demands of jobs, choice of spouse, and desire for new experiences often put brothers and sisters at great distances from each other. The question has often been raised (e.g., Rosenberg & Anspach, 1973) as to whether siblings who are separated geographically can have a viable relationship with one another. The geographic distance that renders a sibling inaccessible depends on a variety of circumstances: the age and health of the siblings, the income level, available sources of transportation, the travel time and costs, and the nature of competing activities and responsibilities. A high–income airline employee with low-cost airfare privileges might find a sibling living 2000 miles away more accessible than a sibling living only 50 miles away might be for an impoverished handicapped person whose only means of transportation was a series of trains and buses. Nevertheless, geographic distance provides a rough indication of the ease or difficulty of sibling visiting.

Several studies have provided information regarding the proximity of siblings of adult and elderly people. Unfortuantely each of the studies has used a somewhat different definition of the sibling or siblings considered, thus making comparisons difficult. Adams (1968) asked about the siblings of the young adults studied who were closest in age; for 29%, this sibling lived in the same city; for 60% this sibling lived within a 100-mile radius. Rosenberg and Anspach (1973) asked about all siblings who resided in the same metropolitan area as the middle-aged and elderly "blue-collar" people they studied. They found that 75% of their 45-54 age group had at least one sibling in the metropolitan area, compared with 64% of the 55-64 age group and 49% of those over age 65. These data indicate a rather strong decline in siblings available within the same city;

however, these data reflect sibling mortality as well as residence patterns. Cicirelli (1980b) studied adults ranging in age from 29-71 (mean age 46.4 years), and asked about the proximity of all siblings for the 85% of the total sample with at least one living sibling. Some 36% of these siblings lived in the same city as the person interviewed, and 56% lived within a distance of 100 miles. The correlation of geographic proximity with age was −.06 and was not statistically significant. These data correspond fairly well with Adams' findings for the closest sibling. Data from Cicirelli's (1979) study of elderly (mean age 73.8 years) showed that 26% of the siblings with whom the elderly person had the most contact lived within the same city and 56% within 100 miles. Again, these findings are not strongly divergent from Adams' findings. One can conclude that for those individuals who have at least one living sibling, about a third have a sibling within the same city and more than half have a sibling within a hundred mile radius. These figures do not appear to change with age. Rosenberg and Anspach's data indicate more than two-thirds of their middle-aged group had siblings in the same metropolitan area; however, their sample was of low socioeconomic status where family members exhibit more limited geographic mobility. Declines in reported sibling proximity with age are largely due to sibling mortality. Taking all these things into consideration, one can conclude that the majority of elderly have a sibling alive and within reasonable visiting distance up to the very end of the lifespan, and the possibility of sibling interaction exists.

Contact With Siblings

Contact with siblings has typically been measured by the frequencies of visiting, telephoning, and letter-writing. Here again, data from several studies are at hand. In Adams' (1968) study of younger adults, 69% of those with a sibling in the same city saw that sibling at least once a week, and 93% saw their sibling at least once a month. When siblings living within 100 miles were considered (excluding those who were in the same city), 12% saw that sibling at least once a week and 65% saw that sibling at least once a month. Many of these encounters took place at the home of their mutual parents. Adams' findings indicate that the frequency of visiting is less for those who live at greater distances. When a somewhat older group of middle-aged adults was considered (Cicirelli, 1980b), 19% of all siblings were seen weekly or more often; 41% were seen at least once a month. The modal visiting pattern, reported for 36% of all siblings, was several times a year (but not as often as once a month). Only 3% of the siblings had not been seen in the two years prior to the interview, and these were living outside the United States. Rosenberg and Anspach (1973) reported visiting patterns only for those middle-aged and elderly adults with a sibling in the same metropolitan area. In the 45-54 age range, 68% saw that sibling weekly or more often, compared with 58% in the 55-64 age range, and 47% of the 65-79 age range.

This indicates a decline in frequency of sibling visiting with increasing age.

In studies dealing with the elderly, Shanas *et al.*, (1968) found that 34% of elderly men and 43% of elderly women in the United States, Denmark, and Great Britain saw a sibling weekly or more often. Also, 39% of men and 44% of women saw a sibling monthly or more often. In a more recent study carried out in seven neighborhoods in Chicago, Bild and Havighurst (1976) found that from 17–30% of the elderly persons they interviewed saw a sibling weekly or more often. Finally, Cicirelli (1979) reported that 17% of the elderly in his study saw the sibling with whom they had the most contact at least once a week; 33% saw their sibling at least once a month.

There is less information about the frequency of telephoning than about visiting. However, the existing evidence suggests that the frequencies of both are rather similar. Bild and Havighurst (1976) found a somewhat greater frequency for telephoning than for visiting, with from 31–43% telephoning a sibling weekly or more often. In Cicirelli's (1979) study of the elderly, 30% telephoned the sibling with whom they had the most contact weekly or more often; 52% telephoned at least monthly. Among the middle-aged adults (Cicirelli, 1980b), only 16% telephoned their siblings at least weekly, and 40% telephoned siblings monthly or more frequently. The modal frequency of telephoning all siblings was several times a year but not as often as once a month.

In regard to letter writing, Cicirelli (1979) found that 51% of the elderly had no correspondence with siblings; 13% wrote at least monthly and 5% wrote weekly. Thus, overall, the frequency of letter writing to siblings was quite low.

Telephoning seems to be a supplement to face-to-face visiting with siblings rather than a substitute for it. Those siblings who live closer to each other also see each other more frequently ($r = .72$), and the more frequently they see each other the more frequently they telephone ($r = .61$) (Cicirelli, 1980b). Similar results were found for elderly siblings as well (Cicirelli, 1979).

Overall, most siblings continue to have contact with each other at least several times a year after they leave home and through their adult years into old age. There is some evidence that contact with siblings declines with advancing age in the latter part of the lifespan, but contact ceases entirely for very few. In late life, as well as throughout the rest of the lifespan, it is a rare event for siblings to lose touch with each other completely.

NATURE OF THE SIBLING RELATIONSHIP

Merely knowing that siblings maintain some degree of contact over the lifespan reveals little about the nature of the relationship between them. The relationship in adulthood has been variously described as one of mutual apathy (with perfunctory participation at family ritual events), exceptional closeness, and enduring rivalry. The course of the relationship has similarly been termed one of continuous decline and one of later life resurgence. In an attempt to reach some conclusion about the sibling relationship, several aspects of the relationship will be taken up in turn.

Social-emotional aspects

Considerable evidence exists that most siblings feel close affectionally and provide psychological support to each other throughout the course of their adult lives. Cicirelli (1980a) asked 100 college women to indicate the strength of their feelings for each of their siblings and their parents, using a 7-point scale ranging from "not at all" to "very, very much." It was hypothesized that the college years would be a period when sibling relationships would be especially strong, with siblings likely to be especially supportive of efforts to establish independence from parents and to take on new roles and values. Four of the items dealing with emotional closeness and support are of particular interest here. These were feelings of closeness, similarity of views, feeling understood, and feeling friendly and relaxed with the other person. Based on responses to all of the items, a "closest" sibling was identified for each subject. Approximately equal numbers of older sisters, older brothers, younger sisters, and younger brothers were identified as the "closest" sibling. The subjects felt more positively toward the "closest," sibling than toward the father (p<.05) on all four items, and felt more positively toward the sibling than to the mother on three of the four, although these differences were not statistically significant. On the average, these college women felt very close to their "closest" sibling, very friendly and relaxed, felt very much understood, and felt their views to be very similar. In an additional analysis in which all siblings were considered, sibling structure variables were related to feelings toward siblings. Birth order and sibling spacing were most strongly related to the feelings toward siblings. Later-born subjects felt more positively toward their siblings than did earlier-born subjects; also, they felt more positively toward siblings who were closer in age. The sex of the sibling was not important for this sample of college women.

In his study of young to middle-aged adults (median age 33 years), Adams (1968) asked about closeness of feeling to the sibling who was closest in age. Responses were measured on a 5-point scale ranging from "not too close" to "extremely close." Adams reported that 48% of those interviewed had a high degree of closeness to their sibling. Closeness, however, was strongly related to sex of the respondent and sex of sibling. Pairs of sisters were closest of all, with 60% reporting a high degree of closeness. By contrast, only 39% of pairs of brothers reported a high degree of closeness. The cross-sex sibling pairs were intermediate in closeness, with 46% reporting a high degree of closeness. Not only did sisters tend to feel affectionally close, more than half reported feeling closer in adulthood than they did when they were growing up. Adams explains the greater closeness of sisters in terms of their role similarity after marriage, when they have common interests in marriage, home, and children. Those siblings who felt close affectionally reported that they communicated with each other, visited, and did things together because they gained enjoyment from each other's company. Feelings of family obligation played relatively little part in these siblings' relationships, whereas obligation was more often cited as a factor in the relationships of siblings who were not close affectionally. Adams also measured value consensus between siblings, and found results closely paralleling those for affectional closeness. Overall, 45% of the subjects of the study reported having a high degree of value consensus with their siblings.

In an as yet unpublished portion of a study (Cicirelli, 1980b) dealing with siblings of middle-aged adults, a 4-point scale ranging from "not close at all" to "extremely close" was used to measure affectional closeness. These adults ranged in age from 29 to 71. Overall, 68% felt "close" or "extremely close" to their siblings, and only 5% did not feel close at all. Further, there was a weak but statistically significant age trend where older adults reported greater closeness of feeling.

Feelings of closeness toward siblings have been found to persist into old age as well. Typically, elderly people feel closer to siblings than to any other relatives except their own children. This is especially true for elderly who are widowed, divorced, childless, or never married. Various authors support the existence of close sibling feelings in old age. Some (Laverty, 1962; Manney, 1975) have observed that siblings draw closer to each other in old age, when children are grown. Cumming and Schneider (1961) found siblings to be close late in life, particularly when spouse and children were gone. Of the three sex combinations, sisters felt the closest, followed by sister-brother, then by brother-brother relationships.

Cicirelli (1979) investigated sibling relationships of elderly individuals over 60 years of age. Of those who had at least one living sibling, 53% reported feeling "extremely close" to the sibling with whom they had the most contact. Another 30% reported feeling "close." The combined figure of 83% for the two response categories is substantially larger than the 68% reported with middle-aged subjects and the 48% reported by Adams with younger adults. At face value, these studies taken in combination suggest that feelings of closeness to siblings increase with increasing age. However, this must be regarded as a tentative conclusion, since there are no longitudinal data on sibling relationships. Different cohorts may be more or less willing to express feelings for their siblings. Also, the society is more open to expression of feelings, especially by men, in recent years, than it was at the time of the Adams study. Finally, differences of method in the studies may account, at least partially, for the differences. It is of interest, nevertheless, that although existing evidence suggests a decline of contact with siblings in the latter portion of the lifespan, there is no corresponding decline in expressed closeness of feeling and there is very possibly an increase.

In regard to sibling structure variables, Cicirelli (1979) found that elderly subjects named a sister as the sibling to whom they felt "closest" more frequently than they did a brother. Also, middle-born siblings were named more frequently than first- or last-born siblings as the "closest" sibling. This, however, may reflect the greater availability of middle-born siblings in the larger families typical of the time period when these elderly persons were born. Similarly, the preference for sisters may be due in some part to the differential death rates for men and women.

As noted earlier, Adams (1968) found that 45% of younger adults in his study reported a high degree of value consensus with the sibling closest in age. Cicirelli (1979, 1980b) used Adams' measure of value consensus with older adults. He found that 49% of middle-aged adults reported that they "agreed completely" or agreed about "most things" with their siblings. For the elderly group, however, 68% reported high value consensus with siblings. This apparently greater degree of value consensus between older siblings may be due to the more homogeneous society in which they grew up.

In further unpublished data from the Cicirelli (1980b) study of middle-aged adults, feelings of compatibility with siblings were explored. When asked how well they got along with their siblings, 78% said that they got along "well" or "very well". Only 4% reported that they got along "not very well" or "poorly." In a similar vein, when asked how much satisfaction they got from the relationship with their siblings, 68% derived "considerable" or "very much" satisfaction from the relationship; 12% reported little or no satisfaction. Another item asked for the extent to which these middle-aged adults felt that they could discuss intimate topics with or ask intimate questions of their siblings. Here, 41% said that they "felt free" to do so, and another 8% said that they could do so often. However, 36% said that they would do so rarely or never. When asked if they talked over important decisions with their siblings, only 8% said that they did so frequently or almost always. At the opposite extreme, 73% indicated that they did so rarely or never. A final item in this group asked about the extent of siblings' interest in things that the interviewee was doing. A "very great" or "moderate" amount of interest on the part of siblings was perceived by 59%; 21% perceived little or no interest. When considering the responses to all these items, high percentages of middle-aged adults report getting along well with their siblings, gaining considerable satisfaction from the relationship, and, to a lesser degree, feeling that their siblings are interested in them. Substantially fewer feel able to discuss topics of an intimate nature with siblings, and very few talk over the important decisions in their lives with their brothers and sisters. Thus, feelings of closeness and compatibility on a global level do not appear to extend to confidences and discussions of a more personal nature. There was no indication of an age trend in these data.

A recent study (Ross, Dalton, & Milgram, 1980) investigated closeness in sibling relationships in late adulthood and old age. Semistructured interviews were conducted in small group settings with from four to six people. Subjects' perceptions of their relationships with siblings were elicited and interview protocols were submitted to content analysis. Although there was only a small number of subjects, some interesting conclusions emerged from the study. For most of the older people interviewed, one sibling was seen as the one to whom they felt "closest." Further, most felt that closeness to their siblings increased as they grew older, especially when a sibling of the opposite sex was involved. Closeness to siblings was viewed as a feeling that had its origins in the family life of childhood. When feelings changed in adolescence or younger adulthood, this most often was felt to be the result of some critical incident. Re-establishing a close relationship with siblings in old age was regarded as an important accomplishment by those who achieved it. Indeed, the salience accorded sibling relationships at this stage of life was impressive. The authors speculated that shared memories and family history were at the heart of the value placed on siblings, as if contact with siblings was able to reactivate the closeness of early family life.

It is clear from the findings of the several studies considered that the majority of siblings tend to remain affectionally close throughout adulthood and old age, and may grow still closer in the last decades of life.

Rivalry

Rivalry between siblings has been written about from the earliest recorded history, although its importance has been minimized or magnified depending on the orientation of the author. With the advent of psychoanalysis, considerable emphasis was placed on sibling rivalry as a major force in child development. For example, Adler (1959) considered the "dethronement" of the older child from a position of being the focus of attention in the family by the birth of a younger sibling as a trauma responsible for feelings of sibling rivalry. Much professional advice is now available to parents on the subject of how to avoid sibling rivalry and how to deal with it.

Feelings of sibling rivalry in childhood seem to be more intense between brothers, particularly when the age difference between them is small (Sutton-Smith & Rosenberg, 1970). Rivalry is least between cross-sex siblings, with sisters in an intermediate position. However, the extent to which such feelings persist when the children mature and leave home has not been well investigated.

In adulthood, Adams (1968) found that brothers reported more competitiveness, ambivalence, and jealousy in their relationships than did any other sibling combination. Sisters reported that their relationship grew closer in adulthood. This was not the case for brothers. The relationship between brothers was the poorest when they were at different occupational levels.

A study by Form and Geschwender (1962) found that workers were more satisfied with their jobs when they felt that they were doing better than their brothers, and least satisfied when they felt that their brothers were in a better occupational position than were they. This sense of competitiveness and comparison between siblings is considered by many to be typical of sibling relationships in adulthood. Troll (1975) concludes that adults use siblings as "measuring sticks" by which to evaluate their own success or lack of it; when a sibling gets too far ahead, the relationship suffers.

In a study of middle-aged adults (Cicirelli, 1981), subjects were asked about the extent to which they felt that they were in competition with their siblings about their accomplishments, their children, and so on. Only 2% reported such feelings frequently or more often, whereas 93% felt such competition rarely or never. When asked about the extent of arguments with siblings, 88% argued rarely or never and only 3% argued frequently or more often. In another item, 89% indicated that their siblings rarely or never acted bossy or dictatorial with them, whereas 3% found that this was the case frequently. These results indicate an extremely low level of sibling competitiveness and conflict, at least on an overt level. Even these weak feelings were found to decline as the siblings grew older.

Allan (1977), who has presented a strong case for the closeness of sibling relationships in adulthood and old age, argued that sibling rivalry appeared to dissipate as the individuals got older. He felt that interaction between siblings was limited in frequency compared to early years, and the nature of the interaction enabled siblings to avoid rivalrous conflicts. If siblings were forced to live together again, or had to work closely together for more reason, he theorized that latent feelings of rivalry would re-emerge. This view is supported by Laverty (1962), who observed elderly people in clinical situations and found that such rivalry was reactivated. Similarly, Berezin (1977) observed frequent quarrels among siblings as they discussed the care of their aged parents. There was an expression of irrational, hostile attitudes in these arguments, which Berezin interpreted as a regression to earlier rivalrous relationships.

Ross and Milgram (1980) conducted small-group interviews with adults ranging from 25 to 93 years of age. Feelings of rivalry with siblings were probed in these interviews. Results indicated that 71% experienced rivalrous feelings with a sibling at some point in their lives, with these feelings most typically arising in childhood or adolescence. Although many people reported that they were able to overcome earlier sibling rivalry, 45% considered their rivalry still active in adult years. Where sibling rivalry persisted in adulthood, it appeared to be nourished by a continuation of family interaction patterns from childhood years. Ross and Milgram's work indicates a much higher incidence of rivalry throughout adulthood than that observed in studies of late adulthood and old age that have been discussed above. It may be that people find it difficult to admit to feelings of rivalry and competition with siblings, as Ross and Milgram suggest, regarding such feelings as immature or unworthy. The clinical type of interview in the small-group setting they used might be more likely to stimulate self-disclosures about rivalry than more traditional interview methods.

Nevertheless, the weight of evidence from most sources indicates a lessening of rivalry with age. Although they report a higher incidence of rivalry, even Milgram and Ross found that earlier feelings of rivalry had diminished for many in adulthood.

Since the findings regarding sibling closeness reveal a high degree of affectional closeness between siblings in the latter part of life, it seems inconsistent for feelings of sibling rivalry to exist at the same time. Troll, Miller, and Atchley (1978) theorize that there is a basic love-hate ambivalence in human relationships, and that strong negative feelings cannot arise where there are not strong positive feelings at the same time. One can speculate on the existence of a closeness-rivalry dialectic between siblings, where a successful resolution of rivalry may lead to growth and new dimensions of closeness in the relationship. Such a process would explain the value that many older people place on the renewal or repair of sibling relationships. On the other hand, one can conceive of rivalry as a feeling that is always latent, appearing strongly in certain circumstances, while closeness is elicited in other circumstances.

Helping Behavior

One aspect of the sibling relationship is the help and support siblings can provide for each other. Irish (1964), Bossard and Boll (1960), and others have delineated the many functions siblings can fulfill in childhood. Among these are help with childhood problems, support in dealing with parents or others outside the family, loans or gifts of clothes, toys, sports equipment, money, and so on. Once siblings leave the family home, helping behaviors continue to some extent.

Adams (1968) found mutual aid between young adult siblings to be relatively infrequent. Helping and receiving help, where it occurred several times a year or more, was observed most often between pairs of sisters and pairs of brothers. It is clear that greater similarity of roles leads to greater help from same-sex siblings. Also, help was more frequent among those siblings who felt close to each other affectionally than among those who were less close.

In middle age, siblings are seen as a source of aid in time of crisis (Troll, 1975), caring for children, sharing household responsibilities, and even making funeral arrangements when this becomes necessary. Most important, they provide a sense of companionship and support to each other when there is a crisis or serious family problem.

For many elderly, siblings can provide a great deal of help. After the death of their mother, older sisters may assume the mother's earlier role in looking after the brothers in the family (Townsend, 1957). Also, following the death of a brother's wife, a sister may assume many of the wife's duties for her brother. To a lesser extent, brothers may take on some of a deceased husband's roles for a widowed sister. Such role substitution helps to explain the growth in closeness to cross-sex siblings that has been observed.

Cicirelli (1979) investigated the extent of help that elderly people received from their siblings. In one part of the study, the elderly interviewees were asked about which kin members they received the most help from for 16 different areas in which help or services could be given. As expected, for most elderly interviewees, children were the primary sources of help. However, siblings were seen as a primary source of help for some elderly. Some 7% of all elderly interviewed reported turning to a sibling as a major source of psychological support; smaller numbers of elderly regarded a sibling as a primary source of reading materials, help with business dealings, source of social and recreational activities, protection, and help with homemaking. More surprising, when the data were examined separately for different age groups, siblings and other kin became more important sources of help as people grew older. These results became even more pronounced when the elderly interviewees were asked to name the kin member they preferred as a source of future help. If occasional and supplementary help from siblings had been considered in this study, the contribution of siblings would surely have been much greater.

Perhaps the most important consideration concerning sibling helping behavior is that siblings stand ready to help one another in time of need, although most people do not call upon this resource frequently. Traditionally, helping behavior within the family flows vertically from parents to children, and later from children back to parents. An individual's primary obligations are to children and parents. However, when the need for help becomes too great for parents or children to handle, or the normal scheme of family obligations is disturbed for some reason (such as loss of a parent or spouse), siblings undertake to fulfill that obligation.

SIBLING INFLUENCE

Since siblings exist and maintain contact in adulthood and old age, there is opportunity for continued sibling influence. However, most studies of sibling influence have been carried out on children and adolescents, so that evidence of influence later in life is scanty.

Two types of sibling influence can be distinguished. The first is an effect of sibling structure variables. Here, a child may be treated differently by virtue of age, sex, and position in the family in relation to the age, sex, and positions of the siblings. Rothbart (1971) presents an example of such differential treatment by the parent. The child's characteristics and behaviors are patterned according to the family structure. A second type of influence arises from the direct influence of siblings upon each other through day-to-day interactions; these too may be patterned by sibling structure. Cicirelli (1972) demonstrated such direct sibling influence in a study of older siblings teaching younger siblings a concept. In comparison to a control group of younger unrelated children, interactions on the teaching-learning task were different for sibling dyads than for nonsibling pairs and depended on sex of child and sex of sibling. Learning outcomes also were influenced. There is no experimental evidence of this sort pertaining to sibling influence in adulthood and old age. Therefore, one is forced to argue the case for sibling influence from effects of sibling structure variables and logical inferences from contemporaneous events.

Much of existing research on effects of siblings in adulthood has dealt with the relationship of birth order to eminence or to psychiatric conditions. Schooler's (1972) critical review of these studies concludes that most of these effects are spurious, due to lack of control of other variables.

Toman's work (1976) has dealt with the theory that the more nearly a marital partner duplicated the sibling relationships of one's youth, the more successful and free from conflict the marriage would be. Thus, for Toman, the best marital partner for the oldest sister of brothers would be the youngest brother of sisters. Toman presents a variety of clinical evidence to support his duplication theorem, as well as personality "portraits" developed for various sibling structure positions. There has been little supporting evidence from other sources, however.

In a recent study of family variables related to locus of control in 200 elderly subjects ranging in age from 60 to 90, (Cicirelli, 1980c), it was found that subjects with more living brothers were more likely to have an external locus of control, whereas those with fewer living brothers were more likely to have an internal locus of control. Further, those older persons who had greater frequency of contact, closeness of feeling, and value consensus with siblings were more likely to have an internal locus of control. (Age, sex, and socioeconomic status were controlled in the statistical analysis.) Thus, the quality of sibling relationships was considered to be an important factor in the maintenance of an internal locus of control. Where the elderly person's efforts at family interactions are reinforced by satisfaction of affective and other needs, the individual maintains a greater sense of efficancy in everyday life. Since brothers have traditionally been less active and responsive in family life, those with more brothers would be less likely to attain satisfaction of these social and affective needs through sibling contact. Close sibling relationships in later life may thus be considered to be an adaptive mechanism, enabling individuals to feel in greater control of events and to feel more motivated to act to improve conditions for themselves.

In an earlier study, Cicirelli (1977) investigated the problems and concerns of 64 elderly men and women who ranged from 65 to 88 years of age. These problems and concerns were identified through content analysis of subjects' responses to stimulus pictures in the Gerontological Apperception Test. The data analysis considered both the number and sex of the elderly person's living siblings. There were two major trends in the results. First, female siblings had a greater influence than male siblings on the older person's feelings and concerns. Second, the effect of sisters on feelings and concerns of aging was different for men and women. Elderly men who had more sisters revealed greater feelings of happiness in life and fewer concerns or threats in areas affecting their basic security in life, such as lack of money, loss of job roles, loss of family relationships, and dealings with younger people. Sisters appear to provide these elderly men with a basic sense of emotional security. For elderly women, sisters were associated with greater concerns with social relationships in dealing with significant others. Elderly women who had more sisters voiced concerns with maintaining social skills, social relationships with people outside the family, helping others in the community, and being able to deal with criticism by younger people. Thus, sisters appear to stimulate and challenge elderly women to maintain their social activities, skills, and roles.

CONCLUSIONS

It is apparent that evidence regarding sibling influence in adulthood and old age is limited. However, some tentative conclusions can be advanced on the basis of existing knowledge.

First, the majority of individuals still have living siblings until the very end (or almost the very end) of their lifespan, although the number of living siblings declines sharply in old age. Thus, for most, the relationship with siblings is of extremely long duration. Contact with siblings is maintained by almost all adults throughout their lives; it is extremely rare for siblings to lose touch with each other. However, contact is somewhat limited in frequency.

Second, most siblings feel close affectionally to each other, with the least closeness between brothers and the most between sisters. It is clear that siblings are capable of true intimacy and extraordinary understanding of one another's problems, although most sibling relationships do not attain this level. Available evidence indicates a growth in closeness in early adulthood, and again in old age when the sibling relationship takes on greater salience. There appears to be increased closeness in cross-sex relationships in later life.

Third, overt sibling rivalry appears to diminish in intensity as people get older, although such rivalry is traditionally greatest between brothers. Greater maturity in outlook and limited frequencies of contact both play a part in allaying such feelings. However, there is evidence that rivalry may be dormant and can be reactivated in such situations of adulthood as caring for aging parents, questions of inheritance, and so on.

Fourth, sisters assume a unique and important role over the entire lifespan. In childhood, sisters are likely to have a caretaking role for younger siblings. In adulthood, relationships with sisters are stronger than those with brothers. Sisters play a major role in preserving family relationships and providing emotional support to their siblings (Troll, 1971).

One view of sibling influence in the last half of the lifespan is that siblings are socialized within the family in early life to behave in certain ways, and these behaviors continue to exist throughout the lifespan. A second view is that siblings continue to socialize each other throughout the lifespan. Siblings in childhood and adolescence can serve as role models and standards of comparison, often serving as "pioneers" into new areas of behavior (Bank & Kahn, 1975). They may serve as role models later on for parenting and grandparenting, successful aging, retirement activities, widowhood, and bereavement. In addition, they can exert pressure to maintain norms and values, and provide reinforcement for desired behaviors. Finally, they can help, challenge, and stimulate one another. Influence through modeling can be a plausible medium for sibling influence in adulthood and old age even when contact is limited, in view of the unusual salience of the sibling relationship for the individuals concerned.

What explains the extraordinary persistance of sibling relationships and influence over time and geographic separation when most peer relationships tend to fade away under similar circumstances? Attachment theory (Ainsworth, 1972; Bowlby, 1979, 1980) can aid in understanding the sibling relationship as well as the bond between mother and child.

According to the theory, the child's attachment can be inferred from its attempts to maintain proximity, contact, or communication with the parent. The child later leaves the parent for varying distances and times to explore the world, returning periodically to renew contact with the parent. Later a protective aspect of attachment develops in which the child desires to care for and protect the attached figure. Attachment does not end with the child's separation from the parental home at the end of adolescence, but endures throughout the lifespan (Antonucci, 1976; Bowlby, 1980; Kalish & Knudtson, 1976; Troll & Smith, 1976). However, the forms of attachment, exploratory, and protective behaviors change as appropriate to the stage of life. In adulthood, feelings of attachment are manifested by periodic communication, visiting, and responses to reunions. Exploratory behavior is shown in the establishment of independent households, or migration for better jobs or adventure. Protective behavior is shown through helping and caregiving behavior that attempts to maintain the survival of the parent and preserve the emotional bond.

Inasmuch as sibling relationships are a part of the total family interaction system, attachment theory can be extended to siblings as well as parents (Troll & Smith, 1976). Although in most cases the young child's siblings do not contribute to basic survival needs, through their association with the parents, feelings of attachment come to be generalized to siblings as well. Of course, siblings can provide direct reinforcement of each other's social (and other) needs in the early years. Siblings can be viewed as part of a total family scene, where feelings of closeness between parents and children can grow to include siblings as well. This interpretation of the development of sibling attachment through early family experience is given some support by the findings of Ross, Dalton, and Milgram (1980). Most of the elderly people whom they studied saw the origins of their feelings of closeness to siblings in their childhood experiences as members of close families. Sibling contact later in life tended to re-evoke these feelings of belonging and family unity. The particular salience sibling relationships in the latter part of life seem to have may be a response to the threat that aging and the death of parents pose to the bond of attachment to the family group of childhood.

Topics of sibling attachment, sibling influence in adulthood and old age, and the more complex dimensions of interpersonal relationships between siblings in later life have not been investigated thus far. The evidence presently available indicates that these areas would indeed be worthy of further study.

ACKNOWLEDGMENTS

Based on a paper presented at the 87th Annual Convention of the American Psychological Association, Divisions 7 and 20, as part of the symposium, "Life-Span Perspectivies on Sibling Socialization," New York, New York, September 1, 1979. Certain of the author's research reported herein was supported by grants from the National Retired Teachers Association—American Association of Retired Persons Andrus Foundation.

REFERENCES

Adams, B. N. *Kinship in an urban setting.* Chicago: Markham Publishing Co., 1968.

Adler, A. *Understanding human nature.* New York: Premier Books (Fawcett), 1959. (Originally published 1929.)

Ainsworth, M. D. Attachment and dependency: A comparison. In J. L. Gewirtz (Ed.), *Attachment and dependency.* New York: Wiley, 1972.

Allan, G. Sibling solidarity. *Journal of Marriage and the Family,* 1977, *39,* 177–184.

Antonucci, T. Attachment: A life-span concept. *Human Development,* 1976, *19,* 135–142.

Bank, S., & Kahn, M. D. Sisterhood-brotherhood is powerful: Sibling subsystems and family therapy. *Family Process,* 1975, *14,* 311–337.

Berezin, M. A. Partial grief for the aged and their families. In E. Pattison (Ed.), *The experience of dying.* Englewood Cliffs, N.J.: Prentice-Hall, 1977.

Bild, B. R., & Havighurst, R. J. Family and social support. *Gerontologist,* 1976, *16,* 63–69.

Bossard, J. H. S., & Boll, E. H. *The sociology of child development* (3rd ed.). New York: Harper, 1960.

Bowlby, J. *The making and breaking of affectional bonds.* London: Tavistock Publications, 1979.

Bowlby, J. *Attachment and loss. Vol. III. Loss: Stress and depression.* New York: Basic Books, 1980.

Cicirelli, V. G. The effect of sibling relationships on concept learning of young children taught by child teachers. *Child Development,* 1972, *43,* 282–287.

Cicirelli, V. G. Relationship of siblings to the elderly person's feelings and concerns. *Journal of Gerontology,* 1977, *131,* 309–317.

Cicirelli, V. G. Social services for elderly in relation to the kin network. Report to the NRTA-AARP Andrus Foundation, May 31, 1979.

Cicirelli, V. G. A comparison of college women's feelings toward their siblings and parents. *Journal of Marriage and the Family,* 1980, *42,* 95–102. (a)

Circirelli, V. G. Adult Children's views on providing services for elderly parents. Report to the NRTA-AARP Andrus Foundation, December, 1980. (b)

Cicirelli, V. G. Relationship of family background variables to locus of control in the elderly. *Journal of Gerontology,* 1980, *35,* 108-114. (c)

Cicirelli, V. G. Interpersonal relationships of siblings in the middle part of the life span. Paper presented at the Biennial Meeting of the Society for Research in Child Development, Boston, April, 1981.

Clark, M. & Anderson, B. *Culture and aging.* Springfield, Illinois: C. C. Thomas Publishing Co., 1967.

Cumming, E. & Schneider, D. Sibling solidarity: A property of American kinship. *American Anthropologist,* 1961, *63,* 498-507.

Form, W. H. & Geschwender, J. A. Social reference basis of job satisfaction: The case of manual workers. *American Sociological Review,* 1962, *27,* 232-233.

Irish, D. P. Sibling interaction: A neglected aspect in family life research. *Social Forces,* 1964, *42,* 279-288.

Kalish, R. A., & Knudtson, F. W. *Human Development,* 1976, *19,* 171-181.

Laverty, R. Reactivation of sibling rivalry in older people. *Social Work,* 1962, *7,* 23-30.

Manney, J. D. *Aging.* Office of Human Development, HEW, 1975.

Rosenberg, G. S., & Anspach, D. F. Sibling solidarity in the working class. *Journal of Marriage and the Family,* 1973, *35,* 108-113.

Ross, H. G., Dalton, M. J., & Milgram, J. I. Older adults' perceptions of closeness in sibling relationships. Paper presented at the 33rd Annual Scientific Meeting of the Gerontological Society, San Diego, California, November, 1980.

Ross, H. G., & Milgram, J. I. Rivalry in adult sibling relationships: Its antecedents and dynamics. Paper presented at the Annual Meeting of the American Psychological Association, Montreal, Canada, September, 1980.

Rothbart, M. K. Birth order and mother-child interaction in an achievement situation. *Journal of Personality and Social Psychology,* 1971, *17,* 113-120.

Schooler, C. Birth order effects: Not here, not now! *Psychological Bulletin,* 1972, *78,* 161-175.

Shanas, E., Townsend, P., Wedderburn, D., Friis, H., Milhoj, P., & Stehouwer, J. *Older people in three industrial societies.* New York: Atherton Press, 1968.

Sutton-Smith, B., & Rosenberg, B. G. *The sibling.* New York: Holt, Rinehart, & Winston, 1970.

Toman, W. *Family constellation: Its effects on personality and social behavior.* (3rd ed.). New York: Springer, 1976.

Townsend, P. *The family life of old people: An inquiry in East London.* Glencoe, Illinois: Free Press, 1957.

Troll, L. E. The family of later life. A decade review. *Journal of Marriage and the Family,* 1971, *33,* 263-290.

Troll, L. E. *Early and middle adulthood.* Monterey, California: Brooks/Cole, 1975.

Troll, L. E., Miller, S., & Atchley, R. *Families of later life.* Belmont, California: Wadsworth, 1978.

Troll, L. E., & Smith, J. Attachment through the life span: Some questions about dyadic bonds among adults. *Human Development,* 1976, *19,* 156-170.

12 Only Children in America

Toni Falbo
University of Texas at Austin

This chapter begins with a brief section describing the social and historical context in which American only children have been placed during the 20th century. I believe that understanding this context is necessary in order to evaluate the psychological literature about only children. This literature has a relatively long tradition within psychology, beginning with early birth order studies (e.g., Ellis, 1904) and continuing to the present. The major part of this chapter reviews the psychological literature about only children. This review is organized into the five topics about only children that have received continued attention from psychologists: intelligence, achievement, interpersonal orientation, self-esteem, and marital success. Throughout this review, I have emphasized the contributions of parental characteristics and parent-child relationships in addition to the effect of a lack of siblings on the development of only children.

THE AMERICAN CONTEXT

Figure 1 (Taffel, 1977) presents information about American fertility trends during the last 60 years. As one can see from this figure, there have been major fluctuations in the percentage of completed American families with one child. Specifically, Figure 1 portrays the percentage of white women by the number of their births completed by the women's 30th year. This cut-off point was selected because the majority of American women have completed their childbearing by this age. The pattern of births for nonwhite women during this period is similar.

In general, the birth patterns shown in Figure 1 indicate that there is an inverse

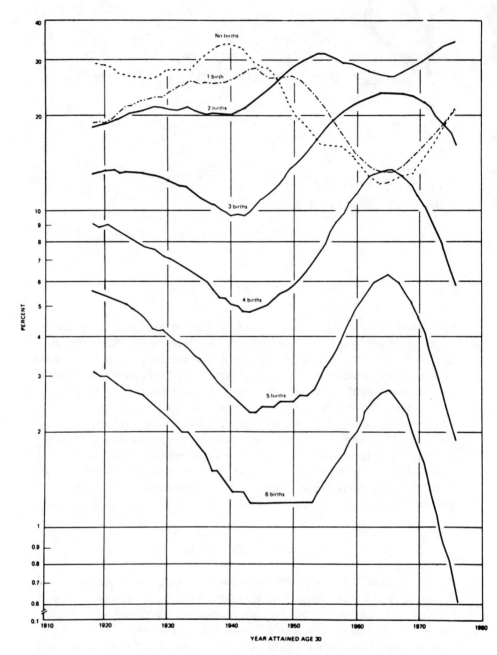

FIG. 1. Percent of white women with specified number of births by exact age 30, January 1, 1918–76 (From Taffell, 1977).

correlation between the percentage of women with just one child and overall fertility. That is, more only children are produced when overall fertility drops. As shown in Figure 1, during the period between 1920 and the early 1940s, the percentage of 30-year-old women with one birth rose from around 20% to about 30%. Simultaneously, the percentage of such women with three to six births dropped. This trend reversed when World War II ended and fertility increased. During this post-War baby boom period, the percentage of women with one child decreased to about 15%. However, in the mid-1960s, this fertility pattern began to reverse again. By the mid-1970s, the percentage of women who had only one child returned to the level found in the early 1920s.

What about the future? Will the percentage of women who complete their family with just one child increase? Among demographers, there is considerable debate regarding future American fertility trends. Some argue that the current low number of births will persist throughout the century (Westoff, 1978). This prediction rests largely on the changing roles of women in America from homemaker to employee and means that the percentage of women with only children will remain stable or slightly increase. In contrast, others (Easterlin, 1978) have asserted that fertility will increase as we approach the 21st century. This prediction is based on the cyclical nature of past American fertility and means that the percentage of women with one child in their completed family would decrease.

Besides speculations regarding fertility, the major evidence available concerning fertility predictions comes from surveys of married women regarding their birth expectations (e.g., U.S. Bureau of Census, 1979a). These predictions support the view that the percentage of women with only children will continue at a relatively high level. In 1971, only 7% of 25–29-year-old married women expected to end their childbearing with one child. By 1979, this percentage had increased to 13 percent (U.S. Bureau of Census, 1979a). Although birth expectations are imprecise forecasts of women's births, such an increase (almost a doubling) of women expecting just one child suggests that more women will be ending their childbearing with a single child.

One of the reasons birth expectations are imperfect indices of future fertility is that fertility is not completely under an individual's control. Factors determining fertility can be divided into voluntary and involuntary categories. For example, women may want more children but are prevented from doing so for health reasons or the death of a spouse. Such fertility determinants would be considered involuntary. Other women may have one child and choose not to have another. This is considered voluntary. Current contraceptive technology has increased the likelihood that women's completed fertility is voluntary. However, as some research suggests, a disproportionate number of women with an only child do not voluntarily place themselves in this fertility category. This research is discussed below.

Factors Promoting One-Child Families

Factors that promote the formation of one-child families are those that generally inhibit fertility. Three such factors are briefly discussed here: war, marital disruption, and economic hardship. First, the fertility patterns shown in Figure 1 suggest that times of war coincide with periods of low fertility. For example, the World War II era is associated with a high percentage of women with one child. However, since wars have only an indirect effect on the current downturn in American fertility, war as a factor promoting the formation of one-child families will not be elaborated in this section.

Second, an important factor promoting the formation of the one-child family is marital instability. A disproportionate number of the one-child families are single parent families (Falbo, 1978a). That is, compared to larger families, one-child families are more likely to have been disrupted by divorce or death. Because marital disruption, particularly divorce, appears to be a contributing factor to the current increase in the percentage of one-child families, this factor will be discussed more fully later in this chapter.

Third, periods of economic stress in the U.S. are associated with declines in fertility. For example, as one can see from Figure 1, the Depression coincided with the formation of a high percentage of one-child families. The recent declines in the American birth rate have been partially attributed to economic factors that both directly and indirectly encourage the formation of one-child families.

The direct effect concerns the increased cost of having children. Recently, an economist has estimated that it costs the average middle income family a total of about $85,000 to rear a child from birth through four years at a public university (Espenshade, 1980).

This direct cost does not include the indirect costs of child care or the costs to women of foregoing or minimizing their employment. The participation of women in the labor force decreases fertility in two distinct ways. First, since the majority of married women are now employed before they have children (U.S. Bureau of Census, 1979b), the benefits of this income and career involvement frequently lead women to postpone childbearing. The longer childbearing is postponed, the greater the chance that a woman will have relatively few children. Second, women who have one child are more likely to be employed outside the home than women with more children (DeJong, Stokes, & Hanson, 1980). Therefore, the financial and personal costs of having additional children is greater for one-child mothers than for those with two or more children.

Factors Inhibiting the Formation of One-Child Families

Currently, in the U.S., the two-child family is considered ideal (Blake, 1974). In contrast, the one-child family is still regarded negatively. According to a Gallup poll taken in 1972, 80% of white Americans indicated that they thought the only child was disadvantaged (Blake, 1974).

Note that only children and their parents have more positive views about only children than do others. The same Gallup poll reported above indicated that only children were much less likely to endorse the statement about the only child disadvantage (Blake, 1974). Similarly, I have found that only children (Falbo, 1978b) and their parents (Falbo, 1978a) rate the amount of suffering only children experience as significantly lower than do others.

Despite the more positive endorsement of only childhood given by only children and their parents, the general American view of the only child is strongly negative. Thompson (1974) points out that only children are viewed as "generally maladjusted, self-centered and self-willed, attention-seeking and dependent on others, temperamental and anxious, generally unhappy and unlikeable, and yet somewhat more autonomous than a child with two siblings [pp. 95-96]." This description suggests that Americans believe children acquire desirable interpersonal characteristics as a consequence of sibling interaction. Therefore, children without siblings are considered to be handicapped in their social development. In fact, the general opinion regarding only children is so negative that the most commonly cited reason for having a second child is to prevent the first from becoming an only child (Solomon, Clare, & Westoff, 1956).

Mothers of Only Children

Given the strong negative stereotype of only children, what self-respecting mother would have a single child? As suggested above, many women reach the end of their reproductive period with an only child for involuntary reasons, such as divorce or health problems. Currently, it is likely that most mothers of only children who have passed their reproductive period fit into this category. However, a strong and possibly growing group of younger parents have chosen this fertility option. Given that such individuals are defying a very strong social stereotype, one might expect them to be distinctive from people with more children.

This section examines the available information regarding the mothers with only children. Overall, the information currently available about mothers of only children is extremely small. First, I will present the evidence regarding the characteristics of married mothers who voluntarily or involuntarily have an only child. Second, I will examine the literature regarding the consequences to both mothers and children of being a member of a single-parent/one-child family.

The evidence about one-child mothers who remain married is limited to two small studies. In fact, one of the studies (Lewis, 1972) contains no information about sample size. In this study, characteristics of one-child mothers were found to vary as a function of the voluntariness of this fertility outcome. Married women who voluntarily had one child were described by Lewis (1972) as coming from nontraditional backgrounds, were more highly educated than other women, and had nontraditional marriages. These women were perceived as highly independent compared to similar women with more children. In contrast, the women who involuntarily had one child came from more traditional backgrounds similar to the backgrounds of women with more children. According to Lewis, women who involuntarily had one child were the most unhappy because such women failed to fulfill their desires for more children.

I conducted the second study that was based on a small sample (N=76) of married mothers of undergraduates (Falbo, 1978a). I examined the psychological characteristics of currently married mothers of only children by comparing them to mothers of more children. Mothers of only children reported having more birth complications than did mothers with more children, a finding that suggests their low fertility was not entirely voluntary. I also found some evidence that one-child mothers were less affiliative than others. Specifically, I found that one-child mothers reported having fewer friends and close friends than mothers of two or more children. The possible significance of this for the social development of only children is described later.

These two studies constitute the current information about mothers of only children. It is painfully clear that a more complete picture of these women, taking into account the voluntariness of their fertility outcome, is needed. It is also obvious that we need to begin collecting data about one-child fathers and one-child families.

The topic of single parents and their single children has received more attention. Unfortunately, the two major works on this topic draw two distinct, if not contradictory, conclusions. The first such work (Weiss, 1979) represents an integration of the results of several small-scale surveys of single parents and generally suggests that the one-child/one-parent family is more problematic than the multi-child/one-parent family. In particular, Weiss argued that with just one child, single parents are prone to either overinvest themselves in their child or to complain about the negative effect their child has on their freedom. In Weiss's view, only children with single parents also suffered more loneliness than similar children with siblings. Finally, Weiss stated that the one-child/one-parent families were more likely to experience aberrations of the parent-child roles than larger families. Specifically, this meant that power was more diffuse, that mothers of only sons were more likely to assume a wife-like role, that mothers of only daughters were more often jealous of their daughter's appearance, freedoms, etc., than single mothers with more children.

In contrast, another, more systematic study of the single-parent/one-child family came to more positive conclusions (Polit, 1980). This study was based on interviews with 90 single mothers of one, two, and three children as well as 20 married mothers of one child. According to Polit (1980), divorced women with one child were found to be less lonely, had fewer financial concerns, were the happiest with their jobs (which were more often of high status), and had a greater sense of well-being than divorced mothers with two or three children.

In terms of Weiss's specific conclusions regarding one-child/one-parent families, Polit's results contradicted or failed to replicate them. In particular, Polit found that few single parent families, regardless of size, showed an overinvestment by parents in their children. However, when such overinvestment was found, it was not concentrated in the one-parent/one-child family. According to Polit, overinvestment was evenly distributed across all the family types in her study, including single-parent/three-child families. In terms of resenting the presence of children, Polit found that some single parents acknowledged that their lives would be easier without children, but this acknowledgment was also found in two- and three-child families as well as one-child families.

Loneliness was not a problem for the only children in Polit's sample. In fact, instead of providing support, siblings were perceived by mothers as having far more hostile than supportive relationships.

Polit's research also indicated that the diffusion of authority was common in single parent families, but no more so in one- than two-child families. However, single mothers with three children were found to have the most restricted division between parent and child roles. In addition, Polit did not observe single mothers taking a wife-like role to their sons, nor did she observe a single incidence of single mothers being jealous of their daughters. However, this may be due to the small number of adolescent children in her sample.

Although only future research will determine which is the more accurate portrayal of the single-parent/one-child family, the disparate conclusions reached by these two investigators are probably due to differences in their research samples. Weiss's sample did not contain a comparison group of two-parent/one-child families; Polit's sample did. Consequently, it is likely that Weiss's conclusions revealed more regarding his and his respondents' fears about only children than their actual outcomes. Also, Weiss's sample included parents who had lost their spouse through death as well as divorce. In contrast, all of Polit's single parents were divorced women. This difference is significant when one considers the outcomes for parents. Specifically, it is possible that one-child mothers who had ended an unsuccessful marriage were more capable of coping with their current status than single parents who had lost their spouse through death.

ONLY CHILDREN

Popular thinking concerning only children has focused on the only child's lack of siblings as the source of any difference between only children and others. However, as I have argued elsewhere (Falbo, 1978a,1978c), it seems plausible that the distinctive attributes of the parents of only children contribute at least partially to the distinctive attributes of their children. In the past, the contribution of sibling absence to the differential development of only children has been emphasized because of the persistent interest in birth order as a topic of psychological investigation and because little evidence has been available about parents of only children.

Throughout the following review, the contribution of parents to the distinctive development of only children is presented and contrasted to the contribution of sibling absence to this development.

Intelligence

A major theory about intellectual development is a good example of the overemphasis of sibling absence as an explanation for only child attributes. This theory, the confluence model (Zajonc & Markus, 1975), concerns the impact of family composition on intellectual development. The confluence model began as an explanation for the repeatedly obtained finding that IQ and family size are inversely related. That is, children from larger families have lower IQs on the average than children from smaller families. On the basis of this negative relationship, one would expect only children to have the highest IQs of all because they come from the smallest families. Unfortunately, the results of three large-scale studies of young adults, conducted in Holland (Belmont & Marolla, 1973) and in the U.S. (Breland, 1974; Claudy, 1976), are consistent in placing only children lower than this prediction. In these studies, only children were found to score at levels comparable to first-borns from three- to five-child families.

The confluence model (Zajonc & Markus, 1975) addresses both the general family size-IQ relationship and the specific only child discrepancy from this relationship. This respected ("Zajonc Defuses IQ Debate," 1976) and popular (Zajonc, 1975) model proposes that intelligence develops as a function of a combination of factors, including the child's maturation and experience within the family. It is through the child's experiences within the family that family size has its effects on intelligence.

The confluence model posits that intellectual development is strongly determined by the level of intelligence present within the family. The level of intellectual functioning of a family is operationally defined as consisting of the average of the absolute intelligence of all family members. Absolute intelligence is uncorrected for age and, because children have lower absolute intelligence levels than adults, the intellectual environment of a family is greater the more adult and fewer child members it has. Consequently, children who grow up in single parent families are disadvantaged relative to children with two parents because the average intelligence level of their family is less than what it would be with two parents in the family.

However, in explaining the lower-than-expected performance of only children, Zajonc and Markus (1975) ignored the fact that only children are more likely to come from single parent families. Instead, Zajonc and Markus proposed that the only child discrepancy was due to the fact that only children have no younger sibling to tutor. This sibling tutoring explanation was proposed and accepted even though there is no evidence that tutoring a younger person results in an intelligence gain for the tutor. Although there is ample evidence that even kindergarten-aged children can tutor younger children, tests of the effects of this tutoring have been limited to studies of the acquisition of social skills and academic content (Allen, 1976). Furthermore, even though the presence of a younger sibling enhances the opportunities for tutoring, there is no evidence about how much tutoring of younger siblings actually goes on within a family.

Therefore, I proposed an alternative explanation for the IQ discrepancy of the only child. Specifically, I suggested that this discrepancy was at least partially explained by the higher incidence of marital disruption among one than multiple child families (Falbo, 1978c). Using National Merit Scholarship Qualifying Test (NMSQT) scores obtained from Zajonc (1977), I found that about 25% of the IQ difference between the mean NMSQT scores for only children and the expected NMSQT scores was explained by an estimated incidence of single parents among one-child families.

Recently, additional evidence supportive of the single parent explanation for the IQ discrepancy of only children has emerged. In 1976, Claudy reported that only children scored lower than children from two-child families on a wide array of intelligence and ability tests (Claudy, 1976). However, more recently, Claudy, Farrell, and Dayton (1979) eliminated one-parent families from the same sample and found that only children either scored better than or no differently from children of two-child families. These results suggest that when family intactness is controlled, the IQ disadvantage of only children disappears.

Achievement

Unlike intelligence, the traditional explanations for the achievement of only children has focused on their relationships with their parents. This is probably due to the fact that only children are like first-borns in their greater achievement. Disproportionate numbers of first- and only-borns have been found among eminent men (Ellis, 1904), the faces on *Time* covers (Toman & Toman, 1970), psychologists (Roe, 1953), and other groups presumably representing achievement. Consistent with these findings, several investigators have found greater academic achievement among only children and firstborns (Guildford & Worchester, 1930; Jones, 1954; Lees & Steward, 1957; Oberlander & Jenkins, 1967; Skouholt, Moore, & Wellman, 1973).

Searches for the psychological factors that account for this birth order effect in achievement have focused on the special relationship onlies and firstborns have with their parents. One branch of this theorizing concerns achievement motivation. Presumably onlies and firstborns achieve more because they are motivated to do so. There is some evidence that supports this supposition. Both Sampson and Hancock (1967), Angelini (1967) and Rosen (1961) found that first- and only-borns scored higher on need for achievement than did later-borns. However, not everyone has found a birth order effect in their need for achievement data (e.g. Rosenfeld, 1966).

Achievement motivation has been thought to originate in the high standards for mature behavior that parents impose on their children at relatively early ages (Rosen & D'Andrade, 1959; Winterbottom, 1958). This approach to explaining achievement motivation is relevant to birth order effects because there is evidence that first- and only-borns receive greater pressure for more mature behavior from parents than do later-borns (Clausen, 1966; Kammeyer, 1967). Consistent with this approach is the finding that only- and first-borns have higher educational aspirations than later-borns (Falbo, 1981).

Another factor that contributes to the achievement of onlies and first-borns is their strong tendency to take responsibility for outcomes. First- and especially only-borns have been found to have a more internal locus of control than later-borns (Crandall, Katkovsky, & Crandall, 1965; Falbo, 1981). To date, there has been little adequate explanation for this finding. Crandall et al. explained their result as due to the tendency of firstborns to take care of their younger siblings. Although this explanation is plausible for first-borns, it fails to explain the fact that Crandall et al. found both first- and only-borns have a more internal orientation than later-borns.

I propose that an adequate, single explanation for the greater internality of first- and only-borns should center on the special relationship only- and first-borns have with their parents. Since firstborns are only children for a limited time, it seems likely that their greater belief in internal control may be related to the increased attention parents give to their first or only child. Because such parents can give their undivided attention to their single child's upbringing, the likelihood that outcomes (i.e., parental rewards and punishments) closely and consistently follow the child's behavior is greater for onlies than for later-borns. It is likely that the closeness and consistency of this contingency reinforces stronger beliefs in internal control among only- and first-borns than among later-borns.

Interpersonal Orientation

This section deals with a set of characteristics that represents the greatest area of popular concern about only children: interpersonal orientation. The stereotype of the only child suggests that only children are thought to lack interpersonal skills. This section is divided into two parts. First, the literature about birth order effects in affiliation is examined and second, evidence regarding peer popularity and styles of peer interaction is debated.

Affiliation.   Parent-child relationships have been frequently presented as the cause of the affiliativeness of only-borns. In some cases, this is probably due to the fact that only children share some affiliativeness attributes with firstborns. In early research on affiliation, Schachter (1959) proposed that onlies and first-borns affiliated more during times of stress than later-borns because in infancy they received more immediate attention from their mothers when they cried than did later-borns. Schachter argued that the mothers of first- and only-borns were more anxious about their babies and therefore responded more promptly to their distress than to the distress of later babies. As mothers developed greater experience with children, they became less anxious and therefore responded less promptly to the cries of subsequent children.

According to Schachter, the result of this differential mothering of early- vs. later-borns was to enhance the expectation among adult onlies and first-borns that other people are comforting in times of stress. Schachter's (1959) early experiment supported this prediction and the general effect has been replicated in field studies (Hoyt & Raven, 1973) as well as with role-playing techniques (Greenberg, 1967).

In terms of nonstress induced affiliation, however, there is some evidence supporting the idea that only children are less affiliative than others. Only children belong to fewer organizations (Blake, 1981; Falbo, 1978a), report having fewer friends (Falbo, 1978b), visit friends and relatives less often (Blake, 1981), and have a less intense social life (Claudy et al., 1979) than others. However, these same only children reported having a comparable number of close friends and leadership positions in clubs (Falbo, 1978b) and feeling as satisfied with their lives and as happy (Blake, 1981) as others.

This lowered affiliativeness among only-borns has also been explained by Conners (1963) as resulting from the strong amounts of affection they receive from their parents. Specifically, Conners argued that because only children suffer less affection deprivation from their parents than do children with siblings, only children are less motivated to affiliate than first- or later-borns. Conners' (1963) birth order study supported his predictions about differential patterns of affiliativeness and affection deprivation. Consistent with these results, Rosenfeld (1966) compared the need for affiliation scores of first- and only-borns and found firstborns to have significantly higher needs for affiliation than only-borns.

Peer Popularity.   On a common sense basis, one would expect sibling experience to have an impact on peer popularity. In fact, research in this area has generally emphasized sibling experience over parental characteristics. For example, Miller and Maruyama (1976) found that onlies and firstborns were selected less frequently as playmates and someone to sit close to by their classmates than were earlier-borns. Furthermore, this birth order difference was found regardless of family size or socioeconomic status. Miller and Maruyama interpreted these results to mean that onlies and first-borns acquire a more autocratic, less interactive style than later-borns because only- and first-borns have no older siblings to interact with.

Unfortunately, these results are contradicted by an earlier study. Sells and

Roff (1963) obtained classmate likeability ratings from same-sex grade school classmates and found that only- and youngest-borns received the highest ratings. It is possible to rectify the discrepant results of the two studies by pointing to the fact that likeability ratings measure different aspects of peer acceptance than playmate and seating selections. However, assuming that there are reliable differences between only- and nononly-borns in terms of peer popularity, it is plausible that parents have some role in the development of these differences. If only children are less affiliative than others, then one would expect them to be less popular than others. Parents could influence this through the affection/affiliation process described by Conners (1963) or through their own example. Recall that, in my study of mothers reported earlier, I found that one-child mothers reported having fewer friends than did mothers of more children (Falbo, 1978a). It seems likely that less gregarious mothers may not encourage their children's peer popularity.

Note that peer popularity is an outcome that leads people to draw inferences about interpersonal behavior. More direct evidence about the interpersonal behavior of only children is needed. More specifically, I think interpersonal behaviors, both verbal and nonverbal, ought to be the focus of future research. As an example of such research, I will present a study I conducted with young adults. The interpersonal behaviors studied here were the play choices in a Prisoner's Dilemma Game (Falbo, 1978b). This abbreviated version of the Prisoner's Dilemma Game consisted of two plays, an initial play and a play in response to another's initial play. In the first play, subjects had to choose between a move that represented a cooperative initiative (both players could win) or a competitive initiative (one subject would win). All subjects were led to believe that they were playing with a fellow subject, when in fact they were playing against the experimenter. Therefore, when the subjects made their second play, it was always in response to a cooperative, initial play actually made by the experimenter. In this second play, subjects had the choice between taking advantage of the initial cooperativeness of their fellow subject (thereby making him/her lose) or making a cooperative play (thereby allowing both to win). My results indicated that the presence of siblings was related to the second, but not the first play choice. Specifically, I found that only-borns were more likely to make a cooperative second play than were people who had siblings. No differences between only- and nononly-borns were found in the initial move.

I explained these results in terms of sibling rivalry. That is, I argued that because only children lack sibling rivalry, they acquire a more trusting style of interaction. Sutton-Smith and Rosenberg (1970) arrived at a similar conclusion. They reasoned that because only children continuously receive help and nurturance from their parents, only children develop the expectation that others are helpful and rewarding. In contrast, children with siblings are more likely to compete with each other for parental rewards and this experience leads them to expect competition from others.

Self-Esteem. Previous research and theory relevant to birth order effects in self-esteem has included a mixture of interpretations, emphasizing both parents and siblings as contributing factors. This mixture of interpretations is matched by a mixture of results regarding only children and self-esteem.

For example, Zimbardo and Formica (1963) based their research on social comparison theory, thich states that an individual's level of self-esteem is determined by the results of a comparison between that individual and others. Zimbardo and Formica reasoned that first- and only-borns compare themselves to their parents, whereas last-borns compare themselves to their older siblings. Since during childhood such comparisons are more invidious for first- and only-than last-borns, Zimbardo and Formica argued that only- and first-borns acquire lower self-esteem than last-borns. The empirical test of this prediction obtained supportive results that were only of borderline significance. Later, Kaplan (1970) had more success. He found that last-borns were more likely to be in the high self-esteem group than were middle- or first- (and only-) borns. Unfortunately, further analysis of Kaplan's findings indicated that the effect was true only for white males from high social class groups.

Other authors have argued that onlies and firstborns would have higher self-esteem than middle- and last-borns because first- and only-borns would receive more unconditional positive regard from their parents than would later-borns. Some support for this prediction was found by Coopersmith (1967). He found that only- and first-born adolescent males were overrepresented in his high self-esteem group. Similarly, Rosenberg (1965) reported that only-borns were more likely to be classified as having high self-esteem than were nononly-borns. However, further analysis of Rosenberg's data indicated that this apparent difference between only- and nononly-borns existed mainly for males, especially Jewish males.

More recently, I compared only children to first-, middle-, and last-borns and found no significant differences between only- and nononly-borns (Falbo, 1981). However, I did find that firstborns scored significantly higher in self-esteem than last-borns but that both only- and middle-borns scored no differently from all others. In explaining this result, I revised the social comparison rationale initially proposed by Zimbardo and Formica. According to this revised view, children develop their sense of personal worth by comparing themselves to their siblings (if present), not to either siblings or parents, as Zimbardo and Formica proposed. Since older siblings are generally more capable, larger, more skilled, etc., than younger siblings, firstborns would come to regard themselves more favorably than would their siblings, and therefore would develop the most positive self-esteem. Conversely, last-borns would have the least positive comparison to their siblings. Therefore, they would develop the least positive self-esteem. Finally, both only- and middle-borns would compare negatively to their older siblings, but positively to their younger siblings, and this mixed comparison would lead middle-borns to the acquisition of moderate levels of self-esteem.

Since only children would not experience this sibling comparison, their self-esteem development would be unaffected by this process and they would develop a moderate level of self-esteem.

In summary, there is no consistent result about self-esteem and only children. I suspect that this inconsistency can be resolved by considering the types of self-esteem measures used, the age of the subjects, and both parental and sibling contributions to the process of self-esteem development.

Marital Success. There are two distinct bodies of literature about marital success that are relevant to predictions regarding only children. One derives from sibling position and the other is based on the transmission of marital instability from parents to their children. Despite this difference, either approach would make the prediction that only children are less likely to have successful marriages than others.

Toman's (1959, 1969) theory asserts that more successful pairings are found among couples who have complementary sibling relationships. For example, Toman (1969) predicted that the marriage of a man with a younger sister to a woman with an older brother would be successful, but the marriage of a man with a younger sister to a woman with only a younger brother would be less likely to succeed. Toman's reasoning is based on the assumption that growing up in a certain sibling position trains one in this role relationship. Thus, the interaction between people with fully complementary siblings is facilitated.

According to Toman, only children are handicapped in mate selection because they have a limited number of possible good matches. Toman argues that since only children have solely their parents to focus on, only children attempt to replicate their relationship with their parents in their marriages. Consequently, only children are best paired with firstborns with opposite sex siblings who take on the role of "parent" for the only child. Given the fact that such firstborns have many other possible good matches, the likelihood that only children never marry or marry inappropriately is increased. Consequently, Toman's theory would predict that only children would be more likely to never marry, or, if married, be more likely to have unstable marriages. Furthermore, even with a proper match, Toman believes that only children prefer to remain childless because only children, in Toman's view, want to remain the undisputed "child" in the family.

Unfortunately, Toman (1959, 1969) provides little empirical evidence to allow an evaluation of his predictions regarding only children. Overall, his sibling replication hypothesis has received some support from studies of dating (Mendlesohn, Linden, Gruen, & Curran, 1974).

The alternate literature bearing on the marriages of only children concerns the tendency of adults with divorced parents to have unstable marriages (Bentler & Newcomb, 1978; Kulka & Weingarten, 1979; Pope & Mueller, 1976). This literature is based on the frequently found correlation between having divorced parents and experiencing marital instability. The underlying reasons for this correlation are basically unknown, although some have speculated that parents "transmit" their own marital instability to their children by means of reducing their children's psychological well-being or changing their children's understanding of the marital role (Kulka & Weingarten, 1979). Since only children are more likely to come from families disrupted by divorce, one would expect only children to experience greater marital instability than others.

Despite the convergence of theory about the marital problems of only children, the current evidence contradicts the prediction. This evidence comes from two separate surveys. The first is a longitudinal survey conducted of high school students in 1960 and 11 years after their expected high school graduation (Claudy, Farrell, & Dayton, 1979). The second analysis was made of a national survey conducted in 1973-1974 of women between the ages of 15 and 44 years (Groat, Wicks, & Neal, 1980).

In the first study, people from one- and two-child families who were living with both their biological parents in 1960 were selected from the larger sample. Stratified by socioeconomic status, this smaller sample was evenly divided by gender and by family size of origin (one- and two-child). Information about marriage was obtained during the 11-year follow-up survey, when the respondents were about 29 years old.

The results of the comparisons of people from one- and two-child families indicated few differences in marriage patterns. Only children were found to have married for the first time at about the same age as people from two-child families. More importantly, the results indicated that the probability of marrying, or of marrying more than once, was unrelated to family size of origin. However, some differences between only and nononly children were found. Only children married more educated spouses (only children also obtained more education), were less likely to be divorced, and desired and had fewer children than did their counterparts from two-child families.

The second study, conducted by Groat, Wicks, and Neal (1980), compared only children to everyone else, controlling for pertinent factors, such as education and parity. In terms of marital outcome, Groat et al. found results that were generally consistent with those reported by Claudy. In particular, there were no differences between only children and others in terms of their age at first marriage, although for men, only children married almost a year later, a difference that approached significance.

However, Groat et al. found that only children were as likely as nononlies to have had a previous marriage at the time of the survey. This contrasts with Claudy et al.'s conclusion that onlies were less likely than nononlies to have been divorced by age 29. An easy reconciliation of these apparently discrepant results rests on a critical difference in the data available to Claudy et al. and Groat et al. First, obviously, Claudy's results were limited to the age of 29—with no information about divorces after that age. The Groat et al. results are based on a wider

(15–44) age range. Second, Claudy's analyses were limited to people from two-parent families, whereas this factor was not controlled in the Groat et al. analyses of marital factors.

Although these two studies provide us with valuable information about the marital success of only children, they leave many questions unanswered. More information is needed about the nature of the marital relationship, e.g., are only children more likely to take the role of "child" relative to their spouse? By examining spouse perceptions and behaviors, one would be better able to determine the relative contributions of parents and siblings to marital success.

SUMMARY AND CONCLUSIONS

Two important sources of only-child differences, parental characteristics and sibling lack, were emphasized throughout this chapter. The relative contribution of each source appears to vary with the attribute being considered. For example, whereas adult only children score less well than one would expect on intelligence, recent evidence suggests that this discrepancy is due to parent and not sibling lack. When the number of parents (one vs. two) is considered, the IQ "decline" of only children is reduced, eliminated, or reversed.

In terms of achievement, only children are generally combined with first-borns and both are found to excel over later-borns. Several explanations for this achievement effect were examined, including achievement motivation and locus of control. Parental attention and expectations are the most likely sources of the greater achievement motivation and internal orientation of only- and firstborns.

Two aspects of interpersonal orientation were examined, affiliation and peer popularity. Speculation regarding the origin of only child characteristics here included both parents and siblings. Only children were found to be like first-borns in exhibiting greater affiliation under stress. However, when not under stress, only children appear to be less affiliative than others. Examinations of the peer popularity of only- vs. other-borns has resulted in conflicting results. More evidence about the peer relationships of only children is needed.

Similarly, there is no consistent picture of the only child's self-esteem. Empirical investigations have placed only children ahead, behind, or at par with others. More research is needed here in order to clarify this self-esteem effect and to determine the contributions of parents and siblings to it.

Finally, the sketchy evidence regarding marital success suggests only children are not at a disadvantage in this area. This conclusion contrasts with the predictions from both the sibling replication and parental transmission theories. More research is needed here, especially to examine the nature of the marital relationships of onlies.

The purpose of including the section concerning the American context in this chapter was to suggest that the psychological characteristics of only children cannot be evaluated without considering their historical and familial contexts. It seems likely that this context has had a significant impact on the development of American only children. Such children, born into an era of economic depression or world war in which only childhood is common, probably developed into adults differently from those only children born into an era of postwar baby boom. Similarly, one would expect only children with single parents to develop differently from only children with two parents who chose the one-child family size. And so on. I am arguing that it may well be a mistake to evaluate today's only children on the basis of information gathered from previous generations. Furthermore, there is little justification for the persistent and popular belief that any difference found between only children and others must be explained wholly in terms of sibling absence. Siblings have an impact on child development, but so do parents and society.

One can argue that one reason so few differences are found between only children and others is that we have not yet examined the important variables. Although this argument has merit, I think it explains only some of the reasons that so many comparisons between only children and others result in no differences. We should admit that many of our psychological measures, especially those dealing with interpersonal characteristics, have little reliability and account for only small amounts of variance in predicting behavior. Furthermore, many of our assessments occur when the subjects are young adults. It seems likely that the distinctive characteristics of only children will be more obvious when we examine younger subjects; that is, children and adolescents. I argue this because it seems likely that the effects of siblings will be more pronounced when siblings are living together as children in the same family rather than when they are living outside their families of origin, as adults.

Finally, I propose that for most psychological variables, the impact of siblings does not follow a simple linear relationship. That is, I suspect that personality characteristics are developed through processes that are not a simple summation of family members. Factors such as age spacing, sex configuration, parental stability and expectations, as well as birth order, interact with each other in complex ways to produce developmental outcomes. In particular, I think that these developmental processes for only children are distinct from those of children who grow up with siblings. Rather than regarding only children as deprived, it is probably more accurate to regard them as enriched with experiences that promote a different course of development. On the basis of current information, it seems that this course of development leads them eventually to many of the same outcomes as those who have siblings. Future research, I hope will avoid making simplistic assumptions about the effects of siblings on development and proceed towards advancing our knowledge about the familial processes that underly development.

REFERENCES

Allen, V. L. *Children as Teachers.* New York: Academic Press, 1976.

Angelini, H. B. Family structure and motivation to achieve. *Revista Interamericana de Psicologia,* 1967, *1*(2), 115–125.

Belmont, L. & Marolla, F. A. Birth order, family size, and intelligence. *Science,* 1973, *182,* 1096–1101.

Bentler, P. M. & Newcomb, M. D. Longitudinal study of marital success and failure. *Journal of Consulting and Clinical Psychology,* 1978, *46*(5), 1053–1070.

Blake, J. Can we believe recent data on birth expectation in the United States? *Demography,* 1974, *11,* 25–44.

Blake, J. The only child in America: Prejudice versus performance. *Population and Development Review,* 1981, *1,* 43–54.

Breland, H. M. Birth order, family configuration, and verbal achievement. *Child Development,* 1974, *45,* 1011–1019.

Claudy, J. G. *Cognitive characteristics of the only child.* Paper presented at the 84th Annual Convention of the American Psychological Association, Washington, D. C., 1976.

Claudy, J. G., Farrell, W. S., & Dayton, C. W. *The consequences of being an only child: An analysis of project talent data.* Final Report (No. N01-HD-82854). Center for Population Research, National Institutes of Health, December, 1979.

Clausen, J. A. Family structure, socialization, and personality. In L. W. Hoffman & M. L. Hoffman (Eds.), *Review of child development research* (Vol. 2). New York: Russell Sage Foundation, 1966.

Conners, C. K. Birth order and needs for affiliation. *Journal of Personality,* 1963, *31,* 409–416.

Coopersmith, S. *The antecedents of self-esteem.* San Francisco: N. H. Freeman, 1967.

Crandall, V. C., Katkovsky, W., & Crandall, V. J. Children's beliefs in their own control of reinforcement in intellectual-academic achievement situations. *Child Development,* 1965, *36,* 91–109.

DeJong, G. F., Stokes, S., & Hanson, S. L. *Long term consequences of childlessness and one child on labor force participation, mobility aspirations, and occupational attainment of married women.* Third progress report, National Institute of Child mental Health and Human Development Contract No. NI-HD-92807, 1980.

Easterlin, R. A. What will 1984 be like? Socioeconomic implications of recent twists in age structure. *Demography,* 1978, *15,* 397–432.

Ellis, H. A. *A study of British genius.* London: Hurst & Blackett, 1904.

Espenshade, T. J. Raising a child can now cost $85,000. *Intercom,* 1980, *8*(9), 1.

Falbo, T. Reasons for having an only child. *Journal of Population,* 1978, *1,* 181–184. (a)

Falbo, T. Only children and interpersonal behavior: An experimental and survey study. *Journal of Applied Social Psychology,* 1978, *8,* 244–253. (b)

Falbo, T. Sibling tutoring and other explanations for intelligence discontinuities of only and last borns. *Journal of Population,* 1978, *1,* 345–364. (c)

Falbo, T. Relationships between birth category, achievement and interpersonal orientation. *Journal of Personality and Social Psychology,* 1981, *41*(1), 121–131.

Greenberg, M. S. Role playing: An alternative to deception? *Journal of Personality and Social Psychology,* 1967, *7,* 152–157.

Groat, H. T., Wicks, J. W., & Neal, A. G. *Differential consequences of having been an only child versus a sibling child.* Final Report (No. NIH-N01-HD-92806), Center for Population Research, National Institutes of Health, April, 1980.

Guildford, R. B. & Worcester, D. A. A comparative study of the only and nononly child. *Journal of Genetic Psychology,* 1930, *38,* 411–426.

Hoyt, M. P. & Raven, B. H. Birth order and the 1971 Los Angeles earthquake. *Journal of Personality and Social Psychology*, 1973, *28*, 123-128.

Jones, H. E. Environmental influence on mental development. In L. Carmichael (Ed.), *Manual of child psychology* (2nd ed.). New York: Wiley, 1954.

Kammeyer, K. Birth order as a research variable. *Social Forces*, 1967, *46*, 71-80.

Kaplan, H. B. Self-derogation and childhood family structure. *Journal of Nervous and Mental Disease*, 1970, *151*, 13-23.

Kulka, R. A. & Weingarten, H. The long-term effects of parental divorce in childhood on adult adjustment. *Journal of Social Issues*, 1979, *35*, 50-78.

Lees, J. P. & Stewart, A. H. Family or sibship position and scholastic ability: An interpretation. *Sociological Review*, 1957, *5*, 173-190.

Lewis, E. J. Psychological determinants of family size: A study of white middle class couples ages 35-45 with zero, one, or three children. *Proceedings of the 80th Annual Convention of the American Psychological Association*, 1972, 665-666.

Mendlesohn, P., Linden, W. L., Gruen, T. S., & Curran, B. Heterosexual pairing and sibling configuration, *Journal of Individual Psychology*, 1974, *30*, 202-210.

Miller, N. & Maruyama, G. Ordinal position and peer popularity. *Journal of Personality and Social Psychology*, 1976, *33*, 123-131.

Oberlander, M. & Jenkins, N. Birth order and academic achievement. *Journal of Individual Psychology*, 1967, *23*, 103-109.

Polit, D. F. *The one-parent/one-child family: Social and psychological consequences.* Final Report, Contract No. N01-HD-82852, American Institute for Research, Cambridge, Massachusetts, 1980.

Pope, H. and Mueller, C. W. The intergenerational transmission of marital instability: Comparisons by race and sex. *Journal of Social Issues*, 1976, *32*, 49-66.

Roe, A. A. Psychological study of eminent psychologists and anthropologists and a comparison with biological and physical scientists. *Psychological Monographs*, 1953, 67(2, Whole No. 352).

Rosen, B. C. Family structure and achievement motivation. *American Sociological Review*, 1961, *28*, 574-585.

Rosen, B. & D'Andrade, R. C. T. The psychosocial origins of achievement motivation. *Sociometry*, 1959, *22*, 185-218.

Rosenberg, M. *Society and the adolescent self-image.* Princeton, N.J.: Princeton University Press, 1965.

Rosenfeld, H. Relationships of ordinal position to affiliation and achievement motives: Direction and generality. *Journal of Personality*, 1966, *34*, 467-479.

Sampson, E. E. & Hancock, F. R. An examination of the relationship between ordinal position, personality and conformity: An extension, replication and partial verification. *Journal of Personality and Social Psychology*, 1967, *5*, 398-407.

Schachter, S. *The psychology of affiliation.* Stanford, Calif.: Stanford University Press, 1959.

Sells, B. and Roff, M. Peer acceptance-rejection and birth order. *American Psychologist*, 1963, *18*, 355.

Skouholt, T., Moore, E., & Wellman, F. Birth order and academic behavior in first grade. *Psychological Reports*, 1973, *32*, 395-398.

Solomon, E. S., Clare, J. E., & Westoff, C. F. Social and psychological factors affecting fertility. *The Milbank Memorial Fund Quarterly*, 1956, *34*, 160-177.

Sutton-Smith, B. & Rosenberg, B. G. *The sibling.* New York: Holt, Rinehart, and Winston, 1970.

Taffel, S. Trends in fertility in the United States. *Vital and Health Statistics Series 21*, Number 28, Washington, D.C.: U. S. Government Printing Office, 1977.

Thompson, V. D. Family size: Implicit policies and assumed psychological outcomes. *Journal of Social Issues*, 1974, *30*, 93-124.

Toman, W. Family constellation as a character and marriage determinant. *International Journal of Psychoanalysis,* 1959, *40,* 316–319.

Toman, W. *Family constellation: Its effects on personality and social behavior.* New York: Springer, 1969.

Toman, W. & Toman, E. Sibling positions of a sample of distinguished persons. *Perceptual and Motor Skills,* 1970, *32,* 825–826.

U. S. Bureau of Census. *Current population reports,* 1979, P-20, No. 350. (a)

U. S. Bureau of Census. *Current Population Reports,* 1979, P-20, No. 336. (b)

Weiss, R. S. *Going it alone.* New York: Basic Books, 1979.

Westoff, C. F. Some speculations on the future of marriage and fertility. *Family Planning Perspectives,* 1978, *10,* 79–83.

Winterbottom, M. R. The relation of need for achievement to learning experiences in independence and mastery. In J. W. Atkinson (Ed.), *Motives in fantasy, action, and society.* Princeton, New Jersey: Van Nostrand, 1958.

Zajonc defuses IQ debate: Birth order work wins prize. *APA Monitor,* May, 1976, p. 1.

Zajonc, R. B. Birth order and intelligence: Dumber by the dozen. *Psychology Today,* 1975, 37.

Zajonc, R. B. Personal communication, November 1, 1977.

Zajonc, R. B. & Markus, G. B. Birth order and intellectual development. *Psychological Review,* 1975, *82,* 74–88.

Zimbardo, P. & Formica, R. Emotional comparisons and self-esteem as determinants of affiliation. *Journal of Personality,* 1963, *31,* 141–162.

13 Sibling Interdependence and Child Caretaking: A Cross-Cultural View

Thomas S. Weisner
University of California, Los Angeles

INTRODUCTION

Some peculiar preoccupations characterize sibling research in the United States and Western Europe. Western views of siblings are limited—one might even say scientifically ethnocentric—because the preoccupations of Western sibling research are by and large the preoccupations of Western society: achievement; status and hierarchy; conformity and dependency; intelligence; rivalry and competition. Now siblings are indeed rivalrous; they often compete fiercely with each other, and age and ordinal position are important for understanding sibling relationships. But these are far from the only important topics. A cross-cultural view suggests a number of aspects seldom considered. Siblings conjointly perform important, responsible domestic tasks and chores essential to the subsistence and survival of the family; they are involved in cooperative child rearing; in defense, warfare, and protection; in arranging marriages and providing marriage payments. Siblings in most of the world strongly influence much of the life course of their brothers and sisters by what they do. They share life crisis and rite of passage ceremonies essential to their cultural and social identity; they take on ritual and ceremonial responsibilities for each other essential to community spiritual ideals. *The sibling group in most societies around the world participates jointly throughout the life span in activities essential to survival, reproduction, and the transmission of cultural and social values.*

One goal of this chapter is to contrast Western and American sibling studies in light of the unique "ecocultural niche" of post-industrial modern society (Bronfenbrenner, 1979; Super & Harkness, 1980). The ecological context has powerful effects on sibling relations around the world. Cross-cultural and comparative material is not qualitatively different from that needed for

305

understanding Western sibling data. On the contrary, the same general principles and antecedent structural variables are relevant in Western studies. The use of cross-cultural material simply brings these variables to our attention. To illustrate this, I focus on data concerning siblings not usually considered in Western family studies: sibling caretaking, marriage, and inheritance. Ones' brothers and sisters play central roles in each of these domains in most of the world.

Cross-Cultural Data

Cross-cultural material directly focused on brothers and sisters—how they relate to one another, how they feel about one another, their relationships as these change throughout the life span, and the causes and correlates of systematic differences in cultural patterns in sibling relationships—is relatively scarce. Why is there so little under the *category* "sibling" in most ethnography? Discovering where material on siblings *is* to be found in ethnographic research suggests part of the answer. Data on sibs are interspersed in sections on kinship studies, studies of family, discussions of bridewealth, bridewealth negotiations, rules of descent, rules regarding the inheritance of property, and occasionally under work and task roles. There might be material under child rearing, child development, or children's play focused on the sibling group; or under initiation ceremonies or other rites of passage, or religious rituals that involve the family group, corporate group, or domestic compound. One might also find material under witchcraft or sorcery, because kinship relationships are often heavily involved in how witchcraft powers are perceived and used in society. Data on siblings also appears in sections describing other social statuses such as age, stage in the life cycle, or sex role differentiation. In short, material on sibling relations per se is to be found throughout cross-cultural research in anthropology, but under topics related to how siblings function in the context of or service of other institutions.

Sibling relations are a somewhat neglected topic also because of the excessive concern in kinship theory with formally recognized, jurally bounded, named groups—corporate kin groups; time-limited ceremonial groups such as initiation groups; age grades; and so forth. Sibling groups usually are influential as a part of the informal flow and routine of the domestic group, not as a formally defined group.

Which Kin Are Classified as "Siblings"?

English-speaking boys and girls call all their brothers by the same term, regardless of age. The same system of classification holds for sisters. Murdock (1980) makes the comparative point:

> To Europeans, terms meaning "brother" and "sister" seem somehow "natural." The foregoing classification, however, reveals that only societies with Type E, comprising fewer than 20 percent of all the world's peoples, actually have

terms that can be glossed as "brother" and "sister"—one more example of anthropology's destruction of ethnocentric illusions! [p. 368]

Now, the importance of sibling terminologies can be seen from several points of view. Terms can produce behavioral differences. The fact that we call our brothers and sisters by only two terms can produce consequences for our behavior towards them. For example, English speakers may emphasize gender in how sibs are treated, and we may relatively neglect age and hierarchy, partly because of how we classify sibs. For example, what if English had only two terms—"older sib" and "younger sib"? (Indeed, some 11 percent of societies have that type of system.) In that case, we might attend more to seniority in sibling relationships, and less to gender.

But sibling terms are more commonly seen as the *outcomes* of cognitive features of mental life, or of social structure, ecology, and environment. Thus, one reason English has the same term for both older and younger brothers is the bilateral nature of descent and inheritance in our society. The relatively egalitarian treatment at marriage for all members of the sibling group, regardless of age, might have a similar effect. These factors, of course, influence how we treat our brothers and sisters quite apart from terminology. Terminology is a reflection of important behavioral, cognitive, and sentimental/affective principles structuring relationships between brothers and sisters.

Sib terms usually also include some kin we call cousins or nephews and nieces. Consideration of this question of "cousin terminology" is beyond the scope of this discussion. Suffice it to say here that the same principles that contribute to differences in sibling terminology—namely age, sex, sex of speaker, cognitive and linguistic principles, and social/structural factors (Kronenfeld, 1974; Nerlove & Romney, 1967)—also contribute to theories of cousin terminology. In most societies, cousins and other kin frequently are grouped in the same categories as are some siblings.

Sibling terms can also be viewed from the point of view of their symbolic or affective meaning, and their extended use in other contexts. The terms brother and sister in English have many such connotations and extended uses, and so does sibling terminology in other societies. In addition, some sibling terms can imply kinds of kin avoidance or intimacy. But these issues take us beyond the sibling group per se.

SIBLING CARETAKING DURING CHILDHOOD: HAWAIIAN AND POLYNESIAN EXAMPLES

Introduction

In much of the world, children spend most of their time after infancy cared for by their older brothers and sisters, not primarily their mothers (Barry & Paxson, 1971; Whiting, 1963; Whiting & Whiting, 1975). The organization of sibling relations, given these kinds of tasks and family responsiblities, differs dramatically from those of urban and industrial societies. In this section, I review a number of themes relevant to sibling care during childhood that illustrate the influence of the ecological niche and the local community on sibling roles and duties. The examples come primarily from Hawaii and Polynesia, and East Africa but the basic patterns apply broadly elsewhere.

Antecedents of Sibling Caretaking: Interdependence

Gallimore, Boggs, and Jordan (1974) developed a series of generalizations based on work with Hawaiian-Americans that synthesize material on the role of the sibling caretaking system in the larger context of shared family obligations:

> "Responsibility is shared and contingencies are placed on groups rather than individuals. The goals involve immediate assistance to others, as opposed to personal development and achievement, and it is assumed that the individual can rely heavily on the group for help in learning new skills and carrying out tasks. [p. 67]."

Interdependence includes household work and chores as well as wages when children reach adolescence and join the work force. Older children contribute more, and girls steadily contribute more than boys.

> For children and adolescents the principal role in the family is defined in terms of material contribution, cooperation, and helpfulness here and now. They are not regarded as trainees for life in another time and place; chore assignments are not designed to foster independence. The work contributed and the wages shared are needed by the family in the present, and young people are expected to do their part. Learning to contribute to the family is preparation for making more not less contributions in the future, with no expectation of a break in the continuity of living arrangements between adolescence and adulthood [p. 81].

Most sibling groups have a "shared-function" rather than a "fixed-role" organizational style [p. 84]. Sharing work and responsibility extends to relationships with parents, peers, and neighbors. Taking turns, substituting, and being interdependent characterizes most sibling groups of this kind. There is also a hierarchy of respect and authority for adults. Obedience to senior siblings, or parents, is extremely important. Successful shared sibling group functioning means that there is no trouble; the system works most smoothly when it goes *un*noticed by adults. Gallimore, Boggs, and Jordan describe this as "benevolent authoritarianism".

These three features of Hawaiian-American families (interdependence, shared functioning, and benevolent authoritarianism) characterize many sibling groups throughout the world. Such systems emphasize cooperation and the flexible allocation of scarce resources. Sibling cooperation, solidarity, and authority of older over younger all flow from this kind of family system.

One of the things about sib care that is most important but least well understood ethnographically is that it is a preeminently shared activity. Sib care nearly always occurs in the context of other activities; it is happening when other people are around, and when other work tasks or chores, games, play, lounging, etc. are going on at the same time. In these contexts sib care is often subsumed under an indirect caretaking hierarchy. The mother may be nearby and apparently not involved in childcare, yet children are watching out for one another knowing that their mother is within shouting distance. Children often play with, help, and discipline one another in the home when the parents are around. The parents seem overtly uninvolved under such circumstances. But their involvement is covert and indirect. This kind of subtle attentiveness to other family members is an integral part of sib care (Ritchie & Ritchie, 1979).

Teaching and learning are often accomplished by graduated stages of participation, and through modeling and imitation of others (Jordan, 1977).[1] Teachers and models are often older children, not parents. Indirect, frequently nonverbal styles of requesting and managing are common.

As infants, children in most Hawaiian and Polynesian families are largely under the direct care of adults (Jordan, 1981; Jordan & Tharp, 1979). Babies receive a good deal of attention from older children also, but do spend most of their time with adults. However, a Hawaiian child as young as one or two may begin to spend a high proportion of time in the company of other children, as the charge of an older child. Most children will be full-fledged members of such a group by age three or four.

Thus, after infancy many Polynesian children are accustomed to spending most of their time with other children rather than with adults or in solitary activity (e.g. Levy, 1968; 1973). They are accustomed to working in a group context with siblings, without immediate adult direction. Although under the supervision of adults, children are expected to be able to carry out their responsibilities without intruding upon adults for help or direction. The group of children is expected to have within itself resources sufficient to carry out tasks that are assigned to it. Adults may relate to the teenage "top sergeant" of a group directly, or just address the group as a whole, rather than talk one-to-one with each individual child.

Hawaiian children acquire skills and knowledge in nonschool settings by participating in activities and tasks with the more competent children of their sibling or companion group (and, to a lesser extent, with adults). This means that they come to learn from a variety of people and that one of their main sources of help, skills, and information is other children. Moreover, they are accustomed to changing roles from that of "learner" to that of "teacher," depending on their competence for a particular function relative to others in the group.

As a consequence, children tend to be highly peer–oriented, and uncomfortable in intensive one-to-one interaction with adults. One would expect that they

---

[1] Portions of this section are drawn from Weisner, Jordan, Gallimore, and Tharp, n.d.

would also have in their repertoire of behaviors well-developed strategies for teaching and learning from peers and near-peers and to be skilled in utilizing a variety of persons as sources of information and help.

Structural Antecedents of Sib Care: Ecology and Demography

What more general conditions tend to promote the occurrence of sibling caretaking? The evidence indicates that factors related to sheer availability and propinquity of family members, as well as a number of institutional pressures, influence the occurrence of sib care at the cultural level. Conditions associated with sibling caretaking include: larger family size; lineal descent and residence patterns; and a daily routine that makes personnel available for sibling care (that is, where older children are available for sibling care during most parts of the day, and there is a heavy, persistent, routinized workload, some of which can be done in or near the home). Societies emphasizing kin and community cooperation in the performance of tasks and chores also tend to be societies that utilize sib care (see Leiderman & Leiderman, 1973; Whiting & Whiting, 1975).

Sib care often functions as a relief and support system for parents and is used as such in order to free parents to perform important subsistence chores or to engage in adult community involvements away from the home. Sib care also provides a training ground for parenting. Girls in particular learn very early the roles required to be an effective caretaker. Girls learn to differentiate different types of infants—their temperaments, cries, maturational stages, and so forth. They have had wide experience with childcare before they become parents themselves. They also have dealt with their brothers and sisters in both a superordinate and subordinate role, a flexible status they will have to carry on throughout life in many other functional areas (marriage arrangements, bridewealth, inheritance, protection for their own children, and so forth). These are all consequences of a "polymatric" caretaking system (Leiderman & Leiderman, 1977; Fox, 1967).

Infancy, early toddlerhood, and later childhood are clearly quite different stages in caretaking style in general and sib care in particular (Barry, Josephson, Lauer, & Marshall, 1980). During infancy mothers are usually involved in infant care and do not often delegate responsibility. If work roles take the mother fairly far from the home, the infant goes with the mother. A mother who works in or near the home can carry her baby on her back. Infant care is delegated more often when women have a moderate distance to travel, allowing a return for feeding. In early toddlerhood, children are more often left with sibs, and are gradually pushed out of the nest, away from the mother's direct involvement. Older children will carry these toddlers, ages 12 months to 3 years old, on their hip or back, often staggering slightly under the weight.

Sibling caretaking, then, is part of a larger childhood experience that stresses interdependence. It is also a form of childcare that is reflected in other institutions in adult life that involve sibling roles—that is, it is not an institution that begins and ends in childhood and exists solely as an aid to parental care or as a means of defense and survival in childhood only. It is also a means to train children to behave in ways and to have expectations and responsibilities towards their siblings that will stand them in good stead throughout life. Sib care provides analogues to patterns of adult life.

Some Social and Personality Correlates of Sib Care

Weisner and Gallimore (1977) have suggested a number of characteristics of child caretakers that might be related to participation in a sibling caretaking system. Children in such a system may show a more diffuse affective style and a diffuse pattern of attachment to adults and other children (but cf. Munroe & Munroe, 1980). The social role responsibilities of older siblings should produce increased social responsibility, increased nurturance toward appropriate targets, earlier and stronger sex role identification, and a more task-specific division of labor (Whiting & Whiting, 1975). These patterns should result from early training for and participation in caretaking hierarchies and family work.

Children gradually are initiated into both charge and caretaker roles, sometimes at the same time. A six-year-old boy may be watched over by his older sister, but also occasionally may be given responsibility for getting his three-year-old brother around the neighborhood. Children learn early both sides of caretaking activities. They learn to take the role of others in the sense of appropriately and responsibly performing caretaking tasks and to respond to others doing the same to them. They learn context-specific, role-appropriate behavior in these ways.

Sib care appears to decrease orientation and involvement with adults, and increases orientation toward a multiage, multisex group of peers and playmates. Along with this decreased orientation toward adults, children do not appear to receive the same ''negotiated rationalizations'' and adult understandings of norms that they would receive if involved in compliance or behavior change with their parents or other adults on a routine basis. Sib care is not usually found along with the elaborate rehearsal of the rules, reasons, rationales, exceptions, and adult understandings Western middle class children acquire in the company of their parents. Children in sib care settings learn through observation in natural contexts. They learn by imitation and mimicry, and through sharing and cooperation, rather than through highly verbal modes.

Qualitative Styles of Sib Care

What is it like to be part of a sibling caretaking hierarchy? It is not possible in this presentation to provide detailed ethnographic, qualitative data, but there are some characteristic patterns presented in the literature.

One finds reports of mimicry by children of adult caretaking patterns. For example, if a mother in the household is stern or talks in a certain way toward a toddler or young child, then the older sister will talk or shout in the same way, usually in the mother's absence. This pattern of sibling care perpetuates parental personality characteristics and individual differences in parenting styles. One also often finds reports of "overmimicry": if the mother talks a lot, the older sib will babble at a younger child; if the mother tends to shout, the child will scream at the younger child on occasion. Thus children will overplay the caretaking role and exaggerate parental styles.

There are also reports of indulgence of the younger sib so as not to incur the wrath of the parent. Indeed, one of the definitions of effective family functioning in a sib care context is that the adults do not notice what is going on and do not need to become involved in child care. Overindulgence can escalate into another pattern: the younger child as "tyrant." The tyranny of younger children over older children—that is younger children making constant demands, generally making life miserable for the older child—has been reported occasionally in the literature. However, the reverse is also reported and appears more common: older children will dominate, tyrannize, harrass, threaten, tease, and neglect to attend to younger children. Older children are more likely to get younger ones to do their work for them than the other way around. They also can be persistently unresponsive or inattentive.

It would be inaccurate to characterize sibling care or the other cooperative responsibilities and involvements of the sibling group as always "happy", or at least beneficent, with a universally shared and collaborative atmosphere. Things are often rough and unpleasant for both older or younger sibs. There are fights, rivalries, and conflicts widely reported. What needs to be kept in mind, however, is that there is an established hierarchy of authority and control, which depends on the daily routine of the family group, the jobs that need to be done, or the times that parents need to be absent or engaged in other activities. These provide constraints on the variations in styles of sib care.

Parents' Views of Sibling Caretaking

How do parents feel about and perceive the functions and meaning of sib care? There has been less research on this area than even that for behavioral outcomes or cross-cultural variability. Weisner, Gallimore, and Tharp (1977) analyzed Hawaiian mothers' reports concerning the importance of children's household chores and tasks, including sib care, and their more general views concerning the values, beliefs, and traits that should be inculcated during childhood. Two dimensions were generated in a factor analysis of the parent reports. The first is a general *child responsibility* dimension. The high end of this dimension included beliefs that it was important for children to be responsible for and care for other children in the family circle. A second dimension clustered together items related to *specific task obligations*—for example, who washes or bathes a child; who feeds it; who gets it up in the morning and ready for school; who takes care of it after school, and makes sure it does not go too far from home, etc. For these specific task dimensions, parents' reports on how often they gave children responsibilities depended more on the specific demographic characteristics of the homes than on a general felt value concerning tasks. General values and specific practices appeared as orthogonal factors in the analysis of the parent interview data.

A sample of urban and rural African mothers in Kenya were asked similar questions concerning how and why they allocate tasks and chores in their family, what they believe the consequences of sib care are, and the extent to which they think such care should be an important part of their family routine (Weisner, n.d.). As in the Hawaiian study, specific task obligations were largely idiosyncratic to the vagaries of birth order and domestic group arrangements for each mother. Unlike the Hawaiian data, however, there was very little diversity in the beliefs concerning responsibility. The African data indicated two different dimensions: a) *maternal control* and authority; and b) *responsibility* for caretaking and its importance. The African mothers, regardless of the general pattern of sib care characterizing their households, believed that they were "in charge" and in control. These mothers believed that sib care functioned in their family circle as an adjunct to their own control and regulation of domestic life. There is a strong cultural belief that sib care is not the transfer of authority to children, but merely the transfer of specific responsibility, under the direction of the mother. The mother's perceptions of sib care in this African sample were not that important family decisions were "shared", but merely that certain tasks and activities were being appropriately delegated to older brothers and sisters.

Mothers differed more on their beliefs concerning the importance of sib care. Mothers who had experienced sib care in their own childhood tended to attach more importance to sib care compared to mothers who had participated very little in sib care activities as children.

In addition, the perception of sib care among these African mothers depends to some extent on the context in which it occurred. Some mothers participated in the Abaluyia custom of child lending; they went to live for a year or more with a grandparent, a mother's sister, or father's sister, in order to help with domestic tasks (usually including child care tasks). For example, a girl often might go to her mother's sister's home when the sister is about to give birth, in order to help her out for awhile. Girls who did child care under these circumstances emphasized it more often and practiced it more often themselves, and also had a strong view that it was a positive and valued activity. On the other hand, mothers who participated in sib care simply as part of the domestic routine in their own households as children gave it somewhat less importance and emphasized the general obligation to be obedient to one's parents.

Children's Perceptions of Sib Care

What of children's perceptions of their child caretaking roles? On this question, the comparative literature is nearly silent. Weisner, Gallimore, and Tharp (in press) report data on a small sample of Hawaiian children's perceptions that they are performing the child caretaking role. The children's reports were compared to a field observer's assessment that sib care was or was not occurring. How does observational evidence for the performance of child caretaking tasks and role behaviors correspond to the child's *felt* role performance? In general, there was a significant relationship between observer judgments and child reports of caretaking; however, disagreement often occurred in situationally ambiguous situations—near home; with the mother; with very few other children around; and for younger children. This result suggests that children clearly do perceive and experience sib care roles between the ages of five and nine, both as charges and as caretakers. However, their understandings are highly situationally specific, and are not dependent simply on the performance of specific caretaking behaviors out of a social context.

Intracultural Variability and Heterogeneity in Sib Care

Much of the material presented so far has been at the cultural level, focused on general patterns of family expectations within a community or tribe or cultural group. How much heterogeneity is there within and between cultures? What is the appropriate level of inference for generalizing about sibling relations?

A study done in Honolulu, Hawaii among Hawaiian-American families practicing sib care clearly shows cultural *homogeneity* in the custom of sib care—yet also finds familial and individual *heterogeneity* in the practice and the experience of sib care.[1] Eight children were selected for intensive study, one boy and one girl from each of the four classrooms at the Kamehameha Early Education Program in Honolulu, Hawaii (Tharp & Gallimore, 1979). Boys and girls were randomly selected from those living in or near a low-income housing area from which many of the children in the school come.

Each child was observed at home 20 times, during the after-school afternoon period. Nearly all children did go home or to their neighborhood setting during this time of day, and observations were less likely to interfere with family meals or activities in the home. Visits to the eight households were done early in the afternoon after the end of school (about 3:00 to 3:45) and later in the afternoon (about 3:45 to 4:30). The 20 visits made to each family were randomized and counterbalanced by household, time of visit (early or late afternoon), and observer.

Some results of this study include:

---

[1]Portions of this section are drawn from Weisner, Jordan, Gallimore, and Tharp, n.d.

1. Sibling caretaking is fairly frequent among urban Hawaiian children; it was observed about a third of the time during the mid-afternoon period, and in those settings where two or more siblings were present together, observers judged that caretaking and responsibility occurred over three-fourths of the time.

2. These estimates are conservative, since shared caretaking with mothers present is underrepresented; these children are not at the ages when most sib care occurs. Infant and toddler care is underrepresented.

3. There is a gradual shift from children being cared for by other children, but not being a caretaker themselves (ages 5–7), to a period when many children experience *both* roles (8–9 and older).

4. Older children are farther from their homes and away from their mothers more often, and thus are recorded as involved in sib care more often.

5. Individual differences in exposure to these facilitative conditions varied widely across our sample of eight children and 20 visits per child; individual differences in the child's direct exposure to sib care were substantial.

6. Although individual children may vary widely in their direct exposure to sib care, either as caretaker or charge, all children are clearly likely to be around peer groups where sib care occurs, and to have friends or cousins who are involved in sib care. It is a familiar pattern to all children.

7. Do children tend to have a homogeneous experience of child caretaking during their afternoons? For instance, are children who are frequently involved in sib care also *regularly* involved in it across our 20 repeated afternoon visits; and are children who are seldom involved in sib care consistently not involved? This level of inference asks about the homogeneity of *intraindividual* experience of sib care by children. Strong cultural consistency could produce homogeneity of experience. To test this, the variance across the 20 observations for each child was computed, and the ratio of the largest to the smallest (Fmax) was calculated. Every one of these F values was significant beyond the $p = .001$ level! Thus, just as for the analysis of variance across families, the children varied significantly in their own experiences across our repeated visits. Culturally homogeneous patterning does not extend to the intraindividual level.

Sibling caretaking is a kind of family and child rearing institution that is very likely to show just this variable pattern as we move from cultural level, community customs, to family–level differences, and finally to individual differences. It is a caretaking style contingent on situational factors (availability of mother and other children; mother's routine and role in the home; sex role training; age and maturation of children, etc.). It depends on a combination of generalized responsibility expectations, as well as the opportunity to have children do specific tasks. This heterogeneity is not due to culture change or the urban milieu; clearly, social changes have an enormous impact on the circumstances that produce sib care, but this impact is on its frequency and style.

FUNCTIONAL ALLEGIANCES OF THE ADULT SIBLING GROUP: MARRIAGE AND PROPERTY

Introduction

Sibling caretaking is not an isolated and specialized institution that merely aids and supplements adult maternal care. It comes into being because it assists families in functioning in the wider community. It is adaptive not only in the sense of producing a more efficient family labor pool. It also encourages the sibling group towards the often tense and strained interdependence I have described; it is part of a shared functioning family system and an affiliative rather than egoistic/individualistic style of achievement and competence. There is also an implicit model of status, hierarchy and sex role obligations that will be continued in later adolescent and adult life. Under some of the same or similar conditions that sustain it in the non-Western world, this kind of sibling group can be found in the West as well—among minority populations; farm families; larger working class families; or in historical accounts of European and early American family and child care arrangements. The institution is a part of a family circle that is perhaps less intensely sentimental than our own, but one that also isolates children less from the worlds of community and work and integrates them into the rhythms of an annual work cycle and a defined life-course. These characteristics of sibling groups do not stop at the end of childhood. On the contrary, they are intensified as children pass into adolescence and adulthood. Sib care mirrors adult sibling group interdependence in matters of marriage and the property needed for survival.

It is difficult for us to imagine the extent to which this is true, given the privacy and even isolation that surrounds our own marriage and family lives, and the relatively minor extent of involvement of brothers and sisters in these events. Marriage decisions, the economic negotiations required for marriages, and the inheritance of property needed for survival are all points in life when one's siblings play a major role, if not a decisive one, in much of the world.

This section illustrates marriage and bridewealth customs that show these kinds of sibling involvements in East Africa and South India. These materials bring home the power of the sibling group throughout the life course—an interdependence that is institutionalized in the rules and regulations concerning marriages, inheritance, and residence, and aided by the patterns of shared functioning learned in childhood through family tasks and chores, and through sibling caretaking.

Marriage Alliances and Siblings: The Case of South Asia

Although brothers and sisters are heavily involved in each other's marriage plans in most cultures of the world, nowhere is this better illustrated than in India and other societies of South Asia. The elaborations of marriage rules and payments of dowry are especially striking, and the theoretical debates about what all this means for society are complex and sharply drawn. The core of this debate starts with the result of every system of prescribed or permitted marriage and descent reckoning that uses siblings and cousins to divide the kindred: some of one's own children and the children of one's brothers and sisters are going to marry each other. At least some of these children are going to marry some other class of cousin. Brothers and sisters live their adult lives arranging and negotiating such marriages. From the point of view of one's descendants, brothers and sisters create alliances between their family group and their brother's or sister's new affinal family group. Another way to express this sibling relationship system is that brothers and sisters retain influence on their descent through marriages between their nieces and nephews. One's mother's brother often is a kinsman subject to special feelings of affection, who receives gifts and has duties and obligations in these systems. Ideology and ritual recognition of these customs elaborate on the rules of alliances and descent.

One consequence of marriage in wide areas of Northern India is the status inequality that immediately attaches to the wife's brother, at least as viewed by the wife's husband and his kin. Mandelbaum (1970) summarizes this contrast in status due to caste differences:

> Over much of northern India he [a brother of a married sister] becomes inferior to his sister's new family. To her he remains one of the closest of the dearly beloved in her childhood home. To her new family he becomes one who, by definition, is to be taken lightly. As she is subordinate to her husband, so is her whole natal family in some degree subordinate to that of her husband. A family that takes in a girl as bride considers itself superior to the family that gives her in marriage [p. 69].

Mandelbaum characterizes the relations between brother and sister in this kind of setting as a "durable bond"—stable, affectionate, open-handed, "without normal reserve or inward calculation [p. 67]."

> In acting as brother to his sister a man also assumes the duties of brother-in-law and of mother's brother . . .
>
> Rivalry figures little in the brother-sister bond, nor is there rivalry between mother and daughter for the affection of son and brother. Because the daughter must soon leave her natal home, her mother is eager that the girl's brother be fond of her. . . . A girl's brother is often the mother's emissary to her [p. 67].

There is an intricacy of strategy and social bonds between siblings involved in such relationships that is not immediately apparent. This is so because the brothers play an important role in accumulating the dowry that their sisters then use in order to marry. This means that men often must defer their own marriage plans in order to save funds for their sisters' marriages. Children are expected to marry in order of birth, but brothers are expected to defer their own marriages in order to assist their elder and younger sisters in getting appropriate husbands. In Tamil parts of Sri Lanka, the traditional expectation is that a brother works to contribute to the dowry fund for his sisters, e.g. contributes part of his earnings, or his labor, to cultivate the family's lands. At some point, of course, the duty of an elder brother has to cease and a younger brother or brothers must take over the responsibility for the remaining sisters (see McGilvray, 1980; 1982).

In systems like these, brothers manage joint property partly in their own interests and partly in order to marry off their sisters. If sisters are married "well", they are more likely to attract large dowries for their brothers' marriages. The husband eventually acts as manager of his wife's dowry brought into his family at the time of marriage, as well as the dwindling inheritance received from the father (in a patrilineal system) or the mother's brother (in a matrilineal one). Accidents of birth order and the sex of one's siblings can make dramatic differences in one's entire life–course due to this interdepencence of brothers and sisters. An oldest son in a bridewealth-paying, patrilineal *African* horticultural society is fortunate indeed if he has several younger sisters following him. He is likely to obtain brideprice payments for himself or from his father to allow him to marry. That same older brother in South India may well be doomed to years of work accumulating wealth that will go to his younger sisters' dowries. Having located a wife, this brother may quietly begin trying to arrange things in his prospective wife's family so that *her* brothers will be sure to contribute towards his future dowry, and try to arrange things so that his future wife's older sisters will marry early and well, to hasten the day when he himself can marry and turn over some of his obligations to his younger brothers and his newly-acquired brothers-in-law.

Mandelbaum (1970) generalizes for much of India that relations between brothers depend on the struggle for property from one's father and/or older brother; on the negotiated intrigues over marriages; and on the accidents of rank and birth order of brothers in the joint family.

> The bond between brothers is taken ideally as a durable and cohesive relationship for cooperative action, second only to the tie between father and son. In actuality the fraternal bond tends to become unstable in time. Brothers of a poor family of low jati [caste] may have little to quarrel about. If they are all laborers or heavily dependent on an overlord, they have little cooperative enterprise of their own. But those brothers who together manage and work the land or jointly provide goods and services are likely sooner or later to fall out [p. 66].

Bridewealth Negotiations and Inheritance in East Africa

Indian marriage customs encourage the children of brothers and sisters to marry each other; dowry payments to daughters are managed by sons-in-law; and marriage is endogamous within castes and occurs within the context of Hindu or

Moslem customs that are a part of world religious traditions. In East Africa by contrast, marriage negotiations just as heavily involve brothers and sisters, but in very different ways. Here, pastoralism and horticulture are practiced by strictly exogamous patrilineal clans; bridewealth is given by the lineage to the wife's husband's lineage at the time of marriage.

Arrangements for marriage in patrilineal, patrilocal, exogamous lineage groups depend on siblings perhaps more than any other category of kin. Sangree (1966) describes the relationships between sibling ties, bridewealth, and marriage among the Tiriki of Western Kenya. Among this group (and many others throughout Eastern and Central Africa) bridewealth is paid by the husband's clan to the wife's, and legitimizes a husband's right to claim the children resulting from the marriage. Bride payment drags over years and years and indeed may never be fully completed. Final payments often are not made until the wife has borne several children, particularly sons to carry on the lineage of the husband. The wife's brother therefore may actually receive the final payments, since the wife's father will often have already died. Sangree (1966) continues:

> Within the homestead the custom of bridewealth fosters a somewhat strained formalistic relationship between a father and his dependent sons while at the same time serving to intensify the brother/sister bond. With cattle received from a sister's marriage a man will generally do one or another of three things, depending on the circumstances: (1) He may use the cattle to pay the bridewealth of an older son; (2) if his father has died, and he is now the head of the homestead, and acting *in loco parentis,* he may use the cattle to pay the bridewealth of a younger brother; (3) if no younger brothers can lay claim to the cattle, and his sons are still young, he may use the cattle to acquire an additional wife for himself . . . . Installments received may be immediately disposed to pay debts contracted in one or even all of the three areas mentioned . . . . The ideal persists in Tiriki that the homestead head will *arrange* things so that an elder son of his may look primarily to the father's younger sisters (to the cattle that their marriage brings into the family homestead) for his bridewealth, and that a younger son may look primarily to his own sisters [pp. 14–15].

Goldschmidt (1976) has published data on the actual participants in brideprice negotiations among pastoral and horticultural Sebei of Uganda. The bride's father's brother(s) were present 92 percent of the time—more often than the bride's father himself (80 percent)! The groom's father's brothers were less often present (25 percent). Fathers usually came along with their brothers to represent their daughter's interests. The groom's own brothers appear 30 percent of the time; neighbors, 35 percent; and the groom himself was present 55 percent of the time. The groom is able to represent himself and to be with brothers, fathers, or neighbors, whereas the bride to be is represented by close male kin, nearly always including her father's brothers and her own brothers.

Sangree (1966) also illustrates the characteristic custom in agnatic lineage systems of delaying finalizing a marriage: "The marriage in Tiriki is only considered truly consummated by the birth of at least three children [pp. 16–17]. If a woman is barren she can be sent back with the demand that bride price be returned. If she has not borne enough children her husband can send her back to her homestead and lengthy negotiations (involving her brothers and her father) would begin concerning why she is not bearing more children, or more sons; whether sorcery is involved; whether more brideprice might need to be paid, and so forth. Thus, "Each sister's child brings a tangible material increase to the homestead of the (mother's brother) [p. 16–17]." Sibling relationships are characterized by such continual small exchanges, requests, and the freedom between siblings of both the same and opposite sex to make such demands of one another. The special bond between brothers and sisters persists throughout life. Brother's children or sister's children are treated warmly, given special hospitality, may visit for long periods of time, expect special gifts, and are called by special terms. These relationships provide social recognition of the profound economic interdependence of brother and sister.

Tiriki agnatic lineage and property relations also illustrate the powerful role that brothers have over one another in the matter of land inheritance (Sangree, 1966);

> At the large post-funeral meeting . . . the grants of land made to mature sons by the father before his death are reviewed and accepted, or contested and revised. The eldest son is generally recognized as the spokesman for those sons not yet matured, and he is usually given the responsibility of distributing the remaining land to the younger sons as they reach maturity, providing the mother or mothers of these immature sons . . . are past childbearing age [p. 24–25].

Clan brothers will also inherit a man's widow. Widow inheritance is a way to care for the widow and children, and increase the size of the clan. Analogous patterns occur for the inheritance of livestock and other property vital to the survival of a sibling, his wife or wives, and children. Sexual access to brothers' wives other than after the death of one's brother occurs in many parts of the world. Wagner (1970) describes such a custom among the Maragoli, close neighbors of the Tiriki.

> Before the birth of the first child the brother of the husband may have occasional sex relations with his wife, which the husband is expected to tolerate. Even after he has children the husband cannot legally accuse his brother of adultery with his wife, but must try to secure his rights by the less drastic means of persuasion or by asking his father to intervene on the strength of his paternal authority [p. 43–44].

East African sibling patterns also illustrate some of the consequences of polygyny and the inclusive classification of "siblings" and "cousins". Most "sibling" groups are not limited to the surviving biological offspring of one couple; "siblings" include cousins, step-siblings, and sometimes other categories of kin. In addition, age and parity make a difference in the conception of the sibling role (see Fortes 1974). Wagner (1970) describes the special role of the eldest son (still more pre-eminently the eldest son of a first wife in a polygynous homestead) as regards his other brothers and his sisters: "The eldest son . . . is entitled to marry first, i.e. he has a preferential claim to the father's cattle for the purpose of paying bridewealth. When he establishes his own household, he usually settles near the parental homestead and becomes 'like a brother to the father', especially as regards his relations with his younger siblings [p. 48–49]."

The eldest son's privileged position becomes effective after he marries and inherits property, and particularly after his father dies, when he may continue to hold property in trust for his younger brothers. As this property is given away by the eldest brother, his position of authority, seniority, and dominance wanes and a greater equality begins to prevail. The elder brother also continues a formal relationship with his sisters, since his and his younger brothers' marriage depend on the bride price they will receive from the marriages of these sisters. He thus retains a closer relationship with these sisters, and with their children, than do other brothers.

Last born children, especially sons, also frequently have unique culturally-defined status. Sangree (1981) has characterized the named, last born son role among the Tiriki: relative indifference to commands of peers and authorities; generosity to others and improvidence in ones own dealings; and a propensity to expect special favors and become enraged when these are not forthcoming (p. 197). Last borns are expected to remain with the parents to help them in old age, and are thought to be "mother's children" more than other children.

Brothers and sisters live under conditions of relative equality when still young. But their daily activities begin to separate when they begin to sleep in different huts in the compound. Both boys and girls sleep in their parents' home until they are about six years old. After that period, boys and girls may sleep in the hut of a widowed grandparent, and a year or two later the boys move into a special bachelor hut vacated by an older brother or friend. The girls go to a special hut for unmarried girls. This usually is a house of an elderly woman, aunt, or grandmother, who is supposed to control moral conduct and assist in the arrangement of marriages. Thus by age eight or so the sibling group is segregated, as are boys' and girls' work roles. Although brothers and sisters do sleep separately and have different work to do, they still eat together frequently with their parents and spend a substantial amount of time together.

In most polygynous societies half-siblings (that is, children of different wives of the same man) live in different huts until they begin to be segregated by sex and they are involved in domestic and garden tasks on the land worked by their own mother (not their stepmothers). At the same time, however, the half-siblings interact constantly around the homestead. Certain formal claims over bridewealth, brideprice, and marriage differentiate these half-siblings. The first wife's first son, for example, occupies a preferential position over other sons.

Similarly, the eldest son of a senior wife may marry a junior wife after the father is dead and might even marry more than one if the father had two wives (Wagner, 1970).

Final Comments

Although very different in culture and in specific customs regarding sibling obligations, marriage, and inheritance, India, Africa, and Polynesia share certain common patterns. There are obligations binding siblings throughout life—but there are emotional tensions, conflicts, and ambivalence built into these shared responsibilities at nearly every point. How are these inherent tensions and ambivalences managed in societies around the world? The cultural defenses and elaborations of sibling hostilities and rivalries attest to the pervasiveness of the problems—and the often dubious efficacy of the solutions within the family circle.

Edgerton (1971) suggests a general hypothesis differentiating horticultural and pastoral societies' modes of conflict resolution within the lineage and domestic group. Pastoralists rely on *spatial* mechanisms for avoiding and resolving conflicts. They and their cattle can move away for lengthy periods. They can take their resource base with them, and can find other groups of kin or age-mates to live with them. Horticulturalists, in contrast, although living in similar agnatic lineage groups, typically cannot do this. They are tied to their land. In previous generations, where land was widely available and cattle were a more important part of a mixed economy, spatial dispute settlements at certain points in the life cycle may have been more readily available. Wage labor migration often provides a modern substitute for this earlier pattern.

In societies where the sibling group will remain in lifelong, face-to-face coresidential community membership groups (whether through marriage, inheritance, or residence rules), conflict control mechanisms will take a different form than in communities where sibs have the option or are compelled to move—that is, where avoidance is compatible with subsistence survival. Strong aggression training, and control of aggression in extended family households is characteristic of many horticultural communities. More frequent use of physical punishment; an emphasis on authority of older over younger members; ritualized avoidances; and projections of witchcraft and sorcery are also common in horticultural communities.

The inevitable conflict between seniors and juniors in the sibling hierarchy is also reflected in social ideology. Jackson (1978) has commented perceptively on the contrast between the social dogma concerning elder and younger siblings, and its common reversal in myth and fiction. The rules of descent and inheritance will place the elder sibling in a position of authority; the elder will be expected to exercise intelligent regulation of the family and the social order, to be socially conservative, restrained, and distant. The younger son has little authority, is formally ineffectual, expected to be self-motivated, irresponsible, foolish. But in myth, fiction, and joking relationships, these dogmas often are reversed: the younger son is brighter, cleverer and triumphant over the older, who is portrayed as bumbling, in a position of influence "only" because of his sibling status. Jackson points to the role of such oppositions in bridging the inevitable gap between social form and variations in individual traits and talents. In this sense, the "real" privilege attached to early birth is as "nonrational" as the "fictional" stories and jokes and myths about the smart younger son outwitting the older. Birth-order position is transformed by cultural rules of inheritance just as it is by mythic inversions of those rules. Such ideologies are not only wish-fulfillment projections of younger sibs deprived of formal power; they are also solutions to the continuing social problem of matching individual talents to socially-prescribed statuses.

In spite of every continuing obligation, however, the full sibling group as a part of the family of origin *does break up*. Sibling relations are increasingly mediated by other relationships (marriage, new parenthood, new economic roles, etc.), and the old ties are diffused by the new family of procreation. Certain unusual exceptions to this (such as the age-villages of the Nyakyusa; see Wilson, 1970) in practice prove the general rule. And most reports of situations where some of the sibling group (both brothers and sisters) continues to live together in the same domestic group, prove to be the result of an excessive "familism," a response to unusual and destructive cultural stress. In such cases, many adults never marry, remain celibate and sexually repressed, and become lonely spinsters and bachelors sharing their aged or dead parents' rooms (e.g. Scheper-Hughes, 1979). Siblings do remain interdependent—but never *exclusively* so; the boundaries of the sibling group are highly permeable.

The passage through adolescence to marriage and parenthood is usually viewed in Western eyes primarily as a separation of children from their parents. Parent-child tension is the central theme of psychodynamic models of family change, and of "new household formation." The sibling care system, and its continuities in the social and affective character of adult roles, suggests another view. It is the transformation of the sibling group, which nurtures and teaches many children in childhood, into the active support adults need as parents and providers, which is the more appropriate and longer-sustained theme.

CONCLUSION

Why Are Sibs Important?

The examples from these Abaluyia subtribes, and from Polynesia and South Asia, illustrate what is the norm throughout most of the cultures of the world: brothers and sisters are decisive participants in each other's fate concerning sexual access, marriage, or property. The same examples could be adduced for work sharing and work groups, ritual obligations, initiation rites, death and mortuary customs, and other domains. The purpose of these examples is not to present an ethnography of sibling involvements in the life span, but rather to illustrate some of the important practical consequences of such involvements in one domain of life. These examples also suggest some of the ways in which childhood roles in the sibling group continue throughout adult life.

Siblings are not the only kin involved in these domains, nor are consanguineal kin the only relatives involved, since neighbors and affines can also participate. But why are sibs so prominent? Why not a random assortment of community members? Why are sibs, who share many highly tension-filled and ambivalent relations (e.g. brothers in Abaluyia lineages), and who struggle in many cases for control of resources, nonetheless so heavily involved in crucial life-course events, especially those involving reproduction?

The sociobiological hypothesis is that those who share their genes are more likely to be involved in relationships of all kinds that promote the survival of close relatives and their offspring. Full siblings share an average of 50 percent of their genes. Is this why island peoples and those living in communities with higher degrees of homozygosity seem so often to engage in especially prominent interdependent relationships with sibs and others (e.g. Freedman, 1979)? The near universality of heavy sib involvements leads one to such speculation, in spite of the high variability in the ways sibling attachments are expressed throughout the lifespan in different cultures. However, homozygosity is everywhere confounded with coresidence, cosleeping, and shared functioning, and these factors are difficult to separate. But there is little doubt that some combination of shared ancestry and social and physical propinquity is involved in the close interdependence of siblings observed throughout the world.

The constant of shared genes cannot explain the variability in the extent of sibling involvement at different points in the lifespan, nor can it easily account for *which* siblings (brothers or sisters, older or younger, cousins or half-sibs, etc.) are the ones with whom one is especially close, or ritually avoids, or inherits wealth from. Most accounts of the cross-cultural diversity in the expression of sibling ties are closely linked to theories of descent and residence patterns around the world, as well as the influence of world religions. Any analysis of these patterns also includes the level of subsistence complexity and the mode of inheriting wealth. These latter factors are not necessarily prior to other influences, but they are everywhere of serious import.

Siblings and the Wider Content

Jack Goody's contrast between "diverging devolution" and "homogeneous inheritance" illustrates the interaction of these social and ecological conditions (1976). Goody distinguishes between inheritance systems where parents' property goes to both sons and daughters (diverging or bilateral systems) and those in which property goes to sons only or to daughters only (homogeneous systems).

The East African examples show the operation of unilineal, homogeneous descent and inheritance; the South Asian examples illustrate devolution; many Pacific/Polynesian societies practice bilateral descent and inheritance. The essence of Goody's hypothesis is that diverging devolution and bilateral inheritance tend to occur in societies with more complex economies, ones that take greater capital investment, have more intensive resource use, and involve the management of relatively scarcer resources. The bilateral/diverging devolution system encourages the preservation of differences in caste, class, and economic status by retaining wealth within the family circle; the unilineal system with partible inheritance tends to equally distribute wealth and resources across the generations and between exogamous clans. Endogamy and the perpetuation of the nuclear family group changes the relationships between siblings, since both brothers and sisters need the valuable resources retained within the family circle. Monogamy, increasing controls over marriage, elaborations on marriage regulations, and intensified investment in the sibling group often are the result. Greater investment in both boys and girls within the family circle is associated in this model with increasing societal *in*equality.

From this point of view, marriage is the institution that reproduces a certain kind of sibling relationship! This connection between marriage and sibs is usually reversed—marriage rules are the phenomenon to be accounted for, along with descent and inheritance, and sibling relations are the result. But it might be fruitful to see this in a more balanced way: the characteristics of sibling roles during childhood, and the functional interdependence of sibs in adult life, are each closely tied to patterns of economic and community survival. These in turn favor certain kinds of descent and marriage rules over others.

These same features of community life are relevant in understanding American family and sibling relations; they are not quaint factors relevant only in the nonindustrial world. The decline in the need for interdependence and shared functioning, and in the maintenance of a single family estate, is the primary underlying feature allowing for the remarkable mobility in the American sibling group. Bilateral inheritance has a great deal to do with the relatively equal investment in boys and girls in our society. The replacement of parents' material wealth with other forms of parental investment early in life, and the lessened importance of having parents' skills transferred to sons, are both of enormous importance for the freedom and egalitarian treatment within the Western sibling group. In subcultural communities or minority groups within the United States that *do* have stronger task pressures, and where the family requires children's shared involvement as part of a sibling group, interdependence often increases. At points in the adult lifespan where questions of inheritance need to be resolved, siblings nearly always *do* reappear. The chronic rivalry and personal possessiveness of middle-class American siblings are not inherent in developmental stages; they are induced by unusually egoistic family pressures that permit us the perhaps unfortunate luxury of letting brothers and sisters go their own ways.

ACKNOWLEDGMENTS

This research has been supported by a number of agencies and institutions: the Kamehameha Schools/Bernice P. Bishop Estate; the Carnegie Corporation through Grant B-3970, and through its support of the Child Development Research Unit of Harvard University and the University of Nairobi; and the Department of Psychiatry and Biobehavioral Sciences, University of California, Los Angeles.

REFERENCES

Barry, H., III, Josephson, L., Lauer, E., & Marshall, C. Agents and techniques for child training: Cross-cultural codes 6. In H. Barry III & A. Schlegel (Eds.), *Cross-cultural samples and codes.* Pittsburgh: University of Pittsburgh Press, 1980.

Barry, H., III, & Paxson, L. M. Infancy and early childhood: Cross-cultural codes 2. *Ethnology,* 1971, *10,* 466-508.

Bronfenbrenner, U. *The ecology of human development.* Cambridge: Harvard University Press, 1979.

Edgerton, R. B. E. *The individual in cultural adaptation: A study of four East African Peoples.* Berkeley: University of California Press, 1971.

Fortes, M. The first born. *Journal of Child Psychology and Psychiatry,* 1974, *15,* 81-104.

Fox, L. K. (Ed.). *East African childhood: Three versions.* London: Oxford University Press, 1967.

Freedman, D. G. *Human sociobiology.* New York: The Free Press, 1979.

Gallimore, R., Boggs, J. W., & Jordan, C. *Culture, behavior and education: A study of Hawaiian-Americans.* Beverly Hills, Calif.: Sage Publications, 1974.

Goldschmidt, W. *Culture and behavior of the Sebei: A study in continuity and adaptation.* Berkeley: University of California Press, 1976.

Goody, J. *Production and reproduction: A comparative study of the domestic domain.* Cambridge: Cambridge University Press, 1976.

Jackson, M. Ambivalence and the last-born: birth-order position in convention and myth. *Man*(n.s.), 1978, *13,* 341-361.

Jordan, C. *Maternal teaching, peer teaching, and school adaptation in an urban Hawaiian population.* Honolulu: The Kamehameha Early Education Program, The Kamehameha Schools, 1977.

Jordan, C. *Educationally effective ethonology: A study of the contributions of cultural knowledge to effective education for minority children.* Unpublished dissertation, University of California at Los Angeles, 1981.

Jordan, C., & Tharp, R. Culture and education. In A. J. Marcella, R. G. Tharp, & T. J. Ciborowski (Eds.), *Perspectives in cross-cultural psychology.* New York: Academic Press, 1979.

Kronenfeld, D. B. Sibling typology: Beyond Nerlove and Romney. *American Ethnologist,* 1974, *1*(3), 489-506.

Leiderman, H. P., & Leiderman. G. F. *Polymatric infant care in the East African highlands: Some affective and cognitive consequences.* Paper presented at the Minnesota Symposium on Child Development, Minneapolis, 1973.

Leiderman, H. P., & Leiderman, G. F. Economic change and infant care in an East African agricultural community. In P. H. Leiderman, S. R. Tulkin, & A. Rosenfeld (Eds.), *Culture and infancy, variations in the human experience.* New York: Academic Press, 1977.

Levy, R. I. Child management structure and its implications in a Tahitian family. In E. Vogel & N. Bell (Eds.), *A modern introduction to the family.* New York: The Free Press, 1968.

Levy, R. I. *Tahitians: Mind and experience in the society islands.* Chicago: University of Chicago Press, 1973.

Mandelbaum, D. G. *Society in India, Volume I; Continuity and change*. Berkeley: University of California Press, 1970.

McGilvray, D. B. *The matrilocal household system of Eastern Sri Lanka*. Unpublished paper, presented at the American Anthropological Association, Washington, D.C., December 1980.

McGilvray, D. B. The mukkuvar Vannimai: Tamil caste and matriclan ideology in Batticloa, Sri Lanka. In D. B. McGilvray (Ed.), *Caste ideology and interaction*. Cambridge: Cambrige University Press, 1982.

Munroe, R. H., & Munroe, R. G. Infant experience and childhood affect among the Logoli: A longitudinal study. *Ethos*, 1980, *8*, 295-315.

Murdock, G. P. Patterns of sibling terminology. In H. Barry III & A. Schlegel (Eds.), *Cross-cultural samples and codes*. Pittsburgh: University of Pittsburgh Press, 1980.

Nerlove, S., & Romney, A. D. Sibling terminology and cross-sex behavior. *American Anthropologist*, 1967, *69*, 179-187.

Ritchie, J., & Ritchie, J. *Growing up in Polynesia*. Sydney, Australia: George Allen and Unwin, 1979.

Sangree, W. H. *Age, prayer and politics in Tiriki, Kenya*. London: Oxford University Press, 1966.

Sangree, W. H. The "last born" (*Muxogosi*) and complementary filiation in Tiriki, Kenya. *Ethos*, 1981, *9*, 188-200.

Scheper-Hughes, N. *Saints, scholars, and schizophrenics: Mental illness in rural Ireland*. Berkeley, University of California Press, 1979.

Super, C. M., & Harkness, S. (Eds.) Anthropological perspectives on child development. *New Directions for Child Development* (Vol. 8). San Francisco: Jossey Bass, 1980.

Tharp, R. G., & Gallimore, R. The ecology of program research and development: A model of evaluation studies. In L. Sechrest, S. G. West, M. A. Phillips, R. Redner, W. Yeaton (Eds.), *Evaluation studies: Review Annual* (Vol. 4). Beverly Hills, Calif.: Sage Publications, 1979.

Wagner, G. *The Bantu of Western Kenya* (Vol. 1). London: Oxford University Press, 1970.

Weisner, T. W. Unpublished field data, no date.

Weisner, T. W., & Gallimore, R. My brother's keeper: Child and sibling caretaking. *Current Anthropology*, 1977, *18*, 169-191.

Weisner, T. S., Gallimore, R., & Tharp, R. G. *Sibling caretaking in an urban Hawaiian setting*. Paper presented at the Society for Cross-Cultural Research, East Lansing, Michigan, 1977.

Weisner, T. S., Gallimore, R., & Tharp, R. G. *Concordance between ethnographer and folk perspectives: Observed performance and self-ascription of sibling caretaking roles. Human Organization* (in press).

Weisner, T. S., Jordan, C., Gallimore, R., and Tharp, R. G. *Cultural homogeneity, familial variability, and educational adaptibility: Sibling caretaking among urban Hawaiians*. Unpublished manuscript, 1981.

Whiting, B. B. (Ed.) *Six cultures: Studies of child rearing*. New York: John Wiley & Sons, Inc., 1963.

Whiting, B. B., & Whiting, J. W. M. *Children of six cultures: A psychocultural analysis*. Cambridge: Harvard University Press, 1975.

Wilson, M. *Good company: A study of Nyakyusa age-villages*. Boston: Beacon Press, 1970.

14 Sibling Relationships in Nonhuman Primates

Stephen J. Suomi
University of Wisconsin, Madison

INTRODUCTION

This chapter is about sibling relationships that are developed by members of various nonhuman primate species. Most nonhuman primate infants grow up in the company of older siblings, and as these infants grow older they usually acquire younger siblings as well. Interactions with siblings constitute one major source of social stimulation for most monkeys and apes, at least until they are adolescents, and in some cases relationships with siblings continue to thrive throughout the whole of their adult lives.

Interest in the study of sibling relationships among nonhuman primate subjects has been a long time in coming for developmental primatologists, much as it has been for those who have studied human infants, children, and adolescents. For many years sibling interactions were largely ignored by most primatologists, for reasons that in retrospect seem quite understandable. Investigators observing natural troops in the field always faced a basic problem of subject identification: the most "popular" species for field studies (e.g., baboons, macaques, and chimpanzees) all lived in complex social groups containing several adult males and females, most of whom were promiscuous. Thus, specification of paternity for any infant was virtually impossible and, as a result, differentiating between the infant's full siblings and maternal half-sibs and between its paternal half-sibs and unrelated or more distantly related peers was likewise all but impossible. Investigators studying primate social development in the laboratory in most cases were observing artificial social groups that contained few if any full-sib pairs. Instead, the emphasis was on studies of infants growing up with access to mothers only, to peers only, or to both (only) (e.g., Harlow & Harlow, 1969). Obviously, neither approach was at all conducive to study of sibling relationships in these species.

A number of changes in methodology and in theoretical orientation in recent years have contributed greatly to a current upsurge in interest in sibling relationships in nonhuman primate species. First, a shift in emphasis from exclusive study of mother-infant interactions to consideration of an infant's entire social network has recently taken place among developmentally oriented behavioral primatologists, very much paralleling (if not actually preceding) the shift that has occurred in human social-developmental research (e.g., Bronfenbrenner, 1979; Lewis & Rosenblum, 1979; Parke, 1979). Second, methodological changes both in the field and in the laboratory have made study of sibling relationships much easier and more obvious than was previously the case. Collection of long-term longitudinal data on the same social groups has provided the most valuable addition to both lab and field studies in this regard. Finally, the emergence of sociobiology as a discipline, with its emphasis on kinship as an important factor in primate social behavior, has clearly contributed to current interest in comparing an individual's social activities directed toward kin with those directed toward unrelated individuals. As a result of these trends, a sizable literature on sibling interactions among nonhuman primates is beginning to emerge (Williams, 1981).

In this chapter I will describe some of the findings from this literature. I will begin by delineating some basic issues that have guided and shaped most of the research carried out to date on sibling interactions among nonhuman primate subjects. I will then examine two quite different theoretical perspectives on the study of sibling relationships, one based primarily on sociobiological principles, the other based on attachment theory and social network considerations. Next, some complications that arise when one tries to compare sibling relationships in different primate species will be discussed. There will follow a description of developmental changes that typically occur in some sibling relationships. I will contrast such developmental changes for marmoset and tamarin infants, who grow up in monogamous nuclear family environments, with those for macaque infants, who typically grow up in social groups filled with promiscuous and prolific adults of both sexes. Finally, I will consider how these nonhuman primate data relate to what we currently know about sibling relationships in human families, and I will outline some strategies for potentially profitable research on this topic in the future.

SOME BASIC ISSUES IN THE STUDY OF SIBLING RELATIONSHIPS

The study of sibling interactions and relationships in nonhuman primates has to date revolved around three basic issues. These issues are in many ways similar to those addressed by the human sibling interaction literature; indeed, they are characteristic of a classic ethological approach to the study of behavior (Tinbergen, 1951). The first issue involves the *description* of sibling relationships as they appear in different primate species and characteristic social structures (Crook, 1972). The second addresses the question of *function:* what role or roles do relationships with siblings play in the social development of an individual monkey, ape, or human, and what does an individual growing up without siblings miss in terms of its social development? The third issue deals with factors that can *influence* the formation and expression of sibling relationships over time, among different social groups, and across different primate species.

An obvious first step in the study of any phenomenon or relationship is to describe it in scientifically acceptable terms. This has clearly been a common goal of the studies of sibling relationships carried out to date in different primate species. Indeed, a description of the nature and frequency of sibling interactions has been a part of virtually every published report of primate sibling relationships. But descriptive data of sibling interactions by themselves turn out to be relatively meaningless unless they can also be compared with similar data on other types of social relationships established by the very same subjects, e.g., those with peers or with adult males. Such comparisons enable one to delineate aspects of sibling interactions that are common to other types of social relationships the individual develops, as well as those aspects (if any) that are unique to relationships between siblings.

For example, Golopol (1979) found that 1- and 2-year-old rhesus monkeys utilized virtually all of the same behavior patterns in their interactions with siblings that they used in their interactions with unrelated peers and with unrelated individuals of the same age and sex as their siblings. Interestingly, the only real differences in the types of behavior displayed toward siblings, as opposed to peers, concerned aggression and sex: these monkeys almost never directed intense aggression, however brief, toward siblings; nor did their play with sibling partners routinely involve motor patterns characteristic of adult copulatory behavior (Golopol, 1979). In contrast, aggression increasingly became part of (male) peer interactions as the participants matured (Suomi & Harlow, 1978); mounting and presenting-like motor patterns were common components of play bouts between rhesus monkey peers (Harlow & Lauersdorf, 1974). In all other categories of behavior, Golopol's subjects' interactions with their siblings overlapped completely with their interactions with peers. However, the relative *proportions* of time allotted for each type of behavior differed between interactions with siblings and interactions with peers. Also, the *pattern of responses* and the *sequencing of interactions* were clearly not the same in sibling and peer interactions. By subjecting interactive data such as these to a series of descriptive analyses, it has been possible to characterize different types of relationships formed by young primates (e.g., Hinde, 1976; Suomi, 1979b), and, as we shall later see, such descriptions can help put sibling relationships in perspective relative to other relationships in the infant's social network (e.g., Lewis & Rosenblum, 1979).

A second major issue basic to the study of sibling relationships in nonhuman primates has concerned the possible *function(s)* of interactions with siblings. Basically, what does a young primate get out of interactions with siblings that it could not acquire or accrue through social relationships with other classes of conspecifics? What does it miss if it grows up without siblings? Put another way, what are the benefits an individual realizes when it is reared with siblings and what are the costs if it is reared without them (and, of course, vice versa)?

Questions of possible function may indeed be important for the study of sibling interactions in nonhuman primates, but providing definitive answers or precise specifications of relative benefits and costs has proven to be rather difficult. For one thing, functions, costs, and benefits are most likely not the same for all sibling relationships (Altmann, 1979). Indeed, *within* any relationship between two siblings there may be different functions of each participant. For example, in marmosets and tamarins, an infant's relationship with an older sibling may serve the function of providing the infant with a substitute caretaker, without which it might perish. The same relationship seems to be serving a different function for the older sibling. Here, the juvenile is obtaining experience as a caretaker—juvenile marmosets who fail to get such experience turn out to be incompetent parents when they have their own offspring (Snowdon & Suomi, 1982). On the other hand, in yellow baboons, substitute caretaking and practice for parenthood do *not* appear to be functions of sibling relationships (Altmann, 1980).

These examples serve to remind us that sibling relationships may encompass mutliple functions and that the same set of functions need not necessarily apply to all sibling relationships, or, indeed, both individuals within a given relationship. It should also be kept in mind that unequivocal determination of function requires experimental manipulation (e.g., Agnew & Pike, 1969), something that has been missing from virtually all studies of primate sibling relationships to date. Thus, the field at present is a long way from being able to specify the functions that any one sibling relationship is providing its participants. Yet, such knowledge is clearly crucial in the long run for fully understanding the significance of sibling relationships.

A third basic issue in the study of sibling relationships in nonhuman primates concerns factors that can influence such relationships. The few systematic studies of sibling relationships carried out to date already are suggesting that these factors are numerous and their interrelationships quite complex. For example, it has been consistently found that the age difference between two siblings can profoundly influence the relationship that they develop with one another—the smaller the age difference, the larger the absolute number of interactions and the greater the proportion of time spent in mutual play activities. It has also been consistently shown that the sex of the older sibling is an important factor—older females are apt to engage in more grooming, but they spend less time in interactive play with young siblings than older males do. Additionally, an interaction between these two factors has been demonstrated—the greater the age differential, the more likely older females will groom their younger siblings and the less likely older males will play with them. To add to the complexity, sex of the *younger* sibling can also influence the development and expression of sibling relationships, as well as interacting with each of the previous two factors separately and together. There are obviously many other factors that can influence sibling relationships, and one can presently only ponder the nature and extent of the interactions among all these factors, in addition to any independent effects each might bring to bear on a given sibling relationship.

Moreover, the manner or mechanisms by which these factors express their influence on sibling interactions can be quite varied. For example, consider how the sex of an infant rhesus monkey can influence the relationship it develops with an older sister. First, there are direct effects: among other things, a male infant will be more likely to try to initiate play bouts and less likely to tolerate being groomed for extended periods than would a female infant (Hinde & Spencer-Booth, 1967; Ruppenthal, Harlow, Eisele, Harlow & Suomi, 1974; Golopol, 1979). There are also more indirect effects: male infants are apt to be more demanding of their mothers than are female infants, and as a result the older female sibling would probably have less direct access to her younger sibling if it were a male than if it were a female (Mitchell, 1968; White & Hinde, 1975.) Also, because male infants seem to attract more attention from group members than do female infants (e.g., Harlow & Lauersdorf, 1974), an older sister is more likely to have a younger sister "to herself" for interactions than she would a younger brother, whose interactions with her would more likely involve other group members as well. Indirect influences of this sort have been described for human children by Lamb (1979), Parke (1978), and Pederson, Yarrow, Anderson & Cain (1979), among others. The inevitable presence of such indirect influences greatly complicates assessment of the manner and extent of any factor's effect on sibling relationships.

Thus, consideration of some basic issues in study and interpretation of sibling relationships in nonhuman primates indicates that a great deal of basic research remains before such issues can be fully addressed and ultimately resolved. Descriptions of sibling interactions need to be placed in the context of the participants' relationships with other members of their social group. Determination of possible functions for sibling relationships requires experimental manipulation along with rigorous observation of such relationships—requirements not met by most of the literature to date. Full consideration of factors that influence sibling relationships in nonhuman primates is likely to be time consuming, for there appear to be many influencing factors and many ways in which such factors can interact with each other in producing a particular empirical finding. Thus, the basic issues that have generated much of the research to date on sibling relationships in nonhuman primates will have to generate a lot more research before such issues can be comfortably settled. In this respect the nonhuman primate literature bears a striking resemblance to literature on the human sibling relationships.

TWO CONTRASTING APPROACHES TO STUDY OF SIBLING INTERACTIONS

While virtually all primatologists who have studied sibling interactions have sought to address the basic issues of description, function, and/or sources of influence, their reasons or rationale for doing so have been mixed. There have been, to date, essentially two major approaches to the study of primate sibling relationships: the *sociobiological* approach and the *attachment theory-social network* approach. Generally speaking, researchers operating from a sociobiological orientation have been most interested in the issue of function, whereas attachment theory-social network adherents have tended to concentrate on descriptive characterizations and sources of possible influence in their empirical studies.

Sociobiologically oriented primatologists have focused their attention on sibling relationships for one primary reason: the genetic similarity of siblings relative to that of others in any primate social group. An individual monkey or ape shares more genes with its siblings than it does with anyone else in the world, except for its biological mother and father (and any offspring it might produce)—and it shares as many genes with its siblings as it does with these close blood relatives. It also has as many genes in common with its half-siblings (both maternal and paternal) as it does with each grandparent (and grandchild)—more than with anyone else besides parents and full siblings (and offspring). For sociobiologists such genetic similarity carries some very important implications for the nature and (especially) the function of primate sibling relationships.

Why should genetic similarity and blood relationships be so important for consideration of social behavior and its development in primates? Sociobiologists believe that much of every individual's behavioral repertoire has been genetically preprogrammed, "selected" by evolutionary pressures to maximize the number of that individual's genes that are successfully passed on to future generations (Wilson, 1975). Dawkins (1976) has cleverly captured much of sociobiology's essence and thrust in his concept of the "selfish gene"—a gene that perpetuates itself by influencing (via natural selection) its "host" organisms to engage in activities that serve to maximize its propagation over time, even if it involves "sacrificing" some of the organisms in the process (or reducing their probability of personal reproductive success). The concept of *altruism* is important for sociobiological interpretations of certain social activities, especially those involving close kin. Trivers (1972), among others, has argued that because close blood relatives share a relatively large proportion of their genes, an individual may engage in behavior that endangers its own livelihood if that behavior enhances the likelihood of survival of close kin by a sufficient amount. Such behavior would not be expected to be directed toward a more distant relative or unrelated cohort because few if any of the subject's genes would likely be shared by such a benefactor. (For one interesting exception, see Trivers, 1971.)

At any rate, sociobiological theory yields some apparently clear-cut predictions about sibling relationships in primates (and in other animals as well). First, although there are theoretical grounds for a certain amount of sibling rivalry to exist, it should generally be less than between unrelated competitors. Moreover, any individual should direct more altruistic behavior toward its siblings than toward anyone else in its social group, except (future) offspring and perhaps its parents. Second, the closer the blood relationships between two individuals, the greater the incidence and intensity of altruistic behavior. Thus, relationships between full siblings should be more likely to involve altruistic interactions than relationships between half-siblings; relationships between half-sibs should incorporate more altruistic behavior than between first cousins. Third, although helping one who shares genes may represent an evolutionarily successful behavioral strategy (Hamilton, 1964), too much sharing of genes can have disastrous consequences: incest carries with it the greatly enhanced probability of lethal or debilitating recessive genes appearing in homozygous form in the offspring. Thus, although siblings would be expected to behave altruistically toward each other, there should also be some mechanism for avoiding incestuous relationships between brothers and sisters or between other close kin of the opposite sex.

Not surprisingly, study of sibling relationships by sociobiologically oriented primatologists has tended to focus on identification of behavior patterns between siblings (and half-siblings) that could be interpreted as being altruistic in nature. The results of many of these studies have been generally consistent with at least some predictions readily derived from sociobiological theory; these results will be reviewed later. Other findings are more equivocal with respect to these predictions, and all of the findings to date lend themselves to alternative explanations on a case-by-case basis. Most current investigators would probably agree with Hrdy's (1976) evaluation that a much better data base is needed before truly rigorous tests of sociobiological predictions concerning sibling relationships in primates can be objectively carried out. Such a data base is currently being accumulated for several nonhuman primate species.

A quite different perspective on sibling relationships in nonhuman primates is provided by an attachment theory-social network framework of study. In this approach, sibling interactions and relationships are not viewed so much in terms of genetic similarity between the participants as they are viewed in terms of their relationships to a common attachment object or objects. In other words, sibling relationships are important not so much because the siblings share many genes but because they share the same mother.

In most primate social groups, individuals who share the same mother are also likely to share many other things besides genes. Siblings are likely to have very early social experiences more similar to one another than to anyone else in the social group. A growing body of primate literature indicates that most primate mothers display highly consistent "styles" of maternal behavior toward successive offspring (e.g., Stevenson-Hinde & Simpson, 1981; Suomi, Eisele, & Chapman, 1982) at least after their first-born infant (cf. Harlow, Harlow, Dodsworth & Arling, 1966; Ruppenthal, Arling, Harlow, Sackett & Suomi, 1976). In addition to having most likely experienced a similar maternal caretaking style, primate siblings share the same source(s) of security—their mutual attachment object(s)—at least until they approach puberty. This means that siblings in most primate species are likely to spend more time in the general vicinity of one another (and, of course, their mother) than they are to unrelated individuals, especially at night (most immature primates sleep in physical contact with their mother whenever permitted) and under conditions of stress and/or danger. Such factors as physical proximity serve to enhance the opportunity for sibling interactions and the development of long-term social relationships between them.

Another important, if not unique, feature shared by siblings in most primate species concerns how the siblings are likely to be treated by the rest of their social group. Numerous field and laboratory studies of social dominance or status within primate social groups structured along matrilineal lines have consistently demonstrated that offspring almost always share their mother's relative status in her group's dominance hierarchy at least until they reach puberty, and, if they are female offspring, they usually continue to share her relative status until she dies (e.g., Kawai, 1965; Lindberg, 1973; Missakian, 1972; Sade, 1967). In other words, in many primate species, an infant's relative social status is determined essentially at birth, and its status is highly likely to be shared by its siblings. In the eyes of the rest of its social group, the infant and its siblings "belong together" because they share the same mother—and therefore the infant tends to be treated like its siblings by other group members, especially unrelated adults.

Thus, attachment theory considerations tend to emphasize the role of the mother or other primary caretakers in explaining the process of social development (Ainsworth, 1979; Bowlby, 1969); sibling relationships are thought to exist largely because of the presence of the mother. On the other hand, social network considerations tend to focus on the infant's relationships with others in its social group and, more basically, on the social composition and underlying role structure of the group (Lewis & Feiring, 1979). Group composition and role structure are thought to have substantial influence on the nature and development of sibling relationships within the group.

For example, consider the case of primate infants who grow up in a social group that lacks peers unrelated to the infants, as opposed to a social group that contains such peers. Numerous studies in both the human and nonhuman primate literature suggest that, when given a chance, infants and children generally prefer to play with age-mates rather than with social partners of a different age (see Maccoby, 1980, and Suomi, 1979a, for a review of these literatures). Thus, in groups containing peers, young primates typically will seek out these peers as their primary playmates. In contrast, interactions with siblings are less apt to involve extended active play bouts; instead, grooming interactions and proximity during feeding periods are much more common between siblings than between peers in these social groups. But in social groups that lack unrelated peers for any one infant, that infant is likely to engage in extensive play bouts with its older and younger siblings in addition to its grooming and feeding bouts with them. Thus, the nature of sibling relationships can be influenced by the nature of the overall social network of which they are a part. Research based on this perspective tends to emphasize description of interactional characteristics of sibling relationships and analysis of social network factors and role structure in terms of possible influence on these relationships.

Using the grossest of generalizations, it is probably not unfair to characterize the sociobiological perspective as one focusing on genetic contributions (ultimate factors) to sibling relationships, whereas the attachment theory-social network perspective seems to be more concerned with environmental contributions (proximate factors); this is, of course, the nature-nurture dichotomy revisited. On the other hand, it should be pointed out that these two theoretical-methodological approaches need not be seen as necessarily mutually exclusive in their interests or in their interpretation of empirical data describing sibling relationships in any given species or group of nonhuman primates. These two general approaches clearly represent different levels of analysis, even when the phenomena under study are the same, but there is no reason why the approaches cannot be made parallel, rather than randomly orthogonal, in their study of sibling interactions. I will return to this point when I describe the development of sibling relationships. First, however, a complication for comparing sibling relationships between different primate species must be considered.

KINSHIP AND SOCIAL STRUCTURE: WHO ARE THE SIBLINGS AND WHO ARE THE PEERS?

Researchers who have studied sibling relationships in human children are usually quick to point out that many factors can influence how siblings interact with one another; by all accounts it is a complex picture. A young child's relationship with his or her siblings is dependent in part on how many siblings there are, how much older or younger they are, what their own social relationships with the mother or father have been, how many peers the child has access to, for how long, and under what conditions, as well as other factors enumerated elsewhere in this book. The human infant or child's relationship with his or her siblings is in large part determined by what the child's social network has to offer. Comparison or generalization from one study to another of findings concerning sibling relationships becomes hazardous if the social networks in the respective studies are substantially different from each other.

Nevertheless, by the standards of the nonhuman primate literature, the large majority of studies of human sibling relationships are amazingly consistent with respect to several aspects of their subjects' social networks. For example, in virtually every human study of sibling relationships, the siblings are full siblings, with the same mother and father. They usually have some access to age-mates who are not related to them, through day care centers, nursery schools, or other institutional social settings for young children. Some of this traditional consistency may change as future studies examine sibling relationships in families in which both parents have divorced and remarried. Here, a child may acquire foster siblings who will not be genetically related and some of these foster siblings may be the same age as the child. If the child's remaining parent has additional offspring by his or her new spouse, the new arrivals will be half-sibs to the child. Clearly, changes in the traditional Western family social structure can very much change the kind of sibling or sibling-like relationships that will develop. Unquestionably, such changes greatly complicate study and interpretation of human sibling relationships.

Such a complication has existed for countless ages in many species of nonhuman primates. The standard Western human nuclear family with mother, father, and offspring who are full siblings is actually the exception across the primate order. Most primate adults do not live as monogamous pairs but rather live in more ''exotic'' social groups where promiscuity on the part of at least one sex of adult is the rule. Sibling relationships among infants growing up in these types of social groups tend to be less straightforward than occurs in the typical nuclear family.

Table 1 lists some of the basic types of social structures that characterize various nonhuman primate species. It also specifies the types of sibling relationships that exist for infants growing up in such groups, as well as characteristics of the rest of the infants' respective social networks, and their long-term status in their natal social group. Although the table is not inclusive, it is representative of most ''standard'' social structures found in the primate order (Crook & Gartlan, 1966); listed in parentheses are some of the most commonly studied primate species (especially with respect to sibling relationships) for each type of social structure.

It is clear from Table 1 that the overwhelming majority of nonhuman primate infants grow up with some exposure to siblings or maternal half-sibs. What differs markedly for infants growing up in the different types of social structures are the *others* in the social group besides mothers and siblings. At one extreme, orangutan infants have no real exposure to any conspecifics except their mothers and siblings until they are adolescents (Horr, 1977). At the other extreme are macaques such as rhesus monkeys, some species of baboons, and chimpanzees.

TABLE 14.1
Social Structure and Sibling Relationships in Different Primate Species

Type of Social Structure	Maternal Siblings	Age-mates	Other Group Members	Long-term Status in Group
Solitary (Orangutan)	No more than one sibling (50%) or maternal half-sibling (25%)	None	None	Both male and female leave maternal "group" prior to adolescence
Monogamous Pairs (gibbons, siamangs)	1–3 full siblings (50%)	None	Father (50%)	Both male and female leave maternal group around puberty
(marmosets, tamarins)	Fraternal twin (50%), full siblings* (50%)	Fraternal twin (50%)	Father (50%)	Both male and female leave maternal group around puberty
1-Male Groups (Hanuman langur, patas monkey, some species of baboons)	Up to several full siblings** (50%)	Paternal half-siblings (25%)	Father (50%), unrelated adult females, paternal half-siblings (25%)	Male leaves natal troop around puberty; female may stay for life
Multi-male multi-female groups (macaques, chimpanzees, some species of baboons)	Up to several full siblings (50%) and maternal half-siblings (25%)	Paternal half-siblings (25%) and unrelated peers	Father (50%), other unrelated adult males and females paternal half-siblings (25%) other unrelated nonage-mate infants and juveniles	Male leaves natal troop around puberty; female may stay for life***

*in some species, there may be some maternal half-sibs (25%).
**some older maternal half-sibs may be present if there has been a recent male takeover of group.
***in chimpanzees, females may leave troop at first estrus, whereas males stay in natal troop.

Rhesus monkey infants born in the wild grow up not only in the presence of their mother and siblings, but also with (usually) maternal half-siblings, paternal half-siblings, nonkin peers, and adolescents and adults of both sexes, some related to any one infant and some not (Berman, 1978; Kaufman, 1966; Lindberg, 1973; Sade, 1967). Thus, although virtually all infants grow up with some exposure to full or maternal half-siblings, the relationships with these siblings are embedded in quite different social networks, almost certainly providing these infants with different forms and amounts of social stimulation.

A second conclusion about primate sibling relationships that can be gleaned from the social structure information in Table 1 concerns blood relationships within the different social structures. It is evident that genetic similarity and attachment object commonality, although not totally independent, are also not perfectly correlated (and thus not perfectly confounded) with one another across different primate species and characteristic social structures. This means that it is possible to identify certain comparisons that directly pit predictions concerning sibling relationships based on sociobiological principles against predictions based on an attachment theory-social network perspective. This fact becomes important when one considers the relative paucity of opportunities to make direct tests of competing theoretical predictions about any social developmental phenomena (cf. Sackett, Sameroff, Cairns, & Suomi, 1981), especially when sociobiology is one of the competing theories.

For example, consider the simplest case in all of Table 1, sibling relationships in orangutans. An orangutan infant in the wild will most likely have limited (< 2 years) exposure to an older sibling (or maternal half-sib), a younger sibling (or maternal half-sib), or both. These various outcomes can take place because: (a) orangutan infants are born to any one adult female orangutan no more frequently than every 2–3 years, and orangutan offspring almost always leave the immediate vicinity of their mothers (and any younger siblings) before they are 5 years old (Horr, 1977); (b) the adult males who are the biological fathers of orangutan infants may never see their offspring as they are growing up, except perhaps in the context of a mating bout; the rest of the time the fathers are living by themselves. Adult male "mating ranges" overlap to some extent. As a result, any one female during her lifetime is usually impregnated by more than one male, and she can also be impregnated more than once by any one male (Horr, 1977). Because adult female orangutans appear to be continually sexually receptive hormonally when not pregnant or nursing, any sexual encounter with any male is highly likely to result in a pregnancy in the wild (Nadler, 1981).

As a consequence, most orangutan infants will grow up with some exposure either to an older full-sibling or a maternal half-sibling. They will also be likely to acquire a younger full-sibling or maternal half-sib before they permanently leave their mothers. From the fact that an infant orangutan shares 50% of its genes with any full sibling but only 25% of its genes with a maternal half-sibling, sociobiological theory would predict more altruism and less sibling rivalry between full-sibling pairs than between infants who were maternal half-sibs. In contrast an attachment theory-social network perspective would predict *no* differences in social relationships between orangutan full siblings and between maternal half-sibs. In both cases the sibs or half-sibs can interact only with their mutual mother and each other. Thus, directly opposite predictions about sibling-half-sibling relationships in orangutans can be derived from sociobiological theory and attachment theory-social network perspectives. Unfortunately, definitive data about such relationships in wild orangutans are not presently available. To date, a major obstacle to obtaining such a data set has involved the extreme difficulty entailed in obtaining the necessary information about the paternity of orangutan infants in the field.

Conflicting predictions about sibling relationships from sociobiological and from attachment theory-social network perspectives become more numerous when one considers the more complex primate social structures listed in Table 1. For example, at least two such conflicting predictions are readily apparent for primate infants growing up in multimale, multifemale social troops in which adults of both sexes are promiscuous. First, these infants are likely to be reared in the presence of siblings related to their mothers, at least in those social troops that are organized along matriarchal lines. (Most multimale, multifemale primate troops are so organized.) The siblings are almost certain to be either full siblings or maternal half-siblings to these infants. A straightforward prediction from sociobiological theory is that there should be more altruistic behavior and less "sibling rivalry" between full siblings, who share 50% of their genes, than between maternal half-sibs, who share the same mother but only 25% of these genes. The prediction based on attachment theory-social network considerations would be that social relationships developed between siblings would not differ appreciably from those between half-siblings—assuming that all adults in the troop were truly promiscuous. The conflict and the resulting differences in prediction are the same as they were in the previous orangutan example.

A second case of conflicting predictions can be found in comparisons between peers (age-mates) of infants who are unrelated to the infants as opposed to being *paternal* half-siblings to them. Attachment theory-social network proponents would have no reason to expect any major differences between unrelated peers as opposed to between paternal half-siblings of the same age and equivalent sex (this would be true only if adult males did *not* interact differentially with offspring vs. nonoffspring infants in the troop, a common assumption of most simulation studies generated to date, e.g., Hausfater, 1981). A sociobiological perspective, of course, would predict major differences between the two sets of relationships because paternal half-sibling age-mates share 25% of their genes whereas unrelated peers are unrelated. A similar prediction would hold for relationships an infant might develop with older paternal half-siblings as opposed to those with unrelated troop members the same age and sex as those older paternal half-sibs (Hrdy, 1976).

As was the case for the previous orangutan example, empirical tests of these contrasting predictions about sibling, half-sibling, and unrelated peer relationships in troop-living primates are crucially dependent on accurate paternity data for the subjects under study. Unlike the case for wild-living orangutans, some definitive data are beginning to emerge. Small and Smith (1981) examined cases of interactions between infants and juveniles in a large, outdoor-living captive troop of rhesus monkeys. Their analysis focused on interactions in which the infant was touched, grabbed, or carried away from its mother, and they included information about each mother's reactions to these interactions involving her infant. Small and Smith (1981) reported that whereas paternal half-sibs and unrelated juveniles initiated these interactions with infants at an approximately equivalent rate (and at a lower rate than full siblings), mothers were significantly *less* likely to restrict such interactions when they involved paternal half-siblings than when they involved unrelated juveniles the same age and sex as the paternal half-sibs. This intriguing finding suggests that somehow mothers are able to differentiate between individuals unrelated to themselves but related to their infants and individuals related to neither themselves nor their infants, although Small and Smith (1981) can offer no specific mechanism for such a discriminative capability.

How could a mother—or, for that matter, her infant—be able to differentiate between paternal half-sibs and individuals unrelated to her infant? One possibility is that each mother was able to associate the paternal half-sib with its own mother, that she had observed procreation between that female and the male who fathered her own infant, and that she could also associate that male with the copulation that produced her own infant. It seems highly likely that rhesus monkey mothers possess the first capability but somewhat less likely that the latter two requirements could be fulfilled by these mothers. (However, the author learned long ago not to underestimate rhesus monkey social perceptual and cognitive capabilities; see Suomi, Harlow, & Lewis, 1970.) Another possibility is that adult rhesus monkey males treat their own offspring differently from nonoffspring, and that adult females can recognize this differential treatment and associate it between their own and other infants (the paternal half-sibs). For such a possibility to be reality it would be necessary not only for fathers to actually engage in such differential treatment (which would additionally entail knowledge of which infants they had fathered and which ones they had not), but also that the mothers could identify such treatment and understand its implications. Some not yet published data strongly suggest that promiscuous primate males indeed proffer preferential treatment to offspring over nonoffspring, even in social groups in which the females are also promiscuous; these data are based on recently developed blood-based determinations of paternity (e.g., Curie-Cohen, 1981). Perhaps these males know something that human males do not.

A third possible mechanism for Small and Smith's (1981) finding has important implications for sibling-nonsibling relationships. It is that the infant and juvenile rhesus monkeys themselves can differentiate their own paternal (as well as maternal) kin from nonkin. How they might do this remains a mystery, but *that* they might be able to make such differentiations perceptually now appears quite likely. Wu, Holmes, Medina, and Sackett (1980), in a provocative study, reported that pigtail macaque infants displayed a preference for paternal half-siblings over unrelated individuals the same age and sex as the half-sibs; the remarkable aspect of this finding was that these preferences were expressed toward half-siblings that the subjects had *never seen before,* i.e., the preference could not have been learned. Actually previous preference studies have demonstrated that socially naive macaque infants can also clearly differentiate adult females from adult males of their own species (Suomi, Sackett, & Harlow, 1970) and adult females of their own species from adult females of other macaque species (Sackett, 1970), even though they have had *no* previous visual or tactile exposure to adults of either sex or any macaque species. Again, the perceptual basis for such "unlearned" social preference patterns is not known, only that such preferences do exist and can be reliably demonstrated. Data such as Wu et al.'s (1980) should bring joy to the hearts of orthodox sociobiologists, for these preference patterns "make sense" from a sociobiological perspective and seem not to require (much) previous social experience for their expression.

At any rate, inspection of Table 1 does reveal a number of areas in which direct comparison of predictions based on sociobiological theory can be made with those based on an attachment theory-social network perspective. In several cases the appropriate data sets required for direct comparison of predictions from these two theoretical frameworks do not presently exist. Still, the information presented in the table can be readily used to identify data sets that would be potentially worthwhile for future studies in this area.

A final point about the social structure-kinship patterns that merits discussion with respect to sibling relationships concerns the dispersion of infants from their natal group prior to adulthood. A quick glance at the far-right hand column of Table 1 reveals that in no species do siblings or half-siblings of the opposite sex both remain in their natal social groups past adolescence. In most species it is the males who leave their natal troop during adolescence and the females who remain, although for chimpanzees the situation is reversed. Also, in all primate species who form monogamous heterosexual pairs and rear offspring within nuclear families, *both* male and female siblings leave their parental nest prior to adulthood. Presumably they do not leave together.

Compelling arguments have been made to the effect that such patterns of natal group exodus by at least one sex of offspring prior to attaining adulthood effectively eliminate the possibility of brother-sister (or half-brother-half-sister) incest occurring. Some authors have gone so far as to suggest that such patterns of natal group exodus were "selected" for the very purpose of sibling incest avoidance (e.g., Hamilton, 1964; Trivers, 1972; Wilson, 1975; Dawkins, 1976). There is no question that sibling incest in primates can and does have disastrous consequences for the offspring resulting from the incestuous relationship. Recent studies of cases of brother-sister incest in laboratory-reared rhesus monkeys have revealed mortality rates during the first six months of life over 10 times greater for offspring of incest than when the parents are not kin to each other (Curie-Cohen, 1981), clearly demonstrating the existence of lethal recessive genes in advanced nonhuman primates and consequently the danger of incest for them. Perhaps it is no accident that the dynamics of most social groups of primates in the field make sibling incest practically impossible to take place under "normal" circumstances.

THE DEVELOPMENT OF SIBLING RELATIONSHIPS:
TWO ILLUSTRATIVE CASES

How do sibling relationships develop in young primates? When do these relationships begin to influence a primate infant's social activities? In what ways does the development of social relationships with siblings parallel the development of social relationships with others, e.g., with peers and others in the group? In what ways do they differ? How long do sibling relationships last among nonhuman primates, and under what conditions are they terminated? Obviously, the specific answers to these questions depend on the primate species and environmental circumstances under consideration, although some effects seem to be quite robust across the primate order. In this section these issues will be examined with respect to the development of sibling relationships in two quite different groups of nonhuman primate species: marmosets and tamarins, who generally grow up in smaller nuclear family groups, and various species of macaques, who live in larger social groupings containing numerous adult males and adult females and their offspring. Direct comparisons between these two species groups will be made whenever possible, although regretably in many instances comparative data do not yet exist or are only available from settings that preclude direct comparison, e.g., laboratory data for marmosets vs. field data for Japanese macaques.

Sibling "Effects" Prior to Sibling Birth

The development of sibling relationships in most primate species begins essentially with the birth of the younger sibling (or maternal half-sib), unlike some other social relationships (e.g., those with peers), which do not emerge until later in the infant's life (Harlow & Harlow, 1965; Suomi & Harlow, 1978). However, the *influence* of a sibling on a young primate's activities can begin *long before the birth of that sibling*—and vice versa. Put another way, "sibling rivalry" can in effect begin before the siblings are born and perhaps before they are even conceived. The best evidence comes from laboratory studies of rhesus monkey infants.

Golopol (1979) examined daily longitudinal behavioral records of rhesus monkeys growing up in artificial nuclear family environments that allowed infants access to their mothers, fathers, siblings, peers, and other unrelated juveniles and adults of both sexes (Harlow, 1971). Using the birth of an infant as a "zero point," Golopol traced the records of its older sibling beginning 12 months prior to the birth of the infant and continuing for 12 months after the infant was born. It was very clear from the data that 1- and 2–year-old rhesus monkeys displayed marked changes in their forms and targets of social activities with the advent of a younger sibling. The remarkable finding was that the greatest change in these activities occurred *not* with the actual birth of the younger sibling but rather 3-4 months *earlier,* when their mothers were in the second trimester of pregnancy.

Prior to their mothers' pregnancy these individuals directed most of their social activities toward peers, and most of those activities involved interactive play bouts (Ruppenthal et al., 1974). When their mothers became pregnant, however, these youngsters' interactions with peers dropped precipitously, and so did their overall levels of play behavior. Thereafter, they spent most of their time in physical contact with or in close proximity to their mothers (who themselves became increasingly inactive as their pregnancy progressed) with grooming and passive contact with mother "replacing" much of the previous play activity. The truly striking aspect of these changes coincidental with maternal pregnancy was that they were apparently independent of the older siblings' ages: 2-year-olds stopped playing with peers and returned to mother statistically as much as did 1-year-olds. Moreover, these changes were not transient. Older siblings' frequencies of interactions with peers and levels of play behavior never did return to their values prior to their mothers' pregnancy, at least not during the first 12 months following the actual birth of the sibling (Golopol, 1979).

Very recent evidence (Snowdon & Cleveland, 1981) suggests that a similar or parallel phenomenon might be occurring in cottontop tamarin "natural" nuclear families. They have found that infants born into laboratory-housed cottontop tamarin groups rapidly increase their play behavior with their twin and older siblings until 4-5 months of age, at which point the incidence of play drops sharply and the amount of contact seeking and maintaining (attachment) behavior directed toward the mother increases almost as rapidly. It is perhaps not coincidental that by this time these infants' mothers are almost always pregnant again. Whether the pregnancy per se is directly responsible for or contributes to such behavioral changes in infant cottontop tamarins remains to be determined.

At any rate, it appears that the coming of a sibling can produce marked changes in an immature monkey's social behavior even before the sibling is born. Such very early "sibling rivalry" effects lend themselves very easily to sociobiological (and other) speculation about possible mechanisms and functions. The most likely mechanism involves the mother. The older infant appears to change its behavioral targets and tendencies as a direct result of its mother's changes in physical appearance, activity levels, and social interaction patterns. As for possible functions, these new findings provide plenty of room for creative speculation concerning not only the older infant but also its mother, sibling-to-be, and other group members.

It is perhaps fitting that there now exists evidence to the effect that the older infant is also capable of "influencing" any potential younger sibling long before the actual birth of the younger sibling. Simpson, Simpson, Hooley, and Zunz (1981) have reported that rhesus monkey infants may be able to *delay* the birth of younger siblings by up to a year's time. Rhesus monkeys are generally seasonal breeders with a relatively short birth season such that most infants are born into any one social group within a period of 2–4 months each year (Kaufmann, 1966; Sade, 1967; Lindberg, 1973). Most reproductively active rhesus monkey females give birth either every year or every other year; thus, a young rhesus monkey will typically get its first younger sibling when it is either one or two years old. Simpson et al. (1981) have presented data suggesting that the behavior of an existing infant can influence whether its mother will become pregnant during the next breeding season or whether she will ''wait'' an additional year before having her next child. Specifically, infants that are active and independent relatively early in development are much more likely to have a younger sibling during the next year than are infants who are relatively inactive and slow to leave their mothers' immediate presence. More rhesus monkey male infants will have a sibling one year younger than themselves than will young rhesus monkey females (Simpson et al., 1981).

Thus, there is evidence that young rhesus monkeys begin to change the focus of their social activities even before a new sibling is born. In essence, this change involves intensifying the previous relationship with the young monkey's mother, largely at the ''expense'' of its interactions with unrelated peers. It can be argued that this change represents the young monkey's attempts to monopolize its mother even before the competition arrives. An equally plausible interpretation is that such behavior serves to ''prepare'' the young monkey for the arrival of its sibling, ''insuring'' that it will henceforth become more socially involved with close kin rather than spending most of its time playing with unrelated peers.

On the other hand, there is also evidence that a young monkey's behavior prior to its mother's next pregnancy can influence when that pregnancy will begin. Active, precocious infants are more likely to have siblings within a year than are slow, dependent infants. Such a ''strategy,'' should it actually exist, might make adaptive ''sense'' in a variety of ways. The demands of a lethargic or highly dependent infant might weaken a mother such that a quick new pregnancy would endanger her health and ultimately the survival of all parties. If males, indeed, are more likely to have younger siblings closer to their own age than females are, it might just be related to the facts that males are more likely to play with and less likely to practice caretaking on younger siblings than are females—and play is most readily carried out with partners close in age whereas caretaking is best practiced on a partner much younger than the practice caretaker.

At any rate, it seems clear that effects of siblings can begin to appear even before the younger siblings are born. The actual mechanisms underlying these effects are not fully understood at present, nor have the extent and longevity of these effects been studied in any detail. The main point is that such effects do occur in at least some primates.

Birth and the Beginning of Sibling Relationships

In most primate species a newborn infant's first social contact with any individual other than its mother is likely to be with an older sibling (or maternal half-sib). Most monkey mothers deliver their infants by themselves; others in their social group may watch the delivery with great apparent interest and some "displacement" behavior (e.g., Gouzoules, 1974), but they do not appear to offer any direct assistance. (Most primate females give birth between the hours of 1:00 AM and 6:00 AM, and perhaps as a result very few births have been witnessed by human observers.) After the birth most mothers will try to keep other group members from touching, holding, or grabbing their neonate. In many species the only contact the mother will permit is contact by an older sibling or maternal half-sib (e.g., Rosenblum, 1971). Even so, with the birth of a new infant these mothers begin to reject contact attempts by older offspring at significantly higher rates than prior to parturition (e.g., Spencer-Booth, 1968; Golopol, 1979; Singh & Sachdeva, 1977).

In most species of nonhuman primates for which appropriate data are available, there appear to be fairly consistent sex differences in efforts by older siblings to contact newborns. For example, young rhesus monkey females seem much more persistent in their efforts to touch and inspect newborn siblings than are young males. These females increase their time spent in contact with their mother and the neonate over levels immediately prior to parturition, while young male siblings decrease maternal contact after the new infant is born. Interestingly enough, the mothers display equivalent rates of rejection or punishment of attempts by male and female older siblings to contact the neonate. However, male infants are more likely to heed the rejections and to seek out the company of other group members, whereas females are more likely to ignore the rejecting acts of their mothers and continue to seek contact with their mothers and the newborn infants (Golopol, 1979). Similar findings have been reported for bonnet macaque youngsters (Singh & Sachdeva, 1977) and in groups of vervet monkeys (Johnson, Koerner, Estrin, and Duoos, 1980).

Marmoset and tamarin species present a special case for consideration of early sibling interactions. Most marmosets and tamarins live in tight-knit nuclear families consisting of mother, father, and 2–3 pairs of offspring. As discussed previously, most pregnancies in these species result in fraternal twins. Thus, each neonate most likely not only has at least one pair of older siblings but also a fraternal twin (although not necessarily of the same sex). It also has a father that takes an exceedingly active role in caretaking activities. In some species of marmosets adult males actually surpass adult females in all aspects of caretaking, except of course nursing (Snowdon & Suomi, 1982).

Given this peculiar (for primates) social network, it is interesting to see who gets the most access to the newborn fraternal twins. Mothers and fathers spend the most time with the neonates, often taking one each. The siblings who end up with the most access to the newborn pair are usually the *oldest* living in the nuclear family—preadolescents who within a year would be leaving the family if they were living in a feral environment (Kleiman, 1979). Juveniles are not allowed extensive contact until the newborns are somewhat older. Also, very early in life the fraternal twins see relatively little of each other, perhaps because they are largely preoccupied with other, older siblings, as well as with each parent. It is only when they grow out of infancy that interactions with their fraternal twin and with juvenile siblings become prominent, superceding interactions with adolescent siblings and parents.

Thus, newborn infants of most primate species receive more contact and attention from siblings or maternal half-siblings than from any other member of their social group except of course, their mother (and father, in species where adult males play major caretaking roles). However, the amount of sibling contact is usually not extensive this early in life, and it is limited by the mother's tolerance of her older offsprings' presence around her and the neonate. Those siblings who get the most access to the neonate are usually approaching reproductive age and soon will have infants of their own to care for. Indeed, there is evidence for a few species (mostly marmosets) that if these older siblings fail to experience such interactions with their newborn brothers or sisters, their subsequent caretaking of their own infants may be deficient (Snowdon & Suomi, 1982). Thus, very early interactions with siblings may be ultimately more important for the older sibling than it is for the newborn.

Sibling Relationships During Childhood

During childhood, a young primate is no longer dependent on its mother for nourishment, and it gradually reduces the amount of time spent in physical contact with her, unless the overall social environment is very unstable or the youngster is unusually insecure (Suomi, 1979a). It also typically spends relatively little time interacting with other adults. Instead, the lion's share of its interactions "replacing" those with the mother earlier in life turn out to involve siblings and peers.

There is increasing evidence that the growth of independence from one's mother can be facilitated by the presence of siblings, especially certain types of siblings. For example, both Rosenblum (1971) and Suomi et al. (1982) have found that laboratory-reared infant macaques growing up in the presence of older siblings leave their mothers earlier chronologically and expand their behavior repertoire more rapidly than do infants without older siblings; in both cases the differences in mother-infant interactions are offset almost entirely by these interactions with older siblings. Berman (1978) has additionally demonstrated that free-ranging rhesus monkey infants with older brothers (or maternal half-brothers) spend more time away from their mothers earlier in life than infants with older sisters (or maternal half-sisters). The basis for this difference appears to lie in the fact that older brothers are more apt to be at a distance from their mother than are older sisters (Sade, 1967; Missakian, 1972), and hence their interactions with infant siblings are more likely to draw the infants away from their mother than interactions with older sisters adjacent to or in contact with her.

At any rate, once a young primate has achieved functional independence from its mother it rapidly develops elaborate social relationships with other youngsters in its social group, including both kin and nonkin. The most prominent behavior in most of these social relationships is social play. Most young monkeys have several playmates, some favored more than others. Virtually every study of play partners among young monkeys growing up in multimale, multifemale groups has found that these subjects play more with siblings (or maternal half-siblings) than they do with nonsiblings the same age and sex as their sibling partners (Berman, 1978; Golopol, 1979; Hanby, 1980; Loy & Loy, 1974; Small & Smith, 1981; Spencer-Booth, 1968, for rhesus monkeys; Fady, 1969, for crab-eating macaques; Yamada, 1963, for Japanese macaques; Estrada & Sandoval, 1977, for stumptail macaques; Rosenblum, 1971; Singh & Sachdeva, 1977, for pigtail and bonnet macaques; Cheney, 1978; Nash, 1978; Owens, 1975, for several species of baboons). However, most of these same studies have also reported that age-mate peers (either unrelated or paternal half-sibs) are the *most* preferred play partners of young macaques and baboons, more so than nonage-mate siblings (or maternal half-sibs). Maccoby's (1980) review of the human literature yields the same conclusion. However, in most other interactions *not* involving social play sequences, e.g., grooming, feeding with, or sitting next to another individual, siblings were clearly the most preferred partner, surpassing the mother in many instances. Nevertheless, it is striking how age-matching considerations can apparently overrule kinship considerations with respect to social play.

The special status of same-aged partners as playmates is particularly evident in cases in which age-mates are also maternal kin, as occurs in marmosets and tamarins. In these species fraternal twin births are the rule (in virtually all other primate species multiple births are exceedingly rare, in contrast to most other mammalian orders, e.g., marsupials, rodents, and carnivores). Thus, most marmoset and tamarin infants enter childhood not only with older siblings but also with a fraternal twin age-mate. However, they do not have any unrelated peers available as potential playmates. Consistent with the macaque data that demonstrate the importance of age equivalence in a playmate, these marmoset and tamarin youngsters play more with their fraternal twin than with any older sibling, and they are more likely to play with an older juvenile sibling than with an older adolescent sibling. In other words, the closer the age match the greater the amount of play between these siblings.

Snowdon and Cleveland (1981) have additionally found that if an infant of these twinning species grows up *without* a fraternal twin (it is not uncommon for one of a twin pair to die during infancy), its overall levels of play behavior with other siblings will be well *below* comparable measures for individuals that have a surviving fraternal twin. In other words, lack of an age-mate partner appears to suppress the expression of play, even that directed toward older individuals. Very similar findings have been disclosed in a laboratory study of rhesus monkeys by Deets (1974), in which infant pairs were cross-fostered to single mothers and these artificial twin pairs were compared with control infants growing up without a "foster twin" but otherwise having access to comparable social stimuli, including other peers. Deets (1974) reported that the foster twin-reared rhesus monkey infants left their mothers earlier chronologically and engaged in more play with peers than did infants reared without a foster twin. In other words, presence of an (unrelated) age-mate associated with one's own mother appeared to encourage earlier independence and more extensive social interactions with others in the social group than if no foster twin were present.

Thus, the bulk of the available evidence suggests that during childhood nonhuman primates who grow up in the presence of siblings (or maternal half-sibs) will develop childhood social relationships with others in their social group earlier; and these relationships will be of a more extensive nature than those formed by infants who grow up in the absence of siblings (or maternal half-sibs). As mentioned earlier, these effects depend in part on the age difference of the siblings. Generally speaking, the smaller the age differential between siblings, the greater will be the facilitative effect of the sibling for any one infant. It should also be mentioned that the exact nature of these effects is dependent on the sex of the respective siblings. For example, Golopol (1979) found that female juvenile rhesus monkeys were more discriminating in their interactions with siblings than were males; females displayed different behavioral interaction patterns toward siblings than they did toward peers, whereas males tended to interact with siblings and with peers in the same fashion or style. Also, several authors have reported that interactions with siblings of the same sex tend to be more frequent and extensive than those involving siblings of the opposite sex. Again, the general resemblance of these findings to those from the human literature is striking.

Sibling Relationships Among Adolescents and Adults

In most primate social groups when an individual becomes an adolescent its relationships with its siblings (and maternal half-siblings) undergo substantial changes. The most characteristic change that occurs for adolescents in virtually all primate species is a marked drop in the incidence of social play, especially with younger siblings. Other changes that transpire depend in large part on the particular species and the sex of the particular adolescent under study.

For example, in marmoset and tamarin groups, interactions between fraternal twins become increasingly rare as the twins approach adolescence, no matter whether the twins are both male, both female, or one of each. Interactions with younger siblings also decline, especially with respect to social play. However, interactions with newborn siblings are substantial and tend to be almost exclusively of a caretaking nature. As was discussed earlier, there is some evidence that such caretaking serves as necessary "practice" for the time when these adolescents will be the primary caretakers of their own infants (Snowdon & Cleveland, 1981). Within a few months of the onset of puberty both adolescent males and females of most marmoset and tamarin species leave their natural nuclear families, in part because of forceful "encouragement" by both of their parents (e.g., Kleiman, 1979). Parallel findings have been reported in nuclear family-living gibbons and siamangs (Fox, 1972). There is little evidence that adolescent siblings of either sex in these species associate with one another to any degree, although the data base to date is quite limited, especially with respect to field data.

The situation for adolescents in most macaque species is somewhat more complex and clearly different for males than it is for females. To begin with, there is virtually complete sex segregation in interactions between adolescent and young adult siblings—male and female siblings (or maternal half-siblings) simply do not interact with each other much at all. In part, this is due to location factors: most adolescent females remain in the general proximity of their mothers, whereas the large majority of adolescent males move to the periphery of their natal troop and may eventually leave the troop permanently. However, even in cases where male and female adolescent siblings are in the same general vicinity, their mutual interactions appear to be severely limited. Stephenson (1975) has presented evidence that brother-sister encounters among Japanese macaques usually elicit strong negative reactions from adults in the troop, and such brother-sister associations are very often disrupted or broken up by disapproving adults of both sexes.

In contrast, same-sex sibling relationships in macaques if anything tend to be *strengthened* during adolescence, especially among females. These relationships are marked less by mutual play as they are by mutual defense and reciprocal grooming bouts. For example, Kaplan (1977) found that rhesus monkey adolescent females living in free-ranging, provisional troops intervened in fights on behalf of a maternal sibling far more often proportionally than they intervened on behalf of nonkin. Watanabe (1979) found the same type of result in troops of free-ranging Japanese macaques; adolescent females were much more likely to groom and interrupt fights involving sisters and maternal half-sisters than they were for unrelated adolescent and juvenile troop members. However, interactions between sisters or maternal half-sisters begin to decline when these females start to have infants of their own (Grewal, 1980), although they tend to stay in relative proximity within the range of the troop (Sade, 1967). There appears to be a well-ordered dominance hierarchy among adolescent and adult female siblings and maternal half-siblings (e.g., Kawai, 1965; Missakian, 1972; Watanabe, 1979; Yamada, 1963). Thus, in most macaque social groups, same-sex sibling relationships between females may last a lifetime, even though the same females may never see their male siblings again once the males have reached puberty.

Less is known about sibling relationships among adolescent macaque males, except that they do not interact much with their older sisters or maternal half-sisters. Many of these males leave their natal group at the onset of puberty and roam about in all-male gangs. It seems very likely that within any one gang there may be several sets of brothers or maternal half-brothers, but the degree to which interaction between these brothers might differ from those between unrelated or more distantly related adolescent males is not presently known. Because adolescent males eventually join other existing troops, it is conceivable that male siblings could eventually become members of the same new troop as young adults (or even as older adults). However, definitive data on sibling relationships among older males do not presently exist.

Thus, most primates undergo a change in their relationships with siblings as they pass through adolescence and enter adulthood. In most species, relationships between siblings of the opposite sex all but disappear with puberty. Indeed, in some species, such as chimpanzees, there is actually clear-cut avoidance of opposite-sexed siblings upon entering adolescence (Pusey, 1980). On the other hand, the nature and extent of same-sex sibling relationships during adolescence depends on the sex of the adolescent, the species it represents, and the social structure of its current resident group. Some same-sex sibling relationships, especially those of female macaques, are likely to last a lifetime.

IMPLICATIONS FOR STUDY OF SIBLING
RELATIONSHIPS IN HUMANS

What can the findings from studies of sibling relationships in different nonhuman primate species tell us about sibling relationships in humans? One must, of course, always be careful when engaging in cross-species generalizations, especially when *Homo sapien* is one of the species involved. Nevertheless, I believe that the emerging nonhuman primate literature can provide considerable insight in the interpretation of data on human sibling relationships, as well as the designing of future studies of sibling relationships in humans. My reasons for this belief are as follows.

First, comparative study of sibling relationships in different species of primates living in groups that differ in basic social structure can provide some perspective for interpretation of human data that is essentially "culture-free." Although almost all primate infants grow up in the presence of siblings or maternal half-sibs, their relationships with these siblings may differ substantially as a function of the social structure in which the relationships are embedded. In spite of these different social structures there are some striking commonalities in certain aspects of these various sibling relationships. That these commonalities in many cases extend to human sibling relationships may facilitate interpretation of these effects as they occur at the human level. On the other hand, demonstrated species differences in sibling relationships as a function of differences in social structure might be useful in an heuristic sense for identifying "culture-free" aspects of human sibling relationships that may be present within families of unconventional structure relative to their overall society.

Second, study of sibling relationships in nonhuman primate species can provide more rigorous tests of predictions from competing theoretical positions than is usually possible or practical at the human level. Sociobiologists such as Dawkins (1976) sometimes argue that human culture has provided some means for "short-circuiting" certain evolutionary trends, and hence tests of sociobiological principles based on human data might not always provide the "purest" or fairest test possible. However, members of many nonhuman primate species characteristically develop complex relationships between not only full siblings but also both maternal and paternal half-siblings, as well as those between less related or unrelated individuals. As was shown for the data summarized in Table 1, it is possible to identify data sets that directly pit predictions from presently popular theoretical perspectives against one another. Indeed, it can be argued that studies of sibling/half-sibling differences in social relationships of nonhuman primates can provide the most exhaustive set of tests of sociobiological principles that could be arranged for any advanced mammalian species.

Finally, I believe that data from studies of sibling relationships in nonhuman primate species can serve to emphasize the fact that relationships between siblings can be incredibly varied and complex. Models of these relationships that fail to take into account such factors as age differential, sex of participants, availability of peers, time of life, and resident social structure are bound to be inadequate. To believe that human sibling relationships might be any less complex would seem to be a disservice not only to the human participants but also to the overall social sophistication of their simian counterparts.

REFERENCES

Agnew, N. M., & Pike, S. W. *The science game.* Englewood Cliffs, N.J.: Prentice-Hall, 1969.

Ainsworth, M. D. S. Infant-mother attachment. *American Psychologist,* 1979, *34,* 932–937.

Altmann, J. *Baboon mothers and infants.* Cambridge, Mass.: Harvard University Press, 1980.

Altmann, S. A. Altruistic behavior: The fallacy of kin selection. *Animal Behaviour,* 1979, *27,* 958–959.

Berman, C. M. The analysis of mother-infant interaction in groups: Possible influence of yearling groups. In D. Chivers & J. Herbert (Eds.), *Recent advances in primatology* (Vol. 1). London: Academic Press, 1978.

Bowlby, J. *Attachment.* New York: Basic Books, 1969.

Bronfenbrenner, U. *The ecology of human development: Experiments by nature and design.* Cambridge, Mass.: Harvard University Press, 1979.

Cheney, D. L. The play partners of immature baboons. *Animal Behaviour*, 1978, *26*, 1038–1050.

Crook, J. H. Sexual selection, dimorphism, and social organization in the primates. In B. Campbell (Ed.), *Sexual selection and the descent of man*. Chicago: Aldine, 1972.

Crook, J. H., & Gartlan, J. S. On the evolution of primate societies. *Nature*, 1966, *210*, 1200–1203.

Curie-Cohen, M. Inbreeding in nonhuman primates. *American Journal of Primatology*, 1981, *1*, 321.

Dawkins, R. *The selfish gene*. London: Oxford University Press, 1976.

Deets, A. C. Age-mate or twin sibling: Effects on monkey age-mate interactions during infancy. *Developmental Psychology*, 1974, *10*, 913–928.

Estrada, A., & Sandoval, J. M. Social relations in a free-ranging troops of stumptail macaques (*Macaca arctoides*): Male-care behaviour. *Primates*, 1977, *18*, 793–813.

Fady, J. C. Social play: Playmates among the young: Observations in *Macaca iris*. *Folia Primatologica*, 1969, *11*, 134–143.

Fox, G. J. Some comparisons between siamang and gibbon behavior. *Folia Primatologica*, 1972, *18*, 122–139.

Golopol, L. A. Effects of the birth of a younger sibling on the behavior of male and female yearling rhesus monkeys. Unpublished M.A. Thesis, University of Wisconsin-Madison, 1979.

Gouzoules, H. T. Group responses to parturition in *Macaca arctoides*. *Primates*, 1974, *15*, 287–292.

Grewal, B. S. Changes in relationships of nulliparous and parous females of Japanese monkeys at Arashiyama with some aspects of troop organization. *Primates*, 1980, *21*, 161–180.

Hamilton, W. D. The genetical evolution of social behaviour. *Journal of Theoretical Biology*, 1964, *7*, 1–52.

Hanby, J. P. Relationships in six groups of rhesus monkeys. II. Dyads. *American Journal of Physical Anthropology*, 1980, *52*, 565–575.

Harlow, H. F., & Harlow, M. K. The affectional systems. In A. M. Schrier, H. F. Harlow, & F. Stollnitz (Eds.), *Behavior of nonhuman primates* (Vol. 2). New York: Academic Press, 1965.

Harlow, H. F., & Harlow, M. K. Effects of various mother-infant relationships on rhesus monkey behaviors. In B. M. Foss (Ed.), *Determinants of infant behaviour* (Vol. 4). London: Methuen, 1969.

Harlow, H. F., Harlow, M. K., Dodsworth, R. O., & Arling, G. L. Maternal behavior of rhesus monkeys deprived of mothering and peer associations in infancy. *Proceedings of the American Philosophical Society*, 1966, *110*, 58–66.

Harlow, H. F., & Lauersdorf, H. E. Sex differences in passion and play. *Perspectives in Biology and Medicine*, 1974, *17*, 348–360.

Harlow, M. K. Nuclear family apparatus. *Behavior Research Methods and Instrumentation*, 1971, *3*, 301–304.

Hausfater, G. Simulation models of primate life-histories and group organization. *American Journal of Primatology*, 1981, *1*, 359.

Hinde, R. A. On describing relationships. *Journal of Child Psychology and Psychiatry*, 1976, *17*, 1–19.

Hinde, R. A., & Spencer-Booth, Y. The behaviour of socially living rhesus monkeys in their first two and a half years. *Animal Behaviour*, 1967, *15*, 169–196.

Horr, D. A. Orangutan maturation: Growing up in a female world. In S. Chevalier-Skolnikoff and F. Poirier (Eds.), *Primate bio-social development: Biological, social, and ecological determinants*. New York: Garland, 1977.

Hrdy, S. B. Care and exploitation of nonhuman primate infants by conspecifics other than the mother. In J. S. Rosenblatt, R. A. Hinde, E. Shaw, & C. Beer (Eds.), *Advances in the study of behavior* (Vol. 6). New York: Academic Press, 1976.

Johnson, C., Koerner, C., Estrin, M., & Duoos, D. Alloparental care and kinship in captive social groups of vervet monkeys (*Cereopithecus aethiops sabaeus*). *Primates*, 1980, *21*, 406–415.

Kaplan, J. R. Patterns of fight interference in free-ranging rhesus monkeys. *American Journal of Physical Anthropology, 1977, 47,* 279–288.

Kaufmann, J. H. Behavior of infant rhesus monkeys and their mothers in a free-ranging band. *Zoologica,* 1966, *51,* 17–28.

Kawai, M. On the system of social ranks in a natural troop of Japanese monkeys. In S. Altmann (Ed.), *Japanese monkeys: A collection of translations.* Atlanta: privately printed, 1965.

Kleiman, D. G. Parent-offspring conflict and sibling competition in a monogamous primate. *American Naturalist,* 1979, *114,* 753–760.

Lamb, M. E. The effects of the social context on dyadic social interactions. In M. E. Lamb, S. J. Suomi, & G. R. Stephenson (Eds.), *Social interaction analysis.* Madison, Wis.: University of Wisconsin Press, 1979.

Lewis, M., & Feiring, C. The child's social network: Social object, social functions, and their relationship. In M. Lewis & L. Rosenblum (Eds.), *The child and its family.* New York: Plenum Press, 1979.

Lewis, M., & Rosenblum, L. A. (Eds.), *The child and its family.* New York: Plenum Press, 1979.

Lindburg, D. G. The rhesus monkey in North India: An ecological and behavioral study. In L. A. Rosenblum (Ed.), *Primate behavior* (Vol. 2). New York: Academic Press, 1973.

Loy, J., & Loy, K. Behavior of an all-juvenile group of rhesus monkeys. *American Journal of Physical Anthropology,* 1974, *40,* 83–95.

Maccoby, E. E. *Social development: Psychological growth and the parent-child relationship.* New York: Harcourt, Brace, Jovanovich, 1980.

Missakian, E. A. Genealogical and cross-genealogical dominance relations in a group of free-ranging rhesus monkeys *(Macaca mulatta)* on Cayo Santiago. *Primates,* 1972, *13,* 169–180.

Mitchell, G. D. Attachment differences in male and female infant monkeys. *Child Development,* 1968, *39,* 611–620.

Nadler, R. *Reproductive behavior in the great apes.* Paper presented at the meeting of the Society for Sex Therapy and Research, New York, March 1981.

Nash, L. T. Kin preference in the behavior of young baboons. In D. J. Chivers and J. Herbert (Eds.), *Recent advances in primatology* (Vol. 1). New York: Academic Press, 1978.

Owens, N. W. Social play behavior in free-living baboons, *Papio anubis. Animal Behaviour,* 1975, *23,* 387–408.

Parke, R. D. Parent-infant interaction: Progress, paradigms, and problems. In G. Sackett (Ed.), *Observing behavior* (Vol. 1). Baltimore: University Park Press, 1978.

Parke, R. D. Emerging themes for social-emotional development. *American Psychologist,* 1979, *34,* 930–931.

Pederson, F. A., Yarrow, L. J., Anderson, B. J., & Cain, R. L. Conceptualization of father influences in infancy. In M. Lewis & L. A. Rosenblum (Eds.), *The child and its family.* New York: Plenum Press, 1979.

Pusey, A. E. Inbreeding avoidance in chimpanzees. *Animal Behaviour,* 1980, *28,* 543–552.

Rosenblum, L. A. Kinship interaction patterns in pigtail and bonnet macaques. In *Proceedings of the Third International Congress of Primatology.* Basel: Karger, 1971.

Ruppenthal, G. C., Arling, G. L., Harlow, H. F., Sackett, G. P., & Suomi, S. J. A ten-year perspective of motherless-mother monkey behavior. *Journal of Abnormal Psychology,* 1976, *85,* 341–348.

Ruppenthal, G. C., Harlow, M. K., Eisele, C. D., Harlow, H. F., & Suomi, S. J. Social development of infant monkeys reared in a nuclear family environment. *Child Development,* 1974, *45,* 670–682.

Sackett, G. P. Unlearned responses, differential rearing experiences, and the development of social attachments by rhesus monkeys. In L. Rosenblum (Ed.), *Advances in primate behavior* (Vol. 1). New York: Academic Press, 1970.

Sackett, G. P., Sameroff, A. J., Cairns, R. B., & Suomi, S. J. Continuity in behavioral development. In K. Immelmann, G. Barlow, M. Main, & L. Petrinovich (Eds.), *Behavioral develop-*

ment: The Bielefeld interdisciplinary conference. New York: Cambridge University Press, 1981, in press.

Sade, D. S. Determinants of dominance in a group of free-ranging rhesus monkeys. In S. Altmann (Ed.), *Social communication among primates.* Chicago: University of Chicago Press, 1967.

Simpson, M. J. A., Simpson, A. E., Hooley, J., & Zunz, M. Infant-related influences on birth intervals in rhesus monkeys. *Nature,* 1981, *290,* 49–51.

Singh, M., & Sachdeva, R. Behavior of juvenile bonnet monkey before and after his mother gives birth to a new baby. *Primates,* 1977, *18,* 605–610.

Small, M. F., & Smith, D. G. Interactions with infants by full siblings, paternal half-siblings, and nonrelatives in a captive group of rhesus macaques (*Macaca mulatta*). *American Journal of Primatology,* 1981, *1,* 91–94.

Snowdon, C. T., & Cleveland, J. Unpublished data, 1981.

Snowdon, C. T., & Suomi, S. J. Paternal behavior in primates. In H. E. Fitzgerald, J. A. Mullins, P. Gage (Eds.), *Child Nurturance* (Vol. 3). New York: Plenum Press, 1982, in press.

Spencer-Booth, Y. The behavior of group companions toward rhesus monkey infants. *Animal Behaviour,* 1968, *16,* 541–557.

Stephenson, G. R. Social structure of mating activity in Japanese macaques. In S. Kondo, M. Kawai, A. Ehara, & S. Kawamura (Eds.), *Proceedings from symposia of the Fifth Congress of the International Primatological Society.* Tokyo: Japan Science Press, 1975.

Stevenson-Hinde, J., & Simpson, M. J. A. Mothers' characteristics, interactions, and infants' characteristics. *Child Development,* 1981, in press.

Suomi, S. J. Peers, play, and primary prevention in primates. In M. Kent & J. Rolf (Eds.), *Primary prevention of psychopathology* (Vol. 3). Hanover, N.H.: University Press of New England, 1979. (a)

Suomi, S. J. Differential development of various social relationships by rhesus monkey infants. In M. Lewis & L. Rosenblum (Eds.), *The child and its family.* New York: Plenum Press, 1979. (b)

Suomi, S. J., Eisele, C. D., & Chapman, S. G. Individual differences in maternal behavior by rhesus monkeys. Manuscript in preparation, 1982.

Suomi, S. J., & Harlow, H. F. Early experience and social development in rhesus monkeys. In M. E. Lamb (Ed.), *Socio-personality development.* New York: Wiley, 1978.

Suomi, S. J., Harlow, H. F., & Lewis, J. K. Effect of bilateral frontal lobectomy on social preferences of rhesus monkeys. *Journal of Comparative and Physiological Psychology,* 1970, *70,* 448–453.

Suomi, S. J., Sackett, G. P., & Harlow, H. F. Development of sex preferences in rhesus monkeys. *Developmental Psychology,* 1970, *3,* 326–334.

Tinbergen, N. *The study of instinct.* Oxford: Clarendon Press, 1951.

Trivers, R. L. The evolution of reciprocal altruism. *Quarterly Review of Biology,* 1971, *46,* 35–57.

Trivers, R. L. Parental investment and sexual selection. In B. Campbell (Ed.), *Sexual selection and the descent of man,* 1871–1971, Chicago: Aldine, 1972.

Watanabe, K. Alliance formation in a free-ranging troop of Japanese macaques. *Primates,* 1979, *20,* 459–474.

White, L. E., & Hinde, R. A. Some factors affecting mother-infant relations in rhesus monkeys. *Animal Behaviour,* 1975, *23,* 527–542.

Williams, J. B. *Kinship behavior in nonhuman primates: A bibliography* (3rd ed.). Seattle: Primate Information Center, 1981.

Wilson, E. O. *Sociobiology: The new synthesis.* Cambridge, Mass.: Belknap Press, 1975.

Wu, H. M. H., Holmes, W. G., Medina, S. R., & Sackett, G. P. Kin preference in infant *Macaca nemestrina. Nature,* 1980, *285,* 225–227.

Yamada, M. A study of blood-relationship in the natural society of the Japanese macaque—An analysis of co-feeding, grooming, and playmate relationships in Minoo-B-troop. *Primates,* 1963, *4,* 43–65.

15 Similarities and Differences Among Siblings

Sandra Scarr
Susan Grajek
Yale University

One of the most curious facts about psychological studies of parents and children is that nearly all investigations focus on differences *among* families. The vast literature on social class, socialization, child rearing styles, and parent-child interaction are based almost exclusively on samples of one child per family. Explanatory variables in these traditions refer nearly always to family or parental characteristics that are shared by children in the same family and thus cannot explain why siblings differ. This fact is curious because most behavioral differences among people are found among siblings *within* families.

The majority of variation in human behavior, be it intelligence, personality, interests, or attitudes, occurs among siblings and not among families. Developmental psychology does not have adequate theories to account for sibling differences (or similarities). We have not taken seriously what Woodworth (1941) observed some 40 years ago: To his surprise, studies of twins and families of biological and adopted children showed that little of the variability in intelligence could be attributed to differences among family environments and that most of the variance lay undissected among siblings reared in the same families. The same statement applies equally well to variability in personality, interests, and attitudes.

This chapter will address the causes of sibling differences and the role that parents play in creating behavioral differences among their children. Parents, it will be shown, create behavioral differences among their children through genetic transmission, rearing environments, and the correlation of genes and environments. The chapter will review theories and research on environmental and genetic differences among siblings and propose a genotype-environmental correlational theory to account for the development of siblings' similarities and differences.

AN OVERVIEW OF THE CHAPTER

Because parents generally rear their own biological offspring, they provide both genes and rearing environments to their children. The children's genes are correlated with the environments provided by the same parents. As an example, brighter, more sociable parents tend to provide more intellectually and socially stimulating environments in the home than less bright and sociable parents, and the offspring of the former are probably more responsive, genetically, to the more stimulating environments than the offspring of the latter parents. This statement applies to the children of such parents, on the average. There are also individual differences among siblings to which parents are responsive, differences that arise both because of the child's individual genotype and because of the parents' response to the child's behavior (Lytton, 1980). Intelligent, sociable parents are likely to be more responsive to the more intelligent and sociable of their children—the match is better. Therefore, the parents can provide an environment that matches the interests and needs of some of the children better than others.

We do not have good theories of environmental differences within families. Only a few variables, such as birth order, child spacing, and sex of siblings have been used to describe within-family differences. The inadequacy of these constructs is evident in the research on their poor fit to sibling differences. There is no adequate environmental theory of the different environments that sibs experience.

There is a perfectly good genetic theory that predicts sibling differences and similarities. The genetic theory of why sibs are similar and different calls upon our certain knowledge of meiosis and conception. Each child in a family receives a random half of each parent's genes, which by chance averages to a common sibling share of about half of their genes. Naturally, some sibling pairs share less than 50% of their genes and others share more than 50%. It may be that some siblings by chance receive as few as 35% of their genes in common, whereas other pairs share as much as 65%. As has been shown with siblings who are dizygotic twins, the degree of genetic similarity, measured by blood group similarity, is regularly related to the sib pair's degree of physical similarity and to a lesser extent to their behavioral resemblance. There is a simple genetic theory of why biological sibs and DZ twins differ physically and behaviorally—because they share only half of their genes on average—and why some sib pairs resemble each other more than others—because they share relatively more of their genes. Given the availability of straightforward ideas about the genetic differences and similarities of siblings, why have psychologists largely ignored genetic theory?

One reason for psychologists' lack of interest in genetic variability is that many have not seen the need to interpret the *causes* of family effects, although most have implied that differences in environments were the exclusive or predominant source. If authoritative parents have more competent children than authoritarian ones, the usual inference is that differences in parental treatment of the children caused the differences in the children.

There are two connected reasons that causal relations in studies of parental socialization and other background differences cannot be interpreted in biological families: First, as Bell (1968, Bell & Harper, 1977) described, the direction of effects in parent-child studies is far from clear, as children determine much of their parents' behaviors toward them; and, second, studies of biological families confound genetic and environmental transmission from parent to child. The first point is probably familiar to most developmental psychologists, but the second may not be.

Briefly, Bell contended that parents' behaviors toward their children are at least in part responsive to the children's behaviors. Because siblings differ in their behaviors, they evoke different responses from their parents and thus receive rearing environments somewhat different from one another. Parents do not arbitrarily impose the same environment on every child, but tailor their behaviors to those of the child. Consider the boisterous, authority-challenging brother, whose shoes are always left in the front hall and whose bath towel is usually found on the floor—both against his parents' repeated requests and commands. The parental response he receives is quite different from that of his self-controlled, orderly, and compliant brother whose neatness and cooperation are a source of joy to his beleaguered parents. Parents who scream at and physically punish one child may be considerate and reasonable with another. They are the biological and social parents of both, but the sibs have both different genes and different environments. One of the reasons they have different environments is because they have different genes.

A second reason that studies of biological families are impossible to interpret is that parents transmit characteristics to their children genetically as well as through the rearing environment. If authoritative parents are shown to have more competent children, is it not possible that the parents are also more competent, a set of characteristics with at least some genetic variability? The offsprings' greater and lesser degrees of competence are likely to result from both genetic and environmental transmission. In addition, more competent parents are likely to provide a rearing environment for all of their children that is more stimulating for the children's development than that of less competent parents. Thus, the genes the child receives are correlated with his parents' genes and the rearing environment they provide. In biologically-related families, it is impossible to disentangle genetic from environmental transmission and the correlation between them.

In adoptive families, on the other hand, the children are not genetically descended from the parents, so that the effects of environmental differences are not confounded with genetic differences among and within the families. Similarities among adopted siblings, who are not genetically related, can be due only to the similarities in their rearing environments and the possible effects of the selective placement of the offspring of two similar natural mothers in the same adoptive home. The effects of such matching of unrelated children are likely to be quite small, as the correlations in the educational levels of the natural mothers of two adoptive studies (Scarr & Weinberg, 1977, 1978) were less than .15. Because education and occupation are about the only kinds of "real" data most adoption agencies have, it is even less likely that effective matching of unrelated children could be accomplished for personality or other behavioral variables.

Clearly, the most important source of similarities among adopted children is the adoptive family's rearing environment. Another way to express the same idea is to say that differences among the rearing environments provided by adoptive families are the source of adoptive siblings' similarities, expressed in correlations between sibs. The differences between the correlations of biological and adopted siblings provide estimates of the importance of genetic differences and genotype-environment correlations, because both kinds of siblings share rearing environments but only biological siblings share genes and gene-environment correlations.

In this chapter, environmental and genetic theories of sibling similarities and differences will be reviewed. We shall show that neither type of theory can adequately account for existing data on sibling similarities and differences. As an alternative, a theory of genotype-environment correlations, which does fit existing data, will be proposed to account for the process by which siblings develop similarities and differences. Differences among siblings' environments and genes, and the correlation of their genetic and environmental differences, will be shown to account for the facts about sibling differences—facts that are not adequately addressed by either a genetic or an environmental theory alone. We contend that it is not useful conceptually or empirically to attempt to separate genetic differences from genotype-environment correlations, because the *process* by which genetic differences come to be expressed in behavior can best be described by three kinds of genotype-environment correlation: A *passive* kind by which genetically-related parents provide the rearing environment; an *evocative* kind by which individuals evoke different responses from others; and an *active* kind of niche-picking that is correlated with genetic differences.

How Different Are Siblings?

Before examining theories that attempt to explain *why* siblings have similarities and differences, it is useful to consider how different siblings actually are. They are far more different than most psychologists seem to think. Studies of sibling similarities and differences reveal that even for measures of intelligence, on which siblings are more similar than on measures of personality or other characteristics, a minority of the variance is common to sib pairs. The typical IQ correlation among siblings is .35 to .50, meaning that 35 to 50% of the variability in IQ is shared by siblings and that 50 to 60% is not. Rowe and Plomin (1981) point out that, even when a correction is made for unreliability of measurement, siblings' IQ differences account for a majority of the variance. In fact, the average IQ difference between siblings is 12 or 13 IQ points, or 4/5 of a standard deviation. The average difference between any two randomly chosen people in the population is only 18 IQ points (Jensen, 1980). Thus, siblings who share half of the same genes and are reared by the same parents have IQ scores that differ by 2/3 the amount of randomly paired people in the population.

For measures of personality, interests, attitudes, and psychopathology, siblings are even more different, compared to random pairs of people (Rowe & Plomin, 1981; Scarr & Kidd, 1982). The typical sibling correlation for such measures is .15 to .20 (Grotevant, 1978; Grotevant, Scarr, & Weinberg, 1977; Rowe & Plomin, 1981; Scarr, Webber, Weinberg, & Wittig, 1981). If the sibling correlation is .20 and the standard deviation of the personality or interest measure is 4.5, which is typical of the Eysenck, Lykken, and Tellegen measures in the Scarr, et al. study, then the average absolute differences between siblings is 4.54 points, or one standard deviation. This value is calculated by a general formula that assumes a normal distribution, an assumption that is met by IQ and personality measures, (Jensen, 1980, p. 459),

$$/\bar{d}/ = (2\sigma\sqrt{1 - r}/ \sqrt{\pi}$$

σ is the standard deviation of the scores, r is the correlation between the siblings, and π is 3.1416. Given that randomly paired people in the population do not have correlated scores, their average absolute differences on personality measures is 5.08 points, hardly a noticeably greater difference from that of siblings.

Lest the reader slip over these results, let us make explicit the implications of these findings: Upper middle-class brothers who attend the same school and whose parents take them to the same plays, sporting events, music lessons, and therapists, and use similar child rearing practices on them are little more similar in personality measures than they are to working class or farm boys, whose lives are totally different. Now, perhaps this is an exaggeration of the known facts, but not by much. Given the low correlations of biological siblings and the near zero correlations of adopted siblings, it is evident that most of the variance in personality arises in the environmental differences among siblings, *not* in the differences among families.

Given the magnitude of sibling differences, we will examine in the next two sections genetic and environmental theories that attempt to account for within-family differences and similarities. In the final section we will describe an emerging theory of genotype-environment correlations.

GENETIC SOURCES OF SIBLING SIMILARITIES AND DIFFERENCES

Simply put, genetic theories of sibling resemblance state that resemblance is determined by the genes siblings have in common. In this section, we shall first review the process of meiosis and conception, because it is a fundamental part of genetic theories of variability. Discussions of research on genetic resemblance among siblings and of the relationship between genetic resemblance and behavioral resemblance among siblings will follow. In the course of these discussions, we shall show that a theory that accounts for sibling similarities and differences on a purely genetic basis does not fit data on intellectual, personality, or interest variation within families.

Biological siblings and dizygotic (DZ) twins have on the average half of the same genes and half different genes. Any genetic account of why siblings are similar and different calls upon established knowledge of meiosis and conception.

In meiosis, the formation of sperms and eggs, the chromosomes are duplicated and subsequently divided into sperms and eggs that contain only half of the parent's gene complement. Instead of the somatic cell number of 46 chromosomes, each germ cell contains only 23 chromosomes, one of each of the 23 pairs for the human species. When egg and sperm meet at conception, each germ cell contains 23 chromosomes that together reestablish in the child the 46 chromosomes that are normal for the species. Thus each child receives exactly half of his genes from each parent, with the exception that sons always receive the larger X chromosome from their mothers and the smaller Y from their fathers.

The familiar story of meiosis and conception contains random events that explain a great deal about sibling similarities and differences. First, the process by which half of the parent's genetic material goes into the germ cell is random selection. Each sibling receives a random half of each parent's genes. This random meiotic process is repeated for each child of the same parents. By chance, therefore, siblings share, on average, half of their genes and do not share the other half.

Second, the way in which genes are transmitted from parent to child has important implications for the distribution of siblings' genetic similarities and differences. Genes are not transmitted individually, but on chromosome segments, pieces of the grandmaternal and grandpaternal chromosomes that have broken apart and rejoined in a process called *crossing over*. Thus, each child receives from each parent 23 chromsomes that are usually combinations of the grandparents' chromosomes. The best estimates of the number of chromosome segments at meiosis range from 65 to 80, with a mean at 73 (Pakstis, 1981). Because crossing over is also a random process that differs from one meiosis to another, siblings' genetic similarities and differences can best be predicted by the repeated random sampling of some 70 to 75 chromosome segments, rather than the overlap in random samples of 23 chromosomes, or thousands of genes. Some sib pairs receive more than half of the same chromosome segments, and others receive fewer than half. The distribution of sibling genetic similarity can therefore be described by the overlap in random samples of 73 or so chromosome segments, each containing many gene loci that are linked together physically on

TABLE 15.1
The Distribution of Sibling Genetic Similarity
With 73 Chromosome Segments at Meiosis

Per Cent of Genes In Common	Per Cent of Sibling Pairs
33 – 35.9	.0003
36 – 38.9	.0027
39 – 41.9	.0252
42 – 44.9	.0789
45 – 47.9	.2324
48 – 50.9	.2584
51 – 53.9	.2207
54 – 56.9	.1404
57 – 59.9	.0329
60 – 62.9	.0070
63 – 65.9	.0010

the segment. Pakstis (1981) generated the following table to demonstrate the variability in sibling genetic relatedness (Table 1).

More than 99% of sib pairs fall in the range of 33 to 66% genes in common; about 70% have from 45 to 54% of the same genes. There is, however, a considerable range and variation in the actual genetic resemblance of sibling pairs.

The random events of meiosis and conception determine two important facts about the genetic resemblance of siblings: (1) On the average siblings have half of the same genes and half different genes; and (2) sib pairs differ in their actual genetic resemblance. Thus, genetic theories about siblings can address both similarities and differences and can predict which sibling pairs will look and behave more similarly than others.

Genetic Resemblance Among Sib Pairs

Siblings who share more of their genes look more similar and are perceived by others as more similar than siblings who have fewer genes in common. Using blood group and serum protein loci, dizygotic twins were typed on 12 different loci in two studies, one a study of 5- to 10-year-old twins (Scarr, 1966; 1969; Pakstis, Scarr-Salapatek, Elston & Siervogel, 1972) and the other a study of 10- to 16-year-old twins (Scarr, 1981; Carter-Saltzman & Scarr, 1977). By correlating the number of blood differences on the 12 independent loci and various measures and ratings of similarity, we could estimate the influence of genetic resemblance on phenotypic similarity. With physical measures, the reverse causation is impossible—how much a pair looks alike cannot determine their blood group resemblance. Table 2 shows the results.

Twin differences at 12 loci that mark only 15% of chromosome segments are a

TABLE 15.2
Correlations between Number of Blood Group Differences
and Physical Differences between Dizygotic Twins in Two Studies

Physical Ratings	r
Zygocity Rating by Examiner[a]	.55*
(1 = surely MZ to 6 = surely DZ)	
Zygocity Rating by Mother[a]	.42*
(1 = surely MZ to 6 = surely DZ)	
Twins' Rating of Physical Resemblance[b]	.34***
Observers' Ratings of Physical Resemblance from Photographs[b]	.25**
Twins' Report of Being Mistaken for Each Other[b]	.18*
Physical Measures[b]	
Stature	.03
Sitting Height	.14*
Skeletal Age	.24***
Height	.23***
Upper Arm Circumference	.10
Tricept Skin Fold Thickness	.04
Skin Reflectance	.01

Note: [a] Data from Pakstis, Scarr-Salapatek, Elson & Siervogel (1972) based on 26 pairs
of DZ twins between the ages of 5 and 10 years.

[b] Data from Carter-Saltzman & Scarr (1977) based on 115 to 140 pairs of DZ
twins between the ages of 10 and 16 years.

Blood group differences in both studies were assessed from 12 blood group and serum
protein loci identified in both articles.

*p < .05   **p < .01   ***p < .001

very rough index of genetic resemblance between siblings. There are statistically
reliable correlations, however, between the number of blood group differences of
siblings and their physical resemblance, especially their appearance. Another
way to look at these data is by comparing the mean number of blood group
differences of dizygotic twins who mistakenly believe they are identical twins
with blood group differences of twins who are uncertain or who disagree about
their zygosity, and those who correctly agree they are fraternal twins. As
Carter-Saltzman and Scarr (1977) reported, the average number of genetic differences at the blood group loci for 13 pairs of twins who mistakenly believe they
are identical is 1.54; for the 34 twin pairs who are unsure or who disagree, the
mean number of differences is 2.41; and for those 76 pairs who correctly believe
they are fraternal, the average number of differences is 3.14. Thus, siblings who
look more alike and who are more likely to think they are genetically identical are
in fact genetically more similar than the average sibling pair.

Similar analyses were attempted in both studies for behavioral differences.
Although the correlations between blood group and behavioral differences were

generally positive, they were most often too low to achieve statistical reliability. With so small a sample of genetic resemblance between siblings, it is not surprising that small correlations were the rule. It is also quite likely that physical resemblance has a greater degree of genetic determination than behavioral similarities, and that more refined measures of sibling genetic resemblance would be required to detect the relationship to behavioral similarities.

Genetic and Behavioral Correlations Among Siblings

The average genetic correlation between siblings is .50, which means that they share half of their genes. If behavioral differences were perfectly heritable and no environmental differences affected them, then one would expect that behavioral correlations between siblings would also be .50 (or a little higher if parents are assortatively mated for the characteristic, because the siblings' genetic correlation would also exceed .50 under these conditions). In other words, there would be a one-to-one correspondence of genetic and behavioral correlations.

Such a model is patently absurd and no one proposes it. Behavioral differences are not completely heritable and they are affected by environmental differences, some it seems more than others. As stated earlier, it is impossible for studies of biological families alone to estimate the relationship between genetic sibling correlations and behavioral correlations, because of the confounding of family environments. By comparing biological siblings with adopted, genetically unrelated siblings, however, one can gain an understanding of the degree to which sibling resemblance is influenced by both the common rearing environment and differences in the rearing environments of the two sibs and the degree to which sibling resemblance rests on genetic similarities.

We hasten to add a caveat on the use of adoptive families to estimate the magnitude of environmental differences in the general population, because adoptive families are an above average group. Differences among adoptive family environments are surely an underestimate of the magnitude of environmental differences among families. By comparing adoptive families to similar biological families, however, it is possible to estimate the proportion of the variance in selected behaviors that are responsive to differences in a range of family environments. That includes about 3/4 of the white population. Similarly, mentally retarded children are seldom adopted; again, comparison with biological offspring of similar families restricts the range of variation studies, but the proportions of variance can be reasonably estimated for an IQ range of 75 to 150.

If genetic differences determined sibling resemblance and environmental differences had no effects, then one would expect biological sib correlations of .50 and adopted sib correlations of .00. No data reported so far approach these values, with the one exception of Scarr and Weinberg's (1978) study of adolescent siblings adopted in infancy, who were compared to biological siblings from similar families. For Wechsler Adult Intelligence Test scores, the biological sib correlation was .35 and the adopted sibling correlation −.03. With a correction for the restriction in range of the IQ scores of both sets of siblings, the biological sib correlation rises to .48 and the adopted sib correlation remains relatively unchanged at −.05. Because this is the only study of late adolescents who were adopted in infancy, it is premature to conclude that IQ differences among siblings depend entirely on genetic differences by the time children reach late adolescence, but that is the most plausible interpretation of the data.

Studies of young adopted children at the average ages of seven to eight (Burks, 1928; Leahy, 1935; Horn, Loehlin & Willerman, 1981; Scarr & Weinberg, 1977) indicate that the family environment is a powerful determinant of sibling resemblance in the early years. In fact, in the later studies in Texas (Horn et al., 1981) and Minnesota (Scarr & Weinberg, 1977), IQ correlations of adopted siblings in the same family were as high as those of biological siblings in the same family. In the Texas study, the sibling correlations for WISC or Stanford-Binet IQ were about .30; in the Minnesota study that used the same measures, the IQ correlations were about .40 for both kinds of siblings. As will be discussed in the final section of this chapter, these results suggest that rearing environments and genetic differences have very different effects on sibling similarity at different stages of development.

Studies of personality resemblance among siblings find that little of the variance is explained by common family environments or shared genes. Adopted siblings hardly resemble each other at all, and biological siblings have personality correlations in the .15 to .20 range. These results indicate that personality variance is larely determined by environmental events unique to individual siblings within the family. The Minnesota study of adolescents (Scarr, Webber, Weinberg, & Wittig, 1981) found adopted sibling personality correlations to have a median of .05, indicating that only 5 per cent of the personality variance was due to environmental differences among families (or to common rearing environment). The biological sibling correlations had a median of .20, also suggesting that neither genes nor common rearing environments could explain much of the personality variance. Similar results have been reported for interests (Grotevant, Scarr, & Weinberg, 1977). Thus, it seems that unlike intelligence, personality variability among siblings is largely determined by unknown environmental differences within the family that lay undissected, as Woodworth said so long ago.

In summary, the research to date suggests that in childhood sibling resemblance on measures of intelligence depends on differences among family environments and very little on genetic differences between siblings. By late adolescence, however, intellectual differences among siblings evidently depend heavily on genetic differences and individual differences within family environments and bear little or no relationship to differences among family rearing environments. Sibling differences in personality and interests appear to be related primarily to differences in the within-family environments of siblings and secondarily to genetic differences.

Thus, none of the data on personality or interest variation fits a model of genetic differences that ignores individual environments. And the data on intelligence suggest that the effects of common rearing environments change from potent to impotent as children grow from early childhood to adolescence. The fact that most of the variability in personality and at least half of the variance in intelligence at any age is due to individual environmental differences within families may not be cause for cheer, because we have no good theories of why siblings experience such different environments.

ENVIRONMENTAL THEORIES OF SIBLING DIFFERENCES

Let us now consider possible environmental sources of sibling differences. Although, in most cases, siblings share the same home, their experiences within that setting may be very different. Environmental theories of sibling differences say that environmental differences within a family are great enough to account for the wide intellectual and personality differences found among siblings. Furthermore, these theories presume that there is a pattern to differences within family environments that is consistent across families. In this section we will begin by differentiating between within-family and between-family variance and outlining the implications of those differences for theories of sibling differences and similarities. We will then review environmental theories of sibling differences and similarities.

Environmental Differences Among and Within Families

Most standard psychological and sociological concepts about families represent environments that siblings share and that therefore cannot account for the vast differences among children in the same family. Social class, parental values, beliefs about child rearing, and so forth are measures of parental and family characteristics that are common to all children in the family. If the goal of the research is to explain *individual* variability in intelligence, personality, and other behaviors, the theories do not contain variables that address the majority of the variance to be explained.

Investigators do not always make explicit *what* variability they are attempting to explain; i.e., whether they are addressing individual differences among groups, such as social classes, schools, or families. If, for example, better educated parents have children who score higher on school tests, there is usually a correlation of about .40 between parental education and children's test scores. The correlation of .40 explains only 16% of the variability in the children's scores. What explains the other 84%, or more conservatively, the other 75% of the reliable variance in children's scores? If one examined the distribution of individual differences in scores, one would find that 59 to 70% of the variability occurs among siblings and not among the children of parents with different educational levels. Thus, parental education is not a variable that can possibly explain more than a fraction of the total variance in children's scores.

Sometimes between-family variables seem to explain more of the total variance than they do because they are used to account for *average* differences among groups rather than total, individual variability. The same educational example will illustrate this point. Suppose one wanted to explain differences in children's test scores by the educational level of the parents whose children attend different schools. The explanatory power of the variable, parental education, will be hugely greater if one averages the children's test scores and their parents' educational levels for each school and then correlates the two averaged variables than if one includes in the analysis all of the individual variability in both measures within each school. Instead of predicting a mere 16% of the individual differences in children's test scores, one can confidently predict 85% of the average differences in children's test scores among schools with averaged parental education. The trick is accomplished by averaging out more than 80% of the variability in the two measures that exists within schools and explaining well the remaining 15% of the total variability that occurs among schools.

There is no problem with the analysis of average differences among schools as long as one remembers what variability one is explaining. The question addressed by the analysis of average differences is, "Do differences among the average educational levels of parents whose children attend various schools predict average differences among schools in children's test scores?" The unit of analysis is the school, not the child, so that the variance that the analysis seeks to account for is a small portion of the total variability in children's test scores. Similarly, the spectacular fits of the confluence model (Zajonc & Marcus, 1975), to be discussed shortly, are made with data that average out individual variability in IQ and fit only the average differences among people by birth order, family size, and spacing. The model has been shown to explain more than 90% of (5% of) the IQ variance.

There are many other examples of confusion between explaining group differences and individual differences, including differences among families. If one averaged the test scores of siblings in families (called the midchild value) and then applied a set of predictors that index between-family differences, one could successfully explain a much greater portion of the remaining variability because one has eliminated the majority of variation that occurs among siblings within families. As before, the total variance explained is much less than it may appear, because one has reduced drastically the amount of variance to be explained and also restricted its possible sources to those that are common to siblings. A more common methodological problem is to sample only one child per family, to predict individual differences with measures of differences among families, and to ignore within-family sources of variability.

With the distinction between within-family and between-family variance clear, we will examine environmental theories of sibling differences. The environmental sources posited by these theories are sibling constellation variables, sibling deidentification, and family environment.

Sibling Constellation Variables

Sibling constellation has been by far the most widely researched environmental source of sibling differences. The variables that describe a sibling constellation are birth order, age spacing, age, and sex of the siblings (both in absolute terms, i.e., male or female, and in relative terms, i.e., same- or opposite-sex). Family size is also considered a sibling constellation variable, but it is a between-family variable, and so could not explain sibling differences. The assumption of sibling constellation research is that different sibling constellations result in different environments for children within families. These environmental differences can then account for cognitive and personality differences between siblings. Furthermore, the same sibling constellation will produce much the same environment in different families.

There is a glaring lack of theory to guide and interpret sibling constellation research. Although plausible explanations are frequently offered for differences in personality and cognitive abilities due to sibling constellation variables, little attempt has been made to organize research findings into a theory. Two exceptions to this theoretical void are the theories of Bossard and Boll (1956) and Parsons and Bales (1955). Both theories are based on a role differentiation hypothesis: that children will develop specific personalities, or roles, in order to distinguish themselves from other family members. The role a child adopts will depend on the roles of other family members. According to Bossard and Boll, role differentiation is greater in larger families because there is more competition for distinctive recognition.

Parsons and Bales' theory of role differentiation is more general than that of Bossard and Boll. According to Parsons and Bales, human personality is created through the process of socialization within the context of the family. The family has a role structure that consists of four role types. These types are the result of the intersection of two axes: the hierarchy or power axis and the instrumental-expressive axis. Family members' position on the former axis is determined by their age, and their position on the latter axis is a function of their sex (males learn to be instrumental, females expressive).

These four role types are a basic pattern common to all families; however, a variety of circumstances can create additional bases of differentiation. Factors with the potential to modify the fundamental four role type structure include the stage of the family cycle, the age difference between the husband and wife, the age differences between the parents and the children, and sibling constellation variables. Although these other areas of differentiation are important to personality development, they are secondary to the differentiation axes of hierarchy and expressiveness-instrumentalism.

The most serious shortcoming of these two role differentiation theories is that they are difficult to apply. They offer little aid to sibling constellation studies, which have not been able to jump from broad theory to complex data. There is potentially a very complex set of relationships among sibling constellation variables, and to date the conflicting data on the relationships of sibling constellation variables have not been organized into a coherent theory.

Zajonc and his colleagues (Zajonc & Markus, 1975; Zajonc, Markus, & Markus, 1979) have presented the only theory claiming to be capable of explaining the relationship between cognitive ability and sibling constellation variables. This theory, the confluence model, states that intellectual performance depends on a child's average intellectual environment, which is determined by the mean mental age of all family members, including the child. A child's average intellectual environment will vary in specified ways according to his birth order, family size, his age, his siblings' ages, and the age spacing between him and his contiguous siblings.

The confluence model offers the attractions of detailed predicted relationships between sibling constellation variables and intellectual performance, and of a potentially useful theoretical paradigm for sibling constellation variables and personality traits. When it has been applied to individual variability, however, it accounts for little of the variance. Galbraith's (1981) criticisms of the confluence model are: a) the discrepancy between the theoretical and mathematical models' predictions; b) the fact that the model does not refer to all birth order positions: actually, only next-to-last and last children are treated by the model; and c) there have been no appropriate tests of the model; although the model seeks to explain within-family differences (thus requiring longitudinal, within-family research), only cross-sectional, between-family data have been used to test it. Galbraith's criticisms of the confluence model prevent its present acceptance as a plausible theory of sibling differences in cognitive ability.

Thus, despite the volume of research, sibling constellation variables do not presently seem to offer an adequate explanation of sibling differences. That such research will continue seems certain, if for no other reason than, as Wagner, Schubert, and Schubert (1979) point out, the "persistence of the scientific belief that effects of sibship constellation exist and can, by diligent research, be identified [p. 67]."

There are other hypothesized environmental sources of sibling differences besides sibling constellation variables. These other sources are different from sibling constellation variables in that they are dynamic variables.

Sibling Deidentification

Sibling deidentification may be a psychological source of sibling differences. Sibling deidentification is the tendency of siblings to perceive themselves to be dissimilar to their siblings (Schachter, Shore, Feldman-Rotman, Marquis, & Campbell, 1976; Schachter, this volume). Schachter and her colleagues obtained judgments of sibling similarity and dissimilarity from college students from two- and three-child families. They distinguished between first pairs (first- and second-born siblings), second pairs (second- and third-born siblings), and jump pairs (first- and third-born siblings). People from first pairs "deidentified" significantly more than people from jump pairs; the deidentification of people from second pairs was at an intermediate level. It was concluded that a psychoanalytic interpretation best fit the results, and sibling deidentification was seen as a way to reduce sibling rivalry.

Although sibling deidentification refers to perceived dissimilarity, the possibility exists that sibling deidentification might result in actual differences among siblings. The possible connection between perceived and actual sibling differences is made more remote by the research of Scarr, Scarf, and Weinberg (1980) on perceived and actual similarities among parents and children. Perceptions did not predict tested similarities on measures of intelligence or personality. Thus, it is unlikely that siblings' perceived similarities would predict actual similarities, and even if they did, there is an equally plausible, alternative explanation: that the siblings were merely accurate perceivers rather than influencers of actual similarity. With dizygotic twins, Scarr and Carter-Saltzman (1979) showed that perceived similarity by the twins themselves was related to actual physical resemblance, rated by observers and measured anthropometrically. Because perceptions of similarity are unlikely to influence actual similarities in sitting height, skeletal age, and physiognomy, we concluded that the twins were accurate perceivers rather than creators of such resemblances. The same point could be made about siblings' perceived and actual similarities, if any correlation were found between them.

Family Environment

Family environment has been studied as a possible source of sibling differences. Most measures of family environment index between family variables, but Marjoribanks (1976a; 1976b) has argued that they may also be a source of within family variation. According to Marjoribanks, family environments may account for sibling differences if parents "create differential learning environments" for their children. This may come about as a result of a change in parents' economic conditions or parents' having learned from experience with previous children how to provide better learning experiences. It is not easy to see how a theory of family environments can be distinguished from genetic differences and genotype-environment correlations without studies of adoptive families.

Within-Family Environmental Differences

Although there is no question that siblings do experience somewhat different environments while growing up within the same family, there is little theory to guide research on the issue. Birth order indexes a small amount of the environmental difference; in most studies of individual differences, birth order accounts for less than 4% of the IQ variance (see Galbraith, 1981), and even less of the variance in personality and other behavioral measures (Scarr, Webber, Weinberg & Wittig, 1981). Given that 50 to 75% of the variance in psychological measures that is not error variance arises between siblings, birth order is not a good index. Sibling spacing is even less adequate (Brackbill & Nichols, in press; Grotevant, Scarr, & Weinberg, 1977; Galbraith, 1981).

Rowe and Plomin (1981) reviewed the causes of environmental variation among siblings and classified them into five types: accidental factors of each sibling's experiences, sibling interaction, family composition, differential parental treatment, and extrafamily network sources, such as peers, teachers, and TV. They concluded that the correlation between any of these between-sibling environmental differences and any behavioral differences is very small. Even more discouraging is the finding that there is no consistent environmental factor that can be extracted to account for the vast sibling differences on all behavioral measures. Rather than despairing of research on sibling environmental differences, however, Roe and Plomin propose that most psychological research on family effects should use behavior genetic designs that include more than one sibling. Although we are not as sanguine in hoping that a general set of environmental variables will be found to account for sibling variability, their advice should serve to curb the excessive claims of those who reach faulty conclusions about the causal importance of environmental variables through studying differences among families.

GENOTYPE-ENVIRONMENT CORRELATIONS

Theories of purely environmental or genetic sources of sibling differences and similarities simply cannot account for data on intellectual, personality, and interest resemblances among siblings. In this section, we will construct an alternative theory of sibling resemblance based upon genotype-environment correlations.

From the previous research of the first author (Scarr, 1966, 1969, 1981; Scarr & Weinberg, 1977, 1978), we were left with two puzzling questions about the nature of sibling differences:

1) By what *process* do monozygotic twins come to be more similar than dizygotic twins in all measurable ways? By the same token, by what *process* do biological siblings come to resemble each other more than adopted siblings?

2) Why do dizygotic twins become *less* similar on measures of intellectual competence from infancy to late childhood? And why do adopted siblings' intellectual correlations *decline* from moderate levels in early childhood to zero in late adolescence? Why do biological siblings retain moderate degrees of intellectual similarity from early childhood into adulthood?

Sibling differences can be allocated to genetic and environmental sources of variance with imprecision by comparing the resemblance of more and less related persons reared together, or by comparing the resemblance of similarly related persons reared in similar and different environments. Familiar comparisons are between monozygotic and dizygotic twins, biologically related and adopted siblings. Behavioral differences among siblings depend on genetic differences and probably on environmental differences between them, but the process by which these differences arise is best described by *genotype-environment correlations.*

Like Chomsky and Fodor (Piattelli-Palmarini, 1980), we propose that the genotype is the driving force behind development and the discriminator of what environments are experienced and what their effects are, because the genotype determines the responsiveness of the person to those environments. Unlike Chomsky and Fodor we do not think that development is precoded in the genes and merely emerges with maturation. Rather, we stress the role of the genotype in determining what environments are actually experienced. The distinction here is between environments to which a person may be observed to be exposed and what is actually grasped by the person. As we all know, the relevance of most aspects of the environment changes markedly with development. The toddler who "catches on" to the idea that things have names and demands the names for everything, to her parents' delight and exasperation, is an example. And so it is with sibling differences: Environments to which both siblings are exposed may have much greater meaning for one than another. The presence in the home of a complete set of carpentry tools may be very important to one child who uses that environment to master complex manual and spatial skills, whereas another ignores the tools in preference for the piano. The siblings' different choices are not unrelated to their own interests and talents, which are related to some extent to genetic differences between them.

Neither environmental nor genetic theories of sibling differences address the process by which siblings come to be similar or different. Both are static accounts that apportion variance at one point in time. The idea of genotype-environment correlations that shift in importance over development is, we think, a dynamic account of how siblings develop similarities and differences that are correlated with similarities and with differences in both their environments and their genotypes.

Passive, Evocative, and Active Correlations

Plomin, DeFries, and Loehlin (1977) described three kinds of genotype-environment correlations that form the basis for a developmental theory. The first, *Passive* genotype-environment correlations, arises in biologically related families and renders all of the research literature on "socialization" uninterpretable. Because parents provide both genes and environments for their biological offspring, the child's environment is necessarily correlated with his genes, because his genes are correlated with his parents' genes, and the parents' genes are correlated with the rearing environment they provide. It is impossible to know *what* about the parents' rearing environment for the child determines *what* about the child's behavior, because of the confounding effect of genetic transmission of the same characteristics from parent to child. Not only can we *not* interpret the direction of effects in parent-child interaction, we also cannot interpret the *cause* of those effects in biologically related families, as discussed earlier.

An example of the passive kind of genotype-environment correlation is reading. Parents who read well and enjoy reading are likely to provide their children with books; the children are more likely to be skilled readers who enjoy the activity, both for genetic and environmental reasons. The children's rearing environment is correlated with the parents' genotypes and therefore with the children's genotypes as well. To a considerable extent siblings share similar environments because they have the same parents who provide a standard of living and an ambience for everyone in the home. On the other hand, it is widely observed that siblings are treated differently by their parents (Lytton, 1980), a fact that can be ascribed to the second kind of genotype-environment correlation.

The second kind of genotype-environment correlation is called *Evocative,* because it represents the different responses that different genotypes evoke from the social and physical environments. Responses to the person further shape development in ways that correlate with the genotype. Temperament is like this: Socially engaging, smiley babies are likely to get more social stimulation than passive, sober infants. In the intellectual area, cooperative, attentive preschoolers probably receive more pleasant and instructional interactions from the adults around them than uncooperative, distractible children.

The third kind of genotype-environment correlation is the *Active,* niche-picking or niche-building sort. People seek out environments they find compatible and stimulating; they live in them, enlarge and deepen them. We all select from the surrounding environment some aspects to respond to, to learn about; and our selections are correlated with motivational, personality, and intellectual aspects of our genotypes.

Changes in Genotype-Environment Correlations With Development

An important part of this theory of sibling differences is that the relative importance of the three kinds of genotype-environment correlations changes over development from infancy to adolescence. In infancy, much of the environment that reaches the child is provided by adults. When those adults are genetically related to the child, the environment they provide—be it mobiles, social interaction, or isolation—is correlated with their own competence and their own genotypes. An infant can selectively attend to what is offered but she cannot do as much seeking out and niche-building; thus, *passive* genotype-environment correlations are more important in infancy and early childhood than they are for older children, who can escape the family's influences and find their own environments to a much greater extent.

Older children and adolescents have many more opportunities than infants and younger children to actively seek out and select their own environments. Both at home and in the larger world, older children can make their preferences known. Most parents are responsive to the different interests and talents of their children: Siblings who like to read are more likely to receive books as gifts; those who prefer sports are more likely to receive sports equipment. Siblings who are good at mathematics are more likely in high school to take advanced math courses than others whose interests and talents lie in languages. And so forth. Older children can be more active in establishing genotype-environment correlations.

Genotype-environment correlations of the *evocative* sort persist throughout life, as we elicit responses from others based on many personal, genotype-related characteristics, from appearance to personality and intellect. Those responses from others reinforce directions our development has taken and make them more so. Escalona (1968) spoke of this in her work on infant temperament. Although genetic differences in temperament are important past infancy, because the genetic program for development continues to prompt developmental change throughout the lifespan, the process she posited by which the infant's temperament evokes reactions in others that reinforce and magnify the initial characteristics of the child is an important type of genotype-environment correlation. Individual differences among siblings in childhood and adolescence continue to evoke different responses from others in their environments. Even the physical environment can play a role in evocative genotype-environment correlations, as some of us cannot gain confidence from successful experiences with tools and manual skills, whereas others do.

We have chosen to emphasize the concept of genotype-environment correlation in this emerging theory for two major reasons: Not only is the concept of genotype-environment correlation a developmental process, but it implies a *probabalistic* connection between a person and the environment. It is more *likely* that people with certain genotypes will receive certain kinds of parenting, evoke certain responses from others, and select certain aspects from the available environments; but nothing is rigidly determined. The idea of genetic differences, on the other hand, has seemed to imply to many that a person's developmental fate was preordained.

Two major questions about sibling differences remained unanswered from the previous research on twins and families. The first question concerned the *process* by which MZ twins come to be more similar than DZs, and biological siblings more similar than adopted siblings. A theory of genotype-environment correlations can account for these findings by pointing to the degree of genetic resemblance and the degree of similarity in the environments that would be experienced by the cotwins and sibs, as shown in Table 3. The expected degree of environmental similarity for a pair is the product of a person's own genotype-environment correlation and the genetic correlation of the pair. For identical twins, the correlation of one twin's environment with the other's genotype is the same as the correlation of the twin's environment with her own genotype. Thus, one would certainly predict what is often observed: That the hobbies, food preferences, choice of friends, academic achievements, and so forth of MZ twins are very similar. The usual theory of environmental differences would have us believe that all of this environmental similarity is imposed on MZ cotwins because they look so much alike. The usual theory of genetic differences does not speak to how the close resemblances arise. We feel more satisfied with the idea that the home environments provided by the parents, the responses the cotwins evoke from others, and the active choices they make in their environments lead to striking similarity in intellectual competence through genotype-environment correlations in their learning histories.

The same explanation applies, of course, to the greater intellectual resemblance of biological than adopted siblings. The environment of one biological sib is correlated to the genotype of the other as 1/2 the correlation of the sib's environment to his own genotype. The same is true for DZ twins. There is a very small genetic correlation between adopted sibs in most studies that arises from selective placement of the offspring of similar mothers in the same adoptive home. More important for this theory, however, is the selective placement of adopted children to match the intellectual characteristics of the adoptive parents. This practice allows adoptive parents to create a passive genotype-environment correlation for their adopted children in early childhood, when the theory says this

TABLE 15.3

	Genetic Correlation	The Similarity of Co-Twins and Siblings' Genotypes and Environments Due to:	
		Passive Genotype-Environment Correlations in Early Development	Passive Genotype-Environment Correlations in Adolescence
MZ Twins	1.00	High	High
DZ Twins	∼ 0.50	High	Moderate
Biological Siblings	∼ 0.50	Moderate	Moderate
Adopted Siblings	0.01	Moderate	Low

kind of correlation is most important. In fact, the selective placement estimates from the studies of Scarr and Weinberg (1976; 1977; 1978) can account for most of the resemblance between adoptive parents and their children.

Selective placement cannot account for the extraordinarily high intelligence correlations found between young adopted sibs. In the study of young adopted children, at an average age of 7 years, the IQ correlation of adopted sibs was .39, equal to that of the biologically related sibs in the same families (Scarr & Weinberg, 1977). Although a straight environmental theory can account for these data by saying that "sibs are sibs are sibs," regardless of genetic resemblance, it cannot account for any other data from the same study. A straight genetic theory founders on the sibling results. The genotype-environment correlation theory needs an adoptive mother who is especially effective in producing environments that evoke from genetically-unrelated children similar motivations and similar learning histories in the early years. As long as such a mother, who wants all of her children to succeed at similar levels, can control the children's learning environments, she could tailor them to suit each child's proclivities. Data from the Texas Adoption Project (Horn, Loehlin, & Willerman, 1979, 1981) fit the genotype-environment correlation theory better than those of the first author. In a sample of all white adopted children, they found a modest level of similarity among adopted sibs that can be nicely explained by the genotype-environment correlation provided by the parents.

The second question left unanswered by previous research concerned the declining similarities of dizygotic twins and adopted siblings from infancy to adolescence. It is clear from Wilson's (1977; Wilson & Harpring, 1977) longitudinal studies of MZ and DZ twins that the DZ correlations of .60 to .75 are higher than genetic theory would predict in infancy and early childhood. For school age and older twins, DZ correlations are usually about .55. Similarly, the sibling IQ correlation of a sample of late adolescents, adopted in infancy, was −.03, compared to the .25 to .39 correlations of the samples of adopted children in early to middle childhood (Scarr & Weinberg, 1978).

Neither environmental nor genetic theories can effectively address these provocative data. How can it be that the longer you live with someone, the less like them you become? One could evoke some ad hoc environmental theory about sibling relationships becoming more competitive, or deidentified, but that would not account for the continued, moderate intellectual resemblance of biological siblings. Genetic theory has, of course nothing to say about decreasing twin resemblance or any resemblance among young adoptees.

The theory put forward here says that the relative importance of passive versus active genotype-environment correlations changes with age. Recall that passive genotype-environment correlations are created by parents who provide children with both genes and environments, which are then correlated. Certainly in the case of DZ twins, whose prenatal environment was shared and whose earliest years are spent being treated in most of the same ways at the same time by the same parents, the passive genotype-environment could certainly account for the high degree of their intellectual similarity.

Biological and adopted siblings do not, of course, share the same developmental environments at the same time because they differ in age. (In fact, in the first year of life, biological siblings' mental development scores correlate only .20-.24 [Nichols, 1972; McCall, 1970]; their IQ correlations rise in early childhood to .35 to .50. This suggests that the early environments of infant siblings are more different than their later environments, and much less similar than the infant environments of DZ twins.) The passive genotype-environment correlation operates for siblings, because they have the same parents, but to a lesser extent than for twins.

MZ twin correlations for intellectual competence do not decline when active genotype-environment correlations outweigh the importance of the passive ones, because MZ cotwins typically select highly correlated environments anyway. DZ pairs, on the other hand, are no more genetically related than sibs, so that as the intense similarity of their early home environments gives way to their own choices, they select environments that are less similar than their previous environments and about as similar as those of ordinary sibs.

Adopted sibs, on the other hand, move from an early environment, in which mother may have produced intellectual similarity, to environments of their own choosing. Because their genotypes are hardly correlated at all, neither are their chosen environmental niches. Thus, by late adolescence, adopted siblings do not resemble each other behaviorally.

Biological siblings' early environments, like those of adopted children, shape similarity through passive genotype-environmental correlations. As they move into the larger world and begin to pick niches, their niches remain moderately correlated, because their genotypes remain moderately correlated. There is no marked shift in behavioral resemblance of biological sibs or for MZ twins as the process of active genotype-environment correlation replaces the passive one.

Thus, a genotype-environment correlation theory includes both environmental *and* genetic sources of sibling similarities and differences and specifies the processes by which those sources shape sibling resemblance.

CONCLUSIONS

A theory of genotype-environment correlations accounts for the data on sibling resemblance by positing a process by which genetic differences result in environmental differences that are correlated with the genotype. Further, it accounts for seemingly discrepant findings in previous research. Lastly, it points the way for further research on sibling differences.

Like Rowe and Plomin (1981) we recommend that developmental psychologists study siblings. To understand how parents affect their children's development, it is crucial to include variation within families, which can be done only by studying more than one child per family. In addition, we need better theories about the nature of variation between siblings. We know that genetic differences account for some of the measured differences between siblings for many behavioral characteristics, but we have inadequate theories of how environmental differences within the family produce additional differences.

We believe that the genetic differences between siblings are correlated with the functional, environmental differences that sibs experience (but not necessarily in the environments to which they are observed to be exposed). This theory suggests several kinds of research on siblings. First, longitudinal studies of the differences in responses that siblings evoke from parents and others would be valuable evidence for one kind of genotype-environment correlation, of which Lytton's (1980) research is a good example. Second, active "niche-picking" (Cole and the Laboratory of Comparative Human Cognition, 1980) can be studied as children build their own environments. Third, longitudinal studies of adopted children, such as the ongoing work of Plomin and colleagues, can provide valuable evidence of the changing influences of family environments on children. Fourth, studies of older adolescents and adults who were adopted in infancy can provide evidence on the long-term effects of environmental differences among and within families and both evocative and active kinds of genotype-environmental correlations.

Perhaps it is more important to consider how such a theory could be falsified. Such evidence could consist of a lack of differential responsiveness of parents to their children, a lack of niche-picking related to siblings' interests and talents, a lack of relationship between degree of sibling behavioral and genetic resemblances, and an increasing effect of passive genotype-environment correlations as children grow older. Such contrary evidence can emerge from the studies recommended above.

We hope that the time has come for developmental psychology to recognize that people, even siblings, are genetically different, and that those differences have implications for behavioral development. Perhaps an emphasis on the important role of the environment in its correlation with genetic differences will make the idea more palatable.

REFERENCES

Bell, R. Q. A reinterpretation of the direction of effects in studies of socialization. *Psychological Review,* 1968, *75,* 81–95.

Bell, R. Q., & Harper, L. V. (Eds.). *Child effects on adults.* Hillsdale, New Jersey: Lawrence Erlbaum Associates, 1977.

Bossard, N. H., & Boll, E. S. *The large family system.* Philadelphia: University of Pennsylvania Press, 1956.

Brackbill, Y., & Nichols, P. A test of the confluence model of intellectual development. *Developmental Psychology,* in press.

Burks, B. S. The relative influence of nature and nurture upon mental development: a comparative study of foster parent-foster child resemblance and true parent-true child resemblance. *Yearbook book of the National Society for the Study of Education*, 1928, *27*, 219-316.

Carter-Saltzman, L., & Scarr, S. MZ or DZ? Only your blood grouping laboratory knows for sure. *Behavior Genetics*, 1977, *7*, 273-280.

Cole, M., & The Laboratory of Comparative Human Cognition. *Niche-picking*. Unpublished manuscript, University of California, San Diego. 1980.

Escalona, S. K. *The roots of individuality*. Chicago: Aldine Publishing Company, 1968.

Galbraith, R. Sibling spacing and intellectual development: A closer look at the confluence models. *Developmental Psychology*, 1982, in press.

Grotevant, H. D. Sibling constellations and sex typing of interests in adolescence. *Child Development*, 1978, *49*, 540-542.

Grotevant, H. D., Scarr, S., & Weinberg, R. A. Patterns of interest similarity in adoptive and biological families. *Journal of Personality and Social Psychology*, 1977, *35*, 667-676.

Horn, J. M., Loehlin, J. C., & Willerman, L. Intellectual resemblance among adoptive and biological relatives: The Texas Adoption Project. *Behavior Genetics*, 1979, *9*, 177-207.

Horn, J. M., Loehlin, J. C., & Willerman, L. Aspects of the inheritance of intellectual abilities. *Behavior Genetics*, 1981, in press.

Jensen, A. R. *Bias in mental testing*. New York: Basic Books, 1980.

Leahy, A. M. Nature-nurture and intelligence. *Genetic Psychology Monographs*, 1935, *17*, 237-308.

Lytton, H. *Parent-child interaction*. New York: Plenum, 1980.

McCall, R. B. Intelligence quotient pattern over age: Comparisons among siblings and parent-child pairs. *Science*, 1970, *170*, 644-648.

Marjoribanks, K. Birth order, family environment, and mental abilities: A regression surface analysis. *Psychological Reports*, 1976, *39*, 759-765. (a)

Marjoribanks, K. Sibsize, family environment, cognitive performance, and affective characteristics. *The Journal of Psychology*, 1976, *94*, 195-204. (b)

Nichols, P. L. The effects of heredity and environment on intelligence test performance in 4- and 7-year-old white and Negro sibling pairs. Doctoral dissertation, University of Minnesota, 1972.

Pakstis, A. A Genetic Model of Sibling Differences. Doctoral Dissertation, University of Minnesota, 1981.

Pakstis, A., Scarr-Salapatek, S., Elston, R., & Siervogel, R. Genetic contributions to morphological and behavioral similarities among sibs and dizygotic twins: Linkages and allelic differences. *Social Biology*, 1972, *19*, 185-192.

Parsons, T., & Bales, R. F. *Family, socialization and interaction process*. New York: Free Press, 1955.

Piatelli-Palmarini, M. (Ed.). *Language and learning: The debate between Jean Piaget and Noam Chomsky*. Cambridge: Harvard University Press, 1980.

Plomin, R., DeFries, J. C., & Loehlin, J. C. Genotype-environment interaction and correlation in the analysis of human behavior. *Psychological Bulletin*, 1977, *84*, 309-322.

Rowe, D. C., & Plomin, R. The importance of nonshared (E_1) environmental influences in behavioral development. *Developmental Psychology*, 1981, in press.

Scarr, S. Genetic factors in activity motivation. *Child Development*, 1966, *37*, 663-673.

Scarr, S. Social introversion-extraversion as a heritable response. *Child Development*, 1969, *40*, 823-832.

Scarr, S. *Race, social class, and individual differences in IQ: New studies of old issues*. Hillsdale, NJ: Lawrence Erlbaum Associates, in press, 1981.

Scarr, S., & Carter-Saltzman, L. Twin method: Defense of a critical assumption. *Behavior Genetics*, 1979, *9*, 527-542.

Scarr, S., & Kidd, K. K. Behavior genetics. In M. Haith & J. Campos (Eds.), *Manual of child psychology: Infancy and the biology of development* (Vol. 2). New York: Wiley, 1982, in press.

Scarr, S., Scarf, E., & Weinberg, R. A. Perceived and actual similarities in biological and adoptive families: Does perceived similarity bias genetic inferences? *Behavior Genetics,* 1980, *10,* 445–458.

Scarr, S., Webber, P. L., Weinberg, R. A., & Wittig, M. A. Personality resemblance among adolescents and their parents in biologically-related and adoptive families. *Journal of Personality and Social Psychology,* 1981, *40,* 885–898.

Scarr, S., & Weinberg, R. A. IQ test performance of black children adopted by white families. *American Psychologist,* 1976, *31,* 726–739.

Scarr, S., & Weinberg, R. A. Intellectual similarities within families of both adopted and biological children. *Intelligence,* 1977, *1,* 170–191.

Scarr, S., & Weinberg, R. The influence of "family background" on intellectual attainment. *American Sociological Review,* 1978, *43,* 674–692.

Schachter, F. F., Shore, E., Feldman-Rotman, S., Marquis, R. E., & Campbell, S. Sibling deidentification. *Developmental Psychology,* 1976, *12,* 418–427.

Wagner, M. E., Schubert, H., & Schubert, D. Sibship-constellation effects on psychosocial development, creativity, and health. *Advances in Child Development,* 1979, 57–149.

Wilson, R. S. Twins and siblings: Concordance for school-age mental development. *Child Development,* 1977, *48,* 211–216.

Wilson, R. S., & Harpring, E. B. Mental and motor development in infant twins. *Developmental Psychology,* 1972, *7,* 277.

Woodworth, R. S. Heredity and environment: A critical survey of recently published material on twins and foster children. *A report prepared for the committee on Social Adjustment.* New York: Social Science Research Council, 1941.

Zajonc, R. B., & Markus, G. B. Birth order and intellectual development. *Psychological Review,* 1975, *82,* 74–88.

Zajonc, R. B., Markus, H., & Markus, G. B. The birth order puzzle. *Journal of Personality and Social Psychology,* 1979, *37,* 1325–1341.

Epilogue: Framing the Problem

Brian Sutton-Smith
University of Pennsylvania

In the pages that follow I discuss the problem of where we should go in future research on sibling development. My point is that we have in the past been ethnocentric in both our choice of variables and in our choice of methodology. Specifically, we have focused on birth order in the family as a source of achievement and generally have investigated it by correlating ordinal position with a limited array of psychometrically assessed variables.

The problem on which this book focuses is that of sibling *relationships* throughout the lifespan. Our intention here is to take a step beyond considering each individual only as he is characterized by a particular birth order or a particular sibling status in isolation from other relationships, or as a product of the mother-infant dyad alone. It has always been a theoretical proclivity and an empirical hazard within psychology to think of individuals as separate beings with their own personal aggregation or integration of traits, abilities, and defenses. In this discussion, I wish to seize upon our present movement away from such philosophical individualism and suggest that in future sibling research we should seek some kind of network analysis as well as a complementation of holistic and analytic methodologies.

But first the data. In the foregoing chapters we have seen that the most powerful current mathematical model of sibling status (Zajonc) requires taking into account the actions of both parents and siblings. Similarly, current studies of infants by Lamb, Abramovitz, and her colleagues Dunn and Kendrick, etc., show the fruitful results of taking into account both sibling and parental role sectors. In addition, many permutations of such interactions have been described here, such as, complementary patterns of neglect and indulgence in which some parental patterns or sibling patterns bind the siblings together and others force them into competitive relationships (Dunn and Kendrick, Banks and Kahn, Schachter). On the other hand, cultural sex roles are seen also to have pervasive influence: with girls being more prosocial with infants, more helpful as child-teachers, and more caring as adults. In addition, those siblings who, because of sibling influences and birth order, appear to be most sex stereotyped (younger brothers with older brothers and younger sisters with older sisters) are the most stable in their own sibling characteristics over time (Rosenberg). Furthermore, the continuation of sibling relationships into later years (Cicirelli, Ross and Milgram), is not only interesting in its own right; it also implies that the kinship networks for young children are much larger than we had supposed. Children also are presumably affected by their parents' siblings as well as by their own grandparents.

Weisner has demonstrated that the emphasis we place on the mother-child dyad is a piece of cultural ethnocentricism. Throughout most societies, siblings exercise a much greater influence over life decisions than we allow. Whether our own practices are only a "pale remnant" of these earlier practices or in fact continue to demonstrate the influence of such siblings is an empirical matter not yet decided. It is not at all impossible that grandparents, uncles and aunts along with parents and siblings contribute in various ways to the calculus of belief, value, character, and competence for any given sibling.

As a personal aside, I am impressed that although neither my father or my mother was much concerned with sports, and both were much opposed to their violence, my mother's brothers had all been highly involved in football and boxing. My brother and I followed their advocacies rather than those of my parents. When it came to occupations, however, my elder brother followed the practice of a farming uncle, whereas I picked up the fantasy of my father to become a professor. The finding that brothers are less close to each other in subsequent years than are sisters (Cicirelli) should not prevent us from looking for the possibility that fateful decisions may nevertheless be determined by the parents' brothers (or for that matter, sisters, or parents). We know that in general males are more likely to be affected by extrafamilial sources than are females. On the other hand, Schachter's data suggest that there are additional dynamics of disidentification that would make some sibling positions more prone to outside influence also. Then again there are the suggestions from the literature in group dynamics implying that even-odd sets of siblings would be given to more or less internal dispute (Bales and Borgatta, 1955) as well as different kinds of coalition (Caplow, 1968), which would in turn lead them to reach beyond the immediate family for guidance and help. The network of potential influences upon the particular child is a complex matter and we need to broaden, not narrow, the gauge of our inquiries, if we are to end up somewhere near the truth.

The extent to which we as investigators are creatures of our own culture is also indicated by the changes in the contents of this volume as compared to earlier volumes on sibling development. Most striking is the current concern with pro-social behavior in the young and caring behavior in the mature. Earlier work focused by contrast on eminence and rivalry. Recent trends in psychology of a more humanistic cast (attachment, altruism, moral development, empathy, rights of subjects) are probably responsible. This broadening of subject matter also helpfully serves to remind us that, as Bossard had said earlier, and Abramovitz and her colleagues do in this volume, siblings generally share the widest range of behaviors. This is an important reminder that, in the 20th century, developmental psychology has generally focused on the child's socialization into public behavior norms and has tended to neglect the socialization of an intimate and private character. Assimilation into modern technological civilization requires a relative subordination of idiosyncrasies of the family, ethnic group, racial group, psychosexual preferences, even in some cases sex role itself. Only recently has there been a general acknowledgment in our field that children have other things to discover than these public norms of competence and appropriate behavior.

Children's folklore as well as their life in peer groups is only partly about such matters (Sutton-Smith, 1981). Our psychology has generally given little attention to the continuing stream of private and intimate life which most people continue to indulge in themselves and without which they feel less than human. When psychologists do deal with such things, it is usually in the clinical context of maladaptation. Fortunately, siblings do this for each other. The chapters by Cicirelli, Ross, and Milgram, and Banks and Kahn are reminders that with our siblings we continue to be "folk" as well as public people.

My argument is that our studies of sibling development have been too "individualistic" in scope, too narrow in content and prejudiced by psychology's role as handmaiden to modern social technology. In defense of this latter proposition, I would suggest that *positivism* in modern psychology is not, as so often criticized, simply a historical anachronism (and it is that); it has also been of great functional value as a vehicle of modern symbolic civilization. We live in an age when measurement of the individual in the abstract (I.Q., GSE, spacial competencies, etc.) can be a useful predictive device in innumerable modern selection and placement situations. The premise that an individual can be assessed in these decontextualized and "mechanistic" ways has actually worked and saves government and industry enormous amounts of money. The disadvantage of this most practical predictive success, however, is that it has prejudiced us against recognizing that this kind of psychology has limited value when used as a general model for discovery purposes where the aim is to provide an explanation of the phenomenon to be investigated. In the present case of sibling studies one could argue optimistically that after thousands of studies we are gradually modifying our limited "predictively" oriented approaches as we discover the limitations of prior work. Or one could say pessimistically that most of that earlier work was vitiated by the premature selection of pertinent variables and the premature quantification of too limited a set of such variables.

Imagine, for example, if instead of those thousands of relatively worthless studies, we now had available thousands of case studies of siblings in context. Imagine, less probably, that they were longitudinal, and involved great amounts of taped (perhaps even video recorded) material across carefully sampled life situations. A sense of their potential value is indicated by the richness of the study reported by Dunn and Kendrick in the present volume. The issue is how to retain some of the systematic quality of description and codification that is characteristic of psychology and at the same time to risk a more ethnographic and far reaching involvement with the families we wish to study. Presumably we need not confine ourselves as anthropologists have typically done to one group or one case although we do need to show some of their same durability of involvement and participation if we are to approach more general explanations of the phenomena at hand. It seems defeating to begin by being detached and neutral in situations where we must use all our resources of feeling and thought to gain a preliminary intuitive feeling for what is happening there.

The time for such "objectivism" comes later, not earlier in the study, and perhaps with families other than those with whom one initiates the study. In sum, I see an urgent need for researchers of sibling interaction to do some intensive and long-term participation, observation, and interviewing with such samples of families as they can reasonably manage. Perhaps what we need here is collaborative work involving groups of researchers, each with their own small segment of cases. It is, in my opinion, too early yet to be doing predictive research on mixed dyads or same-sex dyads, on prosocial or aggressive interactions, until we have established beyond some reasonable doubt that these are indeed the variables worthy of such quantifiable attention. First let us try to *explain* in general what is going on, rather than arrive at some fairly reliable covariances between this variable and that variable without much sense of what it all means. What are the day-by-day events that are different for brothers and for sisters with brothers or sisters? What do grandparents, aunts, and uncles do; what do they say? As children and adolescents make choices, by whom have they been most affected? How do kinship systems, varying as they do within American society by ethnic groups (Chinese, Mexican, Negro, Vietnamese, Irish, Jewish, etc.), have an impact on the immediate relationships of the siblings? How are sex roles as defined by such groups as well as by media norms operative in affecting the day to day interactions of the siblings? Is it that some siblings model positively and some negatively from adults and siblings? Is it that this is more true with some variables than other variables? The present work has the value that it can provide the willing researcher with an inventory of questions with which such an ethnographic assault might well begin.

REFERENCES

Bales, R. F., & Borgatta, E. F. Size of group as a factor in the interaction profile. In A. P. Hare (Ed.), *Small Group Studies in Social Interaction*. New York: Knopf, 1955.

Caplow, T. *Two against one: Coalitions in triads*. Englewood Cliffs, N.J.: Prentice Hall, 1968.

Sutton-Smith, B. *A history of children's play*. Philadelphia: University of Pennsylvania, 1981.

Author Index

Numbers in *italics* denote pages with complete bibliographic information.

Subject Index